WITHDRAWN

CAMBRIDGE STUDIES IN LINGUISTICS

General Editors: B. COMRIE, C. J. FILLMORE, R. LASS, R. B. LE PAGE,
J. LYONS, P. H. MATTHEWS, F. R. PALMER, R. POSNER,
S. ROMAINE, N. V. SMITH, J. L. M. TRIM, A. ZWICKY

Mass terms and model-theoretic semantics

In this series

1 DAVID CRYSTAL: *Prosodic systems and intonation in English**
4 JOHN M. ANDERSON: *The grammar of case**
5 M. L. SAMUELS: *Linguistic evolution**
6 P. H. MATTHEWS: *Inflectional morphology**
7 GILLIAN BROWN: *Phonological rules and dialect variation**
8 BRIAN NEWTON: *The generative interpretation of dialect**
9 R. M. W. DIXON: *The Dyirbal language of North Queensland**
11 MELISSA BOWERMAN: *Early syntactic development**
12 W. SIDNEY ALLEN: *Accent and rhythm*
13 PETER TRUDGILL: *The social differentiation of English in Norwich**
14 ROGER LASS and JOHN M. ANDERSON: *Old English phonology*
15 RUTH M. KEMPSON: *Presupposition and the delimitation of semantics**
16 JAMES R. HURFORD: *The linguistic theory of numerals*
17 ROGER LASS: *English phonology and phonological theory*
18 G. M. AWBERY: *The syntax of Welsh*
19 R. M. DIXON: *A grammar of Yidi*
20 JAMES FOLEY: *Foundations of theoretical phonology*
21 A. RADFORD: *Italian syntax: transformational and relational grammar*
22 DIETER WUNDERLICH: *Foundations of linguistics**
23 DAVID W. LIGHTFOOT: *Principles of diachronic syntax**
24 ANNETTE KARMILOFF-SMITH: *A functional approach to child language**
25 PER LINELL: *Psychological reality in phonology*
26 CHRISTINE TANZ: *Studies in the acquisition of deictic terms*
27 ROGER LASS: *On explaining language change*
28 TORBEN THRANE: *Referential–semantic analysis*
29 TAMSIN DONALDSON: *Ngiyambaa*
30 KRISTJÁN ÁRNASON: *Quantity in historical phonology*
31 JOHN LAVER: *The phonetic description of voice quality*
32 PETER AUSTIN: *A grammar of Diyari, South Australia*
33 ALICE C. HARRIS: *Georgian syntax*
34 SUZANNE ROMAINE: *Socio-historical linguistics*
35 MARTIN ATKINSON: *Explanations in the study of child language development**
36 SUZANNE FLEISCHMAN: *The future in thought and language*
37 JENNY CHESHIRE: *Variation in an English dialect*
38 WILLIAM A. FOLEY and ROBERT D. VAN VALIN JR: *Functional syntax and universal grammar**
39 MICHAEL A. COVINGTON: *Syntactic theory in the High Middle Ages*
40 KENNETH J. SAFIR: *Syntactic chains*
41 J. MILLER: *Semantics and syntax*
42 HARRY C. BUNT: *Mass terms and model-theoretic semantics*
43 HEINZ J. GIEGERICH: *Metrical phonology and phonological structure*

Supplementary Volumes

BRIAN D. JOSEPH: *The synchrony and diachrony of the Balkan infinitive*

* Issued in hard covers and as a paperback

MASS TERMS AND MODEL-THEORETIC SEMANTICS

HARRY C. BUNT
*Department of Language and Literature,
Tilburg University*

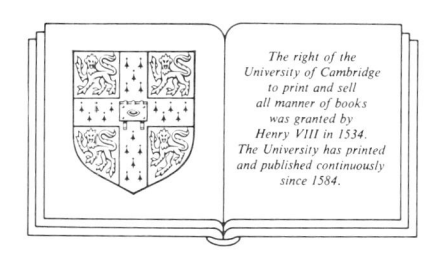

CAMBRIDGE UNIVERSITY PRESS
CAMBRIDGE
LONDON NEW YORK NEW ROCHELLE
MELBOURNE SYDNEY

Published by the Press Syndicate of the University of Cambridge
The Pitt Building, Trumpington Street, Cambridge CB2 1RP
32 East 57th Street, New York, NY 10022, USA
10 Stamford Road, Oakleigh, Melbourne 3166, Australia

© Cambridge University Press 1985

First published 1985

Printed in Great Britain by
J. W. Arrowsmith Ltd., Bristol BS3 2NT

Library of Congress catalogue card number: 84-23831

British Library Cataloguing in Publication Data
Bunt, Harry C.
Mass terms and model-theoretic semantics. –
(Cambridge studies in linguistics, ISSN 0068-676X; 42)
1. Semantics – Mathematics models 2. Logic,
Symbolic and Mathematical 3. Language and logic
I. Title
412   P325.5.M36

ISBN 0 521 25681 X

AS

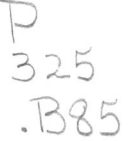

Contents

Preface		ix

PART I
MODEL-THEORETIC SEMANTICS OF MASS TERMS

1	**Introduction**	3
1.1	Semantic issues relating to mass terms	3
1.2	Plan of the book	6
2	**Mass terms**	9
2.1	Mass terms syntactically defined	9
2.2	Mass terms semantically defined	15
3	**Approaches to mass term semantics**	21
3.1	Differences in approaches	21
3.2	Quine's semi-mereological approach	22
3.3	Fully mereological approaches	26
3.4	Mass nouns as denoting substances	29
3.5	Set-based approaches	33
4	**Towards a semantic theory of mass nouns**	43
4.1	Requirements for a semantic theory of mass nouns	43
4.2	The minimal parts hypothesis	44
4.3	The use of mereology	47
5	**Ensemble theory**	53
5.1	Part–whole and member–whole	53
5.2	The part–whole relation	56
5.3	Atoms, unicles, and members	59
5.4	Continuous and discrete ensembles	63
5.5	A model for ensemble theory	66
5.6	Ensembles, sets, and individuals	71

6 Semantic representations based on ensemble theory 73
6.1 Introduction 73
6.2 Amount terms 75
6.3 Language definition and families of languages 81
6.4 The EL type system 84
6.5 The syntax of EL 88
6.6 The semantics of EL 92
6.7 Semantic representations in EL 94
6.8 Notation: summary and some additions 99

7 Two-level model-theoretic semantics 102
7.1 Formal semantics 102
7.2 Model-theoretic semantics 105
7.3 Model-theoretic analysis of natural language 111
7.4 Referential ambiguity and model-theoretic semantics 114
7.5 Two-level model-theoretic semantics 118
7.6 A formal and a referential view of the world 124
7.7 Mass terms in two-level model-theoretic semantics 129

8 Quantification and mass nouns 133
8.1 Introduction 133
8.2 Quantification 137
8.3 Quantification aspects of multi-NP sentences 142
8.4 Quantification representations for count nouns 146
8.5 Quantification in two-level model-theoretic semantics 152
8.6 Mass noun quantification 161
8.7 The representation of mass noun quantification 165
8.8 A grammar for a fragment of English 180

9 Modification and mass nouns 197
9.1 Modification and quantification 197
9.2 Theoretical problems with adjective–mass noun combinations 199
9.3 Empirical facts about adjective–mass noun combinations 204
9.4 The representation of mass noun modification 212
9.5 Augmented phrase-construction grammar for an extended fragment of English 217

PART 2
ENSEMBLE THEORY

10   Axiomatic ensemble theory   233
10.1   The logical system   233
10.2   Ensemble theory built up from a system of axioms   235
       10.2.1   Axiom of transitivity   235
       10.2.2   Axiom of equality   236
       10.2.3   Axiom of unicles   237
       10.2.4   Axiom of extensionality   238
       10.2.5   Axiom of pairing   242
       10.2.6   Axiom of powers   244
       10.2.7   Axiom of merging (or sums)   244
       10.2.8   Axiom (schema) of replacement   247
       10.2.9   Axiom of infinity   251
       10.2.10 Axiom of regularity   252
10.3   Operations on ensembles   252
       10.3.1   Merge   252
       10.3.2   Overlap   252
       10.3.3   Completion   254
       10.3.4   The partition theorem   255
       10.3.5   The Boolean algebra of ensemble operations   256

11   Continuous, discrete, and mixed ensembles   260
11.1   Continuous ensembles   260
11.2   Discrete ensembles   263
11.3   Continuity versus discreteness   266

12   A model for ensemble theory   269
12.1   The model structure   270
12.2   Satisfaction of the ETX axioms   271

13   Ensemble theory, set theory, and mereology   275
13.1   Ensemble theory and set theory   275
       13.1.1   Sets in ensemble theory   278
       13.1.2   Ensembles in set theory   281
13.2   Ensemble theory and mereology   288
       13.2.1   Mereology, or the theory LLG   288

viii *Contents*

13.2.2	Ensembles and individuals	290
13.2.3	LLG individuals in ensemble theory	295
13.2.4	Ensembles in the theory LLG	297

Notes	303
Bibliography	313
Index	319

Preface

This book has grown out of my dissertation, submitted to the University of Amsterdam in 1981. It contains most of the ideas of the dissertation in a revised form, but it also contains a good deal of new material.

New material, that supplements the dissertation at an important point, concerns the description of a model of the axioms of ensemble theory, the generalization of set theory designed for the semantic analysis of mass terms. Section 5.6 contains an informal presentation of a model, and chapter 12 is devoted to the description of a class of models in formal terms. New material relating to ensemble theory can also be found in the final chapter, where a detailed discussion is given of the relation between ensemble theory, classical set theory, and mereology (also known as 'calculus of individuals'). This should prevent such misunderstandings as that ensemble theory is 'another name for mereology' (Roeper, 1983).

Other new material concerns the definition of the general framework in which the semantic analysis is carried out. In this framework two stages of analysis are distinguished: one where the logical semantic aspects of a natural language expression are analysed and one where the referential semantic aspects are analysed in relation to a model of a certain domain of discourse. This has the advantage that the analysis of general, domain-of-discourse independent semantic aspects and that of purely lexical semantic aspects are well-separated components of a single overall framework. Each stage of the analysis results in a representation in a formal language (more than one representation in the case of ambiguities). This gives rise to an interesting treatment of lexical ambiguity and vagueness: content words in the natural language are represented at the nonreferential level by constants of the representation language that preserve the ambiguity and vagueness of the corresponding natural language words; the precise meanings of these words are established by interpretation rules that have the effect of 'translating' these constants into expressions of a second formal language, whose constants have a one-to-one correspondence to entities in the model of the discourse domain. A precise definition of this framework is given in chapter 7 in the terminology of model-theoretic semantics. The relation between the two representation languages, mediating between the natural language and the discourse-domain model, is defined by model-theoretic interpretation rules, where the expressions of the representation language at the referential level serve as interpretations of those of the other representation language. The framework is therefore called 'two-level model-theoretic semantics'.

The most important new material in this book concerns the treatment of ambiguity and vagueness in quantification. The chapter on quantification in my dissertation was primarily meant to illustrate the power of ensemble theory in the analysis of mass noun expressions. As such it may have served its purpose. But it seemed intuitively obvious that the two-level framework had not been fully exploited. The new idea which underlies the treatment of quantification in this book is that the separation of domain-of-discourse dependent meaning aspects from those that do not depend on the domain of discourse is applied to other areas of semantic investigation than that of lexical semantics. For example, the sentence 'The boys carried two pianos upstairs' may have several, quantificationally different readings: one where each of the boys carried each of the pianos, one where the boys collectively carried each of the pianos, one where each of the boys carried a collection of two pianos, etc. All these interpretations are formally possible, but usually not all of them are possible in a given domain of discourse. That depends on whether one considers 18-year-old boys or eight-year-old boys, real pianos or toy pianos, and other such domain-of-discourse dependent considerations. It is therefore attractive to leave such decisions as to whether the boys acted collectively, individually, or in groups to the domain-of-discourse dependent part of the analysis. I have devised a way of doing this, which entails that at the purely formal level of analysis a quantified sentence has a representation which is ambiguous or vague in those quantification aspects on which the natural language sentence is not specific. A sentence like 'The boys carried two pianos upstairs' has only *one* representation at this level, and the number of interpretations it has at the referential level is determined by what the model of the discourse domain says about boys, pianos, and carrying something upstairs. This makes it possible to formulate an articulate analysis of quantifications while at the same time preventing an uncontrolled explosion of interpretations.

The analysis of constructions with adnominal modification, such as 'The pianos carried upstairs by the boys', entails many of the same considerations as that of quantified expressions. I have therefore also devised a new treatment of the ambiguity and vagueness in adnominal modification along the same lines as the treatment of quantification. An interesting minor point which is new in the chapter on modification is the treatment of 'collective modification'. This occurs for instance in the sentence 'John has heavy books in his bag' on the interpretation that the collection of books in the bag as a whole is heavy. This case does not easily fit into a systematic syntactic/semantic analysis, since the adjective 'heavy' is syntactically a modifier of 'books', while semantically it applies to 'the books John has in his bag'.

A new form has also been given to the syntactic/semantic grammar rules, used in the chapters on quantification and modification to describe fragments of English. There were two independent reasons to reconsider the form of the grammar. An anonymous referee for Cambridge University Press had complained about the original form, which had been borrowed from Scha (1981), and asked for a formulation that would be more in line with currently common grammatical formalisms. Moreover, work on a computer implementation of the grammar made it clear that certain changes in the rules would permit more transparent parsing algorithms. The changes that have been made are: (1) the syntactic component of a rule has been split up into three parts: (a) a constituent-structure rule, (b) a condition on syntactic features, and (c) a feature-propagation rule; (2) a form of constituent-structure rule has been designed which is not purely concatenating and which allows a restricted form of context-sensitivity. This grammar, for which I have coined the term 'Augmented phrase-construction grammar', belongs to the class of phrase-structure-based grammar formalisms that includes currently developing formalisms such as Generalized phrase-structure grammar (Gazdar, 1982; Gazdar and Pullum, 1982) and Augmented phrase-structure grammar (Robinson, 1982; cf. Winograd, 1983).

As a study in semantics, this book should in the first place be of interest to linguists and language philosophers. But since the study raises issues concerning the logical and set-theoretical foundations of model-theoretic semantics, it also aims at an audience of logicians and mathematicians. This motivates the division of this book into two parts. Moreover, the semantic analysis of mass terms is partly based on arguments relating to why people express something in one way rather than another, with special attention to the fact that the logical structure of a speaker's apparent beliefs as expressed by his words should be distinguished from the logical structure xii *Preface*

of his actual beliefs. These points, and their far-reaching consequences for the general framework of semantic analysis, may be of interest to psycholinguists. Finally, this study was directly motivated by the problems that arose in an attempt to design a computer program for syntactic and semantic analysis of natural language. The solutions which are presented here, and which are made explicit in the form of grammar rules and interpretation rules for fragments of English, may be of interest to computer scientists and researchers in Artificial Intelligence, who may also be interested in the possible use of ensemble theory in knowledge representation in intelligent systems (see Bunt, 1985). It is because of this wide variety of potential readers that most of the chapters in this book have an introduction at a rather elementary level. Chapter 6, for instance, which discusses the use of ensemble concepts in semantic representations, contains introductory sections on the nature of semantic representations in general and on the definition of representational formalisms. Similarly, chapter 7 contains a general introduction to model-theoretic semantics and ambiguity. My hope is that these sections will enable readers from a variety of academic disciplines to understand the technically more complex material.

I should like to thank a number of people who have contributed directly or indirectly to the realization of this book. In the first place I want to thank my former colleagues at Philips Research Laboratories in Eindhoven for years of fruitful cooperation in the PHLIQA project, where many of the basic ideas in this book were born. My thanks go to Wim Bronnenberg, Jan Landsbergen, Piet Medema, Remko Scha, Wijnand Schoenmakers, and Eric van Utteren. I also want to thank my colleagues and students at the Institute for Perception Research (IPO) in Eindhoven for participating in discussions which helped to shape some of the ideas in this book, for engaging in computer implementation of semantic analysis of fragments of Dutch and English using the two-level framework and the grammar formalism developed here (thereby debugging the corresponding sections in the book), and in general for providing a very pleasant and stimulating working environment. My thanks go in particular to Herman Bouma, Don Bouwhuis, the late Ab van Katwijk, Jurgen van der Linden, Herman Muller, Floris van Nes, Robbert-Jan Beun, Frens Dols and Gemme thoe Schwartzenberg. I feel very fortunate to be in the position to continue my research in the new linguistics department at Tilburg University, in close cooperation with IPO. I also want to thank those with whom I have had fruitful discussions about my dissertation or new ideas incorporated in this book, including my thesis supervisors Hugo Brandt Corstius and Simon Dik; Jens Allwood, Johan van Benthem, Peter van Emde Boas, Jeroen Groenendijk, Sjaak de Mey, Julius Moravcsik, Jane Robinson, and Remko Scha. For comments on some version of the manuscript of this book I thank the anonymous referees of Reidel and Cambridge University Press, Robbert-Jan Beun, Dolf van Wezel and Geraldine Stoneham.

Finally, and most importantly, I want to thank my wife Annette for her careful proof reading of the manuscript and for helping me to bring it to its final form, and in general for helping me to keep going. Without her continuous support this book would not have been written.

PART 1
MODEL-THEORETIC SEMANTIC
ANALYSIS OF MASS TERMS

1 *Introduction*

1.1 Semantic issues relating to mass terms

In many languages we find a grammatical distinction between two classes of common nouns, called 'count nouns' and 'mass nouns'. The following examples illustrate the distinction in English:

(1.1)   a. There's a lot of water in Holland
　　　　　*There's a lot of canal in Holland
　　　　b. How much luggage do you have?
　　　　　*How much suitcase do you have?
　　　　c. Birdie eats 20 rice grains a day
　　　　　*Birdie eats 20 rice a day
　　　　d. The second symphony is fantastic
　　　　　*The second music is fantastic

'Water', 'luggage', 'rice', and 'music' are mass nouns; 'canal', 'suitcase', 'grain', and 'symphony' are count nouns. Mass nouns differ from count nouns in their syntactic as well as in their semantic properties. Syntactic differences are, for instance, that mass nouns do not have a singular and a plural form, do not take number words, and take the determiners 'much' and 'little'; count nouns, on the other hand, take the determiners 'many' and 'few' but resist a number of quantifiers such as 'a great deal of', 'a little bit of'. Semantically, the basic difference is that count terms typically refer to discrete objects, while mass terms typically refer to entities, conceived as continuous. These differences apply not only to bare nouns but also to more complex phrases like 'orange juice', 'cream in your coffee', 'twentieth-century Dutch poetry', etc.; such phrases are called *mass terms*.

This is only a rough, preliminary indication of the count/mass distinction, which will be discussed in detail in chapter 2. There is one qualification that should be made immediately, however, and that is that generally speaking the count/mass distinction cannot be drawn between *words*. In the sentence

(1.2) Mary put 10 grammes of onion in the salad

for example, the word 'onion' figures as a mass term, but in the sentence

(1.3) Mary put half an onion in the salad

the same word figures as a count term. This indicates that the count/mass distinction is not as easily defined as it might appear at first sight. In particular, it casts doubt on the idea that one might get from examples like those in (1.1) that the distinction is a syntactic one. In chapter 2 I shall discuss the problems involved in trying to define the count/mass distinction in syntactic or semantic terms, and offer a definition that is based on syntactic criteria.

Although mass terms are quite common, the study of semantic structures in natural language has so far centred almost exclusively around expressions that contain count terms only. It is only in the last decade that the particular problems associated with mass terms have caught the attention of semanticists, linguists as well as language philosophers, and recently also of computational linguists in the field of Artificial Intelligence.

Mass terms present a variety of semantic problems, that can be divided into two groups. First, there are problems in describing how the meaning of a complex expression containing a mass term is built up from those of its constituents. To give such a description, and to give it with formal precision, is a task for that branch of linguistics called *formal* or *model-theoretic semantics*. One of its central concerns is to offer a precise specification of the truth conditions of sentences, expressed in terms of the denotations of their constituents.

Secondly, there are philosophical problems concerning the nature of the entity denoted by a mass term. Mass terms seem to denote in a different way than count terms, a difference which is often expressed by saying that mass terms do not 'individuate' or 'divide' their extensions, whereas count terms do. Quine has formulated this as follows:

(1.4) To learn 'apple' it is not sufficient to learn how much of what goes on counts as apple; we must learn how much counts as an apple, and how much as another. Such terms possess built-in modes, however arbitrary, of dividing their reference ... consider 'shoe', 'pair of shoes', and 'footwear': all three range over exactly the same scattered stuff, and differ from one another solely in that two of them divide their reference differently, and the third not at all (Quine, 1960: 91).

In the usual formalization of count term denotations, the 'built-in mode of dividing its reference' of a noun like 'apple' is taken into account by construing the extension of the plural noun 'apples' as the set of those individuals called 'an apple'. The member–whole structure of a set is thus used to formalize the individuation of the count term. Since a mass term does not individuate its reference, it would seem that we should not use sets in the same way in formalizing the denotation of a mass term. Indeed, it seems intuitively wrong to ask what members constitute the sets that mass terms like 'orange juice', 'money', or 'music' refer to. Many authors on mass terms therefore believe that we need something other than sets in a formal description of mass term semantics (Quine, 1960; Burge, 1972; Dik, 1973; Parsons, 1970). Several special formalisms and variants of Lesniewski's mereology (also known as 'calculus of individuals') have been suggested. However, abandoning the framework of set theory leads to often underestimated technical problems, as we shall see in chapters 3 and 4.

Most of the literature on mass terms deals with both linguistic and philosophical questions, since an account of the truth conditions of sentences usually entails certain ontological commitments regarding the logical structure of mass noun denotations (see e.g. Bealer, 1975; Laycock, 1975; ter Meulen, 1980; Quine, 1960; Zemach, 1975). In the present study I make an attempt to disentangle the linguistic and the philosophical problems associated with mass terms. To this end I shall present a framework for semantic analysis which makes it possible to interpret mass-noun expressions in a model-theoretic fashion while remaining neutral on philosophical questions. This framework, called *two-level model-theoretic semantics*, distinguishes two levels of analysis: one where the logical nature of the denotations of mass terms (as well as those of other terms) is dictated by purely linguistic considerations, and one where this is dictated by a model of the world, which may be considered as capturing someone's actual ontological assumptions.

I agree with those who believe that we should not use sets for the description of mass term denotations, at least not in the same way as for count terms. I shall argue that we need certain formal concepts not available in classical set theory, both for giving a logical form to the intuition that mass terms do not individuate their reference, and for giving an adequate account of the truth conditions of sentences containing mass terms. I have developed a formalism containing these additional concepts under the name *ensemble theory*. Where set theory is a formalism that defines the formal properties of objects having a member–whole structure, ensemble theory is a formalism defining the formal properties of objects having a part–whole structure. Ensemble theory is set up in such a way that standard set theory is built into it, in the sense that the subset–set relation is treated as a special case of the general part–whole relation. Sets are thus defined in this formalism as ensembles with a special internal structure, which not all ensembles possess. This organization has the advantage that the proposed ensemble-based treatment of mass terms is easily combined with the usual set-based treatments of other semantic phenomena. At the same time, this avoids the technical problems that arise in the use of other non-standard formalisms (see 3.3, 3.4, and 4.3).

The present study deals with those semantic issues that relate specifically to mass terms. Consequently, I do not consider linguistic phenomena that require an intensional framework; I shall argue that these phenomena occur with mass terms in essentially the same way as with count terms. According to Montague (1973), the reason for an intensional treatment of mass terms, even when they occur in a non-intensional context, would be that two mass terms may have empty extensions without having the same meaning. However, this phenomenon is, of course, not specific to mass terms. Therefore, throughout this study only *extensional* interpretations of mass term expressions are considered, and the framework for semantic analysis can be a purely extensional one. This is not a real limitation, though, as it is a technically straightforward matter to intensionalize the treatment by adding functions from reference points to ensembles in the same way as functions from reference points to sets are used in a set-based intensional semantics.

1.2 Plan of the book

From what was said above, it will be clear that ensemble theory plays a central role in the semantic theory of mass terms that I shall propose. In order to be certain that ensemble theory is a formalism as well defined and reliable as classical set theory, I have carried out a full axiomatization of the theory and have provided an interpretation of the axiom system. But since there will be some readers who prefer not to have to work their way through an axiom system, but rather take the logical soundness of ensemble theory for granted, I have divided the book into two parts, where part 2 contains the description and discussion of ensemble theory as a mathematical formalism, while a rather informal exposition of the main points of the formalism is included in the main text in part 1 (chapter 5).

I have indicated above that, although some central examples of mass terms are easy to come by, it is not a simple matter to give a general definition of mass terms. Chapter 2 is devoted to this issue. Various definitions are discussed that have been put forward in the literature, by Jespersen (1924), Quine (1960), and Allan (1980) among others. A definition is offered that is based primarily on syntactic criteria, but which involves semantic considerations as well.

The linguistic literature on mass terms is reviewed in chapters 3 and 4 and the main problems that have not yet been resolved are indicated. It is argued that a successful semantic theory of mass terms should give a formal account of how the meaning of a complex expression, containing a mass noun, is built up from the meanings of its constituents, without violating the intuition that mass nouns do not individuate their reference. Rather, the formalization should give a precise interpretation to what is meant by saying that mass terms do not individuate their reference.

The notion of a semantic representation in a formal language and the use of ensemble concepts in such a representation is discussed in chapter 6. A family of formal languages for semantic representation is defined, based on ensemble theory. This chapter includes a formalization of the 'amount' concept, that is, of the meaning of expressions like 'two litres (of)'; this is needed for an analysis of quantified mass nouns.

After a brief introductory exposition of the aims and methods of model-theoretic semantics in general, the framework for semantic analysis called 'two-level model-theoretic semantics' is described in chapter 7. It is argued that this framework is attractive not only for the analysis of mass terms, but more generally for a systematic treatment of expressions with a semantic structure that has no direct correspondence to a conceptual structure in a domain of discourse.

The power of this framework and the use of ensemble theory are demonstrated in chapters 8 and 9 by giving a detailed account of the phenomena relating to the quantification and modification of mass nouns. Chapter 8 begins with a discussion of the phenomenon of quantification in general, and presents a treatment of quantification for count nouns in classical set-theoretical terms. This is subsequently generalized to an ensemble-based treatment of quantification that includes mass nouns. One of the salient features of this treatment is that, while an articulate analysis of quantification aspects is made, special care is taken to avoid an explosion of the number of readings of quantified noun phrases. This is accomplished by constructing semantic representations in a formal language where some aspects of a quantification may be left unspecified. A formal grammar for a fragment of English is presented, describing how the expressions of the fragment are systematically translated into an ensemble-based formal representation language, and interpreted according to the two-level model-theoretic method.

A treatment of mass noun modification is presented in chapter 9 focussing on modification by adjectives. Empirical data on the grammatical well-formedness of adjective–mass noun combinations are used to investigate the variety of mass noun modification types and the viability of a count/mass distinction among adjectives. A formal grammar is presented for an extension of the fragment of English, considered in chapter 8, which includes modified mass nouns.

Part 2 of the book deals with ensemble theory as a mathematical formalism.

In chapter 10, a detailed description of axiomatic ensemble theory is presented. The basic concepts of ensemble theory are introduced in a systematic manner, and a system of axioms is described from which a number of theorems of fundamental importance about ensembles are derived. It is worth noting that the formulation of axiomatic ensemble theory which is given does not presuppose the notion of a set.

In chapter 11, two special kinds of ensembles, called 'continuous' and 'discrete', are discussed and some of their most important properties are explored. A so-called 'interpretation' or 'model' of the axiom system developed in chapter 10, is described in chapter 12, that is the specification of a collection of objects which are shown to have all the properties described by the axioms. The interpretation proves the consistency of the formalism of ensemble theory, and at the same time shows that ensemble theory has something to offer which is not available in classical set theory.

In chapter 13 a detailed comparison of ensemble theory, Zermelo–Fraenkel set theory, and mereology is presented. It is proved that so-called 'discrete ensembles' are formally indistinguishable from sets, so that ensemble theory can be said to incorporate classical set theory. Moreover, it is shown that ensemble theory may also incorporate mereology, by introducing a special kind of ensemble, the so-called 'individual ensemble', which is proved to be the same formal concept as that of a mereological individual.

2 Mass terms

2.1 Mass terms syntactically defined

There is no general agreement in the literature as to which class of linguistic objects a semantic theory of mass terms should deal with, and whether this class should be defined in syntactic, semantic, or conceptual terms.

Historically, the basis of the distinction between mass terms and count terms is the conceptual delimitation of a certain class of nouns made by Jespersen as follows:

(2.1) There are many words which do not call up the idea of some definite thing with a certain shape or precise limits. I call these 'mass words': they may be either material, in which case they denote some substance in itself independent of form, such as 'silver', 'quicksilver', 'water', 'butter', 'gas', 'air', etc., or else immaterial, such as 'leisure', 'music', 'traffic', 'success', 'tact', 'commonsense', and ... 'satisfaction', 'admiration', 'refinement', from verbs, or ... 'restlessness', 'justice', 'safety', 'constancy', from adjectives (Jespersen, 1924:198).

Jespersen's 'mass words' indicate a linguistically interesting phenomenon in that all these words behave syntactically differently in several respects from such words as 'house', 'ring', 'song', 'day', 'dream', etc. However, there are words that do not 'call up the idea of some definite thing with a certain shape' but yet do not fit into Jespersen's list as far as their syntactic behaviour is concerned; for example, 'dream', 'virtue', 'belief', 'situation', and 'entity'. Also, there are words that fit into the list as far as their syntactic characteristics are concerned, but that do call up some idea of a definite thing; for example, 'furniture', 'footwear', 'fruit', and 'luggage'. Whether a word calls up an idea of some definite thing is therefore not a reliable criterion for defining a linguistic distinction between count nouns and mass nouns. Let us then look for a syntax-based definition.

It turns out to be a tricky matter to define the class of mass nouns on the basis of syntactic properties – so tricky that most authors on mass term semantics avoid the issue (e.g. Parsons, 1970; Burge, 1972; Pelletier, 1974;

ter Meulen, 1980). Parsons writes:

(2.2) A mass term is a term like 'water', 'gold', 'information', 'green ink', 'green ink that has been diluted', etc. ... The task of giving complete and explicit criteria for isolating out mass nouns is a detailed task which I will ignore here (Parsons, 1970:362).

The literature on mass terms contains a number of suggestions concerning cooccurrence restrictions for mass nouns with certain determiners and quantifiers but, with the exception of Bunt (1978), does not provide us with systematic attempts to define mass nouns in syntactic terms.

Grammar text books often take a certain division of the common nouns into mass and count nouns for granted, and mention some constraints on the possible syntactic environments in which the two types of nouns can occur (Gleason, 1965; Quirk *et al.*, 1972). For example, Quirk *et al.* write:

(2.3) 'Bottle', which takes definite and indefinite articles and admits a plural form, is an example of a COUNT NOUN. 'Bread', which takes zero article as well as definite article and indefinite quantifier, but does not have a plural form is a MASS NOUN.... Count nouns, which can be counted ('one pig', 'two pigs', 'several pigs',...), show the speaker as able to distinguish these items as separable entities. Mass nouns, on the other hand, are seen as continuous ('much pork', *'one pork', *'few pork',...) and show the speaker as regarding these substances or concepts as having no natural bounds (Quirk *et al.*, 1972:128–30).

On the basis of this characterization, Quirk *et al.* describe the syntax of English noun phrases, mentioning in passing a number of cooccurrence restrictions for nouns of either type with articles and other determiners, predeterminers, ordinals, cardinals and quantifiers. This is not a very accurate way of doing things since, as we have already seen in the previous chapter, it is, in general, not *words* that can be labelled as count or mass. It would be wrong to think that there is only a limited class of common nouns that can be used both as count nouns and as mass nouns, such as 'cake', 'stone', 'beef', 'ice cream', 'rope'. In fact, almost any 'mass noun' can be used as a count noun with the reading 'kind of...', as sentences (2.4) illustrate:

(2.4) a. Hungary produces many excellent wines
b. I prefer Latin American coffees to most African kinds

This illustrates the phenomenon that mass nouns can be used as count nouns with the reading 'kind of...'. This phenomenon is sometimes attributed only to concrete mass nouns, but it is found for 'abstract' mass nouns as well. The following sentences illustrate this for the abstract mass nouns 'pain' and 'restlessness':

(2.5) a. Back pain is a terrible pain
b. Antonio displays a restlessness that I have observed in many people of this village

On the other hand, most 'count nouns' can be used as mass nouns with the reading '... stuff'. For instance, the word 'apple' occurs as a mass noun in:

(2.6) a. Don't put so much apple in the salad

In 1975, Pelletier invented a hypothetical machine, the 'Universal Grinder', that can chop any object into a homogeneous mass: it turns a steak into steak, an apple into apple, a book into book, etc. Indeed, this suggests that at least for any noun normally used as a count noun referring to concrete objects one can imagine a context in which it would be appropriate to use it as a mass noun. Conversely, we can imagine a machine that takes as input a continuous stream of any substance (wine, linen, etc.), performs inspections according to colour, alcohol percentage, strength, etc., and issues qualifications like 'This is an excellent wine', 'This is a strong linen', etc. The conceivability of this machine, that we might call the 'Universal Sorter', indicates that, in principle, any 'mass noun' can be used as a count noun. (See also Bunt, 1985, section 1.) It would of course be irrelevant to object that the Universal Grinder and the Universal Sorter are only hypothetical machines: for the point made here it is sufficient that such machines can be imagined; we could thus, for example, write a story in which they occur. In such a story we could then have sentences like

(2.6) b. The bookymonster ate all the book that the machine spat out on the floor

A 'mass noun' like 'wine' or 'coffee' undergoes a shift in meaning when used as a count noun, as (2.4) and (2.5) illustrate, and a 'count noun' like 'apple' or 'book' undergoes another shift in meaning when used as a mass noun, as (2.6) illustrates, but that does not alter the fact that *nouns per se* cannot be classified as count or mass.

The fact that most nouns can be used both as count nouns and as mass nouns is interpreted in different ways by different authors. Quirk *et al.* treat such nouns as having dual class membership: ' "Cake" combines the properties of "bottle" and "bread", and is consequently both a count noun and a mass noun.' (1972, p. 128). However, these authors are apparently unaware of the fact that 'bottle' and 'bread' themselves would also have to be assigned dual class membership, and that this is in fact the case for so many nouns that a lexical classification of nouns as being either count or mass or both hardly seems feasible. Yet, one is inclined to say that intuitively speaking nouns like 'book' and 'car' are 'primarily' count nouns, nouns like 'water', 'furniture' and 'wine' are 'primarily' mass nouns, and nouns like 'cake', 'glass', and 'stone' are 'equally much' count noun and mass noun. This point will be taken up again in chapter 9.

Allan (1980) has proposed that 'degrees of countability' be assigned to nouns. For example, he assigns to the nouns 'car' and 'cat' a countability of 100%, to 'lamb', 'cake', and 'coffee' a countability of 82%, to 'admiration' and 'heat' a countability of 14%, and to 'equipment' and 'furniture' a countability of 0%. These figures reflect a noun's readiness to occur as the head of a noun phrase with certain articles, quantifiers, and other determiners.[1] Underlying this approach is the view that a noun as such cannot be classified as 'count' or 'mass', but that such classifications can be given to noun phrases with certain configurations of determiners. This comes very close to saying that the qualifications 'count' and 'mass' can only be applied to a noun as it occurs in the context of certain determiners, a view which is taken by Parsons (1970), Pelletier (1974), and others. I subscribe to this view and thus consider the count/mass distinction as a distinction not among nouns but among noun occurrences.

This leaves us with the task of defining those occurrences of nouns that should be classified as mass occurrences and those that should be classified as count occurrences. In British English, the following syntactic configurations only allow for occurrences of mass nouns:

(2.7) (M1) A noun preceded by the determiner 'much'.
(M2) A noun preceded by one of the quantifiers 'a little', 'a little bit of'.
(M3) A singular noun preceded by an amount phrase, that is, a phrase like '10 kilogrammes of', 'less than five litres of', 'half a cup of'.[2]
(M4) A singular noun preceded by 'enough', by unstressed 'some', or by unstressed 'any'.
(M5) A noun preceded by one of the expressions 'a great deal of', 'a large (small, great, etc.) amount of', 'a large (small, etc.) quantity of'.

Whether a noun occurrence is singular or plural is frequently but not always determined by its morphology, and must, in general, be decided on the basis of the verb forms and pronouns it governs. For instance, the sentence

(2.8) I saw some lamb

(with unstressed 'some') does not contain syntactic clues for deciding whether 'lamb' is singular (and thus used as a mass noun, according to (M4)), or plural; in this respect the sentence differs from:

(2.9) I saw some fish that were jumping out of the net

where the plural verb form 'were' indicates that 'fish' is a count noun here.

It is often said that mass nouns are always singular (e.g. Burge, 1975; Quine, 1960), but there are some exceptions to this, as the occurrences of 'brains', 'oats', and 'mashed potatoes' in the following sentences illustrate:

(2.10) Not so much mashed potatoes please, they're rather salty

(2.11) Just a little oats, please

(2.12) He doesn't have as much brains as Albert

or, in Dutch:

(2.13) Wat een boel watten zijn er gebruikt

(='What a lot of cotton-wool has been used')

It may be added that (M1)–(M5) apply not only to bare nouns but also to nouns with a premodifying adjective or classifier and/or postmodifying relative clause or prepositional phrase – what I shall refer to as 'nominal complexes' (such as 'dirty water', 'orange juice', 'green ink which has been diluted', 'cheese from Friesland').

Next, let us consider some syntactic positions in which only count nouns can occur. The following cases seem to be unexceptionable:

(2.14)   (C1) A noun preceded by one of the quantifiers 'many', 'few', 'fewer', 'fewest', 'a few', 'several', 'numerous'.
   (C2) A noun preceded by one of the determiners 'every', 'each', 'either', 'neither', 'both'.
   (C3) A noun preceded by 'a (large, small, etc.) number of', or 'a single'.
   (C4) A noun preceded by a number phrase, that is, a cardinal number ('one', 'two', 'three', etc.), a fraction ('two-thirds', 'one-and-a-half', etc.), or an expression like 'a dozen', 'a gross'.

It is widely believed that being preceded by the indefinite article 'a(n)' is also typical for a count noun occurrence (see e.g. Quine, 1960; Burge, 1972; Pelletier, 1979; Cartwright, 1975; ter Meulen, 1980). However, Allan (1980) gives some examples to the contrary, such as:

(2.15)   I have a great admiration for Bette

None of the above criteria (M1)–(M5) apply here, but I believe there are reasons to view 'admiration' as a mass noun here, in spite of the occurrence of the indefinite article (see below). The indefinite article has therefore not been included in (C2).

It may be possible to extend the lists (M1)–(M5) and (C1)–(C4) and obtain a more complete catalogue of syntactic positions in which count noun occurrences and mass noun occurrences can be recognized. But, however much effort is put into making up such a catalogue, it will necessarily always be incomplete in the sense that not all noun occurrences *can* be classified on syntactic grounds. In a sentence like

(2.16)   There's no chicken in the yard

there is no way of telling, on purely syntactic grounds, whether 'chicken' is a count noun or a mass noun. The sentence has the two readings

(2.17)   a. There's not a single chicken in the yard
         b. There isn't any chicken in the yard

(with unstressed 'any'); on the first reading 'chicken' is a count noun, on the second it is a mass noun. In other words, 'chicken' in the expression 'no chicken' is ambiguous: it is a count noun on the reading 'not a single chicken', and a mass noun on the reading 'not any chicken' (with unstressed 'any'). This suggests that for occurrences of a noun n in an expression E, which does not contain syntactic criteria for classifying n as a count noun or a mass noun, we might say the following. If E can be paraphrased by an expression E_1 in which n occurs in such a syntactic configuration that it can be classified as a mass (count) noun, then n occurs as a mass (count) noun in E on the reading E_1. Thus, 'chicken' in (2.16) is a mass noun on the reading (2.17a), and a count noun on the reading (2.17b).

Applying this to the sentence considered above (2.15): we can say that, if we agree that 'a great admiration' can be paraphrased by 'much admiration', then on the reading

(2.18)   I have much admiration for Bette

'admiration' is a mass noun in (2.15).

In Bunt [1981a], I have proposed extending the count/mass distinction as based on syntactic criteria by using this paraphrase technique. However, this extension is not without problems, as it may be possible to paraphrase a given sentence in two ways, one with an overt count noun and one with an overt mass noun. The paraphrase technique therefore does not guarantee a consistent classification, and for this reason I now think it is better to stick with the purely syntactic definition given above.

It may be noted that I do not claim the count/mass distinction to be exhaustive. For occurrences of nouns that never appear in any of the syntactic configurations (M1)–(M5), (C1)–(C4) we have no means to classify them as count nouns or mass nouns. This is, for example, the case with 'weather' and 'contents'. Ware (1975) discusses other cases of nouns that seem to resist a count/mass classification.

As we noted already, the count/mass distinction applies not only to occurrences of nouns, but also to occurrences of nominal complexes. For the sake of brevity I shall use the expressions 'mass nouns' and 'mass terms' in what follows as short for 'mass occurrences of nouns' and 'mass occurrences of nominal complexes', respectively, where 'mass occurrence' is defined by the syntactic criteria (2.7).

Another point to notice here is that our definition of mass nouns obviously does not discriminate between 'concrete' and 'abstract' nouns. I do not follow the line that several authors take, who use a definition which is on the one hand based on syntax but on the other hand restricted to 'concrete' nouns (e.g. Burge, 1972; Parsons, 1970; Pelletier, 1974). Both 'abstract' mass nouns and 'concrete' mass nouns are taken here as objects of a semantic theory.[3]

2.2 Mass terms semantically defined

Besides a syntax-based notion 'mass nouns', we also find suggestions in the literature for defining a concept 'mass terms' from a semantic point of view. The general idea is that there is a semantic difference between 'count terms' and 'mass terms' which is found in their way of referring to something: 'count terms' refer to discrete, well-delineated entities, whereas 'mass terms' refer in a diffuse sort of way, without making it explicit how their referents are individuated or 'divided' into individual objects. As Quine puts it, taking the word 'apple' as a (somewhat unfortunate) example of a count term:

(2.19) To learn 'apple' it is not sufficient to learn how much of what goes on counts as apple; we must learn how much counts as an apple, and how much as another.

Such terms possess built-in modes, however arbitrary, of dividing their reference... consider 'shoe', 'pair of shoes', and 'footwear': all three range over exactly the same scattered stuff, and differ from one another solely in that two of them divide their reference differently, and the third not at all (1960, p. 91).

The diffuse, non-individuating way of referring to something, which seems to be characteristic for mass terms, is closely related to the phenomenon that mass terms have the possibility of being used to refer to each of certain objects as well as to these objects as a whole. For instance, if we have the sentence

(2.20) There is some water on the floor

used in a situation where there are several puddles of water on the floor, the term 'water' may refer to each of these puddles as well as to these puddles as a whole. Quine has coined the term *cumulative reference* for this phenomenon, and suggests that it characterizes mass terms semantically:

(2.21) So-called *mass* terms like 'water', 'footwear', and 'red' have the semantical property of referring cumulatively: any sum of parts which are water is water (1960, p. 91).

It is worth noting that the phrase 'any sum of parts which are water is water' can be understood in two ways: it can be understood at a physical level, as an assertion about water, and it can be understood at a linguistic level as an assertion about the use of terms like 'water'. Considerations of a physical nature are, in principle, irrelevant to linguistic theory unless they are shown to be reflected in language (in the truth conditions of sentences, for instance). I therefore assume that the phrase in (2.21) should not be interpreted at the physical level, which is also in line with Quine's calling (2.21) a condition of *reference*. We shall see below that there is a general danger of confusion in the understanding of statements of the kind of (2.21) at a physical or at a linguistic level.

In the characterization of mass terms by the cumulative reference condition there is clearly no restriction to the syntactic category of nouns; it extends, in principle, to all categories of referring terms. As the examples in the quotation indicate, we could consider 'mass adjectives' besides mass nouns, and we could, for instance, also think of 'mass verbs'.

It is not immediately clear that it would be fruitful to distinguish 'mass adjectives' or 'mass verbs'. Moravcsik (1973) notes that the cumulative reference condition would classify 'heavy' and 'large' as 'mass adjectives', whereas 'light' and 'small' would be in a different subcategory ('count adjectives'?), though intuitively one would expect these adjectives to belong to the same semantic subcategory. Whether it is fruitful to distinguish 'mass adjectives' from 'count adjectives' depends on whether such a distinction would have grammatical correlates. There are indications that adjectives not cumulative in reference do not combine well with mass nouns. According to Quine, 'adjectives not cumulative in reference simply tend not to occur next to mass terms' (1960, p. 104). For example, the combination 'small water' in

(2.22) *There is some small water on the floor

seems to be deviant. However, replacing 'small' by 'large', which is cumulative in reference, does not change the situation in this respect. It therefore seems doubtful that cumulativity of reference is what makes the difference. This matter will be taken up again in chapter 9, where the semantics of mass noun modification is discussed.

As for a count/mass distinction among verbs, we should first of all make sure what the cumulative reference condition would mean in this case. For intransitive verbs this seems quite straightforward: a one-argument verb 'V' meets the condition of cumulative reference if, whenever 'V' is truly predicated of two arguments 'x' and 'y', it is also true of 'x' and 'y' considered as a whole. For example, if we take the verb 'melt' for 'V' and if x and y are two portions of snow, then if both x and y are melting one might also say that the portion of snow formed by x and y is melting. Similarly for such verbs as 'flow', 'condense', 'evaporate', 'freeze', etc. These verbs tend to have mass subjects, but it would be wrong to think that this is a correlating syntactic property of these verbs since we also say that ice cubes melt, rivers flow, puddles freeze and evaporate, etc. Alternatively, one could look for verbs requiring a count noun as subject ('count verbs'?). But these are equally hard to find; even for verbs requiring animate subjects the situation is not clear-cut, since they can have animate mass nouns (*sic!*) as subject, as is illustrated by:

(2.23) There's a lot of game on this reserve that lives quite peacefully

Other possibilities, such as verbs requiring a mass noun as direct object, are not any more promising (see Moravcsik, 1973).

Ter Meulen (1980) has proposed a count/mass distinction among verbs that would coincide with a classification into 'activity verbs' and 'performance verbs'; activity verbs are assigned the feature '−count' and performance verbs the feature '+count'. The distinction is defined as follows: 'The difference between activity-verbs and performance-verbs comes out in the fact that performance-verbs do not, whereas activity-verbs do, have sub-events that are denoted by the same verb' (ter Meulen 1980:121). For example, 'to eat' and 'to travel' are activity verbs; 'to prepare dinner' and 'to reach' are performance verbs. Two syntactic correlates of this distinction are mentioned. First, following Hoepelman (1976) it is noted that progressive forms of activity verbs do not always form acceptable verb phrases with bounded temporal adverbs. For instance, the sentence

(2.24) Henry was eating in an hour

is unacceptable, in contrast with

(2.25) Henry was preparing dinner in an hour

Secondly, it is claimed that

(2.26) Nominalizations of verbs can be distinguished into mass-like nominalizations with a −count feature and count-like nominalizations with a +count feature. The nominalization of an activity-verb like 'eating' has all syntactic properties characteristic of mass terms. The determiners 'little' and 'much' are grammatical with 'eating', and a plural form does not really exist, without changing the intuitive meaning to kinds of eating (ter Meulen 1980:124).

Indeed, nominalizations of activity verbs behave like mass nouns in some respects, but it is less clear that nominalizations of performance verbs behave syntactically like count nouns. Does one speak of 'few dinner preparings' or 'many reachings', rather than 'a little dinner preparing' or 'a great deal of reaching'?

In addition, ter Meulen says that a mass noun, when used in such a way that it does not refer to particular instances of its denotation but to an abstract 'substance' (the so-called nominal use; see section 3.5), can only be the subject of a stative verb, that is, a verb denoting a state rather than an event. This is not quite correct, though, in view of such counterexamples as:

(2.27) Gold received atomic number 79

(2.28) Water disappeared from the moon long ago

I think it is fair to conclude that there is no strong evidence that the distinction of 'activity verbs' versus 'performance verbs' should be considered as a generalization of the distinction between count nouns and mass nouns.

Restricting our attention to nouns and nominal complexes then, we may consider how satisfactory the semantic definition of mass terms is which is based on Quine's cumulative reference condition. There are three points of serious criticism that I will discuss here. First, the notions of 'sum' and 'part' are too vague. It is not obvious that the condition, as formulated by Quine, really distinguishes mass nouns from count nouns. For example, if we have two collections of books, when considering them as a whole we again have a collection of books. Since a collection of books may be referred to as 'books', it may be argued that 'the sum of any parts that are books is books'. This is of course not what Quine intended (rather, the idea is that two books, considered as a whole, cannot appropriately be referred to as 'a book'), but it shows that the criterion 'the sum of any parts that are ... is ...' as such is too vague for a reliable definition of mass nouns.

Secondly, it is not obvious that the cumulative reference condition defines a class of terms which is of linguistic interest. We have already seen that the definitions of 'mass adjectives' and 'mass verbs' on the basis of this condition are of dubious value, but there is room for doubts also when we restrict the condition to nominal terms. The reason is that the syntactic phenomena, characteristic for mass nouns, occur equally well with abstract mass nouns as with concrete mass nouns, while there may be doubts about the applicability of the notions 'part' and 'sum' to abstract mass nouns. For instance, Burge writes:

(2.29) abstract mass nouns do not appear to satisfy the semantical criterion that concrete mass nouns satisfy. Mereological concepts simply do not have any straightforward application to these nouns (1972, p. 264).

I believe that the situation is not as simple as Burge suggests, since we do find locutions like:

(2.30)   The last part of my education was the most inspiring

(2.31)   Part of my unhappiness with the situation had to do with the fact that ...

Apparently, we do sometimes talk in terms of education-parts and unhappiness-parts, and surely we can also refer to several of such parts considered as a whole, as in the sentence:

(2.32)   My education at Cambridge and at Oxford together resulted in acquiring a certain manner of thinking rather than in accumulating useful knowledge

It seems to me that there is, in principle, nothing objectionable about the application of the notions 'part' and 'whole' to abstract mass nouns, provided we consider them on the same level of abstractness as the concepts that the nouns refer to.

Finally, although the cumulative reference condition seems to capture a certain semantic property of mass nouns, it is not obvious that it captures the characteristic semantic property. Cheng (1973) suggests another property, which he calls Cheng's condition: 'Any part of the whole of the mass object which is w is w'. This condition is intended to be a condition, not on a term's way of referring to something, but on a term's referent. Cheng believes that, for establishing a definition of mass terms, it is necessary first to study the nature of the entities that mass terms refer to:

(2.33) we can also formulate a general condition for mass terms. Before we do this, we should make clear the general nature of the object to which mass terms apply. We call the object to which a mass term applies a mass object. I think that what characterizes a mass object is the internal uniformity of its discernible composition. Informally speaking, a mass object has a homogeneity of distribution of composing elements which enables us to identify the whole thing by identifying part of the thing or to identify the part by identifying the whole as well as to identify one part by identifying another part (1973, pp. 286–7).

Cheng's condition is unambiguously a condition of an extra-linguistic, physical nature, and should therefore, in my opinion, not be part of a linguistic theory. English and other languages provide us with abundant terms by which we refer to the same objects either by means of a count term or by means of a mass term; moreover, languages differ in what entities are referred to by mass nouns.[4] These facts clearly indicate that the count/mass distinction cannot be viewed as a distinction among objects.

We can turn Cheng's condition into a condition on the way a term refers, instead of a condition on the objects referred to, by reformulating it in similar terms as (2.21):

(2.34) A mass term 'w' has the property that any part of something which is 'w' is 'w'.

I will refer to the condition in this form as the *distributive reference condition*. This condition appears to be equally successful as the cumulative reference condition in capturing a semantic property of mass terms: a part of water, gold, or leisure is again water, gold, leisure. (Any part? This question will be discussed in section 4.2.)

Altogether, I think it is justified to conclude that both the cumulative reference condition and the distributive reference condition expresses a semantic aspect of the way mass terms refer to something, but that it is doubtful whether any one of them captures the essence of non-individuating reference and can be the basis for defining a linguistically relevant notion of mass terms.

3 Approaches to mass term semantics

3.1 Differences in approaches

The various approaches to mass term semantics in the literature differ in one or more of the following respects:

(1) in the class of linguistic objects covered by the term 'mass terms';
(2) in the philosophical standpoint concerning the ontological implications of a semantic theory;
(3) in the formal apparatus that is used.

The differences concerning point (1) will be disregarded to the extent that I shall only consider what the various proposals have to say about mass terms in our sense of the term. As regards the second point, it was already emphasized in chapter 1 that the present study intends to remain neutral on philosophical, in particular, ontological issues as much as possible. This point will therefore be left out of the discussion of the literature insofar as it has no immediate implications for formal semantic analysis.

Concerning the third point, the question invariably turns up whether a mass noun should be viewed as referring to a single, individual entity or to a multiplicity of objects. Does 'water', for example, refer to 'a single though scattered object, the aqueous part of the world' (Quine, 1960, p. 98), or to the class of all portions of water? If the latter view is adopted, the classical apparatus of sets and predicates may be called into action; if the first view is taken, it would appear that something else is needed. For even if we treat 'water' as referring to the single entity formed by all the water in the world, we still have to take into account that this entity has a certain internal structure in order to understand a sentence like:

(3.1) All the water in the Rhine comes from the Alps

Intuitively, the instances of water involved in the quantification and selection in such a sentence stand in a part–whole relation to the totality of all water; many authors therefore invoke for the description of this relation a theory of part–whole, originally developed by Lesniewski under the name *mereology* (Lesniewski, 1929),[1] and reformulated by Leonard and Goodman (1940) under the name *calculus of individuals*. In these calculi a theory of the part–whole relation is developed that leads to a formalized notion of 'sum' or 'fusion' of parts, by means of which an object can be constructed that comprises all the parts in question. Such an object is called the 'mereological whole' formed by these parts, and can be used to formalize the intuitive notion of 'the totality of all water'.

Some proposals for mass noun semantics are formulated within an intensional framework. We shall see, however, that the specific problems that the semantic analysis of mass terms pose are independent of the linguistic phenomena that require an intensional framework (see also section 3.5). Since this study concentrates on the analysis of those phenomena that are specific to mass terms, I shall consider only the extensional parts of these proposals.

The approaches to mass term semantics in the literature which are elaborate enough to allow a detailed comparison can be divided into four groups according to the logical type of the denotation assigned to a mass noun:

1. mass nouns in some syntactic positions denote mereological wholes, in other positions they denote predicates (Quine);
2. in all syntactic positions, mass nouns denote mereological wholes (Moravcsik);
3. mass nouns denote abstract 'substances' in all syntactic positions (Parsons) or in some syntactic positions, while denoting sets of quantities of a substance in other positions (ter Meulen);
4. mass nouns denote sets (Cartwright, Grandy) or predicates (Burge, Pelletier).

I shall review these four groups in the given order.

3.2 Quine's semi-mereological approach

Historically, the literature on mass term semantics can be said to begin with Quine's discussion of the peculiarities of their reference in *Word and Object* (1960). As mentioned in the previous chapter, Quine defines 'mass terms' as those terms that do not 'divide their reference' and are 'cumulative' in reference; accordingly, not only nouns can be mass terms, but also verbs and adjectives.

Quine considers occurrences of mass terms in two syntactic positions: before and after a copula. He argues that mass nouns occurring after a copula, as in:

(3.2) a. This puddle is water
 b. The white part is sugar

should be treated as predicates (general terms):

(3.3) We can view the mass term in these contexts as general terms, reading 'is water', 'is sugar',... as 'is a bit of water', 'is a bit of sugar',... In general a mass term in predicative position may be viewed as a general term which is true of each portion of the stuff in question, excluding only the parts too small to count (1960, pp. 97–8).

On the other hand, when occurring before a copula, as in:

(3.4) Water is a liquid

It is suggested that mass nouns be treated as referring to single entities:

(3.5) In 'water is a liquid', on the other hand, and 'water is liquid', the mass term is much on a par with the singular term of 'Mama is big' or 'Agnes is a lamb'. A mass term used in subject position differs none from such singular terms as 'Mama' and 'Agnes', unless the scattered stuff that it names be denied the status of a single sprawling object (1960, p. 98).

Quine's discussion is rather informal and not explicit about the logical status of the 'single sprawling object' denoted by a mass noun in subject position, but from what he says elsewhere in the book (pp. 61, 98n, 181) we may assume that he conceives this object as the mereological whole made up by all the parts that the predicate, corresponding to the predicative use of the mass term, is true of.

A mass noun in subject position being treated as referring to a single entity, the question arises why a mass noun in predicate position should not be treated in the same way, using a part–whole relation as formal counterpart of the copula. Or, put in mereological terms, if a sentence like 'Water is a liquid' is rendered formally as:

(3.6) LIQUID(W-whole)

where LIQUID denotes the predicate 'is a liquid' and W-whole the mereological whole of all the world's water, why not treat a sentence like 'This puddle is water' as:

(3.7) $p \subseteq W\text{-whole}$

where 'p' denotes 'this puddle' and ⊆ the part–whole relation of mereology, translating the copula 'is'. Instead, Quine proposes to analyse this sentence as:

(3.8) W-pred(p)

where W-pred is the predicate such that W-pred(x) is true of x if and only if x ⊆ W-whole and x is not 'too small to count' (see quotation 3.3). His argument for preferring the analysis (3.8) to (3.7) is that the parts of W-whole that W-pred is true of should not be 'too small to count': the analysis should take into account that the mereological wholes, corresponding to mass nouns in subject position, in general have parts that are too small to be appropriately referred to by the nouns in question. For instance, the parts of a water molecule, the parts of a grain of sugar, or the parts of a chair are not water, sugar, and furniture, respectively. Moreover, the point where this lower limit is reached depends on the noun in question and cannot therefore be accounted for by a general restriction on the part–whole relation.

The idea that lower limits should be acknowledged in mass noun extensions plays a crucial role not only in Quine's own proposal, but also in many other proposals for the semantics of mass terms. I will refer to this idea as the *minimal parts hypothesis* and discuss its significance in detail in chapter 4.

Quine's proposal has already been criticized extensively in the literature (see e.g. Moravcsik, 1973; Pelletier, 1974; Burge, 1972). I restrict myself here to briefly recapitulating the main points of criticism that have been raised.

First, the proposal is incomplete in that it does not treat mass nouns occurring neither before nor after a copula. Thus it may happen as Burge (1972) says about the sentence

(3.9) Phil threw snow on Bill

that 'it would seem natural and intuitive to extend Quine's theory to handle "snow" in this sentence as a singular term'. Thus, the analysis

(3.10) THREW-ON(p, s, b)

is suggested (where 's' is a constant denoting the mereological whole of all snow, 'p' denotes Phil, 'b' denotes Bill, and THREW-ON denotes a predicate corresponding to the throw-action). But, as Burge notes, this would not be a correct analysis of the sentence, assuming that Phil did not throw (the totality of) *all* snow on Bill. To me it seems more plausible that we should apply the predicate-part of Quine's proposal in this case and introduce an existential quantifier in the analysis of the noun phrase 'snow', which would lead to:

(3.11) (∃x)(S-pred(x) & THREW-ON(p, x, b))

Secondly, Quine's theory fails to account for some of the most obvious logical properties of sentences containing mass nouns, even if we restrict ourselves to sentences where mass nouns occur before or after a copula. A classic example (see Moravcsik, 1973) is the theory's failure to account for the inference of

(3.12) This puddle is wet

from the premises (3.13) and (3.14):

(3.13) This puddle is water

(3.14) Water is wet

According to Quine's theory, the premises would be analysed as (3.15) and (3.16), respectively:

(3.15) W-pred(p)

(3.16) WET(W-whole)

and the desired consequence (3.12) would be analysed as (3.17):

(3.17) WET(p)

Since there is no logical relation in the theory between W-pred and W-whole, (3.17) does not follow from (3.15) and (3.16).

For similar reasons, the theory fails to show that the sentence

(3.18) Water is water

is a tautology, for it would be analysed as:

(3.19) W-pred(W-whole)

which is not a tautology, again because of the absence of a logical relation between 'W-pred' and 'W-whole' (example taken from Pelletier, 1974).[2] For further discussion of this kind of problem with Quine's proposal see Burge (1972) and Pelletier (1974); other points of criticism can be found in Parsons (1970) and Moravcsik (1973). Burge summarizes the logical problems with

26 Part 1 *Model-theoretic semantics of mass terms*

Quine's proposal by concluding that 'one must treat mass terms as being either predicates or individual constants but not both, on pain of failing to account for the logical relations binding different sentential occurrences together' (1972, p. 267).

Many of the problems we see here arise because the theory does not specify a logical relation between the mereological whole and the predicate corresponding to a mass noun in different syntactic positions. These problems could be overcome by adding to the theory for each mass noun a postulate of the form:

(3.20) $(\forall x)(M\text{-pred}(x) \leftrightarrow x \subseteq M\text{-whole})$

If these equivalences were accepted, however, it would be simpler to dispense with either the predicates or the mereological wholes altogether, replacing either M-pred by $\subseteq$ M-whole or M-whole by SUM($\{x|M\text{-pred}(x)\}$). It is Quine's minimal parts hypothesis that prevents him from accepting (3.20). According to the hypothesis, (3.20) only holds for those parts of M-whole that are larger than minimal parts. Therefore, we could postulate that

(3.21) $(\forall x)(M\text{-pred}(x) \rightarrow x \subseteq M\text{-whole})$

but not the other way round. Postulates of the latter form are not sufficiently powerful to overcome the difficulties mentioned above.

3.3 Fully mereological approaches

Moravcsik (1973) outlines two alternative proposals in which mass terms in all syntactic positions are treated uniformly as referring to mereological wholes. In both proposals mass nouns in subject position are treated in the same way as in Quine's proposal; the differences are in the treatment of mass nouns in predicate position.

We have seen that the minimal parts hypothesis prevented Quine from analysing a mass noun with extension M-whole, occurring in predicate position, as $\subseteq$ M-whole. Moravcsik suggests two alternative variants of the $\subseteq$ M-whole analysis that would not lead to conflicts with the minimal parts hypothesis.

In the first variant for each mass noun extension M-whole a part M_{SP} is defined that does not contain the parts of M excluded by the minimal parts hypothesis. For instance, for the mass noun 'water' W_{SP} would be the restricted mereological whole made up by all water-parts of at least the size

Approaches to mass term semantics 27

of an H_2O molecule. To say that something 'is water' is then interpreted as saying that it is a part of this restricted whole W_{SP} (rather than a part of W-whole):

(3.22) For any mass term 'F', to say 'x is F' is to say that 'x' is a part of that part of F that has structural properties SP (1973, p. 283).

Moravcsik uses Quine's definition of mass terms, including adjectives, and treats all mass terms alike. A 'mass adjective' like 'red' is thus treated as referring to a restricted mereological whole RED_{SP}.

Quine's 'puddle puzzle' (see (3.12)–(3.14)) can be solved in this proposal. The premises 'This puddle is water' and 'Water is wet' would be analysed as (3.23) and (3.24), respectively:

(3.23) $p \subseteq W_{SP}$

(3.24) W-whole $\subseteq WET_{SP}$

The desired consequence 'This puddle is wet', is analysed as

(3.25) $p \subseteq WET_{SP}$

and this follows indeed from (3.23) and (3.24) since $W_{SP} \subseteq$ W-whole and the $\subseteq$-relation is transitive.

However, this proposal runs into the same problem as Quine's when it comes to accounting for the analyticity of the sentence 'Water is water'. In the present proposal, this sentence would be analysed as

(3.26) W-whole $\subseteq W_{SP}$

which not only fails to be a tautology, but is even false: if it were true it would, in conjunction with $W_{SP} \subseteq$ W-whole, imply

(3.27) W-whole $= W_{SP}$

(in mereology, mutual inclusion means equality; see Leonard and Goodman, 1940, p. 47). This would destroy the very idea that W_{SP} is a restricted part of W-whole. Therefore, (3.26) must be false, and consequently the proposal renders 'Water is water' a *false* proposition.

This obviously could be avoided by analysing 'Water is water' not as (3.26), but as

(3.28) $W_{SP} \subseteq W_{SP}$

which is a mereological tautology. This suggests that it would be better to do completely without the unrestricted W-whole and use only W_{SP}.

Unfortunately, Moravcsik's notion of a restricted mereological whole is not a consistent one. Given a mereological whole M, the restricted whole M_{SP} is meant to include those and only those parts of M that have the property SP. Now suppose we have two parts x_1 and x_2, both part of M_{SP}, then their mereological sum $x_1 + x_2$ is, according to the logic of mereology, also a part of M_{SP}. But, if SP is not conserved under mereological summation, $x_1 + x_2$ will be a part of M_{SP} that does not have the property SP. To avoid such inconsistencies, the property SP must be required to be conserved under mereological summation.

But there is a still greater difficulty. For suppose that x_1 is one of the minimal parts of M that has the property SP. (It was in order to cope with such parts that M_{SP} was introduced.) So $x_1 \subseteq M_{SP}$. Now let x_2 be a part of x_1. From $x_2 \subseteq x_1$ and $x_1 \subseteq M_{SP}$ it follows, due to the transitivity of the $\subseteq$-relation, that $x_2 \subseteq M_{SP}$. Since x_1 is a minimal part having the property SP, x_2 does not have the property SP. Therefore x_2 is a part of M_{SP} that does not have the property SP. To avoid this inconsistency, the minimal parts with property SP must be required not to have any parts at all!

We have to conclude that the notion of a mereological object having as parts those and *only* those entities that have certain properties SP is not a well-defined concept, unless the notion of 'structural properties' or that of 'minimal parts' is constrained in certain ways.

Moravcsik may have had some misgivings about his proposal, as he also suggested an alternative proposal in case the one just outlined should turn out to be untenable. The alternative consists of leaving the mass noun extensions unrestricted but putting the SP-restrictions in the part–whole relation. For every mass noun 'm' a part–whole relation $\subseteq_{SP(m)}$ is introduced, where SP(m) indicates the structural properties of the denotation of 'm'. Using this relation, expressions of the form 'x is m' are analysed as:

(3.30) $x \subseteq_{SP(m)}$ M-whole

Assuming the presence of semantic postulates which ensure that every mass noun extension M-whole has the corresponding property SP(m), this solves the 'Water is water' puzzle, at which the first proposal failed. But this proposal fails at the puddle puzzle. The premises 'This puddle is water' and 'Water is wet' would now be analysed as (3.31) and (3.32), respectively:

(3.31) $p \subseteq_{SP(water)}$ W-whole

(3.32) W-whole $\subseteq_{SP(wet)}$ WET

from which the desired conclusion 'This puddle is wet', now analysed as:

(3.33) $p \subseteq_{SP(wet)} WET$

does not follow, since we have lost the transitivity of the $\subseteq$-relation now that we have the two relations $\subseteq_{SP(water)}$ and $\subseteq_{SP(wet)}$ instead of one single part–whole relation.

The two approaches suggested by Moravcsik thus both run into serious difficulties.

3.4 Mass nouns as denoting substances

Parsons (1970) has proposed an approach to mass term semantics in which all occurrences of mass terms are treated as denoting single entities, as in the approaches suggested by Moravcsik. This proposal differs from all other proposals in the literature both in the formal apparatus that is invoked for the analysis of sentences and in the underlying ontological view. This ontological view has been criticized heavily for its complexity (see e.g. Burge, 1972; Moravcsik, 1973; Pelletier, 1974); in a later paper (1975), Parsons has responded to this criticism and withdrawn some of the details of the original proposal, thereby simplifying his ontology.

Parsons calls the entities, denoted by mass terms, 'substances', and introduces this notion as follows:

(3.34) I will use the word 'substance' in the chemist's sense – to stand for any material (1970, p. 365).

In order to understand what is meant by this notion we must briefly consider Parsons' ontological system, in which entities at three different levels are distinguished: (1) physical objects, (2) 'bits of matter', and (3) substances. Two primitive predicates are introduced, one for relating physical objects to substances and one for relating 'bits of matter' to substances. For instance, a golden ring is conceived of as a physical object consisting of 'bits of matter', some (but not all) of which are 'quantities of gold'. A sentence like:

(3.35) My ring is gold

is analysed as

(3.36) $r\,C\,g$

where 'r' names 'my ring', 'g' names the substance 'gold', and C is the predicate relating the physical object and the substance; C is to be read 'is constituted of' (p. 365). On the other hand, the sentence

(3.37) The bit of matter making up my ring is gold

is analysed as:

(3.38) m Q g

where 'm' stands for 'the bit of matter making up my ring' and 'Q' is the predicate relating the bit of matter and the substance; 'Q' is to be read: 'is a quantity of'.

The notions 'bit of matter' and 'substance', and the relation 'Q' connecting them, are explained as follows:

(3.39) The notion of a bit of matter being *a quantity of* a substance is a primitive notion in my analysis. I can explain it roughly as follows: A substance, like gold, is found scattered around the universe in various places. Wherever it 'occurs', we will have a bit of matter which *is a quantity of* gold. This somewhat vaguely delimits the extension of the relation 'is a quantity of'. Another such delimitation is the following: if it is true to say of an object (a physical object) that it 'is gold', then the matter making it up will be *a quantity of* gold (1970, p. 367).

Parsons admits later that his ontology can perhaps be simplified by dropping the distinction between physical objects and bits of matter (p. 378), which would mean that the relations of constitution (C) and quantity (Q) coincide. However, he insists that physical objects and bits of matter must be distinguished from quantities of a substance. Three arguments are presented to support this view.

First, there is the minimal parts hypothesis. When we consider a golden ring, it is observed that 'if we take sub-atomic parts of the ring ... we no longer have a quantity of gold'. In other words, those and only those bits of matter not excluded by the minimal parts hypothesis are counted as quantities of the substance 'gold'.

Secondly, Parsons argues that a sentence with a modified mass noun, such as

(3.40) All blue styrofoam is granular

cannot be analysed correctly in terms of physical objects only. The argument goes as follows. Suppose we analyse (3.40) as:

(3.41) a. Every blue object that is made of styrofoam is granular or, formally:

(3.41) b. $(\forall x)(BLUE(x) \& x\ C\ s \rightarrow GRANULAR(x))$

Now consider an object, say an ice chest, which was made of pink styrofoam and subsequently painted blue, and suppose blue styrofoam is granular while pink styrofoam is not. Then the ice chest would be an object which is blue and made of styrofoam, but which is not granular. So (3.41) is not a correct analysis of (3.40). Parsons therefore interprets (3.40) as involving a quantification over styrofoam quantities, rather than over physical objects, and analyses the sentence as:

(3.42) a. Every quantity of styrofoam which is blue is granular

or, formally:

(3.42) b. $(\forall x)(BLUE(x) \& x\ Q\ s \rightarrow GRANULAR(x))$

It seems to me that this argument is not conclusive. It is claimed explicitly that quantities of substances are not meant to be abstract entities (Parsons, 1975, p. 517); however, if quantities are conceived as concrete entities, we can have quantities of pink styrofoam painted blue, and so we can have blue quantities of styrofoam which are not granular. Therefore, it is not clear that (3.42) is a more adequate analysis than (3.41).

I think the root of the problem is perhaps not in the ontology of physical objects, bits of matter, and quantities of substances, but in the analysis of the modifier 'blue' (see also chapter 9 on the application of adjectives to mass nouns). Perhaps Parsons would now agree with that, in view of his remarks: 'I now have reservations about the argument, because of the possible unclarity of application of predicates like "blue" to things whose surface color diverges from their interior color' (1975, note 9). A different critique of the argument can be found in Burge (1972).

Thirdly, Parsons argues that physical objects and bits of matter must be distinguished from quantities of a substance because two mass nouns may correspond with spatio-temporally coinciding mereological wholes, formed by the respective bits of matter, while the corresponding substances are not identical. For instance, in some hypothetical world it might be the case that all wood is turned into furniture, and all furniture consists entirely of wood. The mass nouns 'wood' and 'furniture' would then be associated with the same mereological wholes, yet in that world one would not consider the terms as synonymous since we would not call every wood-part 'furniture'.

This argument will be examined in detail in chapter 4, where Pelletier's suggestion is discussed that this argument poses a problem for *any* approach to mass term semantics using mereology or a similar formalism, including the approach I shall propose (Pelletier 1974; 1979). Parsons himself has in fact withdrawn the argument later (1975, p. 519).

The distinction between substances and the mereological wholes of the bits of matter forming objects made of that substance, may remind us of Moravcsik's distinction between restricted mereological wholes M_{SP} and unrestricted M-wholes. In order to compare the two proposals we should consider the formal status of substances more closely.

Unfortunately, Parsons only gives a quasi-formal characterization of the substance notion by means of an analogy. Noting the formal similarity between the sentences

(3.43) Men are widespread

(3.44) Water is widespread

and observing that the count noun case (3.43) is usually viewed as involving a predicate applied to the class of men, Parsons suggests that

(3.45) in general, to talk about substances, we need some sort of higher-order terminology like class terminology in the case of count nouns.... I suggest then, that we introduce a 'substance abstraction operator', on a par with the class abstraction operator. Let us use $\sigma x[...]$ for the substance abstraction operator. Inside the brackets go formulas which are true of quantities of a substance (pursuing the analogy suggested above). The resulting term is to refer to that substance which has as quantities all and only things which the formula inside is true of; i.e., we are to have:

(3.46) $x Q \sigma y[... y ...]$ if and only if ... x ... (Parsons 1970, p. 375).

For instance, the nominal complex 'muddy water' is analysed as:

(3.47) $\sigma x[\text{MUDDY}(x) \& x Q w]$

Parsons' substances play a role similar to that of Moravcsik's restricted wholes M_{SP} in that they are meant to contain those and only those parts not excluded by the minimal parts hypothesis. We have seen that Moravcsik's notion is logically not consistent; is Parsons' substance notion more reliable?

The notions of 'bits of matter' and 'quantities of a substance' are only introduced informally, but it is clear that, when we have two bits of matter m_1 and m_2 which are both quantities of a substance M, then the bit of matter formed by m_1 and m_2 is also a quantity of M, 'formed by m_1 and

m_2' understood as the mereological summation of the individuals m_1 and m_2. This gives rise to exactly the same logical problems as we have seen for Moravcsik's first proposal: there is no reason to assume that the property inside the brackets [... y ...] in a formula like (3.47) is always conserved upon taking the mereological sum. Take, for instance, the property of being small; if m_1 and m_2 are small, the bit of matter that they form together does not need to be small. (See also section 9.2.) Therefore, substances defined by formulas of the form (3.46) in general also contain quantities that do *not* have the property inside the brackets, and consequently the concept of a substance containing those and only those quantities having a certain property is not a well-defined concept.

3.5 Set-based approaches

In this section I discuss the suggestions in the literature for treating mass nouns within a set-theoretical semantic framework. These suggestions can be divided into two groups: (a) those according to which mass nouns are viewed as denoting sets; (b) those according to which mass nouns are viewed as denoting predicates. To the first group belong Cartwright (1965; 1970), Clarke (1970) and Grandy (1973); the second group includes Burge (1972), Grandy (1975) and Pelletier (1974), while ter Meulen (1980) represents a mixture of the two.

The two groups are considered together since, from a formal semantic point of view, a set-based approach and a predicate-based approach are not necessarily different; whether they are depends on what elements the sets in question are meant to contain and what entities the predicates in question are meant to be true of. According to the standard way of interpreting predicate and set constants, it makes no difference whether we translate a sentence like

(3.48)   Socrates is a man

using a predicate constant MAN-pred, as in:

(3.49)   MAN-pred(S)

where S is an individual constant denoting Socrates, or using a set constant MAN-set, as in:

(3.50)   S ∈ MAN-set

since (3.49) and (3.50) have the same truth conditions, namely that the individual Socrates is among a certain set of individuals in the model under consideration. (In the case of (3.49), this is the set of individuals to which the function MAN-pred assigns the value TRUE; in the case of (3.50) this is the set of individuals named by MAN-set.)

This illustrates that the translation from natural language into logical notation in itself is of no theoretical significance: it is merely a convenient way of formulating the truth conditions for natural language sentences. Whether predicate constants or set constants are used in the logical notation is purely a matter of convenience.

Burge (1972) has proposed a *predicate approach* to mass nouns, such that with each mass noun a predicate constant is associated. For a few representative sentences containing mass nouns he considers what their translation in a predicate language would be. For instance, the sentence

(3.51) Snow is white

is treated as involving universal quantification over all objects of which the predicate 'Snow' is true, and is thus rendered in predicate language as:

(3.52) $(\forall x)\text{S-pred}(x) \rightarrow \text{WHITE}(x)$

where S-pred is a predicate constant translating 'Snow', and WHITE a predicate constant translating 'white'.

Burge expresses the opinion that there are mass noun occurrences which it would seem counter-intuitive to treat along these lines, as in the sentence

(3.53) The snow in the garden is two metres high

In such cases he proposes that the mass term be treated as referring to a single entity, and he tries to avoid the logical puzzles that endanger a dual approach by analysing the mass noun as a *complex* singular term, built up with the corresponding predicate. For instance, the word 'water' in the sentence

(3.54) Water is widespread

is translated as:

(3.55) $(iW)(\forall z)(W \text{ overlaps } z \leftrightarrow (\exists x)(W\text{-pred}(x) \& x \text{ overlaps } z))$

According to Burge, this may be read 'The sum (or totality) of all water (. . .). The "overlaps" primitive is borrowed from the calculus of individuals' (Burge 1972, p. 279).

In mereology/the calculus of individuals the 'overlaps' relation is related to the part–whole relation by:[3]

(3.56) x overlaps y $=_D (\exists z)(z \subseteq x \;\&\; z \subseteq y)$

that is, x overlaps with y if and only if x and y have a part in common. Formally speaking, it is a matter of arbitrary choice whether the part–whole relation is taken as primitive and the overlaps relation defined by (3.56), or whether, conversely, the overlaps relation is taken as primitive and the part–whole relation defined (as: x is a part of y if and only if anything that overlaps with x overlaps with y). In other words, the use of the 'overlaps' primitive is formally equivalent to the use of the unrestricted mereological part–whole relation. The individual W defined by (3.55) is identical to the mereological whole W-whole, the sum of all entities of which W-pred is true.

When discussing Quine's approach, we have seen why the use of the unrestricted part–whole relation for interpreting mass predication was rejected: to interpret 'x is water' as 'x $\subseteq$ W-whole' would lead to conflicts with the minimal parts hypothesis. Burge also adheres to this hypothesis (witness his remark that the predicate S-pred applies to portions of snow 'down roughly to the crystals') and consequently does not equate W-pred with the complex predicate '$\subseteq$ W-whole', which is available in his logical language. Indeed, this avoids conflicts with the minimal parts hypothesis, but the use of a primitive predicate constant for each mass noun has the drawback that the theory does not account for any of the specific logical properties of mass term reference, because the logic of mereology does not say anything about these predicate constants. For instance, Burge is unable to show that mass terms refer cumulatively: the theory does not provide a proof of the argument

(3.57) $\left. \begin{array}{l} \text{W-pred}(x) \\ \text{W-pred}(y) \end{array} \right\} \text{W-pred}(x+y)$

where the + sign indicates mereological summation. (Note that Burge's logical language would allow for the alternative representations $x \subseteq$ W-whole and $y \subseteq$ W-whole, from which it would follow that $(x+y) \subseteq$ W-whole.) To ensure cumulativity of reference, a separate postulate is required for each predicate constant that corresponds to a mass noun.

Also, it seems obvious that what is considered as the totality of all water should itself satisfy the predicate of being water, that is, the proposition represented by:

(3.58) W-pred(W-whole)

should come out as an obvious truth. However, Burge's proposal leaves open whether (3.58) is true or false. Again, a separate postulate would be required for each mass noun to guarantee the truth of statements like (3.58).

Of the ways that have been suggested to use *sets* for the denotations of mass terms, there is, in the first place, the suggestion that expressions like 'There is water on the floor', 'This is butter', 'Unload the furniture', be viewed as elliptic for 'There is a puddle of water on the floor', 'This is a dollop of butter', and 'Unload this batch of furniture'. In this view, the mass noun expressions are interpreted as the count noun expressions they are supposed to be abbreviations of. Suggestions to this effect can be found in Strawson (1959) and Clarke (1970). Clearly, the choice of an appropriate 'individuating standard' must depend on the circumstances; for example, 'sugar' will have to be construed as 'lumps of sugar' in some contexts, as 'grains of sugar' in other contexts, and as 'shipments of sugar' in still other contexts. This context-dependence alone makes the proposal rather unattractive; moreover, it runs into fundamental difficulties, illustrated by the following example. If we take some ice cubes from the refrigerator, crush them, and put them into a glass of coke, we may say:

(3.59) The ice in the coke is the same ice that was in the refrigerator before

This would be a true sentence about some ice, yet there is no individuating standard in terms of which we can express this, since the identity stated by the sentence is not an identity of any of the pieces of ice involved, but an identity of the totalities of ice made up of whatever pieces are involved. Further criticism of the attempts in this direction can be found in Cartwright (1965) and Pelletier (1974).

If context-dependent individuating standards do not work satisfactorily, the next move is naturally to look for context-independent individuating standards. Such standards would then have to be artificial, since we just saw that natural standards, suggested by the language ('dollop', 'lump', 'batch', etc.) do not work in general. It is tempting then to think of Quine's minimal parts hypothesis and treat mass nouns as denoting the sets of their minimal parts. 'Water' would denote the set of H_2O molecules, 'furniture' the set of chairs, tables, etc., and 'sugar' the set of sugar grains. I have not seen any serious proposal for such an approach, though it would seem to encounter fewer formal difficulties than the use of context-dependent individuating standards. Presumably, this is due to the fact that such a proposal would so obviously run counter to our intuitions. Even if one were to agree with the minimal parts hypothesis, it is often impossible to actually determine a reasonable set of minimal parts. To consider H_2O

molecules as the referents of 'water' seems quite counter-intuitive; something like 'drops' would seem better, but presents the problem that a drop can be split into smaller drops, so it clearly is not really a minimal part, and the same is true of any other part we can name without making use of technical terms from physics or chemistry. Moreover, for abstract nouns like 'leisure', 'damage', or 'time', for which no minimal parts are assumed to exist, this proposal must fail.

An approach that does not suffer from these problems is to treat a mass term 'm' as denoting the set of all objects that can be said 'to be m'. This approach has been suggested by Cartwright (1965) and Grandy (1973), and it is also the basis of the intensional proposals of Pelletier (1974) and ter Meulen (1980). These proposals assume an ontological category of 'quantities', which is used for the denotation of a mass noun. The most detailed of these proposals has been formulated by ter Meulen (1980; 1981), working out a suggestion made by Montague (1973). Montague suggested that we should distinguish two ways of using a mass noun, for which ter Meulen has coined the terms *nominal* and *predicative*. The nominal use is that of a proper name of an abstract entity, a 'substance', the predicative use that of a predicate which is true of those entities that are 'quantities' of that 'substance'. Examples of the nominal use of a mass noun are:

(3.60)   a. Gold has atomic number 79
         b. Water is a liquid

and examples of predicative use:

(3.61)   a. My tooth is filled with gold
         b. There's no water on the moon

Montague has suggested that different denotations be assigned to nominal and predicative mass nouns: a nominal mass noun would denote a *property* (in the technical sense of the term in possible-worlds semantics), and the same noun used predicatively would denote the *set of quantities* which, in the world under consideration, have that property:

A mass noun β standing alone in predicative position should be regarded as synonymous with 'portion of β'. If a quantifier (for example, 'some', 'all'), a demonstrative, or an adjective phrase accompanies a mass noun, then the mass noun should in that occurrence be taken as denoting the extension of the property usually denoted (Montague, 1973, p. 290).

Nominal and predicative use of a mass term are thus semantically related in that the nominal term denotes the intension of the predicative term.

Ter Meulen takes the phenomenon of nominal and predicative use to be specific to mass terms, and, since nominal mass terms have intensional denotations, she concludes that a formal semantics of mass terms can only be given within an intensional framework. However, I believe the nominal/predicative distinction to have a more general validity. Consider the following three pairs of sentences, that illustrate the nominal/predicative distinction for mass terms:

(3.62)   a. Gold is a metallic element
          b. My tooth is filled with gold

(3.63)   a. Water is H_2O
          b. There's clear water in the lake

(3.64)   a. Silver has atomic number 49
          b. Most of the silver was found again later

The mass nouns in the (a) sentences are used nominally, those in the (b) sentences predicatively. It is not difficult to find sentence pairs with exact parallels for count nouns, such as the following ones:

(3.65)   a. Diamonds are hard carbonites
          b. The ring is ornamented with diamonds

(3.66)   a. A porcupine is not a hedgehog
          b. There's a porcupine in the bath tub

(3.67)   a. Birds are feathered bipeds
          b. Most of the birds returned in spring

The (a) and (b) sentences here differ semantically in exactly the same way as the (a) and (b) sentences with mass nouns above. Just like the mass nouns in the (a) sentences, the count nouns in the (a) sentences do not refer to any specific individuals but to more abstract entities. I therefore consider the nominal/predicative distinction to be a more general one, not specific to mass terms, and one that a semantic theory of mass terms therefore need not pay special attention to. Assuming that nominal use of count and mass terms can indeed be handled in an intensional framework according to Montague's suggestion, denoting the intension of the predicative term, only the proposed treatment of predicative mass terms is relevant for us here.

This takes us back to the proposal that (predicative) mass terms be treated as denoting sets of quantities. The difference between count terms and mass terms is, then, that mass terms denote sets of quantities whereas count terms denote sets of individuals. This raises the question as to what is the difference between quantities and individuals. Montague suggests that there is *no* difference:

(3.68) The question naturally arises whether portions of substances are full-fledged physical objects like tables and rings (together with physical compositions of these). Perhaps. At least I see no clear-cut arguments to the contrary (1973, p. 291).

Ter Meulen deviates from Montague at this point and takes the view that there is a fundamental distinction in that quantities have a homogeneous internal structure, which individuals do not necessarily have:

(3.69) In some respects quantities of stuff are quite like individuals. Individuals are objects in space-time, and so are all quantities of stuff. They are in this sense part of the same physical reality.... But quantities of substances are in many other respects to be distinguished from individuals. The first most striking difference between quantities and individuals is the fact that the quantities of any substance can be divided into smaller parts that are also quantities of the same substance. Similarly the quantities of some substance can become part of a larger quantity of the same substance.... The fact that quantities can be divided into quantities of the same substance together with the fact that any number of quantities of some substance can become part of a new quantity of the same substance is a logical property characteristic of quantities only. This property of quantities, called the *property of homogeneous reference*, has widely been recognized as distinctive of the semantic interpretation of mass terms. A more precise formulation of this property is the following. Any parts of a quantity of x that are themselves quantities of x can become parts of another quantity of x (1980, pp. 67–8).

Ter Meulen accounts for the internal structure of quantities by means of postulates such as the following:

(3.70)   ($\forall$x)($\forall$y)(x <u>part of'</u> y→(P(x)↔P(y)))
       where P is a predicative mass term.

The proposal includes a great number of postulates, three for each mass noun, and various others for substances and quantities. This proposal, and any proposal to the effect that a (predicative) mass term denotes a set of quantities, runs into problems when dealing with certain cases of quantification.

One class of problems arises in the analysis of mass nouns combined with amount expressions such as:

(3.71) 'much water'

(3.72) 'ten litres of water'

Ter Meulen interprets 'much water' as 'many quantities of water' (1980,

p. 90) which is obviously wrong, especially in combination with the non-atomistic view of quantities expressed in quotation (3.69); cases like (3.72) are not considered.

Other problems arise in the analysis of definite descriptions involving mass nouns, like

(3.73) The gold on the table

Let Q_{gold} designate the set of all quantities of gold (the set of all objects that can be said 'to be gold'), and let ONTABLE be a one-place predicate constant. Now we can choose between two ways of analysing (3.73): either we treat 'gold' on a par with a singular count noun, that is, we consider (3.73) as a paraphrase of

(3.74) The golden object on the table

or we treat 'gold' on a par with a plural count noun, that is, we regard (3.60) as a paraphrase of

(3.75) The golden objects on the table

In the first case we would render the noun phrase in predicate language as:

(3.76) $(ix)(x \in Q_{gold}$ & ONTABLE$(x))$

in the second case we have, instead:

(3.77) $\{x | x \in Q_{gold}$ & ONTABLE$(x)\}$

If we choose the first alternative we run into the difficulty that, when there is some gold on the table, it is, in general, incorrect to say that there is *one* quantity of gold on the table since any quantity of gold in general contains many other quantities of gold (cf. Grandy, 1975, p. 483). Thus the analysis (3.63) is incorrect, as is further corroborated by the fact that we can quantify over a noun phrase like (3.60), as in:

(3.78) All the gold on the table was shiny

Montague and ter Meulen suggest that this problem can be solved by introducing into the analysis the concept of 'the largest' of the quantities under consideration. Says Montague:

(3.79) I would take 'the' in 'the gold in Smith's ring' as the ordinary singular definite article, so that 'the X' has a denotation if and only if X denotes a unit set, and in that case 'the X' denotes the only element of that set. But is there not a conflict here? It would seem that there are many portions of gold in Smith's ring. . . . The

Approaches to mass term semantics 41

solution is I think to regard 'in' as in one sense... amounting to 'occupying' or 'constituting'. Then 'gold in Smith's ring' comes to 'gold constituting Smith's ring', denotes the set of maximal portions of gold that are 'in' (in the more inclusive sense) Smith's ring, and hence denotes a unit set (Montague, 1973, pp. 290–1).

He suggests further that the linguistic and extralinguistic context be considered to determine whether volume, weight, or some other dimension should be used for comparing quantities in size. This is, of course, not a real solution of the problem. First, it is unclear what mechanisms could provide the necessary linguistic and extralinguistic contextual information and, most importantly, it seems quite wrong that the analysis of sentences like

(3.80) The snow in the garden is beautiful

should force us to introduce notions such as volume or weight to determine what snow is considered. However, the problem then arises how to construe the notion 'maximal portions of'. Rather, the analysis should be such that this portion is determined by *logical means*, for instance, as that portion of snow which is in the garden and which has all the other portions of snow in the garden as parts. However, this requires a formal part–whole relation among quantities which does not belong to the set-theoretical framework.[4]

The alternative, as mentioned above, is to interpret 'the gold on the table' as 'the set of gold quantities on the table'. The sentence (3.78), 'All the gold on the table was shiny', can now be interpreted in a straightforward way as a universal quantification over this set. But on this approach we run into problems in analysing expressions where a mass noun phrase is the argument of an amount predicate, as in

(3.81) The gold on the table weighs 7 ounces

Suppose we have in our representation language a function WEIGHT which assigns to objects such values as '7 ounces' (for the present we will not bother about the formal status of '7 ounces'; this is discussed in section 6.2). Treating 'the gold on the table' as 'the gold quantities on the table' would lead to the analysis that the sum of the weights of the gold quantities on the table is 7 ounces:

(3.82) $\text{SUM}(\{y|(\exists z)(z \in \{x|x \in Q_{\text{gold}} \ \& \ \text{ONTABLE}(x)\} \ \& \ y = \text{WEIGHT}(z)\}) = 7$ ounces

Of course, this analysis would be wrong in the present case, since the set $\{x|x \in Q_{\text{gold}} \ \& \ \text{ONTABLE}(x)\}$ contains many overlapping quantities whose weights would be counted many times. In order to prevent this from happening we should not apply the WEIGHT function to the elements of the set and then perform a summation of the weights, but we should first perform a 'summation' of the gold quantities involved and then apply the WEIGHT function. However, this 'summation' is an operation that cannot be carried out within a purely set-theoretical framework.

4 Towards a semantic theory of mass nouns

4.1 Requirements for a semantic theory of mass nouns

The previous chapter has provided us with an overview of what has been accomplished so far in the area of mass term semantics and, at the same time, of what problems are still waiting to be resolved. Each of the proposals discussed above is successful in some respects but fails in others. To be completely successful, a semantic theory of mass terms should meet at least the following requirements:

(1) It should give a logical form to the intuition that mass nouns differ from count nouns in that they refer to something 'without individuating'. This involves giving a formal interpretation to such notions as 'cumulative reference' and 'distributive reference'.

(2) It should describe how the meaning of complex expressions containing mass nouns is built up from the meaning of the constituents. This should explain such truisms as 'water is water' and arguments like 'all water is wet', 'this is water' therefore 'this is wet'.

(3) It should fit into an overall framework in which we can also incorporate results of other formal semantic investigations. This is particularly relevant if non-standard formalisms are invoked such as mereology/the calculus of individuals or a formalism of substances.

All the approaches to mass term semantics that we have considered make an attempt, though not always explicitly, to meet the second requirement. Some of these approaches also give due attention to the first requirement, invoking the formalism of mereology in some way or other (Quine, Moravcsik, Burge), or that of substances with its 'quantity-of' relation (Parsons). Two of these proposals have been criticized above for having problems in the logical soundness of the formalism they propose (Parsons' proposal and Moravcsik's first proposal). We have seen that the other three proposals fail to meet the second requirement. Moreover, we shall see that all these proposals suffer from problems concerning the third requirement.

Many of the problems that the various proposals run into are related, directly or indirectly, to the fact that they want to take the minimal parts hypothesis into account. For Quine this was the reason for advocating a 'dual' treatment, where mass nouns in subject position are treated as denoting mereological wholes while mass nouns in predicate position are treated as denoting predicates. For Moravcsik, the minimal parts hypothesis was the reason for proposing the introduction of either restricted part–whole relations $\subseteq_{SP(m)}$ or restricted mereological wholes M_{SP}. For Parsons the minimal parts hypothesis was the reason for introducing, besides 'bits of matter', the logically inconsistent notion of 'substances'.

In view of the enormous impact that the minimal parts hypothesis has had on work in the area of mass term semantics, I think it is worth examining the hypothesis in some detail and discussing its significance for linguistic theory.

4.2 The minimal parts hypothesis

As we have seen, in section 3.2, Quine proposes that mass nouns such as 'water' when occurring in subject position be treated as denoting a mereological whole W-whole ('the aqueous part of the world'). When occurring in predicate position, however, as in

(4.1) This puddle is water

Quine rejects the possibility of doing the same. His motivation for this rejection is that the various occurrences of the copula 'is' in 'This is sugar', 'This is water', 'This is furniture', cannot be interpreted as expressing the same part–whole relation, since each mass noun referent has its own characteristic part–whole structure:

(4.2) there are parts of water, sugar, furniture too small to count as water, sugar, furniture. Moreover, what is too small to count as furniture is not too small to count as water or sugar; so the limitation needed cannot be worked into any general adaptation of 'is' or 'is a part of', but must be left rather as the separate reference-dividing business of the several mass terms (1960, p. 99).

It is thus argued that we should take into account that the parts of a H_2O molecule are not water, the parts of a chair are not furniture, and the parts of a grain of sugar are not sugar, or, in general, that

(4.3)   For each mass noun M there is a specific minimal size that parts of its referent may have in order to count as M.

This is what we have called the *minimal parts hypothesis*.

When discussing the attempts in the literature to define mass terms semantically, using hypotheses like Quine's cumulative reference condition or Cheng's condition, we noted a danger of confusion between an interpretation of these hypotheses on a linguistic level and one on a physical level. Here we have a similar situation. To be precise, the minimal parts hypothesis as it stands allows two interpretations:

(a)   As a hypothesis about the objects denoted by mass nouns (in subject position, at least). As such, it is, of course, correct in many cases: the legs of a chair are not furniture, the vermicelli in the soup is not soup, and physics and chemistry tell us that H_2O molecules are the smallest objects that may count as water, that photons are the smallest quantities of light, etc. On the other hand, what about the minimal parts of the referents of such mass nouns as 'time', 'leisure', 'phlogiston', 'traffic', or 'freedom'?

(b)   As a hypothesis about the use of mass nouns in natural languages. As such, the hypothesis is highly questionable. For instance, the mass noun 'water' has been used for centuries when there was no knowledge of H_2O molecules, and even today our accumulated knowledge about molecules, atoms, energy quanta, photons, phonons, and bits of information has not caused a change in the linguistic role of nouns like 'water', 'energy', 'phlogiston', 'light', 'sound', 'music', or 'news'.

Since we are dealing with the construction of a linguistic semantic theory, which should only account for linguistic facts, I discard interpretation (a) of the minimal parts hypothesis. Concerning interpretation (b), I think all the linguistic evidence points in a direction which is the opposite of this hypothesis: mass nouns provide a way of speaking about things *as if they do not consist of discrete parts*. For some words and some speakers this way of speaking may reflect their real beliefs about the world, as in the case of 'time', 'light' or 'energy'. In other cases, like 'rice', 'sugar', or 'furniture' it is unlikely that any speaker would really believe that the mass noun refers to something non-discrete. However, *nothing in the use of these mass nouns indicates a commitment on the part of the speaker to the existence of minimal parts*.

I therefore hold the view that a linguistic semantic theory should take into account that the use of a mass noun forms a way of speaking about things as if they were homogeneous masses, that is, as having some internal structure, allowing us to refer to certain parts, but without singling out any particular parts and without any commitments concerning the existence of minimal parts. I call this assumption the *homogeneous reference hypothesis*, and formulate it for convenience of reference as follows:

(4.4)   Mass nouns refer to entities as having a part–whole structure without singling out any particular parts and without making any commitments concerning the existence of minimal parts.

I believe that this hypothesis, first formulated in Bunt (1976), expresses in what way mass nouns are semantically different from count nouns. The difference is not in the structure of the entities that mass nouns and count nouns refer to, but in the way in which they refer to these entities.

The homogeneous reference hypothesis has been discussed by ter Meulen (1980; 1981) in a way that illustrates the danger of confusing a physical level and a linguistic level of interpreting statements about mass term reference.

(4.5) The fact that quantities can be divided into quantities of the same substance together with the fact that any number of quantities of some substance can become part of a new quantity of the same substance is a logical property of quantities only. This property, called the *property of homogeneous reference*, has widely been recognized as distinctive of mass terms. A more precise formulation of this property is the following.
The Property of Homogeneous Reference: Any parts of a quantity of x that are themselves quantities of x can become parts of another quantity of x.
In ... it was discussed how mereological theories of the semantics of mass terms take the property of homogeneous reference to be fundamental to the interpretation of mass terms. In Bunt (1978) homogeneous reference is even taken to be a fundamental axiom of the set-theory used in the semantic interpretation of the mass terms. ... It is certainly a property that is characteristic for the denotation of mass terms ... (ter Meulen, 1980, pp. 67–8).

Ter Meulen uses the expression 'property of homogeneous reference' here for a property of *quantities* of substances, that is, for a property on the physical level. It is therefore rather misleading to call this a property of *reference*, and it is incorrect to say that this 'has been widely recognized as distinctive of mass terms'. What has been widely recognized as distinctive of mass terms is what Quine has called the lack of a built-in mode of dividing reference that these terms display; this is, of course, also the essence of the homogeneous reference hypothesis (4.4), which is a *linguistic* hypothesis combining the idea of non-individuating reference with an explicit rejection of the minimal parts hypothesis.

4.3 The use of mereology

We have seen that both Quine and Moravcsik discarded the straightforward application of mereology in view of the minimal parts hypothesis. If the hypothesis is renounced, as I propose to do, the use of mereology deserves to be reconsidered.

An objection against the use of mereology has been raised by Pelletier (1974), using one of Parsons' arguments to distinguish 'quantities of a substance' from 'bits of matter'. The argument is that, if in some hypothetical world all wood were turned into furniture and all furniture consisted entirely of wood, the mass nouns 'wood' and 'furniture' would refer to two mereological wholes, 'W-whole' and 'F-whole', that have the same extension. Therefore,

(4.6) $x \subseteq$ W-whole   iff (if and only if) $x \subseteq$ F-whole

for any 'x'. If we interpret the copula 'is' as the mereological part-whole relation $\subseteq$, we would have the situation that sentences of the form

(4.7) a. x is wood
       b. x is furniture

would be analysed, respectively, as

(4.8) a. $x \subseteq$ W-whole
       b. $x \subseteq$ F-whole

from which it would follow that anything which is wood would be furniture, and vice versa. This would seem wrong, since the legs of a chair are wood but not furniture. Parsons concludes from this that 'bits' and 'quantities' should be distinguished: any 'bit of wood' would be a 'bit of furniture' (bits of matter are conceived of as mereological entities), but not every 'bit of furniture' would be a 'quantity of furniture', and therefore not every 'quantity of wood' would be a 'quantity of furniture'. Pelletier uses this argument to criticize Moravcsik's second proposal, and concludes that it is an objection to *any* attempt to introduce mereological wholes. (Incidentally, the argument is misdirected as an objection to Moravcsik's proposal, since in that proposal the expressions (4.7) would be analysed as:

(4.9) a. $x \subseteq_{SP(w)}$ W-whole
 b. $x \subseteq_{SP(f)}$ F-whole

Since it is not implied that $x \subseteq_{SP(f)}$ F-whole if $x \subseteq_{SP(w)}$ W-whole, it does *not* follow that anything which is wood is furniture.)

How serious is this objection? I believe it is a serious objection only if one adheres to the minimal parts hypothesis. If we replace 'furniture' in the above example by 'sawdust', the problem vanishes. In some hypothetical world in which all wood had been turned into sawdust, the mereological approach would lead to the situation that anything that was wood would be sawdust, and vice versa. Or, formulated more accurately, the truth conditions of any sentence containing the word 'wood' would remain unchanged if 'wood' were replaced by 'sawdust', and vice versa. Now where is the problem? I believe this is just as it should be, as long as we restrict ourselves to occurrences of 'wood' and 'sawdust' in non-intensional contexts. Of course, in an intensional context the replacement of a term by another term having the same extension in some world does not, in general, leave the truth conditions unchanged, but this is a well-known phenomenon that is not specific to mass terms, nor to the use of mereology.

Now it may be argued that the wood–furniture case is different from the wood–sawdust case, since even in a world in which all wood has been turned into furniture and all furniture consists entirely of wood, we would like to distinguish between wood and furniture. In other words, even in that world we should not assign the same extensions to 'wood' and 'furniture'. But then, whatever view is taken on this matter, it is not the business of *formal* semantics to deal with the question of whether two referring terms have the same extension.[1] In the paradigm of formal semantics we just assign a model-theoretic entity to each referring term; if we believe that two terms are synonymous we assign them the same interpretation, if not we assign different interpretations to them. This is perhaps what Parsons had in mind in his later (1975) paper, where he says that it is not up to a semantic theory to deal with the kind of questions raised by the wood–furniture example. I shall return to this point in chapter 7, when a general framework for semantic analysis is outlined, and indicate which part of a semantic theory should deal with questions of this kind.

The mass terms literature contains several other points of criticism on the use of mereology which, upon closer inspection, turn out to be unjustified. One such point, raised by Pelletier (1974) and ter Meulen (1980), is that mereological theories are unable to account for mass noun occurrences in intensional contexts. Most of the mereology-based proposals that have been put forward indeed do not treat intensional occurrences of mass nouns adequately; it is unjustified, however, to say that this is inherent to the use of mereology. If extensional mass terms ('predicative mass terms', in ter Meulen's terminology) are treated as denoting mereological wholes, we can add functions from possible worlds to these extensions in the usual way. A mereological theory can be 'intensionalized' in the same way as a set-theoretical one.

Two other points of unjust criticism have been raised by ter Meulen (1980; 1981). The first point is that mereology-based theories should require an undue number of semantic primitives:

(4.10) semantic theories that employ special set theories or mereology... must employ various primitive relations to account for the relation between individuals, quantities, and substances. These primitive notions do not correspond to any expressions in the syntax of sentences with mass terms (ter Meulen, 1980, p. 194).

Ter Meulen is surely right that a semantic theory should preferably have a minimal number of primitive concepts that have no linguistic counterparts, but are required by the underlying formalism. Mereology as such has only one primitive notion: that of the part–whole relation; any other primitives in mereology-based proposals derive from the linguistic or ontological assumptions that are built into them, and are independent of the use of mereology.

In fact, it is interesting to consider ter Meulen's own proposal in this respect. This proposal, based on standard set theory, contains, besides the set-theoretical part–whole notion (the subset relation), an additional semantic primitive 'part of' which is needed to make sure that her representation language has interpretations with the right properties (see the meaning postulate, quoted earlier as (3.70)). In comparison, a mereology-based theory has the advantage that the primitive 'part of' is supplied by the underlying formalism.

Ter Meulen's second point is brought out clearly in the following quotation:

(4.11) Quantities are part of other quantities just like events are part of other events. Quantities can be reduced to sets of atomic or molecular parts, in what is called an atomistic account. But quantities are not constructions based on such sets, like in mereological theories.... the problem of 'minimal parts' is only a true problem for atomistic theories, which attempt to construct quantities or events from some 'absolute' foundation, i.e. minimal parts or moments of time. The arguments against an atomistic construction of entities, i.e. against mereological theories, can be carried over to arguments against constructions of events (1980, pp. 199–200).

Mereological theories are accused here of being atomistic in character. This is a rather bizarre accusation, since the use of mereology has been inspired in the first place by the wish to analyse mass terms within a non-atomistic formalism. The basic idea underlying the mereology-based proposals is namely that one would like to analyse expressions of the form 'x is (some) M', such as 'this is some water', in such a way that the copula 'is' denotes a part–whole relation; however, the part–whole relation of set theory does not seem attractive for this purpose since it would force one to construe the mass noun denotation as a set, and therefore as an object with an atomistic structure (the singleton subsets being the 'atoms'). Mereological objects, by contrast, do not have an atomistic structure in that mereological wholes do not necessarily have minimal parts. In those mereology-based proposals that are atomistic because they were meant to accommodate the minimal parts hypothesis, special measures have to be taken to introduce atomistic structures. (Moravcsik's introduction of structural properties 'SP' illustrates this clearly.) The accusation that mereology-based theories are atomistic in character, because of the use of mereology, is clearly quite mistaken.

On the other hand, there are problems with the use of mereology which I think are quite serious. One which seems to have gone unnoticed so far, is that mereology does not have such a thing as an *empty* object. This means that mereology cannot be used for describing the extension of a mass term with 'empty reference', such as 'phlogiston', 'water on the moon', or 'unicorn' (in 'I had some unicorn for lunch today'). Montague (1973) has argued that it is the existence of mass nouns with empty extension that requires a complete treatment of mass noun semantics to be intensional; however, if intensions of mass nouns are to be functions from possible worlds to mereological extensions, this means that the absence of an empty mereological object is an equally serious problem for an intensional treatment.

A fundamental problem in connection with any proposal to use mereology has to do with the third requirement, formulated above. Mereology was devised by Lesniewski as part of an attempt to create a sound logical system for the foundations of mathematics. In particular, mereology would, together with the other components of this logical system, constitute an alternative to set theory, which at that time suffered from logical antinomies. Now a fundamental issue to decide when mereology is invoked is whether the other parts of Lesniewski's logical framework are called into play as

Towards a semantic theory of mass nouns 51

well; if not, mereology has to be 'interfaced' with the logical framework of the general semantic theory, which is based on modern set theory. To my knowledge none of the authors on mass term semantics who invoke mereology have paid attention to this problem.

That this is a quite serious problem can be seen from the following example. As mentioned in chapter 2, Quine has proposed that adjectives which are cumulative in reference should be considered as mass terms, and that they should be treated semantically in the same way as mass nouns:

(4.12) in attributive position next to a mass term the adjective must be taken as a mass term: thus 'red' in 'red wine'. The two mass terms unite to form a compound mass term. When we think of the two component mass terms as singular terms naming two scattered portions of the world, the compound becomes a singular term naming that smaller scattered portion of the world which is just the common part of the two (1960, p. 104).

In other words, an adjective–mass noun combination such as 'red wine' is interpreted as denoting the overlap of the mereological wholes denoted by 'red' and 'wine'. Now, what if we have a mass noun modified by an adjective that is not cumulative in reference? Such an adjective would be treated like a count noun, as denoting a set. But since the overlap of a set and a mereological whole is undefined, this does not provide a way of interpreting such adjective–noun combinations. Quine's escape that 'adjectives, not cumulative in reference, simply tend not to occur next to mass terms' (1960, p. 104) is not good enough, as is shown by such examples as:[2]

(4.13) There's some small furniture in the dolls' house

Leonard and Goodman have devised an alternative axiomatization of the logic of part–whole, calling the entities that satisfy these axioms 'individuals'. They claim that their calculus is formally equivalent to mereology, but it should be noted that their axioms are formulated in set-theoretical terms; therefore, their system is formally defined only in combination with set theory. They do not discuss the integration of set theory and mereology explicitly, but the suggestion is that the axioms of the calculus of individuals could simply be added to an axiomatization of set theory.

But this is not satisfactory, even though it may be possible to do it in a formally correct way. The part–whole structure of the individuals has the same logical properties as the part–whole structure of sets defined by the subset relation. Adding the axioms of the calculus of individuals to those of set theory therefore leads to an axiom system in which the same part–whole structure is defined twice: once indirectly, via the axioms for the membership relation, and once directly by the axioms of the calculus of individuals. Moreover, there remain such problems as whether and how the set-theoretical union or the mereological sum could be applied to a mixture of sets and individuals, as would be needed for the representation of certain complex expressions involving both count terms and mass terms, and similarly for intersections. Also, the question arises whether the empty set can play the role of the missing empty individual in mereology.

We thus see that there are certain problems connected with the use of mereology in formal semantics. Nevertheless, I believe that a part–whole relation, as defined in mereology/the calculus of individuals, can play a role in giving a logical form to the intuition that mass terms refer 'without individuating', as well as in giving an account of the truth conditions of sentences with mass terms. We have therefore developed a formalism in which a part–whole relation is defined which is very similar to the part–whole relation of mereology/the calculus of individuals; however, this formalism differs from those calculi in that it includes an axiomatic definition of sets, *viz.* as objects which, besides having this part–whole structure, have some further internal structure. In this sense the formalism, called *Ensemble Theory*, includes set theory. It can therefore be used in formal semantics without entailing the problems of integrating a theory of part–whole with standard set theory.

5 *Ensemble theory*

5.1 Part–whole and member–whole

Ensemble theory is designed around the concept 'part of'. It turns out to be possible to define many useful concepts such as 'union', 'intersection', and 'emptiness' on the basis of a part-of relation. For instance, the 'intersection' of two ensembles can be defined as the 'largest' common part C of A and B, 'largest' in the sense that any ensemble D, which is also a common part of A and B, is a part of C.

The enterprise of designing ensemble theory may be compared to the attempts that have been made in the history of axiomatic set theory to found that theory on the subset relation ($\subseteq$) rather than on the element relation ($\in$); see, for example, Schoenflies (1921) and Wegel (1956). These attempts have not been successful, since it turns out that there are certain statements of fundamental importance that one wants to make about sets, which cannot be expressed in terms of the subset relation. The limitations of what can be done on the basis of the part–whole (subset) relation only become clear when we try to establish the axiom for determining the extensions of a set. It is customary in set theory to posit an 'axiom of extensionality' like:

(5.1a) $A = B \leftrightarrow (\forall x)(x \in A \leftrightarrow x \in B)$

(The precise form of the axiom depends on the details of the logical framework in which the axiom system is formulated; see Fraenkel *et al.*, 1973, pp. 25–30.) We might try to formulate such an axiom in terms of the subset relation, for example, as:

(5.1b) $A = B \leftrightarrow (\forall x)(x \subseteq A \leftrightarrow x \subseteq B)$

that is, two sets have the same extension if and only if they have the same subsets. However, such an axiom is not adequate, as we can see by considering sets with only one element. Suppose $A = \{a\}$ and $B = \{b\}$. Now (5.1b) would say that A and B are co-extensional if they have the same subsets; well, which subsets do they have? A has the subsets ∅ and A, B has the subsets ∅ and B. Trivially, ∅ is a common subset of A and B, so the question whether A = B turns on whether A ⊆ B and B ⊆ A. But that is just what we are trying to establish! So we see that (5.1b) is of no help in determining whether two atomic sets are co-extensional. Of course, what we have to do in this case is to assess whether their *members* are the same. It turns out that the extensionality relations between sets can be described correctly in terms of the subset relation for all sets except for those that are atomic (singletons); for the latter, one must consider their members.

In designing ensemble theory I have attempted to achieve two goals simultaneously. One is to meet the requirement that ensembles have a part–whole structure which is not inherently 'atomistic', the other is to solve the 'interface problem' with classical set theory.

Concerning the 'interface problem', the design of ensemble theory should take the following points into account:

(1) The relation between an ensemble and its parts is already noted to be 'very similar' to that between a set and its subsets. But an ensemble should not have an 'atomistic' structure; in view of the homogeneous reference hypothesis, an ensemble should not necessarily have minimal parts. Therefore, the part–whole structure of an ensemble cannot be quite the same as the subset structure of a set, since a set necessarily has minimal parts (singleton subsets). The similarity and the difference between the two part–whole notions should be made precise.

(2) In order to handle mass terms with empty extensions, like 'phlogiston' or 'ambrosia', there should be an empty ensemble. Moreover, as examples like 'the water on the moon' and 'the pain in my hair' illustrate, every ensemble should have an empty part. It would be most attractive to have only one empty ensemble, in the same way as there is only one empty set in set theory. The question arises whether this empty ensemble is the same object as the empty set. Ensembles, in general, have a different internal structure than sets, but does the internal structure matter when the objects are empty anyway? One would think not, and it therefore seems most attractive to construe the notion of emptiness in ensemble theory in such a way that the empty ensemble can be regarded as the empty set and vice versa.

(3) For sets we have such operations as union and intersection, which have proved to be valuable for the calculation of truth conditions for

complex expressions. Since mass nouns occur in similar syntactic and semantic structures as count nouns, one would like to have counterparts of these operations for ensembles. In mereology there is a counterpart of the union, called 'fusion', but no counterpart of the intersection. (This is due to the fact that mereology does not have a concept of emptiness, so the 'intersection' of two disjoint mereological wholes would be undefined.) If we have ensemble unions and intersections, then what about mixed operations, such as the union of a set and an ensemble? Remember the example 'small furniture' in the previous chapter, that called for the intersection of a set and mereological whole.

The concept of 'atomic ensembles' is defined in order to obtain formal objects with a non-atomistic part–whole structure and solve the 'interface problem' with classical set theory. An ensemble is atomic if it has no other non-empty parts than itself, and is not empty. It turns out that ensembles which are built up of atomic parts are formally indistinguishable from sets. But there are also ensembles which do not have an atomistic structure. These ensembles can be used to model continuous substances. By allowing both kinds of ensembles, we obtain a formalism that includes set theory, but also ensembles without atomistic structures.

The formalism constructed this way has considerable elegance in that it has *one* part–whole relation, of which the subset relation is a special case; that it has *one* empty object, serving both as 'empty ensemble' and as 'empty set'; that it has *one* concept of 'union', which applies to any collection of ensembles, and of which the union of a collection of sets is a special case, etc.

In order to be sure that this formalism is mathematically sound, and does not suffer from internal consistency problems, like Parsons' formalism of substances and Moravcsik's variant of mereology, I carried out a full axiomatization of ensemble theory. This is described in detail in chapter 10. Some of the most important points of the formal definition of ensemble theory are discussed in a rather informal way in the rest of this chapter, along with a few theorems of fundamental importance and the definitions of some concepts which will be useful in the application of ensemble theory to formal semantics.

Setting up a system of axioms and deriving a number of hoped-for results does not form a guarantee that we have defined a logically sound and non-trivial formalism. The axiom system may contain hidden contradictions, in which case it would be possible to deduce just anything; in other words, the question remains whether there are in fact any objects that have the properties postulated by the axiom system. The specification of such objects is what is usually called a *model* or *interpretation* of the axiom system. To remove any possible doubts on the soundness and the power of ensemble theory, a model of the axiom system of ensemble theory is outlined in section 5.5; a more detailed description of a model is given in chapter 12.

5.2 The part–whole relation

At the basis of ensemble theory is a part–whole relation that will be designated by the symbol $\subseteq$. This relation is a primitive of the theory, therefore the elementary logical properties we want it to have must be postulated. One of these properties is *transitivity*: if A is part of B, and B is part of C, then A is also part of C. The 'axiom of transitivity' postulates this property:

(5.2) $(\forall x, y, z)((x \subseteq y \,\&\, y \subseteq z) \rightarrow x \subseteq z)$

Another basic property is that every ensemble should be a part of itself. We will see below that this does not have to be postulated separately, but that it follows as a special case from more general axioms.

An obviously important notion that we should have in the theory is the notion of *equality*. Equality of ensembles is defined as mutual inclusion:

(5.3) $x = y =_D x \subseteq y \,\&\, y \subseteq x$

It will frequently be relevant to consider only those parts of an ensemble that are not equal to that ensemble. It is therefore convenient to define a notion *proper part*, being that y is a proper part of x if y is a part of x not equal to x. This relation is symbolized as $\subset$. Its formal definition is:

(5.4) $y \subset x =_D y \subseteq x \,\&\, y \neq x$

One of the requirements of ensemble theory mentioned above is that there should be a concept of *emptiness*. This is defined as the property of having no other parts than itself:

(5.5) $\text{EMPTY}(x) =_D (\forall y)(y \subseteq x \rightarrow y = x)$

From the transitivity of the part-whole relation it follows that all parts of an empty ensemble are empty. On the basis of axioms which will be considered later, it can be proved that there exists an empty ensemble, and that an empty ensemble is part of every ensemble. From this it follows that there exists only one empty ensemble. It will be designated by the symbol $\emptyset$.

Among the ideas we should be able to express formally in ensemble theory is that of the whole, formed by a number of parts. Suppose, for instance, we have a collection C of three samples of water: w_1, w_2, and w_3. The whole formed by w_1, w_2, and w_3 is that water sample W that has w_1, w_2, and w_3 as parts, and of which every part is made up of water from these three samples. The latter restriction can be formalized as the condition that every non-empty part of W 'overlaps' with (= has a non-empty part in common with) at least one of the samples in the collection C. An ensemble with these properties will be called a *merge* of C. It can be proved that for every collection C of ensembles there is exactly one ensemble which is a merge of C, hence we may speak of *the merge of C*. It is denoted by $\cup(C)$, and if C is a finite collection $x_1, x_2, \ldots, x_n$ the notation $x_1 \cup x_2 \cup \ldots \cup x_n$ is also used.

The merge $\cup(C)$ of a collection C of ensembles is the 'minimal' ensemble having all members of C as parts; minimal in the sense that $\cup(C)$ is a part of any ensemble having all members of C as parts. In the following, the term 'minimal' will be used in this sense: by saying that x is 'the minimal ensemble having property P' is meant that every ensemble y also having the property P has x as a part. The fact that a collection of ensembles always has only one merge is due to its 'minimality': for any property P, such as the property of including all the members of C, there is always at most one minimal ensemble having that property.

The reader who consults chapter 10 for a more precise and formal discussion of these matters will see that the axiom, postulating the existence of a merge for any collection of ensembles, does not in fact speak of collections of ensembles. The term 'collection' is used here only in an informal way, and the term 'set' is avoided. The reason for this is that the ensemble concept is considered to be more general than the set concept: a set is viewed as a special kind of ensemble. Therefore, ensemble theory is formulated in such a way that set-theoretical notions are not presupposed.

An important property of the merge, which is relevant for the application of ensemble theory to formal semantics, is that the merge of a number of parts of an ensemble x is again a part of x (chapter 10, theorem 2.7.3). The merge of a collection of ensembles is the ensemble analogue of the union

58   Part 1 Model-theoretic semantics of mass terms

of a collection of sets. In a similar way we can define an ensemble analogue of the notion of intersection. If C is a collection of ensembles, the *overlap* ∩(C) of C is the minimal ensemble that includes the common parts of all the members of C. An alternative, equivalent way of characterizing ∩(C) is that it is the 'maximal' common part of all the ensembles in C; maximal in the sense that any common part of all the members of C is a part of ∩(C). Again, due to the minimality (maximality) requirement in the definition, there is only one overlap of a collection of ensembles, and hence we may speak of *the overlap of C*.

An ensemble analogue of the set-theoretical notion of complement can be defined as well; it is called *completion*. Given two ensembles x and U such that x ⊆ U, the completion of x relative to U is defined as the minimal ensemble $\bar{x}^U$ such that

(5.6) $x \cup \bar{x}^U = U$

Again, due to the minimality of the completion, it is always uniquely determined.

The operations ∪, ∩, and $^{-U}$ on ensembles have the same properties of associativity, commutativity, and reciprocity as the corresponding operations on sets. More precisely, if C(E) is the collection of all parts of an ensemble E, the sextuple

(5.7) $(C(E), \cup, \cap, ^{-E}, \emptyset, E)$

is a Boolean algebra.

One of the most useful theorems that can be derived from the ensemble axioms is the following (chapter 10, theorem 2.8.5):

(5.8)   For every ensemble x and condition P there exists exactly one ensemble which is the minimal ensemble having the property of including all x-parts for which P is true.

The notation

(5.9) $[z \subseteq x | P(z)]$

is used to denote this ensemble. Its characteristic properties are thus, on the one hand, that it includes all x-parts with the property P:

(5.10a) $(\forall y)((y \subseteq x \,\&\, P(y)) \to y \subseteq [z \subseteq x | P(z)])$

and on the other hand that it is part of any ensemble that includes all x-parts with the property P:

(5.10b) $(\forall w)(((\forall y)(y \subseteq x \ \& \ P(y)) \rightarrow y \subseteq w) \rightarrow ([z \subseteq x | P(z)] \subseteq w))$

It can be proved that the ensemble $[z \subseteq x | P(z)]$ is equal to the merge of those parts of x having the property P. In other words, $[z \subseteq x | P(z)]$ is *the ensemble formed by all x-parts with the property P*.

There is an obvious similarity between the concept of the ensemble $[z \subseteq E | P(z)]$, made up by the parts of E with the property P, and the set-theoretical concept for which the notation

(5.11) $\{z \in S | P(z)\}$

is often used: the set made up by the members of S with the property P. The similarity comes out in the following implications which are valid in set theory and ensemble theory, respectively:

(5.12) a. $y \in S \ \& \ P(y) \rightarrow y \in \{z \in S | P(z)\}$
         b. $y \subseteq x \ \& \ P(y) \rightarrow y \subseteq [z \subseteq x | P(z)]$

It is worth emphasizing that there is also a crucial *difference* between the two notions, namely that the implication in (5.12a) may be reversed, but the implication in (5.12b) may not. That is, in set theory we have

(5.13) a. $y \in \{z \in S | P(z)\} \rightarrow y \in S \ \& \ P(y)$

but in ensemble theory it is, in general, *not* the case that

(5.13) b. *$y \subseteq [z \subseteq x | P(z)] \rightarrow y \subseteq x \ \& \ P(y)$

In particular, from $y \subseteq [z \subseteq x | P(z)]$ we may deduce that $y \subseteq x$, but not that $P(y)$ (chapter 10, theorem 2.8.7).

Ensemble theory is fundamentally different in this respect from Parsons' theory of 'substances', considered in section 3.4.

5.3 Atoms, unicles, and members

We have seen in section 5.1 that it is impossible to develop set theory entirely on the basis of a part–whole relation only, because it is impossible to distinguish one singleton from another.

In view of this, I define the notion of an *atomic ensemble* as follows:

(5.14a) An ensemble is atomic iff it has no other parts than $\emptyset$ and itself, and is not empty.

The notation 'AT(x)' will be used to express that x is atomic; formally:

(5.14b) $AT(x) =_D (\forall y)(y \subseteq x \to (y = \emptyset \lor y = x)) \ \& \ x \neq \emptyset$

I now introduce a second primitive which will have the effect that the whole of set theory can be built into ensemble theory. This primitive is called the *unicle–whole* relation, and is symbolized as $\underline{\in}$. The significance of this relation is expressed by an axiom (the 'axiom of unicles') postulating that on the one hand for every atomic ensemble x there is exactly one ensemble y standing in the unicle–whole relation to x:[1]

(5.15a) $(\forall x)(AT(x) \to (\exists! y)(y \underline{\in} x))$

and that on the other hand there is no such object for an ensemble which is not atomic:

(5.15b) $(\forall x)(\neg AT(x) \to \neg(\exists y)(y \underline{\in} x))$

The unique object, standing in unicle–whole relation to an atomic ensemble x, will be called *the unicle of x*. The word 'unicle' is a contraction of 'unique element'.

With the help of the unicle–whole relation we can formulate an *axiom of extensionality* for ensembles, that tells us when an ensemble x is part of an ensemble y. The axiom stipulates that this is the case whenever all parts of x are parts of y and, in case x is atomic, whenever x's unicle is the unicle of some part of y. In formula:

(5.16) $(\forall x, y)(((\forall z)(z \subseteq x \to z \subseteq y) \lor$
$(\exists z)(z \underline{\in} x \ \& \ (\exists w)(w \subseteq y \ \& \ z \underline{\in} w))) \to x \subseteq y)$

(For technical reasons that cannot be discussed here, the axiom is formulated slightly differently in chapter 10; however, the underlying idea is the same.)

From this axiom it follows immediately that the empty ensemble is part of every ensemble, and that every ensemble is part of itself and hence equal to itself. (The latter point could, alternatively, be taken care of by using a logical system for the formulation of the axioms that includes the equality concept. In that case we would need, instead of definition (5.3), an *axiom* relating the logical concept of equality to the ensemble concept of part–whole.)

Given the primitive relations part–whole and unicle–whole we can define an ensemble concept, corresponding to that of the singleton set containing a given element. From the axiom of extensionality it follows immediately that two atomic ensembles are equal if they have the same unicle. In other words, if x is an (atomic) ensemble with unicle z, then any other ensemble with unicle z is equal to x. An atomic ensemble is thus uniquely determined by its unicle, and so we may speak of 'the ensemble with unicle z'. This ensemble will be called *the singleton (ensemble) of z* and will be designated by {z}. The relation between an atomic ensemble and the singleton of its unicle is captured by:

(5.17) $(\forall x)(AT(x) \to (\exists z)(x = \{z\}))$

The fact that a singleton is uniquely determined by its unicle is expressed by:

(5.18) $(\forall y, z)(z \subseteq y \to y = \{z\})$

As mentioned above, by adding the unicle–whole relation we obtain the full power of set theory. To see this, I use the two primitive relations to define an ensemble counterpart of the element relation in set theory.

A relation called *member–whole*, symbolized as $\in$, is defined by:

(5.19) $x \in y =_D (\exists z)(z \subseteq y \ \& \ x \subseteq z)$

In other words, x is a member of y if and only if x is the unicle of some part of y.

Since the only part of an ensemble that can have a unicle is the singleton of that unicle, we have:

(5.20) $(\forall x, y)(x \in y \leftrightarrow \{x\} \subseteq y)$

Since every ensemble is part of itself, it follows that the unicle of an ensemble is a member of that ensemble. It also follows that the empty ensemble has no members, since in order to have a member z it would need to have an atomic part with z as unicle; however, $\emptyset$ has no atomic parts since all its parts are empty.

Since an atomic ensemble has itself as its only atomic part, it also follows that the unicle of an atomic ensemble is its one and only member. Thus, the singleton {z} has z as its one and only member. It is readily seen that the singleton {z} is the minimal ensemble with member z.

Does the member–whole relation, defined here, represent the same concept as the element relation in set theory? The typical test for this would seem to be whether, for any x and y:

(5.21) $x \subseteq y \leftrightarrow (\forall z)(z \in x \to z \in y)$

In ensemble theory, this equivalence does not hold for all ensembles x and y, however. I shall return to this point below.

Before closing this section I want to mention two concepts in ensemble theory that will be indispensable in its application to formal semantics. The first is the generalization of the singleton concept (the minimal ensemble with one member) to the concept of the minimal ensemble with n members. This should correspond to the intuitive idea of 'collection of n objects'. Since ensemble theory does not presuppose the concepts of set theory, this idea has to be formalized within ensemble theory. To achieve this it is sufficient to postulate that for any two ensembles x and y there is a minimal ensemble having x and y as members. This ensemble, uniquely determined due to its minimality, is called the *pair of x and y* and is designated by {x, y}. Using the notation

(5.22) $(\exists p)(\ldots p \ldots)$

for: there exists a *minimal* ensemble p such that (... p ...), we can formulate the *axiom of pairing*, which postulates the existence of pairs, as:

(5.23) $(\forall x, y)(\exists p)(x \in p \ \& \ y \in p)$

Once we have pairs at our disposal, we can construct triplets, quadruplets, quintuplets, ..., n-tuplets for any n. For instance, the triplet {x, y, z} can be constructed as the merge of the ensemble {{x, y}, {z}}.

The second concept to be introduced here is that of the collection of all parts of a given ensemble. This idea was already used above in an informal way when we discussed the Boolean properties of the merge, overlap, and completion. It is brought into ensemble theory and formalized through the *axiom of powers*, which asserts that for any given ensemble x there is a minimal ensemble having the parts of x as members:

(5.24) $(\forall x)(\exists P)(\forall y)(y \subseteq x \rightarrow y \in P)$

This ensemble, uniquely determined by its minimality, is called *the power (ensemble) of x*, and is designated by $\mathcal{P}(x)$.

By merging the members of $\mathcal{P}(x)$, that is, the parts of x, we obtain x itself again, as it should be:

(5.25) $\cup(\mathcal{P}(x)) = x$

It was already mentioned that the ensemble denoted by $[z \subseteq x \mid P(z)]$, that is, the ensemble made up by the x-parts with property P, is the merge of those parts. We can now express this precisely:

(5.26) $[z \subseteq x \mid P(x)] = \cup(\{z \in \mathcal{P}(x) \mid P(z)\})$

5.4 Continuous and discrete ensembles

We now consider two types of ensemble that are of particular importance for the application of ensemble theory to formal semantics, so-called 'continuous' and 'discrete' ensembles. It is convenient to first introduce a few special cases of the part–whole relation. We already introduced the relation 'proper part of', defined as 'part of and not equal to', and symbolized as $\subset$. Another useful restriction besides 'not equal to' is that of not being empty. I therefore define the relation *non-empty part of*, symbolized as $\subseteq°$:

(5.27) $\quad y \subseteq° x =_D y \subseteq x \,\&\, \neg(y = \varnothing)$

Also useful is the combination of the two restrictions in a relation 'non-empty proper part of'. I call this relation *genuine part of* and symbolize it as $\subset°$. Its formal definition is:

(5.28) $\quad y \subset° x =_D y \subset x \,\&\, \neg(y = \varnothing)$

With the help of these specialized part–whole relations the concept of 'continuity' is defined as follows. An ensemble is called *continuous* if it is not empty and each of its non-empty parts has a genuine part. Formally, x is continuous iff:

(5.29) $\quad \neg(x = \varnothing) \,\&\, (\forall z)(z \subseteq° x \to (\exists w)(w \subset° z))$

In a continuous ensemble one can, so to speak, continue *ad infinitum* to take ever smaller non-empty parts. In that sense, *a continuous ensemble has no minimal parts*. A continuous ensemble differs in this respect from a set: in a set one can take smaller and smaller parts, in the sense of non-empty proper subsets, until one gets down to the atomic subsets, but there it comes to an end.

Since a continuous ensemble does not have atomic parts, it follows that *a continuous ensemble has no members*. If x is a continuous ensemble and y a non-empty part of x then, by the continuity of x, y has a genuine part z. Due to the transitivity of the part–whole relation, this z is a non-empty part of x. Therefore, z too has a genuine part. This means that y satisfies the definition of continuity, and so we may conclude that every non-empty part of a continuous ensemble is continuous.

If we have two continuous ensembles x and y, then their merge $x \cup y$ is also continuous. This is so because, according to the definition of merge, every non-empty part of $x \cup y$ overlaps with x or with y. If, for instance, $z \cap (x \cup y)$ and $z \cap x \neq \varnothing$, then by the continuity of x, $z \cap x$ has a genuine part w. By the definition of overlap, $w \subset° z$ and $w \subset° x$, etc.

Similarly, it can be proved that the overlap of two (or more) continuous ensembles is continuous, and that the completion of a continuous ensemble relative to a continuous ensemble is again continuous. I believe the continuous ensemble is an appropriate concept for modelling entities that do not have atomic parts, such as time, space, and the extensions of many abstract mass nouns.

Continuous ensembles have a kind of antipodes in those ensembles that are called 'discrete'. An ensemble is defined as *discrete* iff it is equal to the merge of its atomic parts. Formally, x is discrete iff

(5.30) $x = \cup(\{x \in \mathcal{P}(x) | AT(x)\})$

Continuous and discrete ensembles are antipodes in that a continuous ensemble is never discrete, and vice versa. A continuous ensemble has no atomic parts, so if it were equal to the merge of its atomic parts then it would be empty. Conversely, if a non-empty ensemble is discrete, the merge of its atomic parts is non-empty, therefore it has at least one such part. This is a part that has no genuine parts, so the ensemble is not continuous. The empty ensemble, not having any atomic parts at all, is trivially equal to the merge of its atomic parts, so $\varnothing$ is discrete.

If x is an atomic ensemble, then its only atomic part is x itself. Thus, the collection of x's atomic parts is, in this case, the singleton $\{x\}$. The merge of $\{x\}$ is, by definition, the minimal ensemble having all members of $\{x\}$ as parts; in this case, that minimal ensemble is just x. Thus, $\cup(\{x\}) = x$. In other words, x is equal to the merge of its atomic parts, that is, x is discrete. In general: atomic ensembles are discrete.

It can be proved that any part of a discrete ensemble is discrete; that the merge of two (or more) discrete ensembles is again a discrete ensemble; that the overlap of two discrete ensembles is again a discrete ensemble; and that the completion of a discrete ensemble relative to a discrete ensemble is again discrete.

An important theorem can be derived from the ensemble axioms:

(5.31a) For every ensemble x and condition P there exists exactly one ensemble which is the minimal ensemble having all members of x for which P is true as members.

(Cf. theorem (5.8)!) To designate this ensemble I shall use the notation

(5.31b) $\{z \in x | P(z)\}$

It can be proved that, for any ensemble x and condition P(z), the ensemble $\{z \in x | P(z)\}$ is discrete (chapter 10, theorem 4.2.4).

A special case is that P(z) is the condition: $z = z$. Thus, given an ensemble x, the ensemble $\{z \in x | z = z\}$ exists and is discrete. Moreover, if x itself is discrete, then it is easily proved that $x = \{z \in x | z = z\}$. This is so because, if x is discrete, it is equal to the merge of its atomic parts. By (5.17) this is equivalent to saying that x is equal to the merge of its singleton parts. By definition, this merge is the minimal ensemble including all singletons $\{z\}$ with $z \in x$. By (5.20), it is also the minimal ensemble containing all members of x. Therefore, if x is discrete it is the minimal ensemble containing all its members. On the other hand, the ensemble $\{z \in x | z = z\}$ is by definition the minimal ensemble containing all members of x which are equal to themselves, hence $x = \{z \in x | z = z\}$.

All this reminds us, of course, of ordinary sets. Are discrete ensembles in fact sets? Does the $\in$ relation, as defined in ensemble theory, represent the same concept as the element relation in set theory? Is the part–whole relation, when applied to discrete ensembles, in fact the subset relation? These questions will be discussed in section 5.6, where we consider the relations between ensemble theory, set theory, and mereology.

Is every ensemble either continuous or discrete? No, there is a third case. The merge of a continuous and a discrete ensemble is neither discrete nor continuous. An ensemble which is neither discrete nor continuous has a continuous part and a non-empty discrete part. Such ensembles are called *mixed*. In fact, continuous and discrete ensembles are special cases; in general, an ensemble has both a continuous part and a non-empty discrete part.

If x is a mixed ensemble, its continuous part (or, more accurately, its largest continuous part) is:

(5.32a) $[z \subseteq x | z \neq \emptyset \ \& \ (\forall y)(y \subseteq^\circ z \rightarrow (\exists w)(w \subset^\circ y))]$

(cf. formula 5.29) and its (largest) discrete part is:

(5.32b) $\{z \in x | z = z\}$

I will use the notation $\mathscr{D}(x)$ for the largest discrete part of an ensemble x, thus:

(5.32c) $\mathscr{D}(x) =_D \{z \in x | z = z\}$

An ensemble is always equal to the merge of its (largest) discrete part and its (largest) continuous part.

5.5 A model for ensemble theory

While going through the above exposition of ensemble theory, the reader has perhaps got the feeling that everything seems to go quite smoothly. Even so, there are two fundamental questions concerning this whole enterprise that have to be faced. The first is whether we can be certain that ensemble theory is a logically sound system, free of hidden inconsistencies, and the second question is whether ensemble theory really offers something not already available in other formalisms such as set theory or mereology. The relations between ensemble theory, set theory and mereology will be discussed in the next section; in this section I shall show that ensemble theory is sound and that it indeed offers us something not available in set theory.

The way to show the soundness of a formal system is to specify a so-called *interpretation* or *model*, that is, a domain of objects with familiar properties and relations, which are shown to satisfy all the axioms. The variables and individual constants (like $\varnothing$) occurring in the axioms are interpreted as denoting objects in the domain, and the relation symbols as denoting relations between those objects. Once it has been established that the objects in the interpretation domain have all the properties expressed by the axioms, it follows automatically that they also satisfy any theorem that can be derived from the axioms.

There is one obvious model for ensemble theory, which consists in taking the class of *sets* as the interpretation domain and interpreting the ensemble primitives $\subseteq$ and $\in$ as the subset relation and the element relation for singleton sets, respectively. It is easily verified that this is indeed a model for ensemble theory, but it is a rather uninteresting one, as the whole point of ensemble theory is to do something beyond what we can do with sets. In the set interpretation, for instance, we get no interpretation for continuous ensembles.

A more interesting model, in which we do have interpretations of continuous ensembles, can be found in terms of *intervals* on the real line. An open interval (a, b), that is, the portion of the real line between two points a and b, the end points not included, always encloses a smaller open interval. Interpreting the $\subseteq$ relation as the enclosure of intervals, open intervals would thus seem appropriate interpretations of continuous ensembles. The merge of two ensembles is then interpreted as 'welding together' the corresponding intervals. For instance, if x denotes the interval (a, c) and y the interval (b, d), then the merge of x and y denotes the interval (a, d), as

(5.34) x: ---- ---●————————●-------------------
               a   c
        y: --------------●————————●---------
                         b   d
       x∪y: -------●——————————————●---------
                   a   d

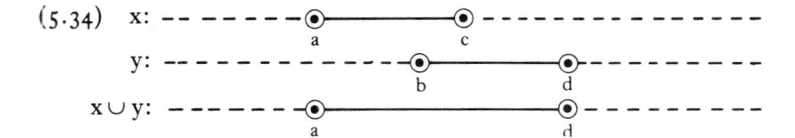

illustrated in (5.34). However, if x denotes the interval (a, b) and y the interval (c, d), disjoint with (a, b), then the merge x∪y comes out as the

(5.35) x: -------●———●-----------------------
                  a   b
        y: ----------------●———●---------
                           c   d
       x∪y: -------●———●---●———●---------
                   a   b   c   d

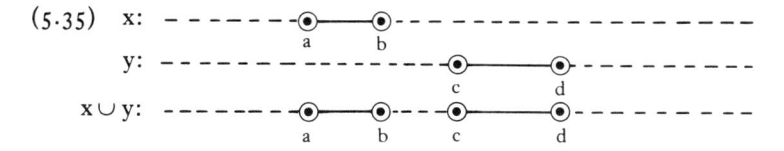

interval series consisting of (a, b) and (c, d) (see (5.35)). Therefore, continuous ensembles should be interpreted more generally as interval *series* (open subsets of R), rather than as single intervals.

Another complication arises because the model should reflect that the completion of a continuous ensemble relative to a continuous ensemble is continuous. The completion of an ensemble x relative to an ensemble z has been defined as the minimal ensemble $\bar{x}^z$ such that $x \cup \bar{x}^z = z$. In the interpretation domain this would mean that $\bar{x}^z$ corresponds to the smallest interval series which, upon welding together with the denotation of x, gives the interval series denoted by z (see (5.36)). We see that the completion of

(5.36) x: ------●———●---●———●-----------
                a   b   c   d
        z: ------●———————————●---------
                a   d
       $\bar{x}^z$: ------------●———●-----------------
                               b   c

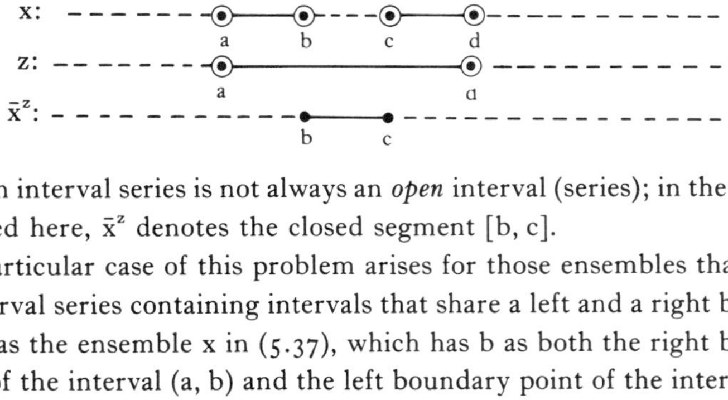

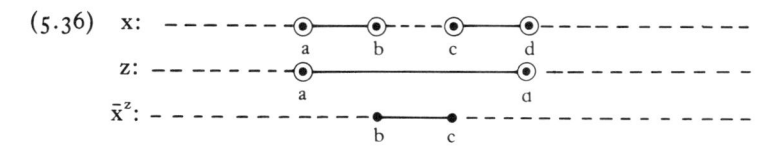

an open interval series is not always an *open* interval (series); in the example depicted here, $\bar{x}^z$ denotes the closed segment [b, c].

A particular case of this problem arises for those ensembles that denote an interval series containing intervals that share a left and a right boundary point, as the ensemble x in (5.37), which has b as both the right boundary point of the interval (a, b) and the left boundary point of the interval (b, c)

(5.37) x: ------●————————●———●---------
                a   b   c
        z: ------●————————————●---------
                a   c
       $\bar{x}^z$: ----------------●---------------
                                   b

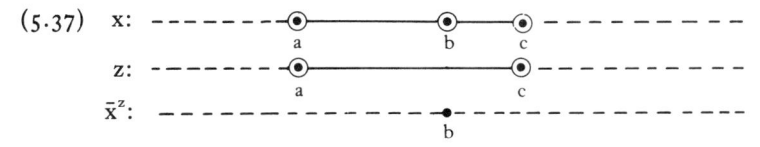

In this case the completion of x relative to z corresponds to a single point (b), and thus not to an open interval series.

To get around these difficulties, I first restrict the interpretation domain for continuous ensembles to interval series containing no intervals with a common left–right boundary point. The interpretation domain, thus restricted, will be referred to as RE (for 'regular–open subsets of R').

But now we must do something about the merge of two ensembles that denote adjacent intervals (or interval series containing adjacent intervals). If the denotation of x contains the interval (a, b) and that of y the interval (b, c), then x ∪ y would denote an interval series with a common left–right boundary point (b), and this interval series would not belong to the domain RE. To remedy this, we interpret the merge of two ensembles in such a way that any common left–right boundary points are *included* in the result

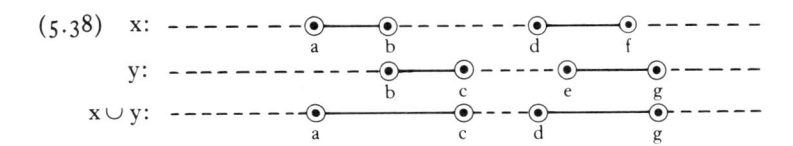

(5.38) x: - - - - - - -●━━━━●- - - - - -●━━━●- - - - -
                       a   b   d   f
         y: - - - - - - - - - -●━━━●- - - -●━━━●- - - - -
                               b   c   e   g
         x ∪ y: - - - - - - -●━━━━━━━━●- - -●━━━━●- - - - -
                             a   c   d   g

of welding the intervals together. Diagram (5.38) illustrates this. With this way of welding intervals together, we at once solve the problem that the completion of a continuous ensemble should be continuous. Example (5.36) illustrates this: the completion $\bar{x}^z$ now comes out in the interpretation domain as the *open* interval (b, c).

So much for the interpretation of continuous ensembles. For discrete ensembles we can construct interpretations in the way usual in set theory, where one starts out with some object 'a' and subsequently builds up {a}, {{a}, a}, etc. The crucial step in the construction of an interpretation for ensemble theory consists in the recognition that *mixed* ensembles are the 'normal' case of an ensemble in the sense that, in general, an ensemble has both a continuous and a discrete part; this can be taken into account in the interpretation by assigning to an ensemble a *pair* consisting of two objects, one interpreting the continuous part and one interpreting the discrete part. Therefore we take the domain U of the interpretation to be a collection of pairs, where one of the elements in a pair is an interval series from RE. The domain is recursively defined by the following two clauses:

(5.39) 1 if z belongs to RE and ∅ is the empty set, then the pair (∅, z) belongs to U;

2 if z belongs to RE and y is a subset of U, then the pair (y, z) belongs to U.

The pairs that form the domain U are assigned to ensembles in such a way that the pair (d_x, c_x) is the denotation of the ensemble x if d_x is the denotation of the discrete part of x and c_x the denotation of the continuous part. Continuous ensembles, having empty discrete parts, are interpreted as pairs $(\emptyset, z)$; discrete ensembles as pairs $(y, \emptyset)$, where $\emptyset$ denotes the 'empty interval series' on the real line (empty subset of R). The empty ensemble has the interpretation $(\emptyset, \emptyset)$.

To interpret the ensemble primitives $\subseteq$ and $\in$, two relations in the domain U are defined. First, using the symbol $\leq$ for the inclusion relation among interval series, a part–whole relation $\subseteq_U$ is defined as follows:

(5.40) $(d_x, c_x) \subseteq_U (d_y, c_y)$ iff d_x is a subset of d_y and $c_x \leq c_y$

Secondly, the relation $\in_U$ is defined as:

(5.41) $(d_x, c_x) \in_U (d_y, c_y)$ iff d_y is the singleton set $\{(d_x, c_x)\}$ and $c_y = \emptyset$

The triple

(5.42) $M = (U, \subseteq_U, \in_U)$

is now a model for ensemble theory. The formal proof of this requires that we verify that all the axioms of ensemble theory are true statements about the domain U if ensemble variables are assigned domain elements as indicated and where, if x and y are ensembles with denotations x' and y', respectively, the elementary statements $x \subseteq y$ and $x \in y$ are interpreted as $x' \subseteq_U y'$ and $x' \in_U y'$, respectively. This is done in detail in chapter 12; here I shall only consider the proofs of three of the axioms that have been mentioned above: the axiom of transitivity (5.2), the axiom of unicles (5.15), and the axiom of pairing (5.23).

Let x, y, and z be three ensembles such that $x \subseteq y$ and $y \subseteq z$. The axiom of transitivity then asserts that it is implied that $x \subseteq z$. To verify that this axiom is satisfied in the interpretation $M = (U, \subseteq_U, \in_U)$ we have to do the following.

Let $x' = (d_x, c_x)$ be the denotation of x, $y' = (d_y, c_y)$ that of y, and $z' = (d_z, c_z)$ that of z. We have to show that from the premises $x' \subseteq_U y'$ and $y' \subseteq_U z'$ it follows that $x' \subseteq_U z'$. Well, $x' \subseteq_U y'$ means that d_x is a subset of d_y and $c_x \leq c_y$; likewise, $y' \subseteq_U z'$ means that d_y is a subset of d_z and $c_y \leq c_z$. From the transitivity of the subset relation it follows that d_x is a subset of

d_z, and from the transitivity of the interval inclusion relation that $c_x \leq c_z$. Therefore $x' \subseteq_U z'$.

The axiom of unicles speaks of atomic ensembles; before we can verify this axiom, we should therefore consider what objects in the interpretation domain correspond to atomic ensembles.

Atomic ensembles are discrete, so they denote pairs $(a, \emptyset)$, with $a \neq \emptyset$. The definition of an atomic ensemble stipulates that every non-empty part of it equals it; in the interpretation domain this means that for every pair $(b, \emptyset)$ with $b \neq \emptyset$, if $(b, \emptyset) \subseteq_U (a, \emptyset)$ then $(b, \emptyset) = (a, \emptyset)$. By the definition of $\subseteq_U$, this means that every non-empty subset b which is a subset of a is equal to a. In other words, any element of a is also an element of any non-empty subset of a. Together with $a \neq \emptyset$, this implies that 'a' can only have one element: $a = \{e\}$. Therefore, atomic ensembles correspond to pairs of the form $(\{e\}, \emptyset)$.

From the definition of the $\in$ relation it follows immediately that e is the one and only object in U such that $e \in_U (\{e\}, \emptyset)$, and that for pairs (d, c) which are not of the form $(\{e\}, \emptyset)$ there is no object p such that $p \in_U (\{e\}, \emptyset)$. This is precisely what the axiom of unicles says.

In the axiom of pairing we see the member–whole relation among ensembles. This relation is defined in terms of the primitives $\subseteq$ and $\in$, therefore the interpretation of these primitives as the relations $\subseteq_U$ and $\in_U$ in the domain U determines the relation in U corresponding to $\in$. This relation, symbolized as $\in_U$, is the following:

(5.43) $(a, b) \in_U (c, d)$ iff $(a, b) \subseteq_U (e, f)$ for some pair (e, f) such that $(e, f) \subseteq_U (c, d)$

To verify the axiom, let x and y be ensembles with denotations $x' = (d_x, c_x)$ and $y' = (d_y, c_y)$. We now have to show that there is a $\subseteq_U$-minimal object in the domain U that contains both x' and y'.

Since both x' and y' are elements of U, the set $\{x', y'\}$ is a subset of U. Therefore, by the definition of U (5.39), the pair $(\{x', y'\}, \emptyset)$ belongs to U. This pair is the object we are looking for; let us call it p'. We must prove that $x' \in_U p'$ and $y' \in_U p'$, and that $p' \subseteq_U q'$ for every q' in U such that $x' \in_U q'$ and $y' \in_U q'$.

Since the singleton set $\{x'\}$ is a subset of the set $\{x', y'\}$, it follows from the definition of $\subseteq_U$ that $(\{x'\}, \emptyset) \subseteq_U p'$. By the definition of $\in_U$, $x' \in_U (\{x'\}, \emptyset)$. Therefore $x' \in_U p'$. Similarly $y' \in_U p'$. Now suppose $x' \in_U q'$ and $y' \in_U q'$. Then $(\{x'\}, \emptyset) \subseteq_U q'$ and $(\{y'\}, \emptyset) \subseteq_U q'$. If q' is the pair (d_q, c_q), this means that x' and y' are subsets of d_q, therefore x' and y' are elements of d_q, hence the set $\{x', y'\}$ is a subset of d_q, hence the pair $(\{x', y'\}, \emptyset) \subseteq_U q'$; in other words $p' \subseteq_U q'$.

5.6 Ensembles, sets, and individuals

A discrete ensemble can be proved to be completely determined by its members, that is, for any two discrete ensembles x and y:

(5.44) $\quad x \subseteq y \leftrightarrow (\forall z)(z \in x \rightarrow z \in y)$

(The proof can be found in chapter 11, theorem 2.7.) This means that the classical axiom of extensionality for sets holds for discrete ensembles as well. Does this mean that discrete ensembles are in fact sets? The answer is yes. In chapter 13 I give a proof of this allegation, which goes along the following lines.

Let ETX be the list of axioms defining ensemble theory. Let ETX* be ETX extended with the 'axiom' saying that all ensembles are discrete. By adding this axiom we restrict ensemble theory to a formalism dealing with discrete ensembles only. Let ZFX be the list of axioms defining classical Zermelo–Fraenkel set theory. Then all the axioms of the list ZFX can be derived from ETX* and vice versa. This means that every theorem in set theory is also a true statement about discrete ensembles, and everything that is true about discrete ensembles is true about sets. In other words, *discrete ensembles are indistinguishable from ordinary sets*. The axiom systems ETX* and ZFX define the same formalism.

The formalism defined by the axiom system ETX* is a subformalism of ETX, since ETX* was constructed by adding an axiom to ETX, which means that the objects satisfying the axioms of ETX* will certainly satisfy the axioms of ETX (a discrete ensemble is an ensemble). Since ETX* is a way of defining sets, we may say that *set theory is incorporated in ensemble theory*.

The part–whole relation as defined by the axioms of ensemble theory has the same logical properties as that defined in mereology, so one might well ask what differences there are. One point of difference we have seen is that there is an empty ensemble, which is a part of every ensemble, whereas in mereology there is no empty object. In addition, a non-empty ensemble which has no proper parts is, by definition, atomic and, therefore, by the axiom of unicles, it has a unicle. This is a point of difference with mereology. In ensemble theory the unicle concept is introduced via the notion of atomicity, which we could introduce in mereology by defining a mereological individual as atomic if it has no other parts than itself. But since the part–whole relation is the only relation in mereology, an 'atomic individual' does not have any internal structure. This difference can be removed, if desired, by relaxing the axiom of unicles in ensemble theory. As it stands, it stipulates that every atomic ensemble has a unicle and that all other ensembles do not have unicles. This may be relaxed to saying that an ensemble which is not atomic does not have a unicle, which is a way of saying that an atomic ensemble may have a unicle but is not required to have one. We then get two kinds of atomic ensembles, with and without a unicle. The latter can be proved to have precisely the same properties as mereological individuals (see section 13.2). Therefore, if so-desired not only set theory but also mereology can be incorporated into ensemble theory.

6 Semantic representations based on ensemble theory

6.1 Introduction

The semantic analysis of a natural language expression often takes the form of providing a formal notation that is meant to represent the semantic structure of the expression. The survey of the literature on mass term semantics given in chapter 3 contains numerous examples of this. Such a formal notation is then called a *semantic representation* of the sentence. Chapters 7 to 9 will be concerned with the use of ensemble-based semantic representations in a linguistic semantic theory.

The use of formal semantic representations has the advantage that one is forced to be precise and explicit. As Lyons (1977) puts it: 'when one is converting statements of ordinary language into some supposedly equivalent symbolic representation, one is forced to examine the ordinary language statements with more care than one might otherwise have done; and, as a consequence, instances of ambiguity or imprecision may be detected which might otherwise have passed by unnoticed' (Lyons, 1977, p. 139). In particular, formal semantic representations are often useful for making explicit under what conditions a natural language sentence expresses a true assertion, that is, for representing its *truth conditions*.

When semantic analysis takes the form of providing semantic representations in some formal notation system, the choice of that system is one of crucial importance. The use of a particular system always has the effect of putting oneself into a straitjacket: such a system has a very limited set of formal concepts, such as the concepts of set theory, in terms of which everything is expressed. Once a particular representational formalism has been chosen, the desire to express everything in that formalism often has the effect that simplifications or slight distortions of one's intuitions about certain semantic structures in the natural language sneak in. I think this is in fact the case with the set-based proposals for the semantics of mass noun expressions that we have discussed in chapter 3. The choice of a set-based representational formalism, as far as it has been a deliberate choice at all, is based primarily on the circumstance that set theory is a familiar formalism. The enterprise of developing ensemble theory can be seen as an attempt to break away from the ties of set-based representational formalisms and to develop a formalism that is more tailored to our intuitions about semantic structures in natural language.

A well-defined notation system is in itself, of course, a language, a formal language with its own syntax and semantics. The analysis of natural language using semantic representations, when pursued in a systematic fashion, therefore, takes the form of *translating* ordinary language into a formal language. This approach has gained popularity in linguistics since the pioneering work of Richard Montague, who gave an analysis of certain classical problems in semantics by describing the translation of the expressions of a fragment of English into a formal language, designed for the purpose (see Montague, 1974). In this approach the precision and explicitness associated with the use of formal semantic representations have been attained fully, since (a) the representational formalism is rigorously defined, and (b) the translation procedure systematically assigns to every expression in the natural language fragment one or more (in the case of ambiguity) expressions in the formal language. The truth conditions of any natural language sentence in the fragment are thus precisely determined. I shall follow this approach and define the translation of fragments of English into formal languages designed for the purpose of providing adequate representations of English expressions containing count terms as well as mass terms. This will be the subject of chapters 8 and 9.

In the next chapter, I shall discuss the theoretical status of semantic representations. In the present chapter, I define a formal language for semantic representation in which ensemble concepts are used.

As a preliminary indication of the kind of semantic representations that will be used, consider the notation introduced in the previous chapter in (5.9):

(6.1) $[x \subseteq E | P(x)]$

Theorem (5.26) told us that, for a given ensemble E and predicate P, the ensemble denoted here is made up by those parts of E for which P holds. The use of ensembles in semantic representations will be such that a mass noun is translated into an expression that denotes an ensemble. If SNOW is a formal-language constant translating 'snow' and INGARDEN a predicate translating the phrase 'in the garden', the expression

(6.2) $[x \subseteq \text{SNOW}|\text{INGARDEN}(x)]$

will represent the phrase 'the snow in the garden'.

The notation (6.1) was introduced in the previous chapter as just a 'notation convention'. In this chapter I shall be more precise, defining a formal language in which the syntax and semantics of this notation are described. This language will be called *Ensemble Language* (EL).

When I discuss the systematic use of EL in the analysis of mass noun expressions in chapters 8 and 9, one of the central points of interest will be the analysis of quantification in relation to mass nouns. To analyse quantified mass terms we shall have to consider expressions containing so-called *amount terms*, expressions like 'five litres', 'two gallons of', etc. To my knowledge, no representational formalism has yet been developed in which this kind of expression can be represented adequately. Therefore, I first take a brief excursion into the semantics of amount terms, and present an analysis of these terms that will be the basis of their representation in EL.

6.2 Amount terms

By an 'amount term' I understand a phrase consisting of a numeral and a unit, such as 'two litres', 'five tons', 'two and a half teaspoons'. These expressions are also known as 'measure phrases'.

Two important syntactic positions in which amount terms occur are those that we might call *predicative* and *attributive*. In predicative position the amount term functions either as one of the arguments of a verb, as in

(6.3) a. The sand weighs five tons
       b. This book costs 10 dollars

or as the value of a function noun, as in

(6.4) a. The weight of the sand is five tons
       b. The price of this book is 10 dollars

In attributive position, on the other hand, the amount term precedes a noun or more complex nominal constituent (but not a noun phrase, see below); in English, as well as in French and other Romance languages, a partitive particle usually connects the amount term and the nominal term, as in

(6.5) a. Five tons of sand
       b. Two teaspoons of soy sauce

76 Part 1 Model-theoretic semantics of mass terms

In this case the amount term functions as a determiner, in much the same way as a number with a count term. Parsons (1970) calls the amount terms used predicatively 'isolated amount terms' and uses 'applied amount terms' for phrases consisting of an amount term, a partitive particle, and a mass term. (The possibility that an amount term is applied to a plural count term is not considered.)

There is a third syntactic position in which amount terms may occur, namely in front of a partitive particle plus a noun phrase:

(6.6) Five tons of the sand

This use of the amount term is similar to that of a numeral in expressions like 'Three of the boys'. For a detailed study of amount terms in the framework of transformational syntax see Klooster (1972).

From a semantic point of view, the treatment of amount terms which is proposed here has a platonistic basis in that amount terms are considered as having denotations which are abstract mathematical objects, similar in many ways to numbers. I call these entities 'amounts'. I shall begin now by considering the nature of these abstract amounts, and subsequently suggest a way of using these in the semantics of predicative and attributive amount terms.

Amounts share with numbers the feature that they have a certain arithmetic: under some conditions, amounts can be added, subtracted, and compared to size; moreover, an amount can be multiplied by a number. For example, 7 kilometres minus 200 metres is equal to 6 kilometres plus 800 metres; 7 kilometres is more than 3 miles, but 7 kilometres is neither more nor less than 7 kilogrammes. Numbers of kilometres, metres and miles can be compared, added and subtracted because these units belong to the same *dimension*, in this case the dimension of distance.

Units of the same dimension are numerically related: a kilometre is 1000 metres, a mile is 1·6 kilometres, etc. The possibility of performing algebraic manipulations with amounts of the same dimension depends on the existence of these numerical relations among units. Because of these relations, one can convert from one unit to another. I therefore call the numerical factors relating the units of a dimension the 'conversion factors' of that dimension.

For a given set of units, the conversion factors can be specified by means of a function assigning to each pair of units the factor that must be taken into account upon conversion from the one to the other. I call such a function a *conversion function*. For instance, for the dimension of distance the conversion function F_d would say F_d(mile, kilometre) = 1·6. Conversion

Semantic representations based on ensemble theory

functions have certain interesting properties which will be important in the formalization of the amount concept.

A conversion factor is always a positive real number, so given a set of units SU_d the conversion function F_d has the domain $SU_d \times SU_d$ (the set of all pairs of units from SU_d) and takes values in $\mathbb{R}^*$, the set of positive real numbers. Now if one is to convert from a unit u_1 to a unit u_2, one may always go via a third unit u_3: the conversion from u_1 to u_2 can be calculated by first converting from u_1 to u_3 and subsequently from u_3 to u_2, and the outcome should be independent of u_3. Therefore, the conversion function F_d has the property that, for any x, y, $z \in SU_d$:

(6.7) $\quad F_d(x, y) \cdot F_d(y, z) = F_d(x, z)$

where the dot represents ordinary multiplication of numbers. By analogy with transitive relations, I call a function satisfying (6.7) *transitive*. The set of all transitive functions from $A \times A$ into $\mathbb{R}^*$ will be designated by $Tr[A]$.

Two useful properties of such functions are the following. First, taking $y = x$ in (6.7) we obtain

(6.8) $\quad F_d(x, x) \cdot F_d(x, z) = F_d(x, z)$

Dividing on both sides by $F_d(x, z)$ we obtain

(6.9) $\quad F_d(x, x) = 1$

Secondly, taking $z = x$ in (6.7) we obtain

(6.10) $\quad F_d(x, y) \cdot F_d(y, x) = F_d(x, x)$

Hence, by (6.9),

(6.11) $\quad F_d(x, y) = F_d(y, x)^{-1}$

I shall call a set of units plus a conversion function a 'dimension'.

Definition 6.1. A *dimension* D is a pair (SU_d, F_d) such that
  (i) SU_d is a non-empty set, the elements of which are called *D-units*;
  (ii) F_d is a function belonging to $Tr[SU_d]$, called the *conversion function of D*.

We are now almost prepared to take the step to the precise definition of the amount concept. When we think about the denotation of an amount term like '25 kilos', the first thing that comes to mind is probably the pair consisting of the number 25 and the unit denoted by 'kilo'. But '25 kilos' and '2500 grammes' denote the same amount, which would not come out this way. However, we can use conversion functions to construct appropriate denotations out of number–unit pairs as follows.

The conversion function F_d of a dimension $D = (SU_d, F_d)$ defines a relation between pairs consisting of a non-negative real number and a D-unit as follows:

(6.12) $(n_1, u_1) =^D (n_2, u_2)$ iff $n_1 \cdot F_d(u_1, u_2) = n_2$

From (6.7) to (6.11) it follows that the relation $=^D$ is an *equivalence relation*; therefore, if $\mathbb{R}^*$ is the set of non-negative real numbers, the relation defines a partitioning of the space $\mathbb{R}^* \times SU_d$ into equivalence classes (see e.g. Birkhoff and Bartee, 1967). The proposal is now to take these equivalence classes as the formalization of the concept 'amounts of the dimension D'. I designate the set of these equivalence classes by A_d. Formally, then, an amount of the dimension D (a 'D-amount') is defined as follows.

Definition 6.2. Given a dimension $D = (SU_d, F_d)$, a *D-amount* is an element of the partitioning of $\mathbb{R}^* \times SU_d$ into equivalence classes defined by the relation $=^D$.

Example: Three of the units of volume and their conversion factors are: litre, pint, and gallon, with 1 litre being equal to 1·76 pints and 1 pint being equal to $\frac{1}{8}$ of a gallon. This can be modelled formally by the dimension:

(6.13) $V = (SU_v, F_v)$, where:
  $SU_v = \{litre, pint, gallon\}$.
  $F_v = \{((litre, pint), 1·76),$
    $((litre, gallon), 0·22),$
    $((litre, litre), 1),$
    $((pint, litre), 0·57),$
    $((pint, gallon), 0·13),$
    $((pint, pint), 1),$
    $((gallon, litre), 4·55),$
    $((gallon, pint), 8),$
    $((gallon, gallon), 1)\}$.

An example of a V-amount is now the equivalence class:

(6.14) $\{(1·14, litre), (2, pint), (0·25, gallon)\}$

I shall say that the elements of an amount *represent* that amount; for instance, (2, pint) and (0·25, gallon) both represent the amount (6.14). The notation $(n, u)_d$ will be used to designate the D-amount represented by (n, u).

The conversion function F_d can be used to define an ordering relation $>^D$ between pairs (n_1, u_1), (n_2, u_2) in a way similar to the use in defining the equivalence relation $=^D$. The definition is:

(6.15) $(n_1, u_1) >^D (n_2, u_2)$ iff $n_1 \cdot F_d(u_1, u_2) > n_2$

In terms of the relation $>^D$ an *ordering* relation $>$ between D-amounts is now defined as follows:

(6.16) $a_d > a'_d$ iff $(\exists x \in a_d)(\exists x' \in a'_d)(x >^D x')$

For instance, the amount $(2, \text{litre})_v$, is greater than the amount $(3, \text{pint})_v$ if V is the dimension of example (6.13), since

(6.17) $(2, \text{litre}) \in (3 \cdot 52, \text{pint})_v$

and $(3 \cdot 52, \text{pint}) >^D (3, \text{pint})$.

For any two D-amounts a_d and a'_d, it is either the case that $a_d > a'_d$ or that $a'_d > a_d$ or that $a_d = a'_d$. The ordering, defined by (6.16), is thus a total one. This way of comparing amounts will be the basis of an analysis of expressions like 'more than two litres of milk', 'weighing less than five hundred kilogrammes', etc.

Addition and subtraction of amounts of the same dimension can be defined along the same lines as their comparison. The reader is referred to Bunt (1978) for a discussion of these and other formal operations on amounts.

One last formal point about amounts that must be mentioned here is the existence of so-called 'null amounts'. This notion is defined as follows.

Definition 6.3. The *null amount* of a dimension D is the D-amount represented by $(0, u_i)_d$ for arbitrary D-unit u_i.

I use the notation $\emptyset_d$ for the null amount of D. For this definition to be meaningful, it must define the same null amount independent of the unit u_i that occurs in the definition. It is easily seen that, for any $n \in \mathbb{R}^*$, $u_i \in SU_d$:

(6.18) $(n, u_i) \in \emptyset_d$ iff $n = 0$

Therefore,

(6.19) $(0, u_i)_d = (0, u_j)_d$

for any $u_i, u_j \in SU_d$; hence the null amount of D is indeed uniquely determined by definition 6.3.

Null amounts play a role in the formalization of the amount concept given here, as we shall see below. They could conceivably also play a role in the semantic analysis of expressions like

(6.20) There's no hot water

I will explicitly avoid using null amounts for this purpose, however, as I think the analysis of such expressions should preferably not force us to choose a particular dimension in which amounts are measured. (See further chapter 8.)

D-amounts are intended to be useful in the semantic analysis of quantified mass noun expressions: we want to measure such things as samples of water, sand, furniture, and luggage (but also collections of apples, books, chairs and suitcases) along such dimensions as weight and volume. In the formal semantic representations we thus want to express relations between ensembles and D-amounts, and an obvious way of doing this is by means of functions, defined on ensembles and having D-amounts as values. In order to be suitable for this purpose, such a function must have certain logical properties.

Consider an ensemble E and a dimension D along which parts of E are to be measured. A function μ, defined on the set $\mathcal{P}(E)$ of E-parts and having A_d as its value range, is suitable for expressing the 'measure' of E-parts along dimension D only if it has the following properties:

1. μ has the null amount $\varnothing_d$ as value only when applied to the empty E-part $\varnothing$.
2. When applied to the merge of two (or more) non-overlapping E-parts, the value of μ is the sum of the values that μ has for each of the parts.
3. When applied to an atomic part of E, the value of μ is the same as when applied to the unicle of that part.

I call a function satisfying these requirements a *measure function*. Formally, a measure function for E-parts is defined as a function μ from $\mathcal{P}(E)$ to the set A_d of amounts of a dimension D, such that:

(6.21) a. $(\forall x, y \subseteq E)(x \cap y = \varnothing \rightarrow \mu(x \cup y) = \mu(x) + \mu(y))$
b. $(\forall x \subseteq E)(x \neq \varnothing \rightarrow \mu(x) > \varnothing_d)$
c. $(\forall x \subseteq E)(\mu(\{x\}) = \mu(x))$

This concept of a measure function is a relatively straightforward extension of the usual mathematical concept of a measure function (see e.g. Halmos, 1950).

With the help of measure functions and amounts as developed here, we can analyse amount terms in predicative and attributive positions as follows. Let μ_w be a measure function, applicable to the parts of an ensemble E, and having as values amounts of the dimension W (weight). Let x be a part of E. A statement of the form

(6.22)   x weighs n pounds

containing the predicative amount term 'n pounds', is analysed as having a semantic representation of the form

(6.23) $\mu_w(x) = (n, \text{pound})_w$

On the other hand, an expression of the form

(6.24)   n pounds of E

containing an attributive amount term, is analysed as denoting a part y of E such that $\mu_w(y) = (n, \text{pound})_w$.

We already noted that measure functions can also be applied to discrete ensembles, such as a collection of apples. The application of μ_w to a set of two apples a_1, a_2 illustrates the role of the properties (6.21) required of a measure function. Since $\{a_1, a_2\} = \{a_1\} \cup \{a_2\}$ and the sets $\{a_1\}$ and $\{a_2\}$ are disjoint, by (6.21a) we have

(6.25) $\mu_w(\{a_1, a_2\}) = \mu_w(\{a_1\}) + \mu_w(\{a_2\})$

so that, by (6.21c), the total weight of these apples is the sum of their individual weights:

(6.26) $\mu_w(\{a_1, a_2\}) = \mu_w(a_1) + \mu_w(a_2)$

Below, I shall introduce amounts and measure functions into a formal semantic representation language; their use will be considered in chapter 8, where quantified mass terms are analysed.

6.3 Language definition and families of languages

We are now in a position to consider the definition of a formal language for semantic representation that includes ensemble concepts and provisions for representing amounts. First, there is a minor terminological point that has to be settled, having to do with what we mean by a language. In formal conceptions of natural language, a language is often considered to be defined by three parts: (i) the lexicon, (ii) the syntax, and (iii) the semantics. In this conception, the lexicon lists all the lexical items with their syntactic categories and features and with their lexical meanings. The syntactic and semantic components are usually considered to be lexicon-independent: the syntactic rules are in terms of syntactic categories and syntactic features, but do not mention individual lexical items, and similarly for the semantic rules. On this view, the lexicon is thus a completely separate 'module' in the language definition that could be replaced by another one without anything else having to change. When we are dealing with natural languages, it is of course not realistic to think that there are any two languages that differ solely in their lexical parts. But in the case of formal languages the situation is different.

Formal languages that have the same syntactic and semantic definition parts but differ in their lexical parts are sometimes said to belong to the same *family of languages*, but are also sometimes loosely called *a language*. It is, for instance, not uncommon to speak of 'predicate language' or 'the language of predicate calculus', thereby meaning any language with the syntactic and semantic structures considered in the logic of predicate calculus.

What is defined in this chapter, and called 'EL' (Ensemble Language), is a language in the latter sense of the word. Actually, the syntax and semantics of a family of formal languages will be defined, particular 'instances' of which will be considered in later chapters. Since the choice of the constants of EL is of no concern at this point, it is convenient to forget about the EL lexicon for a while and proceed as if we are considering just one language.

It was mentioned above that since ensemble theory is an extension of set theory in the sense discussed in section 5.6, in principle, any formal language defined on the basis of set theory can be extended to include ensemble constructions. As a starting point, I have taken here a set-based language that has been developed for the purpose of semantic representation in an Artificial Intelligence project which was carried out between 1972 and 1979 at Philips Research Laboratories in Eindhoven. This project has resulted in a computer program that responds to questions in English, typed on a keyboard. For a description of this program, called PHLIQA1, and its representation language, see Bronnenberg *et al*. (1980). A language somewhat simpler than EL, obtained by adding ensemble constructions to the PHLIQA representation language, has been described in Bunt (1979). The language EL as described below, with some extensions that are of no relevance here, is used for semantic representation in a natural language dialogue system called TENDUM which is being developed in a joint project of the Institute for Perception Research in Eindhoven and the Computational Linguistics Research Unit at Tilburg University (see Bunt, 1984a; Bunt *et al.*, 1984).

The view that a language can be characterized by a lexicon, syntax and semantics, corresponds to a rather abstract conception of language that many linguists are not entirely happy with. It may be argued that part of the definition of a language should concern the way the language is spoken and written and functionally used. How a language is spoken and written is only partially described by the syntactic component and the lexicon, and in the tripartite definition there is no part at all relating to how the syntactic/semantic structures defined by the other components may be used in actual communicative situations. In other words, there is no place for *pragmatic* considerations. In the definition of a formal language there is never any serious concern for how the language is to be spoken or written. Formal languages are simply not spoken; conventions for their writing usually form part of their syntax or they remain implicit, and pragmatic considerations seem irrelevant since formal languages are not used for communication. (There are only marginal exceptions to this in artificial languages for communication between humans and computers.) However, if the study of pragmatic aspects of natural languages develops to a similar level of precision as has been attained in formal semantics, the inclusion of pragmatic aspects of natural language expressions in their formal representations becomes relevant. The most natural way of achieving this would seem to be the addition to the language definition of a pragmatic component in relation to a formalized model of communication. (See Bunt, 1981b for some steps in this direction.) However, pragmatic aspects will be left out completely in the present study of mass nouns, and so the traditional conception of a language as defined by its syntax, semantics, and lexicon will be adopted here. It is the basis for the definition of the fragments of English considered in chapters 8 and 9.

The definition of EL will be seen to contain, besides the syntax and semantics, a part that formalizes considerations which in linguistic theory are commonly found either in the form of selection restrictions in the syntactic component, or in the form of semantic features in the semantic component. It is the type of consideration that certain verbs, like 'breathe' and 'live', require a subject which is 'animate'. In formal languages similar considerations are often formalized with the help of the concept of *semantic types*, also simply called 'types'. A type is associated with each expression of the language, which indicates the sort of entity denoted by the expression. The way in which types are associated with EL expressions will form part of the definition of the EL syntax; in the next section we first consider the nature of types and their internal structure.

6.4 The EL type system

The (semantic) type associated with an EL expression indicates the kind of entity denoted. In saying what kind of entity is denoted we can distinguish two aspects, a *logical* aspect and a *referential*, domain-of-discourse-dependent aspect. The former aspect is concerned with the logical structure of the denotation, that is, with questions such as whether something is an individual, a set of individuals, a continuous ensemble, a property, a set of properties, etc. The latter aspect is concerned with whether an expression denotes a person, a machine, a piece of furniture, a water sample, etc., and reflects a categorization of the objects in the domain of discourse. The type system now has a set of atomic types, one for each category of objects in the discourse domain, and a variety of ways of building up complex types out of atomic ones to represent the logical aspects of a denotation.

This is formalized by defining a simple formal language in which types are expressed, the *EL type language*. The simplest expressions of this language are the names of the semantic categories distinguished in the discourse domain (the atomic types). From these, more complex expressions may be built up, representing complex types, according to the following syntactic rules.

(6.27) Syntactic rules of EL type language

1. There is a finite set T_A of constants called *atomic types*. Every atomic type is a type.
2. If $\underline{t}$ is a type, then $S(t)$ is a type.
3. If $\underline{t}$ is a type, then $E(t)$ is a type.
4. If $\underline{t}_1$ and $\underline{t}_2$ are types, then $(t_1 \rightarrow t_2)$ is a type.
5. If $\underline{t}$ is a type, then $Tr(t)$ is a type.
6. If $\underline{t}$ is a type, then $amt(t)$ is a type.
7. If $\underline{t}_1, \ldots, \underline{t}_n$ are types, then $\langle t_1, \ldots, t_n \rangle$ is a type for any integer $n > 0$.
8. If $\underline{t}_1, \ldots, \underline{t}_n$ are types, then $\cup (t_1, \ldots, t_n)$ is a type for any integer $n > 0$.[1]

It was said that atomic types are names of categories of objects in the domain of discourse. It is customary in formal semantics to consider objects like numbers and truth values as not belonging to the discourse domain proper, however, and according to that convention we should say that atomic types are either names of object categories in the discourse domain or names of categories of elementary mathematical objects. Types of the latter kind I shall call *formal atomic types*, the others *referential atomic types*. What referential atomic types are included in the set T_A of atomic types thus varies from discourse domain to discourse domain; concerning the formal atomic types I shall assume that the following ones are included: truthvalue, integer, real, string.

The definition of the EL type language also has a semantic part, of course. This consists of a set of rules that assign to each type a set of entities called the *domain* of that type. The entities that form these domains are constructed from elementary mathematical objects and objects in the discourse domain. The discourse domain is assumed to be categorized in such a way that all objects of the same category are part or member of an ensemble, which may be discrete, continuous or mixed. This categorization is in accordance with the type system in the sense that as many ensembles $E_1, E_2, \ldots, E_m$ are distinguished as there are referential atomic types in T_A; moreover, these ensembles are assumed to be mutually disjoint. Such a collection of ensembles $C = \{E_1, E_2, \ldots, E_n\}$ will be called a *categorization* of the discourse domain. The starting point of the semantics of the type language is now that (1) to every referential atomic type t_i an ensemble in the categorization is assigned; this assignment is formally described by a function D_{at}, and (2) to every formal atomic type a set of elementary mathematical objects is assigned, again by the function D_{at}. On this basis, a domain is assigned to every type by means of a set of rules, recursively defining the *domain assignment function* D, as follows.

(6.28) Semantic rules of EL type language

1. To every referential atomic type t_i an ensemble $D_{at}(t_i)$ is assigned in the categorization of the discourse domain.
   To every formal atomic type a set of elementary mathematical objects is assigned as follows:
   – D_{at}(truthvalue) = {TRUE, FALSE}
   – D_{at}(integer)   = $\mathbb{Z}$, the set of integer numbers
   – D_{at}(real)   = $\mathbb{R}$, the set of real numbers
   – D_{at}(string)   = the set of alphanumerical strings.
   For any atomic type, $D(\underline{t}) = \mathscr{D}(D_{at}(\underline{t}))$
   That is, the domain assigned to an atomic type $\underline{t}$ is the maximal discrete part of $D_{at}(\underline{t})$; see (5.32c).

2. $D(\underline{S(t)}) = \mathscr{P}(D(\underline{t}))$
3. $D(\underline{E(t)}) = \mathscr{P}(D_{at}(\underline{t}))$ if $\underline{t}$ is atomic, otherwise $\mathscr{P}(D(\underline{t}))$
4. $D(\underline{t_1 \to t_2}) = D(\underline{t_2})^{D(\underline{t_1})}$

   That is, the domain is the set of all functions from the domain of $\underline{t_1}$ to the domain of $\underline{t_2}$.
5. $D(\underline{Tr(t)}) = Tr[D(\underline{t})]$

   That is, the domain of such a type is the set of transitive functions from $D(\underline{t}) \times D(\underline{t})$ into $\mathbb{R}^*$ (see section 6.2).
6. $D(\underline{amt(t)}) =$ the class of partitions of the space $\mathbb{R}^* \times D(\underline{t})$ into equivalence classes.
7. $D(\underline{\langle t_1, \ldots, t_n \rangle}) = D(\underline{t_1}) \times \ldots \times D(\underline{t_n})$
8. $D(\underline{\cup (t_1, \ldots, t_n)}) = D(\underline{t_1}) \cup \ldots \cup D(\underline{t_n})$

The reader familiar with the techniques of model-theoretic semantics will recognize here, in fact, a description of the model theory of the type language.

In what sense do the rules (6.28) constitute the semantics of the type language, that is, in what way do these rules express the 'meaning' of the types? Types are meant to indicate what sort of object an EL expression denotes. Suppose, for instance, that 'John' is an EL expression (simply a constant), to which the EL definition assigns the referential atomic type person. Let the domain of discourse be categorized in such a way that a discrete ensemble PERSONS is distinguished, associated with the type person by (6.28(1)). The domain associated with the type person is then, by (6.28(1)), the set of persons: $D(\text{person}) = \mathscr{D}(\text{PERSONS}) = \text{PERSONS}$. Therefore, the fact that 'John' has the type person means that the set PERSONS is associated with 'John'; the nature of this association, sometimes called that of *possible denotation* (see e.g. Montague, 1970), will be made precise in the semantic part of the EL definition, but the general idea may be clear by now: the domain of the type of an EL expression is the set to which the denotation of the expression must belong. So, indeed, the type of an EL expression indicates the category of object denoted.

Let us also consider briefly the kinds of objects corresponding to complex types.

— Types of the form $\underline{S(t)}$ (set types) have domains consisting of sets of elements of the domain of $\underline{t}$. Thus, an expression of type $\underline{S(\text{person})}$ has a denotation belonging to the set $\mathscr{P}(\text{PERSONS})$, that is, it denotes a set of persons.

— Types of the form $\underline{E(t)}$ (ensemble types) have domains consisting of the parts of the ensemble $D_{at}(\underline{t})$ in case $\underline{t}$ is an atomic type, and consisting of the parts of the ensemble $D(\underline{t})$ if $\underline{t}$ is not atomic. It follows that, for non-atomic type $\underline{t}$, the domains of the complex types $\underline{S(t)}$ and $\underline{E(t)}$ coincide. But for an atomic type $\underline{t}_i$ the domains are different: if $\underline{t}_i$ corresponds to the ensemble $E_i(=D_{at}(\underline{t}_i))$ in the categorization of the discourse domain, then for the set type we have

(6.29a) $\quad D(\underline{S(t_i)}) = \mathcal{P}(D(\underline{t}_i)) = \mathcal{P}(\mathcal{D}(D_{at}(\underline{t}_i))) = \mathcal{P}(\mathcal{D}(E_i))$

while for the ensemble type

(6.29b) $\quad D(\underline{E(t_i)}) = \mathcal{P}(D_{at}(\underline{t}_i)) = \mathcal{P}(E_i)$

Note that this implies that, for any type $\underline{t}$:

(6.29c) $\quad D(\underline{S(t)}) \subseteq D(\underline{E(t)})$

The domain of a type $\underline{S(t)}$ is thus always a subset of the domain of the type $\underline{E(t)}$. This may be considered to reflect the fact that a set is a special case of an ensemble, and that a set type is therefore more restrictive than an ensemble type. By assigning the type $\underline{E(t)}$ to an EL expression we say that the possible denotations of the expression are the parts of a certain ensemble; by assigning it instead the type $\underline{S(t)}$ we say, more restrictively, that the possible denotations are the *discrete* parts of that ensemble.

Relations between types such as the one between $\underline{S(t)}$ and $\underline{E(t)}$ are expressed formally by a relation called *type inclusion*.[2] If the type-inclusion relation, symbolized by $<_t$, holds between two types $\underline{t}_1$ and $\underline{t}_2$ then the domain of $\underline{t}_1$ is always a subset of the domain of $\underline{t}_2$:

(6.30) $\quad \underline{t}_1 <_t \underline{t}_2 \to D(\underline{t}_1) \subseteq D(\underline{t}_2)$

— Types of the form $(\underline{t}_1 \to \underline{t}_2)$ have domains consisting of total functions from the domain of $\underline{t}_1$ to the domain of $\underline{t}_2$. Thus, an expression of type (person → integer) may denote any function from persons to integers, such as 'age'.

— Types of the form $\underline{Tr(t)}$ have domains consisting of the transitive functions defined on pairs of which both arguments belong to the domain of $\underline{t}$, and having positive real numbers as values. These types are convenient for the formal treatment of amounts.

— Types of the form $\underline{amt(t)}$ have domains consisting of partitions of the set $\mathbb{R}^* \times D(\underline{t})$, the set of pairs (n, u) where n is a non-negative real number and u an element of the domain of t̲, into equivalence classes. These are the objects introduced in section 6.2 in the formalization of the amount concept.

— Types of the form $\langle t_1, \ldots, t_n \rangle$ have domains consisting of n-tuples whose first element is from the domain of t_1; whose second element is from the domain of t_2; ...; and whose nth element is from the domain of t_n. Thus, an expression of type ⟨person, person⟩ may denote any pair of persons.

— Types of the form $\cup (t_1, \ldots, t_n)$ have domains which are the unions of the domains of $t_1, \ldots, t_n$. Thus, an expression of type ∪(integer, real) may denote any integer or real number (the union of the sets of the integers and the real numbers is the set of its possible denotations).

6.5 The syntax of EL

The syntax of EL defines the class of expressions belonging to the language. In addition, the syntax assigns a type (an expression of the type language) to every expression of the language. An EL expression is either a *term*, that is, a constant or a variable, or a complex expression. The complex expressions are recursively defined in terms of simpler expressions. They are always of the form:

(6.31) brc(sel$_1$: E$_1$, ..., sel$_n$: E$_n$)

where E$_1$, ..., E$_n$ are EL expressions, brc is the 'branching category' of the expression, which is a name of the semantic relationship between E$_1$, ..., E$_n$, and sel$_1$, ..., sel$_n$ are the 'selectors' belonging to the branching category; the selectors are names of the roles played by the constituents E$_1$, ..., E$_n$ in the semantic relationship brc. For example, one of the branching categories of EL is function application, with the selectors 'fun' and 'arg'; application of a function 'F' to an argument 'a' is represented in this form by:

(6.32a) application(fun: F, arg: a)

As well as 'branching category' I shall also use the term 'construction'.

The recursive definition of the complex expressions consists of a set of rules of the following form:

(6.33) If $E_1, \ldots, E_n$ are expressions of the language and their types fulfil the conditions C_k, then $\underline{brc}_k(sel_{k1}: E_1, \ldots, sel_{kn}: E_n)$ is an expression of the language, and its type is constructed from the types of $E_1, \ldots, E_n$ by the operation F_k.

EL expressions can be represented as trees, with constants and variables as terminals, branching categories at the non-terminal nodes, and selectors as labels on the arcs. Such a tree form is convenient for internal representation in a computer, and may be preferred by some readers because of its visualization of the syntactic structure, which in EL will be seen to always coincide with the semantic structure. But as, surely, the syntactic/semantic structure of an expression may also be read off immediately from the notation with branching category names and selector names, as (6.32a) illustrates, I will not use the tree notation here. (For the use of the tree form see Landsbergen and Scha, 1977; Bunt, 1981b, chapter 7.)

Many readers may find the use of branching categories and selectors rather cumbersome, making EL expressions difficult to read. I shall therefore introduce a way of writing EL expressions in a more familiar sort of 'algebraic' notation, using various kinds of brackets and other delimiters. For instance, the application of a function 'F' to an argument 'a' is written as

(6.32b) F(a)

instead of (6.32a). The use of branching categories and selectors has, apart from its function in computer representation, mainly the advantage that an expression explicitly displays its syntactic and semantic structure, which is convenient in giving a rigorous description of the syntax and semantics of the language. The reader who is not primarily interested, at least at this point, in the details of the language definition, may skip the remainder of this section and the next section. In section 6.8 a summary is given of the syntactic constructions of EL with their 'algebraic' notation and an informal explanation of their semantics.

EL is a highly complex language, in both its syntax and its semantics. In order to describe the syntax in an easily readable way I shall leave out some of the details on the types assigned to EL expressions (see notes 2 and 3), and I shall use the following terminology in formulating the type restrictions on the constituents combined by the syntax rules to form complex expressions.

1. 'function expression F' will be used as short for: 'EL expression of type $(\underline{t}_1 \rightarrow \underline{t}_2)$, with arbitrary types $\underline{t}_1$ and $\underline{t}_2$.'

2. 'predicate expression P' will be used for: 'EL expression of type ($\underline{t} \to \underline{\text{truthvalue}}$), with arbitrary type $\underline{t}$.'
3. 'proposition expression p' will be used for: 'EL expression of type $\underline{\text{truthvalue}}$.'
4. 'set expression A' will be used for: 'EL expression of type $\underline{S(t)}$, with arbitrary type $\underline{t}$.'
5. 'ensemble expression E' will be used for: 'EL expression with a type $\underline{E(t)}$ or a type $\underline{S(t)}$, with arbitrary $\underline{t}$.'
6. 'tuple expression T' will be used for: 'EL expression of type $\underline{\langle t_1, \ldots, t_n \rangle}$, with arbitrary sequence of types $\underline{t_1}, \ldots, \underline{t_n}$.'
7. 'numerical expression n' will be used for: 'EL expression of type $\underline{\text{integer}}$ or $\underline{\text{real}}$.'
8. 'unit expression u' will be used for: 'EL expression of type $\underline{\langle t, Tr(t) \rangle}$, with arbitrary type $\underline{t}$.'
9. 'amount expression a' will be used for: 'EL expression of type $\underline{\text{amt}(t)}$, with arbitrary type $\underline{t}$.'
10. 'F is applicable to A' means that A and F have such types that the possible denotations of A belong to the possible domains of the function F.

The type restrictions that the definition of EL imposes on the various constructions can be expressed formally by a predicate TR, defined with the help of the type-inclusion relation introduced above. For example, for the function application construction the predicate is defined by:[3]

(6.34) TR($\underline{\text{application}}$, $\underline{t}$, $\underline{t}'$) = TRUE iff $\underline{t} = (\underline{t_1} \to \underline{t_2})$ for some types $\underline{t_1}$, $\underline{t_2}$, and $\underline{t}' <_t \underline{t_1}$

After these preliminaries, I list the syntactic rules defining the class of well-formed EL expressions.

(6.35) Syntactic rules of EL[4]

0. Every EL constant and variable is an EL expression, called a *term*. Particular choices of constants will be considered in subsequent chapters. There are denumerably many variables of every type.
1. As complex expressions, we have the basic operations of the λ-calculus: λ-abstraction and function application.

1(a) If x is a variable and E is an EL expression, then $\underline{\text{abstraction}}$(var: x, descr: E) is a function expression. It is also written as: (λx: E).

1(b) If 'F' is a function expression and 'a' is an EL expression, such that F is applicable to a, then $\underline{\text{application}}$(fun: F, arg: a) is an EL expression. It is also written as: F(a).

Semantic representations based on ensemble theory 91

2. We have some logical operations involving propositions. If p and q are proposition expressions, so are:
2(a) non(arg: p), also written as ¬p,
2(b) conj(1: p, 2: q), also written as p & q,
2(c) disj(1: p, 2: q), also written as p ∨ q.
3. We have universal and existential quantification. If A is a set expression and P a predicate expression, applicable to the elements of A, then:
3(a) universal-quantification(forall: A, holds: P) is a proposition expression.
3(b) existential-quantification(forsome: A, holds: P) is a proposition expression.
4. A number of constructions relating to ensembles. Let $E, E_1, \ldots, E_n$ be ensemble expressions and $S, S_0, S_1, \ldots, S_n$ set expressions.
4(a) power(arg: E), also written as $\mathscr{P}(E)$, is a set expression.
4(b) cartesian-product(1: $E_1, \ldots$, n: E_n), also written as $E_1 \times \ldots \times E_n$, is a set expression.
4(c) union(1: $E_1, \ldots$, n: E_n), also written as $E_1 \cup \ldots \cup E_n$, is an ensemble expression.
4(d) unionstar(reference: S_0, el$_1$: $S_1, \ldots$, el$_n$: S_n), also written as $\cup^*(S_0; S_1, \ldots, S_n)$, is a set expression.
4(e) If P is a predicate expression, then selection(head: S, mod: P) is a set expression.
4(f) If P is a predicate expression, then partselection(head: E, partmod: P) is an ensemble expression.
4(g) If E is an ensemble expression and e an EL expression, then membership(member: e, ensemble: E) is a proposition expression. It is also written as e ∈ E.
4(h) If E is an ensemble expression and e an EL expression, then inclusion(part: e, whole: E) is a proposition expression. It is also written as e ⊆ E.
5. Some constructions relating to discrete ensembles only.
5(a) If $a_1, \ldots, a_n$ are EL expressions, then set(1: $a_1, \ldots$, n: a_n), also written as $\{a_1, \ldots, a_n\}$, is a set expression.
5(b) If A is a set expression, then card(arg: A), also written as #(A), is an expression of type integer.
5(c) If A is a set expression and F a function expression then iteration(for: A, apply: F) is a set expression.
6. Some miscellaneous operations.
6(a) If A and B are EL expressions, then equality(arg$_1$: A, arg$_2$: B), also written as A = B, is a proposition expression.

92 Part 1 Model-theoretic semantics of mass terms

6(b) If C is a proposition expression and A and B are arbitrary EL expressions then <u>conditional</u>(if: C, then: A, else: B) is an EL expression. It is also written as C → A|B.

6(c) If $F_1, \ldots, F_n$ are EL expressions denoting functions with non-overlapping domains, then <u>function-union</u>(1: $F_1, \ldots,$ n: F_n) is a function expression. It is also written as '$F_1 f \cup \ldots f \cup F_n$'.

6(d) If $e_1, \ldots, e_n$ are EL expressions, then <u>n-tuple</u>(1: $e_1, \ldots,$ n: e_n), also written as $(e_1, \ldots, e_n)$ is a tuple expression.

6(e) If T is a tuple expression, then <u>element</u>$_i$(arg: T), also written as T_i, is an EL expression.

6(f) If n is a numerical expression and u a unit expression, then <u>amount</u>(num: n, unit: u), also written as n–u, is an amount expression.

The parts of the syntactic rules that specify the type of an expression being constructed, together form the recursive definition of a function that, when applied to an EL expression, delivers its type (see note 3). This function will be called TYPE.

6.6 The semantics of EL

The semantics of EL systematically assigns values (or 'denotations') to EL expressions. First, a value is specified for every term (constant or variable); for the constants this specification forms part of the EL lexicon; for the variables this is a matter of arbitrary choice provided that the value of a variable belongs to the domain of the type of the variable. The choice of values for the variables is arbitrary in the sense that the value of an EL expression without free variables (what is called a 'closed' expression) is independent of the values of the variables occurring in it. The assignment of values to the constants and variables is formally described by a function V_t, called a *term valuation*. Secondly, values are assigned to complex EL expressions by means of a set of recursive rules, organized in such a way that for each syntactic rule there is a corresponding semantic rule. If the syntactic rule says that an expression <u>brc</u>$_i$(sel$_{i1}$: $E_1, \ldots,$ sel$_{in}$: E_n) may be formed from the simpler expressions $E_1, \ldots, E_n$ (observing certain type restrictions), then the corresponding semantic rule specifies how the value of the newly formed expression follows from the values of subexpressions $E_1, \ldots, E_n$.

Altogether, the semantic rules constitute a recursive definition of the *valuation function* V. (The term valuation V_t is introduced separately to obtain a proper recursive definition of the valuation function.)

Semantic representations based on ensemble theory 93

(6.36) Semantic rules of EL

0. To any term e a value $V_t(e)$ is assigned, such that $V_t(e) \in D(TYPE(e))$. For constant terms this assignment forms part of the EL lexicon, for variable terms it is a matter of arbitrary choice. The valuation function V is defined for terms by: $V(e) = V_t(e)$.

1(a) V(abstraction(var: x, descr: E)) is the function assigning to any element a in the domain of the type of x the denotation that E has for that term valuation V'_t which only differs from V_t in that $V'_t(x) = a$.

1(b) V(application(fun: F, arg: a)) = V(F)(V(a)), that is, the result of applying the function V(F) to V(a).

2(a) V(non(arg: p)) = TRUE if V(p) = FALSE, otherwise $V(\neg p)$ = FALSE.

2(b) V(conj(1: p, 2: q)) = TRUE if both V(p) = TRUE and V(q) = TRUE, otherwise FALSE.

2(c) V(disj(1: p, 2: q)) = TRUE if V(p) = TRUE or V(q) = TRUE or both, otherwise FALSE.

3(a) V(universal-quantification(forall: A, holds: P)) = TRUE if application of the predicate V(P) yields TRUE for each element of V(A), otherwise it is FALSE.

3(b) V(existential-quantification(forsome: A, holds: P)) is TRUE if application of the predicate V(P) yields TRUE for at least one element of V(A), otherwise it is FALSE.

4(a) $V(\underline{power}(arg: A)) = \mathcal{P}(V(A))$.

4(b) V(cartesian-product(1: A_1, ..., n: A_n)) = $V(A_1) \times ... \times V(A_n)$, that is, the set of n-tuples $(a_1, ..., a_n)$ where a_i is a member of A_i.

4(c) V(union(1: A_1, ..., n: A_n)) = $V(A_1) \cup V(A_2) \cup ... \cup V(A_n)$.

4(d) V(unionstar(reference: S_0, el_1: S_1, ..., el_k: S_k)) = {x ∈ $V(S_0)$|x = $V(S_i)$ or x ∈ $V(S_i)$ for some i such that $1 \leq i \leq k$}, that is, the set of those members of $V(S_0)$ which are either equal to one of the values $V(S_1), ..., V(S_k)$ or a member of one of these.

4(e) V(selection(head: A, mod: P)) = {x ∈ V(A)|V(P)(x)}, that is, the subset of V(A) formed by those elements of V(A) for which the predicate V(P) is TRUE.

4(f) V(partselection(head: A, partmod: P)) = [x ⊆ (A)|V(P)(x)], that is, the subensemble of V(A) made up by those parts of V(A) for which the predicate V(P) is TRUE.

4(g) V(membership(member: e, ensemble: E)) = TRUE if V(e) is a member of V(E), and FALSE otherwise.

4(h) $V(\underline{inclusion}(\text{part: } e, \text{whole: } E)) = \text{TRUE}$ if $V(e)$ is a part of $V(E)$, and FALSE otherwise.

5(a) $V(\underline{set}(1: a_1, \ldots, n: a_n)) = \{V(a_1), \ldots, V(a_n)\}$, that is, the set consisting of the elements $V(a_1), \ldots, V(a_n)$.

5(b) $V(\underline{card}(\text{arg: } A)) =$ the cardinality of $V(A)$.

5(c) $V(\underline{iteration}(\text{for: } A, \text{apply: } F)) = \{x | (\exists y \in V(A)) \; V(F)(y) = x\}$, that is, the set of those objects which the function $V(F)$ yields when applied to the elements of $V(A)$.

6(a) $V(\underline{equality}(\text{arg}_1: A, \text{arg}_2: B)) = \text{TRUE}$ if $V(A)$ is equal to $V(B)$, and FALSE otherwise.

6(b) $V(\underline{conditional}(\text{if: } C, \text{then: } A, \text{else: } B) = V(A)$ if $V(C) = \text{TRUE}$, otherwise it is $V(B)$.

6(c) $V(\underline{function\text{-}union}(1: F_1, \ldots, n: F_n))$ is the function which assigns to any argument in the union of the domains of the functions $V(F_1), \ldots, V(F_n)$ the result of applying that function among $V(F_1), \ldots, V(F_n)$ which is applicable to it. By the syntactic definition of the branching category, there is always precisely one such function.

6(d) $V(\underline{n\text{-}tuple}(1: a_1, \ldots, n: a_n)) = (V(a_1), \ldots, V(a_n))$, that is, the n-tuple consisting of the values of each of the elements $a_1, \ldots, a_n$.

6(e) $V(\underline{element}_i(\text{arg: } T)) =$ the ith element of the tuple $V(T)$.

6(f) $V(\underline{amount}(\text{num: } n, \text{unit: } u)) =$ the equivalence class of all number–unit pairs which, according to the conversion function specified by the second component of $V(u)$, are equivalent to the number–unit pair consisting of $V(n)$ and the first element of $V(u)$.

Note that this semantic definition is in accordance with the types that the syntactic rules (in particular those parts that define the type assignment function TYPE) assign to the complex expressions, in the sense that to any complex expression E a denotation $V(E)$ is assigned which belongs to the domain of the type of E:

(6.37) $V(E) \in D(\text{TYPE}(E))$

This is a consistency requirement on the definition of the language.

6.7 Semantic representations in EL

In the beginning of this chapter, I said that mass noun expressions like

(6.38) The snow in the garden

would be represented in EL by expressions of the form

(6.39a) $[x \subseteq \text{SNOW}|\text{INGARDEN}(x)]$

In this representation, SNOW is an EL constant of type $\underline{E(t)}$ for some appropriate type $\underline{t}$, say snow. INGARDEN stands for an EL predicate, be it a simple constant or a complex expression, of type $(E(\text{snow}) \rightarrow \text{truthvalue})$. Expressions of the form (6.39a) have been introduced in the exposition of ensemble theory (see (5.8)), but they do not in fact belong to the class of expressions defined by the EL syntax as described by (6.35). In (6.35), a number of notation conventions have been introduced to allow the writing of EL expressions without branching categories and selectors, in what we called an 'algebraic' notation. Similarly, expressions of the form of (6.39a) are intended as a more traditional sort of notation for the following EL expression:

(6.39b) partselection
                (head: SNOW,
                partmod: abstraction
                    (var: x,
                    descr: application
                        (fun: INGARDEN,
                        arg: x)))

Let us consider the representation (6.39) of a mass noun expression in the light of our discussion of the peculiarities of mass term reference in earlier chapters.

In section 3.1 we have come across the question whether a mass noun should be considered as referring to a single object or to a class-like multiplicity of objects. For instance, does 'water' refer to 'a single, though scattered object, the aqueous part of the world' (Quine, 1960) or to the class of all portions of water? We have seen that definite descriptions involving mass nouns give rise to conflicting intuitions on this point. In expressions like

(6.40) The flowers in the garden

(6.41) The snow in the garden

we have, on the one hand, the intuition that the mass noun phrase has a denotation structurally similar to that of the count noun phrase, and is thus class-like, while, on the other hand, it seems natural to view the snow in the garden as 'one thing', especially if it has been swept on a heap; the latter view is presumably related to the fact that the phrase is syntactically singular. This 'one thing' is what Montague had in mind when he suggested representing definite descriptions with mass nouns by 'the maximal portion of ...' (see (3.79)).

Ensemble theory now gives us the instruments to formalize the idea of 'maximal portion' or 'one thing', while at the same time retaining the structural similarity between the denotations of 'The snow in the garden' and 'The flowers in the garden'. We have seen in the previous chapter that the ensemble denoted by (6.39) is the unique object made up of the snow samples which are in the garden. Or, to put it differently, it is the merge of all the snow samples in the garden. Now if s_1 and s_2 are two such samples, their merge $s_1 \cup s_2$ is another one. Therefore, the entire ensemble denoted by (6.39) is also in the garden:

(6.42) INGARDEN($[x \subseteq$ SNOW$|$INGARDEN$(x)]$)

Moreover, it is the *maximal* snow sample which is in the garden, for if s is any such sample then $s \subseteq$ SNOW and INGARDEN(s), therefore s belongs to the set $\{x \in \mathcal{P}(\text{SNOW}) | \text{INGARDEN}(x)\}$. We have seen that (6.39) is the merge of this set, and by the definition of the merge of a set of ensembles all the ensembles involved are part of the merge. Therefore, $s \subseteq [x \subseteq$ SNOW$|$INGARDEN$(x)]$.

Note that this argument depends on the assumption that the merge of two samples of snow in the garden is again a sample of snow in the garden, that is, the predicate INGARDEN has the property:

(6.43) INGARDEN(x) & INGARDEN(y) $\rightarrow$ INGARDEN(x $\cup$ y)

This property is called the *cumulativity* of the predicate (Bunt, 1980a, after Quine, 1960). It may seem rather a coincidence that we have a predicate with that property, but this is not quite so. I shall argue in chapter 9 that a predicate which does not have the property of cumulativity cannot be used to restrict a continuous ensemble in a sensible way. For instance, 'light' (not heavy) is such a predicate; it cannot be used in a definite description such as 'The light sand from this bag' in the same way as 'The dry sand from this bag' to identify certain sand. I think that the intuition that a definite description refers to the 'maximal portion' satisfying the predicate does not apply to descriptions involving predicates like 'light'.

The class-like character that the denotation of 'The snow in the garden' also has, is brought out by the close similarity between its EL representation and that of (6.40), compare

(6.44) $[x \subseteq \text{SNOW}|\text{INGARDEN}(x)]$

(6.45) $\{x \in \text{FLOWERS}|\text{INGARDEN}(x)\}$

The similarity of these representations reflects the similarity of the concepts they express: $[x \subseteq E|P]$ denotes the ensemble made up by the E-parts that satisfy the predicate P, $\{x \in E|P\}$ denotes the ensemble made up by the E-members that satisfy P. So the only difference is, one might say, that in the one case we consider the objects that stand in part–whole relation to E, in the other case those that stand in member–whole relation to E. As already mentioned in section 5.2, the similarity comes out further in that the following implications are both valid:

(6.46) $y \in E \ \& \ P(y) \to y \in \{z \in E|P(z)\}$

(6.47) $y \subseteq E \ \& \ P(y) \to y \subseteq [z \subseteq E|P(z)]$

But, then again, we have seen that there is also an important difference, in that the implication (6.46) is also valid from right to left, but (6.47) is not. That is, from $y \subseteq [z \subseteq E|P(z)]$ it does not follow that $P(y)$. It is for this reason that the present proposal does not run into the logical problems we have seen with Parsons' proposal involving substances, and with Moravcsik's proposal involving restricted mereological wholes.

In chapter 2 I have argued that the fundamental difference between mass nouns and count nouns is that count nouns individuate their reference but mass nouns do not: they refer to something as having an internal structure that can be described as a part–whole structure, without singling out any parts in particular. And, especially, without carrying the assumption that there are 'minimal' or 'atomic' parts. This view was summarized in chapter 4 as the *homogeneous reference hypothesis*. The precise role of this hypothesis in our semantic theory will be discussed in the next chapter, but it may be clear already at this point that the use of ensembles in the way just indicated is precisely in accordance with the homogeneous reference hypothesis. Representing the mass noun 'snow' in EL by the ensemble constant SNOW we are in effect saying that 'snow' refers to an entity which has the part–whole structure of an ensemble and therefore does not need to have minimal parts. The same is true of the denotation of the complex mass term 'The snow in the garden' as represented by (6.39).

Closely related to the homogeneous reference hypothesis are two conditions on mass term reference that we have come across in chapter 2, the *cumulative reference* condition (2.21) and the *distributive reference* condition (2.34). Ensemble theory provides us with logical devices for formalizing these conditions. They contain the informal terms 'sum', 'part', and 'is m' for a mass noun m (such as 'is water'), which can be formalized in ensemble-theoretical terms as follows. The term 'part' and the copula 'is' in expressions 'is m' are interpreted as the $\subseteq$ relation of ensemble theory; the term 'sum' is interpreted as the merge. The cumulative reference condition

(6.48)   Any sum of parts which are m is m

is thus formalized as

(6.49) $(\forall s)((s \in \mathcal{P}(M)) \rightarrow \cup(s) \subseteq M)$

where M designates the ensemble denoted by the mass noun m and the variable s ranges over the set of parts of M. In words, (6.49) says that the merge of any collection of parts of M is a part of M.

Similarly, the distributive reference condition

(6.50)   Any part of something which is m is m

is formalized as

(6.51) $(\forall x)(x \subseteq M \rightarrow (\forall y \subseteq x)(y \subseteq M))$

The formulas (6.49) and (6.51) are both *theorems* in ensemble theory that hold for any ensemble M. The proof of (6.49) follows from theorem (5.25) combined with the fact that a set of which all members are parts of M must be a subset of $\mathcal{P}(M)$. The validity of (6.51) is a direct consequence of the transitivity of the $\subseteq$ relation. We thus see that the use of ensemble theory in the way indicated here is in accordance with both the cumulative reference condition and the distributive reference condition.

It may be useful to consider briefly also the use of the EL construction called 'amount' for the representation of amount terms. Using again the example of a dimension illustrated by (6.13), we want to represent an expression like 'Two pints' in such a way that it denotes the volume amount

(6.52) $\{(1 \cdot 14, \text{litre}), (2, \text{pint}), (0 \cdot 25, \text{gallon})\}$

To achieve this, we introduce an EL constant PINT and use the amount construction defined by (6.35) and (6.36), rule 6f:

(6.53a)   <u>amount</u>(num: 2, unit: PINT)

or, in 'algebraic' notation:

(6.53b) 2-PINT

The unit constant PINT has the type ⟨volume, Tr(volume)⟩, where volume is an atomic type with $D_{at}(\underline{volume}) = SU_v$. The value of PINT consists of the pair (pint, F_v) where 'pint' belongs to SU_v and F_v is the transitive function defined on $SU_v \times SU_v$ by (6.13). According to the semantic definition of the amount construction as given in (6.36) rule 6f, the representation (6.53) then denotes the set of number–unit pairs which, according to the conversion function F_v, are equivalent to the pair (2, pint). By (6.13), this is the set (6.52).

6.8 Notation: summary and some additions

In the definition of the class of well-formed expressions of EL in (6.35) I have indicated a number of notation conventions for writing EL expressions in a familiar, 'algebraic' sort of way, using a variety of brackets and special punctuation symbols instead of names of branching categories and selectors. A similar notation was used in the previous section when (6.39a) was introduced as a convenient abbreviation of (6.39b). In this section I recapitulate the definition of the class of EL expressions in this algebraic notation together with an informal explanation of the semantics of the various constructions. Moreover, I introduce a number of convenient abbreviations like (6.39a).

Notation	Meaning
(λx: E)	The function which, applied to an argument a, has as value the value of the expression E, when all occurrences of the variable x in E are replaced by a.
F(a)	The application of the function F to the argument a.
¬p	The negation of the proposition p (not p).
p & q	The conjunction of the propositions p and q (both p and q).
p ∨ q	The disjunction of the propositions p and q (either p or q or both).
$\mathcal{P}$(A)	The 'power set of A', that is the set having the parts of A as its members.
$A_1 \times \ldots \times A_n$	The 'cartesian product' of the ensembles $A_1, \ldots, A_n$, that is, the set consisting of those n-tuples of which the first element belongs to A_1, the second to A_2, etc.
$A_1 \cup \ldots \cup A_n$	The union (or merge) of the ensembles $A_1, \ldots, A_n$, that is the smallest ensemble that has all these ensembles as parts.
$\cup^*(A_0; A_1, \ldots, A_n)$	The 'unionstar' of the ensembles $A_1, \ldots, A_n$ given the 'reference ensemble' A_0. For explanation see section 8.4 (8.72).

100 *Part 1 Model-theoretic semantics of mass terms*

Notation	Meaning
$a \in E$	a is a member (or 'element') of E.
$a \subseteq A$	a is a part of A.
$\{a_1, \ldots, a_n\}$	The set consisting of $a_1, \ldots, a_n$.
$\#(A)$	The 'cardinality' (number of elements) of A.
$a = b$	a is equal to b.
$c \rightarrow a\|b$	If c is true then a, otherwise b.
$(a_1, \ldots, a_n)$	The n-tuple consisting of $a_1, \ldots, a_n$.
T_i	The ith element of the n-tuple T.
n–u	The amount made up by n units u.

The following additional abbreviations will be used:

Notation	Meaning
$F(a_1, \ldots, a_n)$	The application of a function F to a tuple $(a_1, \ldots, a_n)$ of arguments. The unabbreviated notation would be: $F((a_1, \ldots, a_n))$.
$a_1 > a_2$	Infix notation for $>(a_1, a_2)$, that is a_1 greater than a_2. Similarly for other relations.

$[x \subseteq A \| P]$	The ensemble made up by those parts of A that have the property P. The full EL expression would be:
	partselection
	  (head: A,
	   mod: abstraction
	    (var: x,
	     descr: P))

$(\forall x \in A: P(x))$	All members of A have the property P. The full EL expression would be:
	universal-quantification
	  (forall: A,
	   holds: abstraction
	    (var: x,
	     descr: application
	      (fun: P,
	       arg: x))),

$(\exists x \in A: P(x))$	There is a member in A that has the property P. The full EL expression would be:
	existential-quantification
	  (forsome: A,
	   holds: abstraction
	    (var: x,
	     descr: application
	      (fun: P,
	       arg: x)))

$(\forall x \subseteq A: P(x))$	All parts of A have the property P. The notation is short for: $(\forall x \in \mathcal{P}(A): P(x))$

Semantic representations based on ensemble theory 101

Notation	Meaning
$(\exists x \subseteq A: P(x))$	There is a part of A that has the property P. The notation is short for: $(\exists x \in \mathcal{P}(A): P(x))$
$\{x \subseteq A \mid P(x)\}$	The set of those parts of A that have the property P. The notation is short for: $\{x \in \mathcal{P}(A) \mid P(x)\}$

$proj_i(S)$	S denotes a collection of n-tuples; $proj_i(S)$ denotes the collection of the ith elements of these tuples. The full EL expression would be:
	iteration
	  (for: T,
	  apply: abstraction
	    (var: x,
	    descr: element$_i$(arg: x)))
	Example: $proj_2\{$(John, Mary), (Bill, Anne), (Bert, Betty)$\} = \{$Mary, Anne, Betty$\}$.

$\mathcal{P}_n(S)$	The collection of those subsets of S that have exactly n members. The notation is short for: $\{x \in \mathcal{P}(S) \mid \#(x) = n\}$.
$\mathcal{P}_{plur}(S)$	The collection of those subsets of S that have more than one member (the 'plural subsets' of S). The notation is equivalent to: $\{x \in \mathcal{P}(S) \mid \#(x) > 1\}$.
S^*	The set consisting of the elements and the plural subsets of S. The notation is short for: $S \cup \mathcal{P}_{plur}(S)$. Example: $\{$John, Mary, Anne$\}^* = \{$John, Mary, Anne, $\{$John, Mary$\}$, $\{$John, Anne$\}$, $\{$Mary, Anne$\}$, $\{$John, Mary, Anne$\}\}$.
$\exists_n x \in S: P(x)$	There are exactly n elements in S that have the property P. The notation is equivalent to: $\#(\{x \in S \mid P(x)\}) = n$.
$\exists! x \in S: P(x)$	There is exactly 1 element in S that has the property P. The notation is equivalent to: $\exists_1 x \in S: P(x)$ and to $\#(\{x \in S \mid P(x)\}) = 1$.
N	The predicate of having N members. Short for: $(\lambda x: \#(x) = N)$. See for example, formula (8.95b).

7 Two-level model-theoretic semantics

7.1 Formal semantics

In the previous chapter we considered the concept of a semantic representation in a formal language. We now turn to the status of such representations in a linguistic theory, in particular, in a theory that aims at a precise and systematic description of the meanings of natural language expressions. The branch of linguistic study that deals with the construction of such a theory is called 'formal semantics'.

Using semantic representations of the kind described in the previous chapter, a declarative sentence is represented by what we called a 'proposition expression': an expression in the representation language of type truthvalue. Such an expression has two possible values: true and false. The semantic structure of the sentence is made explicit in the way this proposition expression is built up, which, in turn, determines under what conditions the expression is true or false. Therefore, the study of semantic structures in natural language sentences is closely related to the study of *truth conditions*.

It is often thought that the study of truth conditions is the primary or even the only aim of formal semantics. For example:

(7.1) the aim of a syntactic theory is to define in a rigorous way . . . the concept of *well-formedness*, semantics has as its main aim to define . . . the concept of *truth* for a language with respect to interpretations (Guenthner and Rohrer, 1978, p. 1).

(What is meant by 'interpretations' in this quotation will become clear in the next section.) Accordingly, the term 'truth conditional semantics' is sometimes used as synonymous with 'formal semantics'. I think this is an unduly restricted view of the domain of formal semantics, however, which is probably due to the fact that declarative sentences form the traditional domain of linguistic study and, perhaps, also to the fact that formal languages have been used traditionally by logicians for establishing the truth or falsity of propositions. When we consider the assignment of semantic representations to natural language expressions other than declarative sentences, we see that truth conditions are special cases of something more general. To take an example from the previous chapter, the noun phrase 'The flowers in the garden' is represented by a set expression, that is, an EL expression with a type of the form S(t), such as S(flower). This means that the expression denotes a set of flowers. In the semantic representation

(7.2) {x ∈ FLOWERS | INGARDEN(x)}

we see the semantic structure of the noun phrase spelled out: from the set of all flowers, called FLOWERS, those elements are selected that satisfy the predicate INGARDEN. This makes explicit that 'in the garden' is interpreted as a restrictive modifier. The representation thus specifies in a formal way how the denotation of the phrase 'The flowers in the garden' is determined by the denotations of the constituents 'flowers' and 'in the garden'. This is more generally what formal semantics is about: it studies the way the denotations of complex phrases are determined by those of their constituents. The study of truth conditions is a special case of this, truth values being denotations (or important aspects of denotations) of declarative sentences.[1] Rather than saying that formal semantics is the study of truth conditions, we might say that it is the study of *denotation conditions* (a term suggested by Hausser, 1980).

A fundamental decision in describing how the denotation of a complex expression is determined by those of its constituents, concerns the treatment of the denotations of the atomic constituents. Should they be analysed further, in terms of semantic primitives which are 'subatomic' compared to the natural language, and if so, how should they be chosen? And if not, then we have to face the problem that atomic constituents, that is, words, mostly have a wide variety of possible denotations; if we do not use 'subatomic' semantic primitives, then how can we distinguish the various denotations of a word and how can we relate and distinguish the denotations of one word from those of another, semantically related word? Guenthner and Rohrer formulate this problem as follows:

(7.3) A major problem which remains to be solved concerns the 'depth' of the logical analysis of natural languages. Even though almost everyone agrees that the quantificational, temporal, modal, spatial subsystems of natural languages should be viewed as consisting of logical constants, there is quite a lot of disagreement about the analysis of verbs, nouns and adjectives. In other words, is the meaning difference between nouns, say, in a natural language to be accounted for in a logical semantics? Or should it rather be left to what has elsewhere been called 'empirical semantics' (cf. Putnam, 1975) (Guenthner and Rohrer, 1978, p. 6).

Thomason gives a firm negative answer to this question:

(7.4) It is the business of semantics to account for meanings. A central goal of this account is to explain how different kinds of meaning attach to different syntactic categories; another is to explain how the meanings of phrases depend on those of their components. . . . *But we should not expect a semantic theory to furnish an account of how any two expressions belonging to the same syntactic category differ in meaning* (Thomason, 1974, p. 48, his italics).

On this view, a linguistic semantic theory should not be expected to tell us the differences in meaning between words of the same syntactic category since, in order to explain such differences as those between the common nouns 'unicorn' and 'rhinoceros', or between the adjectives 'mauve' and 'magenta', it would be necessary to draw upon all sorts of human knowledge. As Thomason argues,

(7.5) The task of explaining the particular meanings of various basic expressions will obviously presuppose, if not factual information, at least a minutely detailed terminology for classifying things of all kinds. Perhaps even pictures or a museum of representative specimens would have to be counted as 'terminology' . . . . At any rate, lexicography will have to borrow concepts from all areas of knowledge and practice: astronomy, jurisprudence, cuisine, automotives, pigeon breeding, and so forth (Thomason, 1974, pp. 48–9).

It is clear that there are strong arguments for clearly separating the study of individual word meanings from that of the meanings of complex expressions. These two areas of semantics are often referred to as *lexical*, or *referential semantics*, and *logical semantics*, respectively. The term *formal semantics* is also used as synonymous with logical semantics, and I shall use formal semantics in this way. Formal semantics, in this sense, is indeed 'formal' in the strict sense of the word, as it deals purely with those aspects of the meaning of an expression that are due to its structure, to its 'form'. In this conception, formal semantics does not deal with individual word meanings.

However, we must immediately qualify this statement. First, the statement is only correct for words that refer to real world entities or mental objects. It belongs to the territory of formal semantics to give an account of the meanings of words like 'all', 'some', 'each', 'not', 'and', etc.; words that do not refer to entities in some domain of discourse but that have a *logical function*. We should thus distinguish between *referring words* (or *referential words*) and *function words*, and say that formal semantics should be expected to deal with the meanings of function words but not with those of referential words.

Second, we have to be precise in the use of the word 'words' in this context. This term has several distinct uses (see Lyons, 1977, pp. 7–22), two of which are relevant to consider here. In the sentence:

(7.6) The Danish words 'hus', 'huset', 'huse', and 'husene' are different forms of the word 'hus'

we see two different senses of the word 'word'. 'Words' in the sense in which 'huset', 'husene', etc. are words is synonymous with *word forms*. Words in the more abstract sense, in which word forms are forms of the same word, are sometimes called *lexemes*. Words in this sense do not occur in sentences, only word forms do. Word forms, such as verb forms, inflected noun forms, superlative forms of adjectives, or diminutive forms of nouns, may have an internal structure that has similar semantic consequences as syntactic phrase structure. We should therefore distinguish between *formal and referential aspects of word forms*, the referential aspects being carried by the lexeme of which we have a form, and the formal aspects by the function elements in the word form. Thus, the dividing line between the territories of formal semantics and referential semantics is not between referential words and function words, but between referential lexemes and function elements, where the latter may be either complete function words or functional parts of word forms.

Taking these qualifications into account, we can say that the goal of a theory of formal semantics is to specify the denotations of complex expressions in terms of those of their constituents, down to the level of the smallest referential elements. This goal is also pursued in formal logic in the definition of formal languages, and its pursuit is called *model-theoretic semantics*. The study of formal semantics has in recent years taken the form of applying the ideas of model-theoretic semantics to natural languages. Let us therefore briefly consider the aims and methods of model-theoretic semantics.

7.2 Model-theoretic semantics

The method of model-theoretic semantics, the foundations of which were laid by Tarski (see Tarski, 1936), was originally developed as a tool for giving a precise and systematic account of the semantics of artificial languages as used in formal logic, such as the languages of the propositional calculus and the predicate calculus. The method is based on the following assumptions.

(7.7) (i) The syntactic rules of the language define a class of expressions, the 'correct' or 'well-formed' expressions of the language. Every such expression has a value, also called denotation. The semantic rules have the task of specifying the denotation of every well-formed expression.

(ii) The denotation of a complex expression is completely determined by the denotations of its well-formed subexpressions (Principle of Compositionality).[2] It can thus be computed from those denotations by means of a recursive function. The semantic rules should embody a definition of that function.

(iii) The denotations of the atomic well-formed expressions, which are the constants and variables of the language, cannot be computed; they should therefore be listed.

The assignment of values to the constants of the language has a different significance than the assignment of values to the variables. This is because variables, by their very nature, can be bound by quantifiers and other logical operators, and once a variable in an expression is bound by some operator, the denotation of the expression no longer depends on that of the variable. This is most easily illustrated by an example in a simple predicate language. Consider the expression

(7.8) $(\forall x)P(x)$

where P is a predicate constant. The semantic rules will say that this expression has the value TRUE if and only if the predicate P holds true for any value that can be assigned to x. Clearly, it is irrelevant what value the semantic rules have listed for x; this value does not play a role in the truth conditions of (7.8).

An expression in which all the variables are bound by some operator is called a 'closed' expression; the value of a closed expression is independent of the values that the semantic rules list for the variables, as (7.8) illustrates. The only situation where the values of variables are relevant is when we have an 'open' expression with an unbound, or 'free' variable, as in

(7.9) $\text{EUROPEAN}(x) \rightarrow \text{SCANDINAVIAN}(x)$

Here, the semantic rules of the language will say that the expression has the value TRUE if and only if the consequent is TRUE if the antecedent is TRUE; that is, either the value of x does not satisfy the predicate EUROPEAN or it satisfies both the predicates EUROPEAN and SCANDINAVIAN. Clearly, the value of x does play a role in this case.

The difference in significance between the values of the variables and those of the constants is usually brought out in the formalization of the assignment of these values. It is common practice to do this, as follows. A mathematical structure which contains (a) a specification of the objects to be used as values of constants and variables, and (b) an assignment of such objects to the constants of the language is called a *model* or *interpretation* of the language; in its simplest form it is a pair

(7.10) M = (D, f)

where D is a set called the *model structure*, containing the possible values, and f is a function assigning a value to each of the constants; this function is called the *model assignment*. Note that a model does not specify the values of variables; it is, therefore, only a basis for determining the values of closed expressions. To be able to compute the values of open expressions as well, another function is introduced that assigns values from D to the variables. This function is usually designated by g. The complete basis for determining the values of any well-formed expression of the language thus consists of a model M extended with such a function g.

The complete model-theoretic semantic definition of a language now looks as follows.

(7.11) (i) The specification of a model M;
(ii) The specification of a function g assigning values to variables;
(iii) The recursive specification of how the denotation of any complex expression is determined by those of its subexpressions.

The model structure was introduced here as a specification of the objects which are the possible values of constants and variables. It is usual, however, to consider objects of a logical or mathematical nature, such as truth values and numbers, as not belonging to the model structure D. Rather, the model structure is meant to contain only those possible values that belong to a certain domain of discourse, and to allow the values of constants and variables to be either objects specified by D, or logical or mathematical entities. By 'objects specified by D' are meant, in the first place, the elements contained in D, but also the structures that can be built up from those. For instance, a relation constant, like BROTHER, has as value a set of pairs consisting of elements in D. More generally, the values of constants and variables, as far as they are not logical or mathematical entities, are either individual objects in D or structures like sets, n-tuples, etc. built up from those. Altogether, one might characterize the model structure as the *source* of the non-mathematical, domain-of-discourse-dependent values of the constants and variables. Moreover, since the value of a complex expression is built up from those of its constituents, and thus ultimately of the values of the constants and variables, it follows that the model structure is really the source of the values of *any* expression of the language.

The model structure D of a model M = (D, f) used in the semantic definition of a language L was said to contain those possible denotations of L-expressions which belong to a certain domain of discourse. By 'domain of discourse' we mean the collection of objects that we want to make statements about in the language L. What are these objects? They are precisely the elements of the model structure D: the primary motivation to exclude mathematical and logical objects like numbers and truth values from a model structure is that we are not making statements about these; rather, we use them in formulating statements about objects in D – the objects in the discourse domain. (Of course, the situation is different if the aim is to make assertions about mathematical or logical objects.) We can thus regard the model structure as a specification of the objects that populate the discourse domain. A discourse domain is in a certain state of affairs: the objects in the domain have certain properties and relations. When we make a statement in L, we say something about the properties or relations of some objects; therefore, we say something about the state of affairs in the discourse domain. Whether a statement in L is true thus depends on the state of affairs in the discourse domain.

The relation between true statements and the state of the discourse domain can also be viewed in the opposite direction: the state of affairs in the discourse domain is determined by what statements in L are true. If we know the truth of every possible statement in L, then we know the state of the discourse domain. Since the definition of the semantics of L determines which statements are true, it can be viewed as a representation of the state of affairs in the discourse domain. Now a statement is either compound or simple; if it is compound, then its truth value is determined by its component statements, therefore, the truth of compound statements contains no information on the state of the discourse domain beyond what is conveyed by the truth of the elementary statements it is composed of. So the state of affairs is represented by those parts of the semantic definition of L that determine the truth of elementary statements. These are the parts (i) and (ii) in (7.11) where the functions f and g are specified. In other words, *the state of the discourse domain is represented by the assignment of denotations to the terms of the language*.

So far, I have described the most usual way of organizing the model-theoretic semantic definition of a formal language, and considered only the simplest kind of models. In a slightly different setup, the assignment of the values to the variables is included in the model, which is then either a triple

(7.12) $M = (D, f, g)$

or a pair

(7.13) $M = (D, V_t)$

where V_t is the combination of f and g in a single function, assigning values to all *terms*, that is, constants and variables. Such a function is called a *term valuation* (cf. section 6.6). If this organization is used, the semantic definition has two components instead of three, namely the parts (i) and (iii) of (7.11). We have seen that the functions f and g together represent a state of affairs in the discourse domain specified by D. Therefore a model of the form (7.13) represents the discourse domain and its state. In this sense, it may be called *a model of the discourse domain*. We shall return to this point in section 7.6.

Another point where things may be organized differently is in the model structure D. Instead of being a single set containing all the objects in the discourse domain, the model structure may consist of a collection of sets $\{D_1, D_2, \ldots, D_n\}$. This is the case with models for so-called *many-sorted* languages, languages in which the terms have different types. As we have seen in section 6.4, the type of a term indicates what sort of object is denoted. Using the terminology developed in chapter 6, the referential atomic types $\underline{t}_i$ have a one-to-one correspondence with the sets D_i in the model structure.

The reader who has worked his way through the definition of the language EL in the previous chapter will have noted that many of the same considerations turn up here in a more general form. We have seen that the definition of EL presupposed a categorization $C = \{E_1, E_2, \ldots, E_m\}$ of the discourse domain, which served as the source of the values of the constant and variable terms and thereby of the complex EL expressions. This categorization plays the role of the model structure in a model of the form (7.13), where the term valuation is the function V_t in (6.36) rule 0. In model-theoretic terminology, the semantics of EL is thus defined relative to the model

(7.14) $M_{EL} = (\{E_1, E_2, \ldots, E_m\}, V_t)$

The semantic rules (6.36), rules 1–6, form the recursive part of the model-theoretic definition (component (iii) in the description (7.11)). The definition of EL thus exemplifies the model-theoretic method as applied to formal languages.

Incidentally, the definition in section 6.4 of the EL type language (henceforth ELTL) *also* exemplifies the model-theoretic method. From the semantic rules (6.28) of ELTL it follows that the categorization $C = \{E_1, E_2, \ldots, E_m\}$ plays a double role, as it is also the source of the values of the ELTL expressions, values which were called 'domains'. The role of the term valuation is played in this case by the assignment D_{at} of domains to atomic types. (Since ELTL has no variables, the term valuation coincides with the specification of the values of the constants.) The full definition of EL can thus be viewed as consisting of the definitions of *two* languages, EL and ELTL, and the relation between them. This relation is established by the function TYPE, that relates one ELTL expression to each EL expression. In terms of their models, EL and ELTL are related as follows:

(7.15)   a. EL has a model $M_{EL} = (\{E_1, E_2, \ldots, E_m\}, V_t)$;
        b. ELTL has a model $M_{ELTL} = (\{E_1, E_2, \ldots, E_m\}, D_{at})$
        c. $V_t(t) \in D_{at}(TYPE(t))$ for any term EL term t for which TYPE(t) is atomic (cf. 6.37).

The definition of EL illustrates in particular the following important aspects of a language definition using the model-theoretic method.

(1) A model assigns semantic values only to the basic expressions of the language (the terms: constants and, possibly, variables).

(2) The values of complex expressions are defined by means of rules that determine recursively how the value of a complex expression follows from those of its subexpressions.

(3) *There is a one-to-one correspondence between syntactic rules and semantic rules.* This has the advantage of ensuring that the semantic rules cover the entire language.

(4) The semantic rules capture the formal semantic aspects of the language, as they account for the semantic consequences of the syntactic structures of complex expressions.

(5) Types play a role similar to that of syntactic categories: the syntactic rules specifying how complex expressions may be built up from simpler ones are expressed in terms of conditions on the types of the constituents. Moreover, the rules describe how the type of a complex expression follows from the types of its subexpressions, thus providing the information necessary for knowing how the complex expression may be used as a building block in other complex expressions.

7.3 Model-theoretic analysis of natural language

When we consider the application of the model-theoretic method to the analysis of natural language, we encounter several problems that arise from the differences between formal and natural languages. The first and most obvious difference is that a formal language, in contrast to a natural language, is the product of a definition. For natural languages there are no definitions, only partial, *post hoc* descriptions. In particular, formal languages have a rigorously defined syntax, while for natural languages we only have incomplete descriptions of syntactic regularities. A common strategy in model-theoretic studies of natural language is, therefore, to restrict oneself to a 'fragment' or 'sublanguage' of a natural language. A limited vocabulary and a set of syntactic rules are chosen, which define a fragment of a natural language. As in the case of a formal language, a set of semantic rules is then specified having a one-to-one correspondence with the syntactic rules. The semantic rules thus describe the semantic structure of the expressions belonging to the fragment. This approach has been followed by Montague (1970a; 1970b), Bennett (1975; 1978), ter Meulen (1980), Thomason (1972), and many others.

Another difference is that the expressions of a natural language are sequences of words, while the expressions of a formal language usually contain auxiliary symbols such as various sorts of brackets and special symbols marking the syntactic structure. The definition of the class of well-formed EL expressions in (6.35) illustrates this: every EL expression, if not just a term, contains a branching category and selectors that spell out the syntactic structure.

A third important difference is that, most of the time, natural language expressions are ambiguous in a variety of ways. Formal languages, by contrast, have been developed as tools for expressing something in a precise and unambiguous manner. This difference has various implications for the application of model-theoretic methods to natural language semantics, implications that depend on the nature of the ambiguity. At least three different types of ambiguity are to be distinguished in this connection, called *referential*, *syntactic*, and *structural semantic* ambiguity.

Referential ambiguity occurs when a referential word has more than one possible meaning. For instance, the sentence

(7.16) I looked at the bank

has alternative readings due to the ambiguity of 'bank' (as a financial enterprise or a river bank). The consequences of referential ambiguity are discussed in the next section. I prefer to use the term 'referential' ambiguity over the more usual 'lexical' ambiguity, since non-referential words like 'the' and 'and' can also be argued to be lexically ambiguous, but this is not an ambiguity of reference.

Syntactic ambiguity has its origin in the circumstance that natural language expressions are 'just' sequences of words, without explicit indications of the syntactic structure. It is therefore often possible to assign more than one syntactic structure to an expression. A noun phrase like

(7.17) A man with a donkey with a red hat

is syntactically ambiguous since the phrase 'with a red hat' can be a modifier either of 'a donkey' or of 'A man with a donkey'. In this example, the ambiguity is a matter of constituent structure, and can be brought out by different ways of 'bracketing' the sentence:

(7.18) a. (A man)(with(a donkey with a red hat))
        b. (A man with a donkey)(with a red hat)

Different possibilities of bracketing form a rich source of syntactic ambiguities.

There are also cases of syntactic ambiguity of a 'deeper' nature. Two classical examples are:

(7.19) Flying planes can be dangerous

(7.20) I heard the shooting of the hunters

In (7.19) the ambiguity is caused by the fact that 'flying' can be both a participle (an adjectival verb form) and a gerund (a nominal verb form); this distinction comes out clearly in the sentences

(7.21) Flying planes are dangerous

(7.22) Flying planes is dangerous

In the case of (7.20) the ambiguity is caused by the fact that 'shoot' may be used both transitively and intransitively, and that 'the hunters' may be either the subject of 'the shooting', used intransitively, or the object in the transitive use. Both in (7.19) and in (7.20) the ambiguity cannot be expressed in different ways of grouping the words into larger constituents.

Two-level model-theoretic semantics 113

The third type of ambiguity mentioned above, that of structural semantic ambiguity, is illustrated by the sentence:

(7.23) These books are heavy

The ambiguity is here that 'heavy' can be interpreted either collectively, as a predicate of the collection of books as a whole, or distributively, as a predicate of each of the individual books in the collection. In cases like this, the source of the ambiguity is that the concepts that the words refer to can be related semantically in different ways, while there is no reflection of this relation in the syntactic structure. It is therefore a purely semantic kind of ambiguity, and it is, in contrast to referential ambiguity, a structural one. Ambiguities of this kind will be discussed extensively in chapters 8 and 9.

Syntactic ambiguity is one of the major reasons why the model-theoretic method is usually applied to natural languages in a different way than to formal languages. Applying the method to a natural language in the way we have seen for formal languages would mean that we list the denotations of the referential words (of a certain fragment) and devise a set of semantic rules, one for each syntactic rule of the fragment, which together form a recursive characterization of the denotation of any expression of the fragment. If the expression is syntactically ambiguous it can be 'parsed' in more than one way, that is, different sequences of syntactic rules apply, and so the semantic rules produce more than one value for it. This approach has been followed in Montague (1970a). However, a more perspicuous and manageable system is obtained if the denotations of the natural language expressions are obtained indirectly, via a translation into semantic representations in a formal language. The formal language is then interpreted in the standard model-theoretical way. Syntactically ambiguous sentences now have more than one translation into the formal language. This has become the usual way of applying the techniques of model-theoretic semantics to natural languages, and this is also my approach in the subsequent chapters.

The indirect model-theoretic interpretation of a natural language fragment can be described with the same precision as the direct method. Given a natural language fragment NL_o and a formal representation language L_f, the translation is performed by a procedure which is defined as follows.

(7.24) (i) The class of well-formed expressions in L_f (the possible semantic representations) is specified;

(ii) For each NL_o word its translation into L_f is specified. This is formally described by a function T_f that assigns to each word a semantic representation;

(iii) For each NL_o syntactic rule a corresponding translation rule is specified, describing how the translation of the complex NL_o expression is built up from the translations of the constituents.

The reader will no doubt have noted that this definition is structurally very similar to the description, above, of the model-theoretic semantic interpretation of a language. Indeed, from a purely formal point of view there is no difference at all. If we simply equate a language with the class of its well-formed expressions, as is often done, then the pair MT consisting of L_f and the function T_f in (ii) form a *model*

(7.25) $\quad \text{MT} = (L_f, T_f)$

with model structure L_f and model assignment T_f. In other words, the translation from NL_o into L_f is nothing else than a model-theoretic interpretation of NL_o using semantic representations in L_f as values.

Combining the formal definition of the NL_o–L_f translation with the model-theoretic definition of the L_f semantics gives us a rigorous definition of the indirect interpretation of NL_o.

7.4 Referential ambiguity and model-theoretic semantics

We have seen that the translation into semantic representations involves the specification of the semantic representation of each word (or more accurately, lexeme) of the natural language fragment. Such a specification is usually combined with the specification of syntactic properties of the lexemes and called a *lexicon*. The phenomenon of referential ambiguity is often ignored altogether in model-theoretic studies of natural language. In the beginning of this chapter we have seen some arguments why it may be reasonable to consider the study of referential ambiguity as not belonging to the realm of formal semantics; yet, if we take the latter seriously we should be able to indicate how studies of formal and referential semantics fit together in an overall framework of semantic analysis. As the definition of the translation from natural language to semantic representations requires a specification of the translations of the referential words, ignoring the phenomenon of referential ambiguity takes the form of assigning just one representation to each referential word, tacitly assuming that there is no referential ambiguity in the fragment under consideration (see e.g. Montague, 1970b).

The ambiguity of a constant cannot, of course, be accounted for by assigning it different denotations in different models. This is most clearly illustrated by sentences in which the same word occurs with different meanings, such as

(7.26) He took the money to the bank on the bank of the Thames

Clearly, we can only get the desired reading here if we have more than one denotation available for the word 'bank'. If referential ambiguity is not to be ignored, the only possibility would seem to be that we assign more than one lexical entry to a referentially ambiguous word, one for each word meaning. This approach has been taken, for instance, by Bennett (1978). Thus, the word 'bank' is given two lexical entries, each with their own translation into L_f. A sentence like

(7.27) The cuckoo flew over the bank

is thus assigned two semantic representations.

However, this approach goes against the doctrine of formal semantics which says, as we have seen, that formal semantics should deal only with the formal semantic structures of natural language expressions. The two readings of (7.27) have the *same* semantic structure, therefore the sentence should be assigned only *one* representation.

We are thus led to the conclusion that if, on the one hand, we do not want to lose any of the referentially different readings of (7.27) but, on the other hand, we want to assign only one semantic representation to the sentence, then *the representation must preserve the referential ambiguities* in the sentence. The representation should thus contain terms with the same referential ambiguities as the corresponding natural language words. Consequently, the language L_f of the semantic representations must be *a formal language with ambiguous constants*. Moreover, if all the referential ambiguities in a natural language fragment NL_o are to be preserved, then there must be a one-to-one correspondence between the referential words of NL_o and the constants of L_f.

The idea of a formal language with ambiguous constants has been explored in the PHLIQA project, mentioned in the previous chapter (see

Landsbergen and Scha, 1979). The ambiguity of the constants gives rise to technical complications in the language definition, which will be considered below; as the above arguments show, the idea seems to be quite attractive from a theoretical linguistic point of view.

The ambiguity of its constants has the consequence that, in the model-theoretic definition of the representation language, sets of values are assigned to constants instead of single values, and that the recursive rules for evaluating complex expressions become correspondingly more complicated. For example, instead of the rule which says that the denotation of an application expression $F(x)$, with a function expression F and an argument expression x, is the result of applying the function denoted by F to the argument denoted by x, we now have the more complicated rule saying that the value of $F(x)$ is the set of all values that result from applying one of the functions denoted by F to one of the arguments denoted by x. That is, instead of the rule

(7.28) $V(F(x)) = V(F)(V(x))$

(see (6.36), rule 1b) we now get the rule

(7.29) $V(F(x)) = \{y | \exists F_i \in V(F): \exists x_i \in V(x): F_i(x_i) = y\}$

The situation is complicated further by the fact that not every one of the functions in the collection $V(F)$ is necessarily applicable to every one of the objects in the collection $V(x)$. The following example illustrates this. Consider the expression

(7.30) The age of this chair

where we distinguish two meanings of 'chair', that of article of furniture and that of president of a meeting. Suppose, further, that two interpretations of 'age' are distinguished, one in terms of year of manufacture and one in terms of year of birth. Let (7.30) be assigned the single semantic representation

(7.31) AGE(CHAIR)

where AGE and CHAIR are L_f constants with the referential ambiguities we assumed for 'age' and 'chair'. Distinguishing the different interpretations by an index which is either 'a' (for 'animate') or 'i' (for 'inanimate'), we thus have:

(7.32) $V(AGE) = \{age_a, age_i\}$
       $V(CHAIR) = \{chair_a, chair_i\}$

Of the four possible combinations of values from these collections, only two are meaningful; we want the value of (7.30) to be

(7.33) $\{age_a(chair_a), age_i(chair_i)\}$

rather than the set of all four combinations. This illustrates a general problem that turns up in the semantic definition of a language with ambiguous constants: the recursive rules are now formulated in terms of sets of values of which some combinations should be ruled out as not meaningful.

The natural instrument for ruling out undesirable combinations is that of a type system, as we have seen in the previous chapter. However, the notion of a type as it has been introduced earlier applies only to expressions of a language, not to their values; that is, *unless these values are expressions of a language*. We have seen above that the formal specification of the assignment of semantic representations to natural language expressions is in fact nothing other than a model-theoretic interpretation with L_f expressions as values; this idea can be used once again, now in the semantic definition of L_f. I therefore introduce a second formal language, called L_r ('r' for 'referential'), which has typed, unambiguous constants that have a one-to-one correspondence with the objects in the discourse domain, originally intended as denotations of L_f expressions. We then specify the semantic definition of L_f in model-theoretic terms as a translation into L_r. Since L_r is a language with unambiguous constants, its semantic definition can be given in the usual model-theoretic way, described in the previous section. I will take, for the languages L_f and L_r, two members of the family of Ensemble Languages, defined in the previous chapter. These two members, designated as EL_f and EL_r, differ only in their constants: EL_f has potentially ambiguous constants, one for each referential word of the natural language fragment under consideration; EL_r has unambiguous constants, one for each possible interpretation of a natural language term in the domain of discourse that is considered. The domain of discourse is reflected, as we have seen earlier, in the model structure that is used (see (7.15)); in this case, this is the model structure used in the definition of EL_r. Altogether, this means that we have now arrived at the following schema for the semantic interpretation of natural language expressions (see (7.34)).

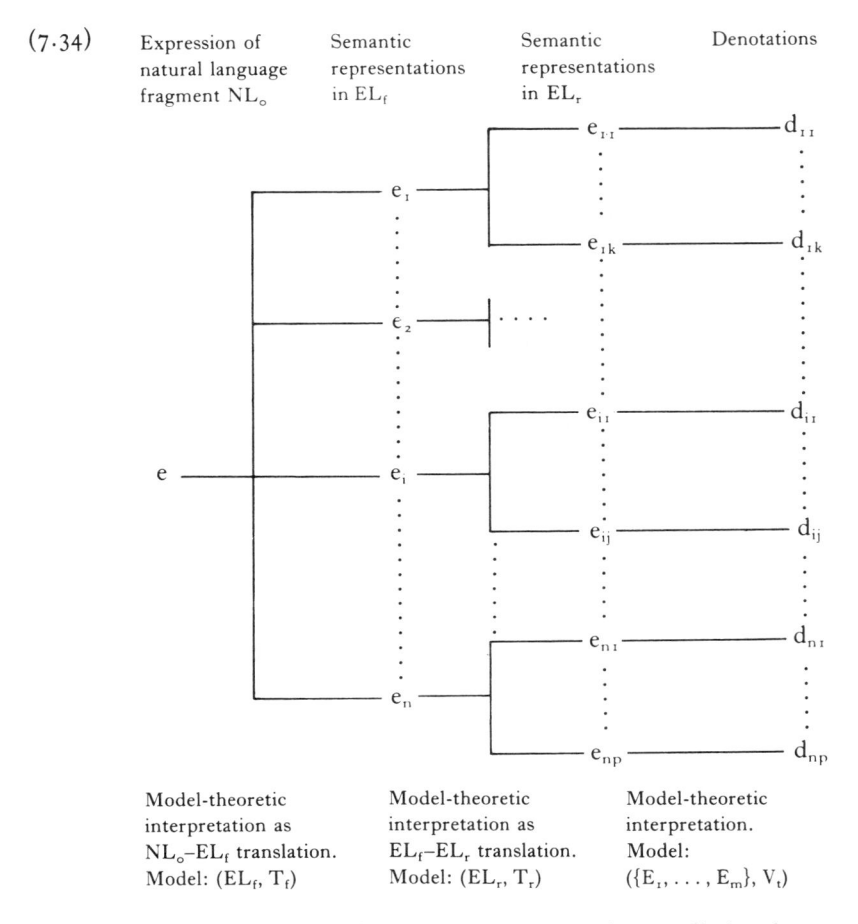

118 Part 1 *Model-theoretic semantics of mass terms*

(7.34)

Expression of natural language fragment NL_o	Semantic representations in EL_f	Semantic representations in EL_r	Denotations

```
                              ┌─ e₁₁ ─────── d₁₁
                     ┌─ e₁ ───┤    ⋮
                     │        └─ e₁ₖ ─────── d₁ₖ
                     │
                     ├─ e₂ ───┤ ····
                     │
                     │        ┌─ eᵢ₁ ─────── dᵢ₁
    e ───────────────├─ eᵢ ───┤    ⋮
                     │        └─ eᵢⱼ ─────── dᵢⱼ
                     │
                     │        ┌─ eₙ₁ ─────── dₙ₁
                     └─ eₙ ───┤    ⋮
                              └─ eₙₚ ─────── dₙₚ
```

Model-theoretic interpretation as NL_o–EL_f translation. Model: (EL_f, T_f)	Model-theoretic interpretation as EL_f–EL_r translation. Model: (EL_r, T_r)	Model-theoretic interpretation. Model: $(\{E_1, \ldots, E_m\}, V_t)$

Since there are two levels of semantic representation mediating between natural language expressions and their denotations here, rather than one, as is usual, I call the semantic analysis following this schema *two-level model-theoretic semantics*. In the next section I shall discuss some of the formal properties of this method.

7.5 Two-level model-theoretic semantics

Two-level model-theoretic semantics is essentially the model-theoretic formalization of the linguistically relevant part of a method of semantic analysis that has been developed in the PHLIQA project on natural-language question-answering by computer, mentioned above. The development of the method, called *multi-level semantics*, has been the collective effort of those participating in the project, namely Wim Bronnenberg, Harry Bunt,

Jan Landsbergen, Piet Medema, Remko Scha, Wijnand Schoenmakers and Eric van Utteren. The method has been described informally in Medema et al. (1975); the most complete description can be found in Bronnenberg et al. (1980); see also Scha (1976), Landsbergen (1976), and Bunt (1981a). Multi-level semantics was devised as a multi-stage process of semantic analysis useful for bridging the gap between natural language expressions and the contents of a conventional computer data base. Though multi-level semantics was originally not conceived within the model-theoretic framework, it contained the essential ingredients: values are assigned (derived from the computer data base and serving as answers) to natural-language expressions (in this case English questions) by translating them into a formal language of which the expressions are evaluated recursively. The translation is carried out in a number of steps, each resulting in an expression in a different member of the same family of formal languages, where the first step is the construction of a representation in a formal language with ambiguous constants.

The use of more than one level of representation in formal languages is particularly elegant if those languages are chosen as different members of the same language family, differing only in their constants (like EL_f and EL_r). In that case the translation from one language to another can take the simple form of replacing the constants of one language by their translations in the other (which are, in general, complex expressions). Thus, if the 'source language' of the translation has unambiguous constants, then the recursive part of the translation can be described by a single rule defining a translation function T_{st} as follows. Let us assume that source and target language are members of the Ensemble Language family, designated by EL_s and EL_t, respectively. If

(7.35) $\underline{brc}(sel_1: e_1, \ldots, sel_n: e_n)$

is an EL_s expression with branching category $\underline{brc}$ and selectors $sel_1, \ldots, sel_n$ then

(7.36) $T_{st}(\underline{brc}(sel_1: e_1, \ldots, sel_n: e_n)) =$
         $\underline{brc}(sel_1: T_{st}(e_1), \ldots, sel_n: T_{st}(e_n))$

The recursion ends at the EL_s terms, for which T_{st} coincides with the specification of their translation in the non-recursive part of the translation definition (see (7.24)).

If the source language has ambiguous constants however, as in the case of EL_f, then the recursive part of the translation is complicated in the way we have seen when we considered the model-theoretic interpretation of a

120 Part 1 Model-theoretic semantics of mass terms

language with ambiguous constants (see (7.29)). Since the EL_f–EL_r translation is, formally speaking, nothing other than a model-theoretic interpretation using EL_r expressions as values, the same complication now turns up in the transformation rules. Thus, if T_r is the specification of the value sets of the ambiguous EL_f constants, the translation of, for instance, an application expression is described by the rule

(7.37) $T_{fr}(\underline{application}(function: F, argument: a)) =$
    $\{y \mid y = \underline{application}(function: F_i, argument: a_i)$
    $\& \ F_i \in T_r(F) \ \& \ a_i \in T_r(a)\}$

(cf. (7.29)). The translation of any complex expression can still be described by a single recursive rule which, however, is more complicated than (7.36):

(7.38a) $T_{fr}(\underline{brc}(sel_1: e_1, \ldots, sel_n: e_n)) =$
    $\{y \mid y = \underline{brc}(sel_1: Z_{1i}, \ldots, sel_n: Z_{ni}) \ \&$
    $Z_{ji} \in T_{fr}(e_j) \text{ for } 1 \leq j \leq n\}$

There is the further complication that only those combinations of the possible constant translations should be accepted which are in accordance with the type restrictions of the target language. This is accomplished by adding to the recursive translation rule the type restriction pertaining to the branching category of the expression that is translated. Taking again the example of an application expression, the type restriction stipulates that the type of the argument subexpression satisfies the type-inclusion relation with the domain part of the type of the function subexpression (see (6.34)). Using the type restriction predicate TR, introduced in section 6.4, we can describe the translation of complex EL_f expressions still by a single recursive rule, which now runs as follows:

(7.38b) $T_{fr}(\underline{brc}(sel_1: e_1, \ldots, sel_n: e_n)) =$
    $\{y \mid y = \underline{brc}(sel_1: Z_{1i}, \ldots, sel_n: Z_{ni}) \ \&$
    $Z_{ji} \in T_{fr}(e_j) \text{ for } 1 \leq j \leq n$
    $\& \ TR(\underline{brc}, TYPE_r(Z_{1i}), \ldots, TYPE_r(Z_{ni}))\}$

The addition of type checking to the translation rules can be avoided by requiring the translation of the EL_f constants to satisfy a condition on the relation between the type of a constant and those of its translations. EL_f and EL_r each have their own type languages which are again chosen as two members of the same family, in this case the ELTL family, defined in the previous chapter. Let us designate these two members by $ELTL_f$ and $ELTL_r$. The EL_f syntax thus defines a function $TYPE_f$ from EL_f expressions to $ELTL_f$ expressions, and similarly the EL_r syntax defines a

Two-level model-theoretic semantics 121

function $TYPE_r$ from EL_r expressions to $ELTL_r$ expressions. Between the respective type languages a translation function TT is defined by specifying for each $ELTL_f$ constant its $ELTL_r$ translation (which is a unique translation, since there is no ambiguity in the type languages), and defining TT for any $ELTL_f$ expression as that expression which is obtained by replacing any $ELTL_f$ constant by its $ELTL_r$ translation. The relations between the various languages are represented schematically in (7.39).

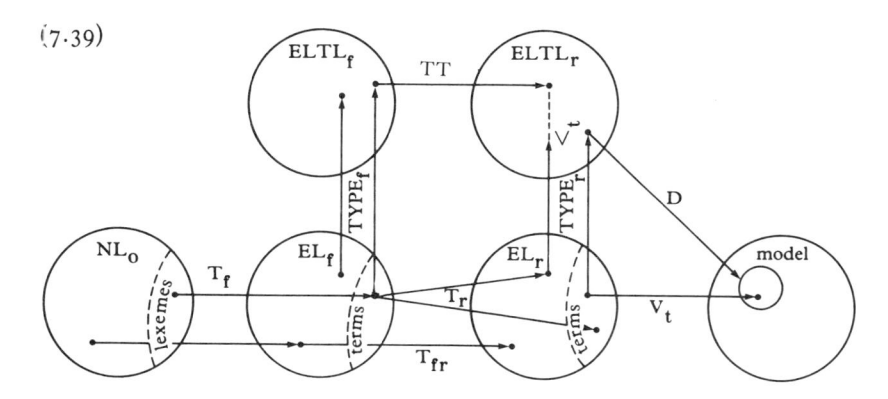

(7.39)

Note that the type translation is defined in such a way that it preserves type inclusions and other formal relations between types. This is because such a relation can only hold between two types t_1 and t_2 if the same atomic types occur in certain syntactic patterns in the type structures of t_1 and t_2; now the structures are completely untouched by the type translation, and each atomic type is replaced uniformly by the same translation. In particular, the type restrictions for the various constructions of a language of the EL family remain satisfied under type translation; thus for every branching category,

(7.40) $TR(\underline{brc}, \underline{t}_1, \ldots, \underline{t}_n) \rightarrow TR(\underline{brc}, TT(\underline{t}_1), \ldots, TT(\underline{t}_n))$

The condition on the translation of EL_f constants which guarantees the correctness of the translation of any EL_f expression is the following.

(7.41) For every EL_f constant c and any $z \in T_r(c)$,
 $TYPE_r(z) <_t TT(TYPE_f(c))$

Fulfilment of this condition guarantees correctness of the translation of any EL_f expression[3], since the constructions of an EL language all have the following properties:

(1) The type restrictions of all branching categories are 'transparent'

for the type-inclusion relation in the sense that, if $\underline{brc}(sel_1: E_1, \ldots, sel_n: E_n)$ is a well-formed expression whenever $TYPE(E_1) = \underline{t}_1, \ldots, TYPE(E_n) = \underline{t}_n$, then it is also a well-formed expression if $TYPE(E_1) = \underline{t}'_1, \ldots, TYPE(E_n) = \underline{t}'_n$ such that $\underline{t}'_i <_t \underline{t}_i$. Thus, for every branching category $\underline{brc}$,

$$(7.42) \quad \left. \begin{array}{l} TR(brc, \underline{t}_1, \ldots, \underline{t}_n) \\ \underline{t}'_1 <_t \underline{t}_1, \ldots, \underline{t}'_n <_t \underline{t}_n \end{array} \right\} \rightarrow TR(brc, \underline{t}'_1, \ldots, \underline{t}'_n)$$

(2) Type inclusions propagate through a construction in the sense that, if a construction builds up an expression of type $\underline{t}$ when applied to subexpressions of types $\underline{t}_1, \ldots, \underline{t}_n$ then, when applied to subexpressions of types $\underline{t}'_1, \ldots, \underline{t}'_n$ with $\underline{t}'_i <_t \underline{t}_i$, the resulting expression has a type $\underline{t}'$ such that $\underline{t}' <_t \underline{t}$. Thus, for every branching category $\underline{brc}$,

(7.43) If $e = \underline{brc}(sel_1: e_1, \ldots, e_n)$ and $e' = \underline{brc}(sel_1: e'_1, \ldots, e'_n)$, with $TYPE(e'_i) <_t TYPE(e_i)$ for $1 \le i \le n$, then $TYPE(e') <_t TYPE(e)$

These properties imply that, if the translation of the constants meets the condition (7.41), then so does the translation of complex expressions:[4]

(7.44) For any EL_f expression e and EL_r expression $z \in T_{fr}(e)$, $TYPE_r(z) <_t TT(TYPE_f(z))$

We have now seen how we can work with a level of semantic representations built up from ambiguous constants, obtaining the desired interpretations by means of a simple, carefully constrained translation: a single recursive rule which replaces the ambiguous constants by appropriate unambiguous translations does the whole job.

Two-level model-theoretic semantics owes its name to the fact that the assignment of a denotation to a natural language expression takes place via two intermediate stages of representation. The EL_r representations can be said to constitute a 'deeper level' of analysis than the EL_f representations, as they incorporate the results of referential semantic analysis in addition to those of the purely formal analysis at the first stage. One may therefore speak of two *levels* of analysis.

It may be thought that the two-level system, while elegant from a logical or a theoretical linguistic point of view and, owing to its modularity, attractive from a computational point of view, is unattractive from a psycholinguistic point of view. It would seem implausible that in the analysis of a natural language sentence one should first construct a representation of the formal structure of the sentence and fill in the appropriate referential elements only in a later stage. It is important to realize that this is not what the two-level method says, however. The description of the two-level analysis framework given above is a *mathematical* one, in terms of functions and their decomposition; there is still a variety of ways in which this can be cast in *algorithmic* terms and implemented on a processor, be it an animate or an inanimate one. One possibility out of many, and perhaps the one that comes to mind first after the above description of the method, is that an incoming sentence is first translated into EL_f and the resulting expressions subsequently translated into EL_r. Another possibility is, for instance, that the EL_f translation of an incoming word is immediately looked up in the EL_f–EL_r dictionary and its EL_r translations are stored as a 'semantic feature' of the word; when a larger constituent is to be formed this feature can be used for semantic checking, thereby constraining the application of grammar rules. Moreover, as soon as a certain rule is applied, those EL_r translations of the constituents that would violate the type restrictions can be deleted. In this way the available referential knowledge is used in an early stage in the analysis process. Viewed in time, this is in fact no longer a two-stage process, but a process consisting of alternating steps of the natural language–EL_f and EL_f–EL_r translation.

An essential point of the two-level model-theoretic method, which will be found in any implementation, is that a referential word with several meanings that are syntactically indistinguishable has a single, referentially ambiguous representation from where its unambiguous 'instances' can be found. This has the attractive consequence that lack of detailed referential knowledge does not have to block further linguistic processing. Suppose, for example, the following sentence fragment is to be processed:

(7.45)   Last week, when I travelled from Brussels to Amsterdam, I saw a Dutch...

The possible continuations of this fragment include, for instance, the words 'town', 'flag', 'girl', and 'aeroplane'. What is meant by 'Dutch' is rather different in each case: a Dutch town is a town in Holland, a Dutch flag is a flag symbolizing Holland, a Dutch girl is a girl with Netherlands' nationality, and a Dutch aeroplane is made in Holland. Clearly, 'Dutch' has a variety of meanings, from which the appropriate one can only be selected if one knows how the sentence continues. Yet it would seem implausible that the lack of this information should block the syntactic and semantic structure-building operations involving the word 'Dutch' for the sentence fragment. But it seems equally implausible that we should be forced to choose a particular interpretation of 'Dutch' at this point. In the two-level framework it is possible to suspend making decisions about the referential aspects of a word, building up a semantic structure with the ambiguous EL_f constant. In the implementation outlined above, where referential semantic information is carried along with the words as semantic features, the appropriate meaning of 'Dutch' is selected when information becomes available on the type of object that it is applied to. This implementation has been realized in a version of the TENDUM computer-dialogue system mentioned in section 6.3.

7.6 A formal and a referential view of the world

We have seen in section 7.2 that the components of a model $M = (D, V_t)$ represent a domain of discourse (D), a state of affairs in that domain being represented by the assignment of denotations to terms (V_t). We have also seen, in section 6.6, that the type definition of a language determines the possible denotations of the terms: for any term c, the term valuation has to satisfy the condition

(7.46) $V_t(c) \in D(TYPE(c))$

The assignment of types to the terms thus determines the possible term valuations V_t and, since a term valuation represents a state in the discourse domain, the types determine the possible states of the discourse domain. For instance, suppose that EL_r has a function constant PARENTS of type (person → ⟨person, person⟩). The EL_r term valuation is then required to meet the condition

(7.47) $V_t(PARENTS) \in D((\text{person} \rightarrow \langle \text{person, person} \rangle))$

By the semantic rules (6.28) of the type language, this means that PARENTS denotes a function which assigns to a person a pair of persons. The possibility is thus excluded that the discourse domain should be in a state of affairs where someone would have more than two or less than two parents.

In the two-level model-theoretic framework a domain of discourse is represented by the model of EL_r, and the assignment of types to the EL_r constants and variables determines the possible states of the domain. A natural language sentence that describes a situation in the domain which is impossible, according to the EL_r model, cannot be represented in EL_r

since it would give rise to an expression in which the EL_r type restrictions are violated. In this way the definition of the representation language at the referential level embodies a view on what natural language sentences can possibly mean in relation to a given domain of discourse. One might say that the instruments of the representation language are chosen in accordance with a view on what is possible in the discourse domain, and the meaning of a natural language sentence cannot be something impossible. The following example illustrates this. Suppose we have a function constant AGE in EL_r, of type (person → integer), which is used in the representation of sentences about a person's age. Suppose, moreover, that EL_r has no other terms for representing ages. Now the sheer fact that AGE has the type of a function from persons to integers means that we are committing ourselves to the following views on the universe of discourse:

(7.48) (1) an age is an integer
        (2) only individual persons have ages
        (3) a person has only one age

As a result of these commitments, the sentence

(7.49) Eric and Jasper are aged 12 and 4

cannot be interpreted as asserting that Eric and Jasper each have the two ages 12 and 4. Similarly, the sentence

(7.50) Martin and Jasper are four years old

cannot be interpreted as saying that the age of four years is a collective property of the duo Jasper–Martin. Also, the sentence

(7.51) Astrid is aged nine-and-a-half

is uninterpretable, since an attempted representation like

(7.52) *AGE(Astrid) = 9.5

would violate the EL_r type restriction. Similarly, if MOTHER is an EL_r constant of type (person → person) the sentence

(7.53) Astrid's mother is 34

cannot be interpreted as

(7.54) *MOTHER(Astrid) = 34

This illustrates how the possible interpretations of natural-language sentences are restricted by the assumptions on what is possible in the discourse domain, embodied in the definition of the representation language at the referential level.

The definition of EL_f, on the other hand, is domain-of-discourse-independent, as the EL_f terms have the full referential potential of the corresponding natural-language words. Still, the definition of EL_f also embodies a view on what natural language sentences can possibly mean.

We have not yet considered the types of EL_f expressions, although it was assumed in the previous section that EL_f and EL_r have different referential atomic types. (For referential versus formal atomic types see section 6.4.) The referential atomic types of EL_r represent basic semantic categories in a domain of discourse but those of EL_f do not, as EL_f is domain-of-discourse-independent. The atomic types of EL_f therefore have to be extremely general. The only choice which is guaranteed to be general enough at this point, and truly domain-of-discourse-independent, is to have only one referential atomic type. I will therefore assume that there is one referential atomic type at the formal level, called *entity*. This makes the definition of EL_f indeed completely domain-of-discourse-independent. The reason why EL_f still imposes certain restrictions on the possible interpretations of natural language sentences is that most EL_f constants have a complex, rather than an atomic type. The following examples illustrate the consequences of this point.

Suppose we translate intransitive verbs as constants of type (entity → truthvalue), that is as one-place predicate constants. This would allow us to interpret a sentence like

(7.55) Mickey and Pluto are walking

as WALK(Mickey) & WALK(Pluto). However, this would not allow us to interpret a sentence like

(7.56) Mickey walks Pluto

where we have a transitive sense of 'walk'. If we want to be domain-of-discourse-independent at the formal level, and therefore be able to handle the transitive case as well, then we either have to distinguish two senses of 'walk', each with its own EL_f translation, or else we have to give the EL_f translation a more 'liberal' type, namely

(7.57) ((entity ∪ ⟨entity, entity⟩) → truthvalue)

Suppose we translate transitive verbs as constants of type (⟨entity, entity⟩ → truthvalue), that is as two-place predicate constants. This would allow us to represent a sentence like

(7.58) Eric lifted the boat

in EL_f. It would also allow us to represent the sentence

(7.59) Martin and Jasper lifted the boat

on the distributive reading where both Martin lifted the boat and Jasper lifted the boat, but not on the collective reading where Martin and Jasper together lifted the boat. The representation of that reading would require an EL_f constant of type $(\langle S(entity), entity\rangle \to truthvalue)$. Similarly, the representation of

(7.60) Eric lifted the boat and the paddles

on the reading where the boat and the paddles are lifted together, would require an EL_f translation of type

(7.61) $(\langle entity, S(entity)\rangle \to truthvalue)$

that is, an interpretation where the direct object of 'lift' is a set of things. To handle all these cases, plus the double collective one in

(7.62) Jasper and Martin lifted the boat and the paddles

we either have to provide four lexical entries for 'lift', each with its own EL_f translation, or else we have to give the EL_f translation a more 'liberal' type, namely

(7.63) $(\langle entity \cup S(entity), entity \cup S(entity)\rangle \to truthvalue)$

The decision as to how liberal we make the type of an EL_f constant or, alternatively, how many EL_f translations we provide for a natural language word, determines what readings of natural-language sentences can be represented. A decision like the one to include in EL_f a single translation for 'lift' with the type (7.61) amounts to incorporating in EL_f the view that only an individual entity can lift something, which may be a set of things. Note that this should be a domain-of-discourse-independent decision. At the formal level of analysis we thus have a similar situation as at the referential level, namely that the definition of the representation language embodies a view on what is possible, except that at the formal level this view is not restricted to a particular domain of discourse but is of a very general nature.

The general view of 'the world' which is embodied in the definition of the representation language at the formal level of analysis I call the *formal view of the world*. Every well-defined representation language embodies such a view. The richer the language, the wider the range of semantic structures in natural language expressions that can be represented, and the broader the formal view of the world. Ideally, the representation language covers precisely the range of semantic structures in natural language expressions; in that case we could say the formal view of the world is that which is embodied in the natural language itself.

It should be noted that a formal view of the world manifests itself in *any* system of semantic analysis where domain-of-discourse-independent representations are constructed, regardless how the representation language is defined. This is because a formal-semantic, domain-of-discourse-independent representation is meant to capture those and only those semantic aspects of natural language expressions that are due to the morphosyntactic structure and the occurrences of function words (quantifiers, determiners, etc.) Words that differ in their referential aspects, but are identical in their formal aspects (which means that they may occur in the same syntactic configurations, because they belong to the same syntactic category and have the same syntactic features) are thus translated into distributionally equivalent EL_f constants. Since the distribution of an EL_f constant is determined by its type, this means that two natural language words that differ only in their referential aspects correspond to EL_f constants of the same type. (In Montague grammar this phenomenon turns up in the fact that the syntactic category of a word determines the type of its translation in Intensional Logic.) On the other hand, the type of a constant determines its possible denotations; therefore two words that differ only in their referential aspects have the same possible denotations. The following example illustrates the consequences of this point for the formal view of the world. Consider the sentences:[6]

(7.64) The whistle is blowing

(7.65) The wind is blowing

These sentences have the same formal organization, and thus differ in their EL_f representation only in the constants translating 'whistle' and 'wind', respectively. Sentence (7.64) is thus analysed just like (7.65), as saying that a certain entity, the wind, satisfies a certain predicate: to be blowing. This means that, independent of how the representation language is defined, at the formal level we are committed to an analysis in terms of an object called 'the wind', independent of its blowing. Is this an awkward side-effect of the two-level framework?

I think not. I think it is correct to say that in (7.65) we speak *as if* there is an object 'wind' which is doing some blowing. It is for this reason that a question like

(7.66)   What does the wind do if it doesn't blow?

can arise. This view is suggested by the linguistic form of sentences like (7.65) and (7.66), and it is therefore appropriate that this is reflected in the formal view of the world incorporated in the EL_f level. Such speaking 'as if' should, of course, be distinguished from a speaker's actual beliefs about the world; these are accounted for at the referential level when it comes to what words like 'wind' actually refer to.

Clearly, a formal view of the world is, in general, not how a speaker really views the world. To express a speaker's real beliefs we must consider the concepts referred to by the referential words and how they are related. This takes place at the level of EL_r. The definition of this level, in particular that of the EL_r model, can be viewed as a specification of a speaker's actual view of the world or some restricted domain of discourse. I call this view as incorporated in EL_r the *referential view of the world*.

We shall see in the next section that the distinction between a formal and a referential view of the world is of fundamental importance in the semantic analysis of mass nouns.

7.7 Mass terms in two-level model-theoretic semantics

I have stipulated in chapter 4 that the use of a mass noun constitutes a way of referring to something as if it is a homogeneous mass, as opposed to a discrete collection of objects. The linguistic evidence supporting this view, summed up in the homogeneous reference hypothesis (4.4), is the same for all mass nouns: the count/mass distinction is a *formal* phenomenon, not a referential one. Although we may have different actual beliefs about the 'homogeneity' of the referents of such words as 'furniture', 'luggage', 'computing equipment', 'shoe polish', 'time', or 'rice', from a formal semantic point of view these mass nouns should all be treated alike. In other words, in our two-level framework all mass nouns should be treated *at the formal level* as referring to entities as having a part–whole structure, without any commitments concerning the existence of minimal parts. This is regardless of our actual beliefs about mass noun referents. Actual beliefs about the world simply play no part at the formal level: this level is completely determined by the formal semantic structures found in natural language sentences. (It follows, in a way which is perhaps still more compelling than the way we argued in chapter 4, that Quine's minimal parts hypothesis, being based on actual beliefs about the physical structure of the real world, cannot play a part in a formal semantic theory.)

We can now use ensemble theory to give a logical form to the formal view of the world in which mass nouns refer to entities as having a part–whole structure without further commitments regarding their internal structure. At the formal level we represent mass nouns by constants denoting *general ensembles* without any restrictions as to whether they are discrete, continuous, or mixed. In doing so we make precisely those commitments which, according to the homogeneous reference hypothesis, are carried by mass nouns.

At the referential level, on the other hand, we interpret mass nouns in accordance with our actual beliefs about the world. A mass noun whose referent is actually believed to be discrete is represented by an EL_r expression denoting a discrete ensemble; a mass noun whose referent is actually believed to be continuous is represented by an EL_r expression denoting a continuous ensemble; and a mass noun whose referent is actually believed to be of a mixed character is represented by an EL_r expression denoting a mixed ensemble.

To illustrate how this works, suppose we want to treat the mass noun 'furniture' as denoting a discrete ensemble at the referential level. Assume, further, that we are dealing with a domain of discourse in which chairs and tables are the only articles of furniture. At the referential level, 'furniture' thus refers to the discrete ensemble formed by the union of the set of chairs and the set of tables, denoted by the EL_r constants $CHAIRS_r$ and $TABLES_r$, respectively. At the formal level, 'furniture' is represented by the constant $FURNITURE_f$, denoting a general ensemble. Now consider the interpretation of the noun phrase

(7.67) The furniture in this room

At the formal level we analyse this as the ensemble made up by all FURNITURE-parts which are in this room, that is, as the ensemble:

(7.68) $[x \subseteq FURNITURE_f | IN_f(x, ROOM_f)]$

where IN_f and $ROOM_f$ are constants of the formal level, representing the spatial 'in' relation and 'this room'. To take into account that we only have chairs and tables as furniture in our discourse domain, the constant FURNITURE$_f$ is translated into the EL$_r$ expression CHAIRS$_r \cup$ TABLES$_r$. To translate (7.68) into EL$_r$, the constants IN$_f$ and ROOM$_f$ are also replaced by their EL$_r$ translations. IN$_f$ is translated into

(7.69) $(\lambda y: (\forall z \in y_1: IN_r(z, y_2)))$

The variable y in this expression ranges over 2-tuples; y_1 designates the first element of the 2-tuple y, and y_2 the second element. IN$_r$ is a two-place predicate constant which may be applied to such arguments as a pair consisting of a chair and a room. The expression (7.69) represents a two-place predicate applicable to argument-pairs (y_1, y_2), where y_1 designates a *set* of chairs and tables and y_2 a room. Indicating the EL$_r$ translation of ROOM$_f$ by ROOM$_r$, we obtain the following EL$_r$ translation of (7.68):

(7.70a) $[x \subseteq CHAIRS_r \cup TABLES_r | (\lambda y: (\forall z \in y_1: IN_r(z, y_2))(x, ROOM_r))]$

Note that the EL$_r$ representation has the same overall structure as the EL$_f$ representation. Since 'furniture' corresponds at the referential level to the union of the sets of chairs and tables, we would like the EL$_r$ representation of (7.67) to be simply a set expression. Well, it is. The notation $[x \subseteq A | P]$ has been defined for any ensemble A; in particular, it is also defined if A is a set (discrete ensemble). We have seen in chapter 5 that $[x \subseteq A | P]$ is the merge of all parts of A for which P is true (theorem (5.26)). Therefore, (7.70a) is equivalent to

(7.70b) $\cup (\{x \subseteq CHAIRS_r \cup TABLES_r | (\lambda y: (\forall z \in y_1: IN_r(z, y_2)))(x, ROOM_r)\})$

In other words, the EL$_r$ representation of 'the furniture in this room' denotes the union of those sets consisting entirely of chairs and tables which are 'in this room'. It is easily seen that (7.70b) is equivalent to the simpler form

(7.70c) $\{z \in CHAIRS_r \cup TABLES_r | IN_r(z, ROOM_r)\}$

This is precisely what we wanted.

Generally speaking, the use I shall make of ensemble theory is such that, in the formal semantic analysis of mass noun expressions, ensembles and the $\subseteq$ relation play the role that sets and the $\in$ relation play in the analysis of count noun expressions. The above example (7.68) illustrates this: the formula

(7.68) $[x \subseteq \text{FURNITURE}_f | \text{IN}_f(x, \text{ROOM}_f)]$

representing the mass noun phrase 'The furniture in this room' is the ensemble-theoretical counterpart of the set-theoretical expression

(7.69) $\{x \in \text{CHAIRS}_r | \text{IN}_f(x, \text{ROOM}_f)\}$

which represents the count noun phrase 'The chairs in this room'. Similarly, the sentence 'All the furniture is in this room' can be represented in ensemble-theoretical terms as:

(7.70) $\forall x \subseteq \text{FURNITURE}: \text{IN}_f(x, \text{ROOM}_f)$

This is the ensemble-theoretical counterpart of:

(7.71) $\forall x \in \text{CHAIRS}: \text{IN}_f(x, \text{ROOM}_f)$

which represents the sentence 'All the chairs are in this room'.

8 Quantification and mass nouns

8.1 Introduction

In this chapter and chapter 9 I discuss in some detail the application of ensemble theory to the analysis of mass noun expressions within the framework of two-level model-theoretic semantics.

To begin with, let us consider in what ways mass nouns occur in English and how we can deal with various types of occurrence in a systematic way. Three important types of mass noun occurrence are as follows.[1]

A. As the head of a so-called 'basic noun phrase', a noun phrase that has no premodifying or postmodifying adjectives, prepositional phrases, or relative clauses (see Quirk *et al.*, 1972, chapter 4, and below). Examples of such occurrences are:

(8.1) Do you have *cheese*?

(8.2) Waiter, *my soup* is cold

(8.3) *All this furniture* is Danish

(8.4) *The butter* is melting

(8.5) Mary bought *2 kilogrammes of cheese*

B. As modified by an adjective, prepositional phrase or relative clause. Examples of such occurrences are:

(8.6) This ring is made of *pure gold*

(8.7) They have *furniture made in Denmark*

(8.8) The *sweet, hot chocolate* warmed us

C. As a bare noun after the copula 'is'. Examples are:

(8.9) This puddle *is water*

(8.10) What you see there *is gold*

By combining the analysis of mass nouns in these three 'basic' types of occurrence, we obtain an analysis of mass nouns in complex noun and verb phrases.

Concerning mass noun occurrences after the copula 'is' we may recall, from the discussion in chapter 3, Quine's refusal to analyse (8.9) 'This puddle is water', as

(8.11) $p_o \subseteq$ WATER

(where p_o abbreviates the semantic representation of 'this puddle', WATER denotes a mereological whole, and $\subseteq$ denotes the part–whole relation of mereology), because of his adherence to the minimal parts hypothesis: the object denoted by p_o might be 'too small to count as water'. Since in our two-level framework the minimal parts hypothesis is irrelevant at the formal level, an analysis like (8.11) is acceptable if the $\subseteq$ symbol is interpreted as the part–whole relation of ensemble theory and WATER as denoting an ensemble. 'Being water' is thus analysed as being a part of the totality of all water.

In chapter 3, where we have discussed the approaches to mass term semantics in the literature, we have considered a number of sentences with intuitively obvious logical properties to expose the strengths and weaknesses of the various proposals. Most of these sentences involve quantifications or modifications, so their discussion will have to wait until we have treated these phenomena; at this point we may consider the example

(8.12)   Water is water

interpreted as saying that the totality of all water is water. (This sentence formed a problem for Quine's and Burge's proposals, in which it does not come out as a necessary truth.) With the ensemble-theoretical interpretation of 'being water' given above, this sentence is now analysed simply as

(8.13)   WATER $\subseteq$ WATER

which is a logical truth in ensemble theory.[2]

Modified mass nouns (occurrences of type B) are studied in chapter 9, where the emphasis is on combinations of a noun and a single adjective. Single adjective–noun combinations are the simplest form of modification, the understanding of which is basic to the analysis of syntactically more complex forms of modification.

The consideration of mass nouns modified by adjectives gives rise to intriguing questions about the grammatical well-formedness of adjective–

Quantification and mass nouns

mass noun combinations. Sentences such as

(8.14) *There is big onion in the salad
(8.15) *There is small rope in the drawer

seem to be ungrammatical at a purely syntactic level, that is, independent of the interpretations of the nouns and adjectives involved, while a sentence like

(8.16) Remove all the heavy sand from the yard but leave all the light sand

seems to be deviant,[3] unless 'heavy' and 'light' are understood as 'heavy kind of' and 'light kind of', respectively, that is, as referring to specific weight rather than weight in the ordinary sense. The question thus arises as to what adjective–mass noun combinations are deviant, and in what terms these deviances should be described.

The study of adjective–mass noun combinations has an independent motivation in that it may shed some light on two recurring issues in the mass terms literature:

(a) Should the concept of 'mass terms' be extended to include 'mass adjectives'? We have seen in chapter 2 that Quine and Moravcsik have suggested doing so; however, the consequences of such a move have hardly been explored so far.

(b) Related to a possible distinction between 'mass adjectives' and 'count adjectives' are the co-occurrence restrictions that seem to obtain for certain adjectives and mass nouns, as illustrated by (8.14)–(8.16). Quine has suggested that only adjectives which are cumulative in reference can modify a mass noun, but we have seen in chapter 2 that the situation is not as simple as that. The question is therefore what, precisely, are the co-occurrence restrictions for adjectives and mass nouns?

In the discussion of mass noun modification in chapter 9, I shall argue that a correct treatment of mass noun modification requires the distinction of several semantically different types of modification which closely parallel the types of quantification distinguished in the present chapter. Moreover, it will be argued that two subcategories of mass nouns should be distinguished. These distinctions will form the basis for both describing the grammatical constraints on adjective–mass noun combinations and defining 'mass adjectives'.

136 Part 1 Model-theoretic semantics of mass terms

Mass noun occurrences of type A, as the head of a basic noun phrase, are occurrences as the rightmost element in a sequence of determiners followed by a noun. The determiners of English can be subcategorized as 'predeterminers', 'central determiners', and 'postdeterminers', according to the relative positions they may occupy. Table (8.17) illustrates this.[4]

(8.17)

Predeterminer	Central determiner	Postdeterminer	Head
All	the	little	butter
Both	these	two	days
Half	my		salary

Count nouns and mass nouns differ considerably in the determiners they take. Some illustrative examples are:

(8.18) a. Both suitcases are heavy
b. *Both luggages are heavy

(8.19) a. Several jewels were stolen
b. *Several jewellery were (was) stolen

(8.20) a. Each participant baked three cakes
b. *Each participant baked three cake

(See also the syntactic criteria for identifying mass nouns and count nouns, discussed in section 2.1.)

Semantically, these differences are evidently related to the fact that mass nouns do not individuate their reference; therefore, one wouldn't know how to count the luggage, cake and jewellery in (8.18b), (8.19b), and (8.20b). In order to indicate quantity in the case of a mass noun one must, for the same reason, choose a certain dimension and unit of measurement (weight/grammes, volume/litres, value/dollars, etc.). The role of numerals in NPs with count noun heads is thus played by amount phrases ('100 grammes of', 'two litres of', etc.) in NPs with mass noun heads. Analogous to 'vague' numerical quantifiers for count nouns, like 'many' and 'several', are vague amount phrases like 'much' and 'a great deal of', which are vague in two respects: they do not specify in which units or even in which dimension we are to measure amounts of the mass noun extension, and they also have the same kind of vagueness as 'many' and 'several' in not being precise about the number of units under consideration.

Amount phrases can of course be used with count nouns as well (2 kilogrammes of apples). The difference between count nouns and mass nouns in expressing quantity is that count nouns have a linguistically indicated 'default' dimension and unit of measurement, that of counting individuals (for measuring apple amounts, for instance, the default dimension is number of apples, and the default unit is apple); for mass nouns no such dimension and unit exist. Numerical quantification over a count noun and amount quantification over a mass noun have different implications for the existence of entities in the extension of the noun. Compare the sentences:

(8.21)   There are 5 onions in the salad

(8.22)   There is 5 grammes of onion in the salad

Sentence (8.21) claims the existence of five objects in the extension of 'onions in the salad'; (8.22), by contrast, has no implications for the existence of particular onion-parts. It would of course be wrong to say that 5 onion-parts, each measuring 1 gramme, are claimed to be in the extension of 'onion in the salad'. If (8.22) is true, then there are *infinitely many* onion-parts in the salad that weigh one gramme, since the onion can be divided into such parts in infinitely many ways. For the same reason it is absurd to propose that the mass noun quantifier 'much' be analysed as 'many quantities of', as has been done by ter Meulen (1980, p. 90).

I claim that, in principle, any proposal for the analysis of count noun quantification in set-theoretical terms can be generalized to an ensemble-theoretical one that includes mass noun quantification. Quantification is a complex phenomenon which is still only partly understood in the case of count nouns, therefore, before turning to the analysis of quantified mass nouns I begin with a discussion of the phenomenon of quantification in general. I shall then outline a treatment of quantification for count nouns in set-theoretical terms. This treatment is subsequently generalized to an ensemble-theoretical one that includes mass noun quantification.

8.2 Quantification

Quantification is a complex phenomenon that occurs whenever a nominal and a verbal constituent combine to form a higher constituent, where the verbal constituent denotes a predicate which is applied to arguments supplied by the nominal constituent. This always gives rise to a number of considerations such as (1) What exactly are the objects that serve as predicate arguments? (2) How many objects are involved in true predications? (3) How many objects are considered as potential arguments of the predicate? The following examples illustrate this.

(8.23) a. These books are heavy
b. Four of these books are heavy
c. Most of these 12 books are heavy

Sentence (8.23a) illustrates that the question of which objects are the arguments of the predicate deserves serious consideration; in this case, the question is whether these are individual books or the collection of books as a whole. The question of how many objects the predicate is true of is explicitly addressed in (8.23b) and (8.23c); in (8.23a) this is an implicit consideration. (The assertion involves at least two books.) The question how many objects are considered as potential arguments is explicitly addressed in (8.23c).

The various aspects of quantification are closely related to the semantic functions of determiners. Determiners can have different functions, such as indicating quantity ('five books', 'many books') or specifying the range of reference of the head of the noun phrase by making it definite ('my books', 'the books') or indefinite ('a book', 'some books'). The semantic function of a determiner depends on its syntactic position in a determiner sequence; as mentioned in the previous section, a full-fledged basic NP has the layout:

(8.24) predeterminer + central determiner + postdeterminer + head noun

The determiners in such a sequence have different semantic functions. In the NP

(8.25) All my four children

for instance, the central determiner 'my' restricts the range of reference of the head noun 'children' to the set of my children; the predeterminer 'all' indicates that a predicate, combined with the noun phrase to form a proposition, is associated with all the members of that set, and the postdeterminer 'four' expresses the presupposition that the set consists of four elements. This set is determined by the central determiner plus the denotation of the head noun. It will be convenient, in the discussion to follow, to have a term designating this set (or, if the head is a mass noun, this ensemble). I will use the term *source* for this purpose.[5] In the case of an NP without central determiner the source is the denotation of the head noun. Concerning the functions of predeterminers, central determiners and postdeterminers it thus appears that we can say, in general, that the central determiner contributes to the determination of the source, the postdeterminer indicates the presupposed quantity of the source, and the predeterminer indicates the quantity of that part of the source that is involved in a predication; for the latter aspect I use the term *source involvement*.

The determiners that indicate amount or quantity are called *quantifiers*.[6] When we try to classify the quantifiers according to the scheme predeterminers–central determiners–postdeterminers, we see that they do not fall into one single category. In English, some quantifiers such as 'all' and 'both' are predeterminers: they occur to the left of articles and other central determiners. Other quantifiers, such as 'many', 'few', and 'several', are postdeterminers: they occur to the right of central determiners. Then there is a third group of quantifiers, including 'each', 'every', 'some', 'no', and 'much', that can occur neither to the left nor to the right of central determiners, and for this reason are usually classified as central determiners (see e.g. Leech and Svartvik, 1975, section 550). This classification captures some of the co-occurrence restrictions among determiners; however, the classification of the 'each/every group' of quantifiers as central determiners is somewhat arbitrary as far as co-occurrence restrictions go, since they are mutually exclusive not only with central determiners but also with predeterminers, so they might as well be classified as predeterminers. Their classification as predeterminers is more attractive from a semantic point of view, since it has the effect that all central determiners (articles, possessives, WH-determiners, and demonstratives) have the semantic function of determining, together with the head noun, the source of a quantification. Each of the three positions in a determiner sequence then correlates with a semantic aspect of quantification: central position with source determination, pre-central position with source involvement indication, and post-central position with presupposed source size indication.

As quantifiers give a quantitative indication, either of the presupposed source size or of the involvement of the source in a predication, an important question is what indication of quantity or amount a quantifier in fact gives. This is, in general, a very complicated matter, that I will not go into in any detail (see e.g. Bennett, 1974, chapter 4).[7]

Another important aspect of quantification is illustrated by the following pair of sentences:

(8.26)   a. The chairs were lifted by all the boys
          b. The chairs were lifted by each of the boys

Due to the semantic difference between the quantifiers 'all' and 'each of', these sentences differ in the following respect. Sentence (8.26a) is unspecific as to what each individual boy did: it only says that the chairs were lifted and that all the boys were involved in the lifting, but it does not specify, for instance, whether every one of the boys lifted the chairs or all the boys together lifted the chairs. Sentence (8.26b), on the other hand, says unambiguously that every one of the boys lifted the chairs. The quantifiers 'all' and 'each (of)' thus both indicate complete involvement of the source, but they differ in their determination of how a predicate ('lifted the chairs') is applied to the source. 'Each' indicates that the predicate is applied to the individual members of the source; 'all' leaves open whether the predicate is applied to individual members, to groups of members, or to the source as a whole. To designate the way in which a predicate is applied to or 'distributed over' the source of a quantification, I will use the term *distribution*.

We have seen that a sentence like

(8.27) a. These books are heavy

has the following readings, which differ in distribution:

(8.27) b. Each of these books is heavy
c. Together these books are heavy

These readings are often referred to as the 'distributive' and the 'collective' reading (see e.g. Dik, 1975). They can be represented in EL_f by (8.28a) and (8.28b), respectively:

(8.28) a. $\forall x \in \text{THESE-BOOKS}: \text{HEAVY}(x)$
b. $\text{HEAVY}(\text{THESE-BOOKS})$

The quantifications in (8.27b) and (8.27c) have the same source and the same source involvement; they only differ in how the predicate 'heavy' is distributed over the source. A way of expressing the distribution of a quantification is by specifying the class of objects that the predicate is applied to, and how this class is related to the source. In the distributive case this class is precisely the source; in the collective case it is the set having the source as its only element. I shall refer to the class of objects that the predicate is applied to as the *domain* of the quantification. Clearly, the domain of a quantification is always closely related to the source; in fact, the distribution of a quantification over an NP denotation can be viewed as specifying how the domain can be computed from the source.

Where domain = source I shall refer to *individual* distribution; where domain = {source} I shall refer to *collective* distribution.

Individual distribution and collective distribution are not the only possible types of distribution. Consider the sentence

(8.29)   All these machines assemble 12 parts

This sentence may describe a situation in which certain machines assemble sets of 12 parts, that is, a situation where we have a relation between individual machines and groups of 12 parts. If PARTS is the set denoted by 'parts', the direct object quantification domain is $\mathscr{P}_{12}$(PARTS), the subset of $\mathscr{P}$(PARTS) containing only those subsets of PARTS that have 12 members (cf. section 6.8). Designating the machines denoted by 'these machines' by THESE-MACHINES, we can represent this reading of (8.29) by

(8.30) $\forall x \in$ THESE-MACHINES: $\exists y \in \mathscr{P}_{12}$(PARTS): ASSEMBLE(x, y)

I call this type of distribution *group distribution*. The numerical quantifier in this case indicates the group size. We thus see that a predeterminer can have yet another function than that of indicating source involvement.

In a sentence like

(8.31)   The crane lifted the pipes

there is no indication as to whether the tubes were lifted one-by-one (individual distribution), two-by-two (group distribution with group size 2), one-or-two by one-or-two (group distribution with group size ≤2), ..., or all in one go (collective distribution). The quantification is unspecific in this respect. In such a case I will say that the distribution is *unspecific*. If S is the source of the quantification, the domain is, in this case, the set consisting of the elements of S and the subsets of S that contain more than one element.[8]

Assigning unspecific distribution to a quantification is in fact a way to avoid having to say that a quantification is many-ways ambiguous, having besides a collective and an individual reading also all logically possible group readings. Articulate analyses of quantification are generally in danger of ambiguity explosions, as we shall see below.

I shall refer to 'collective quantification' instead of 'quantification with collective distribution', of 'individual quantification' instead of 'quantification with individual distribution', etc. In keeping with established terminology, I will also use the term 'distributive quantification' instead of 'individual quantification'.

So-called 'generic quantification', which occurs in sentences like

(8.32) a. Lions are carnivores
b. Water is uninflammable

will be left out of consideration here since it is highly questionable whether this phenomenon can be treated adequately in an extensional framework (see e.g. Dahl, 1978).

8.3 Quantification aspects of multi-NP sentences

So far, we have only considered quantification aspects relating to single noun phrases. When we turn to sentences with two or more NPs which all interact with the same verbal constituent, we encounter quantification aspects that relate to more than one NP, the most important being that of *relative scope*. The classical example of this phenomenon is the difference in meaning between the sentences

(8.33) Every person in this room speaks two languages

(8.34) Two languages are spoken by every person in this room

In the most plausible reading of (8.33) it is asserted that everyone in the room speaks more than one language, whereas in the most plausible reading of (8.34) there are two languages that each person in the room is said to speak. In (8.33) the quantification over persons is analysed as having wide scope and that over languages as having narrow scope, in (8.34) it is the other way round. Relative scopes are brought out very clearly in a logical representation like

(8.35) $(\forall x \in \text{PERSONS})[(\exists_2 y \in \text{LANGUAGES})[\text{SPEAK}(x, y)]]$

(8.36) $(\exists_2 y \in \text{LANGUAGES})[(\forall x \in \text{PERSONS})[\text{SPEAK}(x, y)]]$

where square brackets are used to indicate the scope of quantifiers, and where the quantifier $\exists_2$ is used to represent 'there are two'. (See also section 6.8.)[9]

There is a general tendency in English and in many other languages to interpret the quantifications in multi-NP sentences as having scopes that decrease with the left-to-right order of the NPs. The sentences (8.33) and (8.34) illustrate this. But this is no more than a tendency; sometimes the preferred reading of a sentence has quantifications with relative scopes that do not correspond to the left-to-right order, as the following examples show:

(8.37) Three beers did each man drink

(8.38) Two boys gave three flowers to four girls

(In the latter sentence, left-to-right order of relative quantification scopes would mean that each of the flowers is given to four different girls.)

Some determiners have *inherent* scope properties in that they always give rise to quantifications with wider (or narrower) scope than other quantifications and scope-bearing elements, such as negations. For instance, WH-determiners like 'which' and 'what' always have wide scope.

In a sentence where more than one NP enters into a quantified relation via a verbal constituent we must distinguish two ways in which a quantifier can express source involvement. Compare the following one- and two-NP sentences:

(8.39) Five ships were lifted

(8.40) Both cranes lifted five ships

(8.41) Two cranes lifted five ships

In the first of these sentences five ships are involved, as indicated by the quantifier 'five'. In the second sentence the number of ships involved can be any number between five and ten, depending on whether some of the ships were lifted more than once; in this case the quantifier 'five' indicates the source involvement of the object-NP quantification per element of the subject-NP quantification domain. In such a case I will say that the quantifier indicates *local source involvement*. Sentence (8.41) is ambiguous as to whether each of two cranes lifted five ships (subject NP is individually quantified) or two cranes together lifted five ships (subject NP is collectively quantified). In the first case 'five' is again a local source involvement indicator, in the second it indicates *global* or *total source involvement*.

A quantifier in a collectively quantified noun phrase, such as '12' in the sentence

(8.42) 12 men conspired

indicates the size of the collection of objects from the quantification source that serves as argument of a predicate or relation. Thus, (8.42) may be read as

(8.43) A group of 12 men conspired

and may be represented in EL_f as

(8.44a) $\exists x \in \{s \in \mathcal{P}(MEN) | \#(s) = 12\}: CONSPIRE(x)$

or, in the notation with subscripted power set symbols used above as

(8.44b) $\exists x \in \mathcal{P}_{12}(MEN): CONSPIRE(x)$

This is in fact the group reading of sentence (8.42); see also (8.30). However, I do not consider this to be the preferred analysis of the sentence. It seems to me that there is a slight difference in meaning between (8.42) '12 men conspired' and (8.43) 'A group of 12 men conspired' in that the latter leaves open the possibility that more than one group of 12 men conspired, as the representation (8.44) with an existential quantifier brings out clearly, whereas the former sentence on the preferred reading says that precisely one group of 12 men conspired. I will call the former the *strong group reading* and, to distinguish it clearly from what has been called a 'group reading' up to now, I will call the latter the *weak group reading*. (There is, of course, also the difference between (8.42) and (8.43), that (8.42) leaves open whether the 12 men conspired as one group or, for instance, in two groups of six. That is, (8.42) also admits an interpretation with unspecific distribution.) On the strong group reading the quantifier in (8.42) has a *double* function: it indicates both group size and total source involvement. This means that the following representation is appropriate:

(8.45) $\#(\cup(\{x \in \mathcal{P}_{12}(MEN) | CONSPIRE(x)\})) = 12$

It should be noted that the assignment of relative scopes influences the total source involvements of the various quantifications. For the NP with widest scope the total source involvement is simply as indicated by the corresponding quantifier, but for an NP with narrower scope this is not so, as (8.33) and (8.38) show.

A form of multi-NP quantification which is often overlooked is one where several NPs have quantifications with equally wide scope. Consider the sentence

(8.46) Three boys kissed three girls

The most plausible reading here is one where both NPs have individual quantification and where both numerals express total source involvement. This is the 'total–total' reading of the sentence (Partee, 1975) which I shall call, following Scha (1981) the reading with *cumulative quantification*. It can be paraphrased by

(8.47) The total number of boys who kissed a girl is three, and the total number of girls kissed by a boy is three

A correct EL_f representation would thus be

(8.48) $\#(\{x \in BOYS | \exists y \in GIRLS: KISS(x, y)\}) = 3$ &
$\#(\{y \in GIRLS | \exists x \in BOYS: KISS(x, y)\}) = 3$

A slightly different form of multi-NP quantification which to my knowledge has not been considered before in the literature, is illustrated in the following example. Suppose two basketball teams, WINNERS and LOSERS, play a match. LOSERS wins, surprisingly enough, by 100–90. Two of LOSERS' players are outstandingly productive: together they score 99 points. A newspaper report of the match may now contain the following headline:

(8.49) Two players score 99 points

The intended meaning is not the cumulative reading, as neither the total numbers of players who scored is two, nor the total number of points scored is 99. Rather, the intended meaning can be paraphrased by

(8.50) There is one set of two players who scored 99 points in all

I will say that this reading has *subcumulative quantification*; it can be represented in EL_f by

(8.51) $\exists! z \in \mathscr{P}(\{y \in PLAYERS \times POINTS | SCORE(y)\}):$
$\#(proj_1(z)) = 2$ & $\#(proj_2(z)) = 99$

Here, y is a variable that ranges over pairs consisting of a player and a point, and z is a variable that ranges over sets of such pairs; $proj_1(z)$ denotes the set of first elements (the players) in the collection of pairs denoted by z, and $proj_2(z)$ the set of second elements: the points. (See section 6.8 for the definition of this notation.)

The distinction of cumulative and subcumulative interpretations leads to two additional types of quantification in multi-NP sentences besides the combinations of distributive, collective, unspecific, and group quantifications of the individual NPs with all possible relative scopes. Note that an NP can only have group quantification if it contains an explicit quantifier (numerical determiner), and that both cumulative and subcumulative quantifications tend to arise only if all the NPs contain explicit quantifiers.

8.4 Quantification representations for count nouns

In the previous section I have occasionally suggested possible EL_f representations of some types of quantification. I shall now do this more systematically and consider how the suggested representations can be generated within a grammar. The main purpose of doing this is to introduce the kind of semantic representations in an Ensemble Language that would seem appropriate for the various quantification types distinguished above; at the same time, it will become clear that these representations could easily be generated by grammars in the style of the PTQ grammar (Montague, 1973) or the grammar for analysing quantification suggested by Barwise and Cooper (1981). The examples used in this section are only meant to illustrate the possibilities of Ensemble Languages as a tool for representing quantification aspects; I shall therefore refer loosely to 'EL representations' rather than EL_f or EL_r representations. In the next section I will offer a particular proposal for analysing quantifications within the framework of two-level model-theoretic semantics and for constructing EL_f and EL_r representations, thereby paying special attention to the question of how many quantificationally different readings of natural language sentences should be distinguished.

Count nouns will be treated here as denoting sets. To a noun like 'girl' we thus assign an EL constant (GIRLS) of type S(entity). Noun phrases are objects that combine with an intransitive verb to give a sentence; this is reflected in logical terms by treating verbs as denoting predicates and noun phrases as denoting functions from predicates to truth values. For example, we represent

(8.52)   each girl

by the function expression:

(8.53a) $(\lambda P: \forall x \in GIRLS: P(x))$

Such a representation can be constructed from the representations of 'each' and 'girl' by treating determiners as functions from sets of individuals to NP denotations. Thus, to 'each' we assign the representation

(8.54) $(\lambda X: (\lambda P: \forall x \in X: P(x)))$

(A capital X is used to indicate that the variable has a set or ensemble type.) This is again a function expression; by applying it to GIRL, we obtain:

(8.53b) $(\lambda X: (\lambda P: \forall x \in X: P(x)))(GIRL)$

Quantification and mass nouns 147

By the operation, known in the theory of λ-calculus as *λ-conversion*,[10] this can be simplified to the equivalent form (8.53a). To obtain the representation of the sentence

(8.55) Each girl smiles

we assign to the verb form 'smiles' the EL constant SMILE, of type (entity→truthvalue), and apply the function expression (8.53a) to the argument SMILE. After λ-conversion, this leads to the representation:

(8.56) $\forall x \in \text{GIRLS}: \text{SMILE}(x)$

This illustrates how the representation of a one-NP sentence with distributive quantification can be constructed.

Distributive quantification can also arise with numerical quantifiers, as in:

(8.57) Three girls smile

For such cases we can construct EL representations with a similar structure as (8.56) by using subscripted quantifiers (see above, and section 6.8). If we assign to 'three', as a determiner, the representation

(8.58) $(\lambda X: (\lambda P: \exists_3 x \in X: P(x)))$

we obtain, in the same way as in the previous example, the representation

(8.59) $(\exists_3 x \in \text{GIRLS}: \text{SMILE}(x))$

Collective quantifications can be represented by means of predicates applied to the source set as a whole. The use of such a representation is in accordance with arguments that have recently been put forward in the linguistic literature, showing that a theory of quantification in natural language should include quantifiers that range over sets of sets (see Gil, 1982). For example, the collective reading of the sentence:

(8.60) All men gather

can be represented by

(8.61) GATHER(MEN)

Here, GATHER is a predicate of type (S(entity)→truthvalue). This representation can be obtained from the representations of 'all' and 'men' by assigning to 'all', among other representations, the following one for the collective reading:

(8.62) $(\lambda X: (\lambda P: P(X)))$

As before, this is a function expression that can be applied to the argument MEN, with the result (after λ-conversion):[11]

(8.63) $(\lambda P: P(MEN))$

Combined with the representation of 'gather', this leads to the representation (8.61).

This is similar for strong group quantification in a sentence with a numerically quantified NP, as in the example (8.42) '12 men conspired'. The representation (8.45), suggested above, can be obtained by assigning '12', as a determiner, a strong group reading in which it indicates both group size and total source involvement, represented by

(8.64) $(\lambda X: (\lambda P: \#(\cup(\{x \in \mathcal{P}_{12}(X) | P(x)\})) = 12))$

The case of weak group quantification, where a numerical quantifier indicates group size only, can be dealt with in a similar way, leading to the representation

(8.65) $(\lambda X: (\lambda P: \exists x \in \mathcal{P}_{12}(X): P(x)))$

All this is fairly conventional, and can easily be extended to sentences with more than one noun phrase. For instance, Scha (1981), who used semantic representations similar to the ones considered here, has suggested a two-stage parsing process where the first stage consists in constructing a representation of the sequence of noun phrases in a sentence, and the second stage in combining this representation with that of the verb to obtain the sentence representation. Applied to the sentence

(8.66) Every person speaks two languages

this would go as follows. Suppose the NPs 'every person' and 'two languages' are represented by

(8.67) a. $(\lambda P: \forall x \in PERSONS: P(x))$
        b. $(\lambda P: \exists_2 y \in LANGUAGES: Q(y))$

From these, the representation (8.68b) is constructed for the 'noun phrase

Quantification and mass nouns 149

sequence' (8.68a):

(8.68) a. (every person, two languages)
b. $(\lambda R: (\lambda P: (\forall x \in PERSONS: P(x)))(\lambda x_1:$
$(\lambda Q: (\exists_2 y \in LANGUAGES: Q(y)))(\lambda x_2:$
$R(x_1, x_2))))$

The latter representation is applied as a function to the verb representation. After simplifying the formula by λ-conversion, this leads to the sentence representation

(8.69) $\forall x \in PERSONS: \exists_2 y \in LANGUAGES: SPEAK(x, y)$

The relative scopes of the quantifications correspond in this approach to the order of the NPs in the noun phrase sequence; readings with relative scopes that deviate from the order of the NPs in the sentence can be constructed by generating permutations of the noun phrase sequence.

We have not yet considered the representation of quantifications with unspecific distribution. In such a quantification, if S is the source, the quantification domain is a mixture consisting of the elements and plural subsets of S. Using the notation $\mathcal{P}_{plur}(S)$ to denote the collection of those subsets of S that contain more than one element (see also section 6.8), the quantification domain is thus

(8.70) $S \cup \mathcal{P}_{plur}(S)$

which I will also abbreviate as S^*. For example, in the unspecific reading of

(8.71) Five boats were lifted

the quantification domain consists of individual boats and sets of two or more boats. There is a technical difficulty in this case in representing the source involvement correctly, which is determined by the number of boats that were involved either individually or as a member of a set of boats involved collectively. To count the number of boats involved we cannot, of course, simply apply the cardinality function $\#$ to the involved part of the quantification domain, as in the case of a distributive quantification, nor can we use the $\#$ function after first applying the union operator, as in the case of a collective quantification (see 8.45). What we need is a combination of the ways in which the source involvement is expressed in the distributive and collective cases. To this end I shall introduce a union-like operator $\cup^*$ which has two arguments, a set S, and a set X consisting of members and subsets of S. The operator yields as value the set of those members of S which are either members of X or members of a member of X. Thus, if $X = \{x_1, x_2, \ldots, x_k, X_1, X_2, \ldots, X_n\}$ with $x_1, x_2, \ldots, x_k \in S$ and $X_1, X_2, \ldots, X_n$ subsets of S,

(8.72) $\cup *(S, \{x_1, x_2, \ldots, x_k, X_1, X_2, \ldots, X_n\}) =$
$\{x_1\} \cup \{x_2\} \cup \ldots \cup \{x_k\} \cup X_1 \cup X_2 \cup \ldots \cup X_n$

With the help of the $\cup *$ operator we can represent the unspecific reading of (8.71) as

(8.73) $\#(\cup *(\text{BOATS}, \{x \in \text{BOATS}^* | \text{LIFTED}(x)\})) = 5$

This representation can be constructed by assigning to 'five' as a determiner, besides the representations already mentioned for distributive and group readings, another representation for unspecific readings:

(8.74) $(\lambda X: (\lambda P: \#(\cup *(X, \{x \in X^* | P(x)\})) = 5))$

We have seen two types of quantification that may occur in sentences with two or more noun phrases, especially if they all have an explicit numerical quantifier: cumulative and subcumulative quantification. As an example of cumulative quantification we have considered the sentence (8.46) 'Three boys kissed three girls', on the reading paraphrased by: (8.47) 'The total number of boys who kissed a girl is three, and the total number of girls kissed by a boy is three'. The problem with cumulative quantification is that it is hard to find a formal representation that has a close enough structural correspondence to the English sentence that it can be derived in a systematic way from the English surface structure. The representation considered in the previous section, namely

(8.48) $\#(\{x \in \text{BOYS} | \exists y \in \text{GIRLS}: \text{KISS}(x, y)\}) = 3 \;\&$
$\#(\{y \in \text{GIRLS} | \exists x \in \text{BOYS}: \text{KISS}(x, y)\}) = 3$

illustrates this problem: it bears a structural resemblance to the paraphrase (8.47), but it is structurally very different from the original sentence, and therefore difficult to derive. Scha (1981) has suggested analysing cumulative quantifications as having the cartesian product of the sources associated with the respective NPs as quantification domain. For the present sentence this leads to the representation:

(8.75) $(\lambda u: \#(\text{proj}_1(u)) = 3 \;\&\; \#(\text{proj}_2(u)) = 3)$
$(\{x \in \text{BOYS} \times \text{GIRLS} | \text{KISS}(x)\})$

Quantification and mass nouns 151

The variables u and x here take elements from the cartesian product BOYS×GIRLS as values. As before, $\text{proj}_1(u)$ denoted the set of first elements in the collection of pairs denoted by u, and $\text{proj}_2(u)$ the set of second elements (see section 6.8). This representation is constructed by generating intermediate representations for both the sequence of NP heads and the sequence of quantifiers. In the present example, these two sequences and their representations are

(8.76) a. (boys, girls)
        b. BOYS×GIRLS

for the NP head sequence, and

(8.77) a. (three, three)
        b. $(\lambda u: \#(\text{proj}_1(u)) = 3 \ \& \ \#(\text{proj}_2(u)) = 3)$

for the quantifier sequence. These representations are subsequently combined by a special rule in the grammar that constructs a noun phrase sequence from a noun sequence and a quantifier sequence, with the result

(8.78) $(\lambda R: (\lambda u: \#(\text{proj}_1(u)) = 3 \ \& \ \#(\text{proj}_2(u)) = 3)$
        $(\{z \in \text{BOYS} \times \text{GIRLS} | R(z)\}))$

The application of this representation as a function to the representation of the verb leads, after λ-conversion, to the representation (8.75).

For subcumulative quantification we can do something similar. Let us consider again the example from the previous section, namely (8.49) 'Two players score 99 points', on the reading paraphrased by (8.50) 'There is one set of 2 players who scored 99 points in all'. The EL representation

(8.51) $\exists! z \in \mathcal{P}(\{y \in \text{PLAYERS} \times \text{POINTS} | \text{SCORE}(y)\}):$
        $\#(\text{proj}_1(z)) = 2 \ \& \ \#(\text{proj}_2(z)) = 99$

can be constructed from the same intermediate structures representing noun sequence and quantifier sequence, as in the case of cumulative quantification, but now using a different rule for constructing a noun phrase sequence from them, with the representation

(8.79) $(\lambda R: \exists! z \in \{y \in \text{PLAYERS} \times \text{POINTS} | R(y)\}:$
        $\#(\text{proj}_1(z)) = 2 \ \& \ \#(\text{proj}_2(z)) = 99$

This representation, applied as a function to the verb representation SCORE, gives us (8.51).

8.5 Quantification in two-level model-theoretic semantics

In the previous sections we have seen a variety of quantificationally different readings that sentences with one or more noun phrases may have, how they can be represented in an Ensemble Language, and how these representations may be constructed by the rules and lexicon of a grammar. We have distinguished distributive, collective, unspecific, cumulative, subcumulative, weak, and strong group quantifications, and it is clear that any theory of quantification in natural language must be able to represent and generate these distinctions. However, a treatment of quantification that generates the corresponding representations is in great danger of what might be called a *quantification ambiguity explosion*. By this I mean that the incorporation in the grammar of the lexical distinctions and semantic rules necessary to enable the generation of the various representations has the effect that virtually every sentence is assigned a multitude of readings that differ in some quantification aspect.

In a discussion of syntactic and semantic aspects of ambiguity, Partee (1975) considers the number of readings of the sentence

(8.80) Three Frenchmen visit five Russians

and, designating 'Three Frenchmen' by NP_1 and 'five Russians' by NP_2, distinguishes the following eight readings.

(8.81) 1. A group of three F's visits a group of five R's. Both NPs have group distribution; the reading where NP_1 has wide scope and the one where NP_2 has wide scope are logically equivalent.
2. A group of three F's visits five R's. NP_1 has group distribution, NP_2 has individual distribution. NP_1 has wide scope.
3. As (2), but NP_2 has wide scope.
4. Three F's visit a group of five R's. NP_1 has individual distribution, NP_2 has group distribution. NP_1 has wide scope.
5. As (4), but NP_2 has wide scope.
6. Three F's visit five R's. Both NPs have individual distribution, NP_1 has wide scope.
7. As (6), but NP_2 has wide scope.
8. A total of three F's paid visits to a total of five R's. Cumulative reading: both NPs have individual distribution, three and five are the respective total source involvements. NP_1 and NP_2 have equally wide scope.

Quantification and mass nouns 153

These readings are summarized in table (8.82), where the number of scope-differentiated readings is given for each combination of the distributions of the two quantifications, and where the noun phrase with wide scope is indicated. The numbers in (8.82) are based on a distinction of only two

(8.82)

NP₁ \ NP₂	Individual	Group
Individual	3 NP₁ NP₂	2 NP₁ NP₂
Group	2 NP₁ NP₂	1 NP₁ or NP₂

types of distribution, individual and group. If we add the unspecific distribution, the distinction between weak and strong group readings and the subcumulative reading, this table will grow and the figures it contains increase as in table (8.83). We see that the number of readings increases

(8.83)

NP₁ \ NP₂	Individual	Group	Unspecific
Individual	4	4	2
Group	4	4	4
Unspecific	2	4	2

from eight to 30. Are we to conclude that sentence (8.80) is 30 ways ambiguous, as far as quantification is concerned? The analysis of the following sentence, which is formally identical to (8.80), may help us to answer this question.

(8.84) Two boys carried two pianos inside

Like visiting, carrying may be done individually or collectively, and objects may be carried individually or collectively. Formally, (8.84) therefore has, for example, the reading where each of the boys carried a collection of two pianos. But in view of what we know about piano transportation, this reading does not deserve serious consideration, and there is, in fact, only one reading that really does: the one where two boys together carried each of two pianos.

This suggests that, just as with other kinds of ambiguity, bringing in referential semantic information is the natural way to eliminate ambiguities that arise on formal grounds. We have seen in the previous chapter that bringing in referential considerations is, in principle, alien to semantic analysis of natural language in the model-theoretic paradigm, but that it can be given a proper place in two-level model-theoretic semantics. The suggestion naturally arises that within the latter framework a grammar should generate the EL_f representations of all the formally possible readings, and the EL_f–EL_r translation should act as a filter with the effect that only those interpretations which are referentially acceptable in a given domain of discourse reach the EL_r level.

It would be more attractive, however, to let referential considerations play a more *constructive* role than merely that of excluding certain formally admissible interpretations. For consider, once again, the example

(8.71) Five boats were lifted

To be able to generate representations of the various types of quantification distinguished above, the grammar needs to provide the following four representations of 'five' as a determiner:

(8.85) a. $(\lambda X: (\lambda P: \exists_5 x \in X: P(x)))$
b. $(\lambda X: (\lambda P: \exists x \in \mathcal{P}_5(X): P(x)))$
c. $(\lambda X: (\lambda P: \#(\cup(\{x \in \mathcal{P}_5(X) | P(x)\})) = 5))$
d. $(\lambda X: (\lambda P: \#(\cup^*(X, \{x \in X^* | P(x)\})) = 5))$

These are the representations of the distributive reading (cf. (8.59)), the weak group reading (cf. (8.65)), the strong group reading (cf. (8.64)) and the unspecific reading (cf. (8.74)), respectively. The presence of these representations in the lexicon will have the effect that sentence (8.71) is four-ways ambiguous at the formal level of analysis. This strikes me as unfortunate, for its seems to me that this sentence is in fact not ambiguous at all, not even at the formal level. The sentence just says that a total number of five boats were lifted in whatever way, leaving open whether this happens individually, groupwise, or still otherwise. But if this is correct then a formal semantic representation should also say just that and thus *leave the distribution of the quantification open*. Referential semantic information should then be used in a constructive way to specify the distribution.

We have seen in the previous chapter that referential considerations can be brought in in two-level model-theoretic semantics by the technique of using ambiguous constants at the formal level, which are disambiguated in the translation to the referential level. This technique can also be employed to construct representations where the distribution of a quantification is left open.

To see how this can be achieved, consider first the four readings of the sentence (8.71) 'Five boats were lifted' that correspond to the four readings of 'five', given in (8.85):

(8.86) a. $\exists_5 x \in \text{BOATS}: \text{LIFTED}(x)$
b. $\exists x \in \mathcal{P}_5(\text{BOATS}): \text{LIFTED}(x)$
c. $\#(\cup(\{x \in \mathcal{P}_5(\text{BOATS}) | \text{LIFTED}(x)\})) = 5$
d. $\#(\cup^*(\text{BOATS}, \{x \in \text{BOATS}^* | \text{LIFTED}(x)\})) = 5$

The source involvement of the quantification, which is expressed in different ways in these representations, can be expressed uniformly in all cases by using the $\cup^*$ operator. This is shown in the following representations, which are equivalent to those in (8.86):

(8.87) a. $\#(\cup^*(\text{BOATS}, \{x \in \text{BOATS} | \text{LIFTED}(x)\})) = 5$
b. $\#(\cup^*(\text{BOATS}, \{x \in \mathcal{P}_5(\text{BOATS}) | \text{LIFTED}(x)\})) \geq 5$
c. $\#(\cup^*(\text{BOATS}, \{x \in \mathcal{P}_5(\text{BOATS}) | \text{LIFTED}(x)\})) = 5$
d. $\#(\cup^*(\text{BOATS}, \{x \in \text{BOATS}^* | \text{LIFTED}(x)\})) = 5$

Note that the representations (8.87b) and (8.87c) bring out clearly that the difference between weak and strong group readings comes down to whether a determiner like 'five' is interpreted as 'at least five' or as 'exactly five'.

The representations (8.87) can be viewed as the result of applying λ-conversion to expressions of the form:

(8.88) $(\lambda z: N(\cup^*(S, z)))(\{x \in D | P(x)\})$

where S represents the source of the quantification (in this case the set BOATS) and N the numeral 'five', interpreted either as 'at least five' or as 'exactly five', and represented as (8.89a) or (8.89b):

(8.89) a. $(\lambda y: \#(y) \geq 5)$
b. $(\lambda y: \#(y) = 5)$

The source involvement of the various quantification types in (8.87) is thus represented uniformly by a subexpression of the form

(8.90) $(\lambda z: N(\cup^*(S, z)))$

The representations (8.87) all contain a subexpression of the form $\{x \in D | \text{LIFTED}(x)\}$, where D represents the quantification domain. These subexpressions contain the source representation S in a way dependent on the distribution of the quantification. Earlier in this chapter we have distinguished the following cases:

(8.91) a. individual distribution: $D = S$
b. collective distribution: $D = \{S\}$
c. (k-)group distribution: $D = \mathcal{P}_k(S)$
d. unspecific distribution: $D = S \cup \mathcal{P}_{plur}(S) = S^*$

We can clearly regard the various forms that the expression D may take as the result of applying λ-conversion to expressions of the form

(8.92) $\delta(S)$

where δ is one of the following expressions:

(8.93) a. $\delta = (\lambda X: X)$
b. $\delta = (\lambda X: \{X\})$
c. $\delta = (\lambda X: \mathcal{P}_k(X))$
d. $\delta = (\lambda X: X \cup \mathcal{P}_{plur}(X))$

In all cases δ denotes a function which, applied to a quantification source, gives us the quantification domain, so we can view δ as a representation of the distribution of the quantification. I therefore call the function denoted by δ the *distribution function*.

A technical detail is that (8.93c) does not constitute a proper handling of the group size (k). Formally, we have to make δ a function of two arguments, one of which is the group size. Moreover, the group size is not always just a number, like five, but may be a more complex numerical constraint as in the sentence 'Between ten and 20 men conspired'. This means that, instead of (8.93a)–(8.93d) we get the following EL_r instances of the distribution function:

(8.93) e. $\delta = (\lambda k, X: X)$
f. $\delta = (\lambda k, X: \{X\})$
g. $\delta = (\lambda k, X: \{z \in \mathcal{P}(X) | k(z)\})$
h. $\delta = (\lambda k, X: X \cup \mathcal{P}_{plur}(X))$

Inserting $D = \delta(K, S)$ into (8.88), where K represents a numerical constraint, we obtain the following general form of the EL_f representation of a quantification:

(8.94) $(\lambda z: N(\cup^*(S, z)))(\{x \in \delta(K, S) | P(x)\})$

For the example, 'Five boats were lifted', we thus get the following representation, if 'five' is interpreted as 'exactly five':

(8.95a) $(\lambda z: (\lambda y: \#(y) = 5)(\cup^*(BOATS, z)))$
  $(\{x \in \delta((\lambda y: \#(y) = 5), BOATS)|LIFTED(x)\})$

or, using the notation

(8.96) FIVE $=_D (\lambda y: \#(y) = 5)$

introduced in section 6.8, and performing λ-conversion:

(8.95b) FIVE$(\cup^*(BOATS, \{x \in \delta(FIVE, BOATS)|LIFTED(x)\}))$

This representation can be generated by the rules and lexicon of a grammar as follows. The number 'five' is represented in the lexicon as an item of syntactic category *number* with EL_f representation '5'. To this item, a rule applies constructing a syntactic structure of category *numeral* with EL_f representation $(\lambda y: \#(y) = 5)$, which we also wrote as FIVE. To this structure a rule applies that constructs a syntactic structure of category *determiner* with EL_f representation

(8.97) $(\lambda X: (\lambda P: FIVE(\cup^*(X, \{x \in \delta(FIVE, X)|P(x)\}))))$

A rule constructing a syntactic structure of category *noun phrase* from a *determiner* and a *nominal* (in the simplest case: a noun) applies to 'five' and 'boats', combining their representations by applying (8.97) as a function to the noun representation BOATS. After λ-conversion, this results in:

(8.98) $(\lambda P: FIVE(\cup^*(BOATS, \{x \in \delta(FIVE, BOATS)|P(x)\})))$

A rule constructing a *sentence* from a *noun phrase* and a *verb* applies to 'five boats' and 'were lifted', combining their EL_f representations by applying (8.98) as a function to the verb representation LIFTED. After λ-conversion, this results in (8.95b).

The most important point about this representation is that the distribution aspect of the quantification has an explicit representation, localized in the distribution function δ. Now the EL_f–EL_r translation techniques described in the previous chapter can be used to make the number of quantificationally different readings of the sentence that we want to distinguish depend on referential considerations. Suppose the sentence 'Five boats were lifted' is interpreted relative to a domain of discourse in which we have such boats and lifting facilities that it is impossible that more than one boat is lifted at a time. Let this be taken into account by the fact that the EL_r predicate $LIFTED_r$ has such a type that it can only apply to individual boats, not to sets of boats. Assuming that the EL_f constant BOATS has the single EL_r translation $BOATS_r$ and that LIFTED has the single translation $(\lambda z: LIFTED_r(z))$, the translation rules will 'attempt' to construct the four EL_r representations of (8.95b) that correspond to the four translations of δ. However, only the translation

(8.99) $FIVE(\cup *(BOATS_r, \{x \in BOATS_r | LIFTED_r(x)\}))$

will indeed be generated, since in all other cases the translations of δ, BOATS, and LIFTED would violate the type constraints of the target language (see section 7.5).

If in addition to or instead of the distributive reading we want to generate another reading of the sentence at the referential level, then we extend or modify the translation function for LIFTED accordingly. For instance, we can obtain the reading with unspecific distribution by adding the following translation of LIFTED, built up with the help of the 'function union' construction defined in sections 6.5 and 6.6:

(8.100) $T_{fr}(LIFTED) \ni$ <u>function union</u>$(1: LIFTED_r, 2: COLLIFTED_r)$

where $COLLIFTED_r$ is an EL_r predicate applicable to sets of boats. The function at the right-hand side of (8.100) can be applied to individual boats as well as to sets of boats.

We have thus developed a method of analysis which avoids the generation of a multitude of readings at the EL_f level, independent of referential considerations; instead, different readings are generated from a single EL_f representation only insofar as they are relevant from a referential point of view.

To illustrate the method, let us consider one more example, the treatment of the quantificational ambiguity in the sentence

(8.101)   These books are heavy

'These' is a central determiner with a deictic function in determining the quantification source, which I will designate by $BOOKS_d$, and with a function as indicator of the source involvement, which is complete (each element of the source is involved, at least in this example). The noun phrase 'These books' therefore has the EL_f representation

(8.102) $(\lambda P: \cup *(BOOKS_d, \{x \in \delta(\lambda y: y = BOOKS_d, BOOKS_d) | P(x)\})$
          $= BOOKS_d)$

The EL_f representation of the sentence is then, after λ-conversion,

Quantification and mass nouns 159

(8.103) $\cup^*(\text{BOOKS}_d, \{x \in \delta(\lambda y: y = \text{BOOKS}_d, \text{BOOKS}_d) | \text{HEAVY}(x)\})$
$= \text{BOOKS}_d$

To translate this into EL_r, suppose that there is an EL_r predicate DHEAVY_r, applicable to individual books, and a predicate CHEAVY_r applicable to sets of books. We assign to the EL_f constant HEAVY the translations:

(8.104) $T_{fr}(\text{HEAVY}) = \{\text{DHEAVY}_r, \text{CHEAVY}_r\}$

If BOOKS_{dr} designates the EL_r translation of BOOKS_d, the four possibilities of the quantification domain denoted in EL_f by $\delta(\lambda y: y = \text{BOOKS}_d, \text{BOOKS}_d)$ are, according to (8.93):

(8.105) a. $(\lambda X: X)(\text{BOOKS}_{dr}) = \text{BOOKS}_{dr}$
b. $(\lambda X: \{X\})(\text{BOOKS}_{dr}) = \{\text{BOOKS}_{dr}\}$
c. $(\lambda X)(\{x \in \mathscr{P}(X) | (\lambda y: y = \text{BOOKS}_{dr})(x)\})(\text{BOOKS}_{dr})$
$= \{x \in \mathscr{P}(\text{BOOKS}_{dr}) | x = \text{BOOKS}_{dr}\}$
$= \{\text{BOOKS}_{dr}\}$
d. $(\lambda X: X \cup \mathscr{P}_{plur}(X))(\text{BOOKS}_{dr})$
$= \text{BOOKS}_{dr} \cup \mathscr{P}_{plur}(\text{BOOKS}_{dr})$
$= \text{BOOKS}_{dr}{}^*$

Note that in this case the third possible translation of δ is equivalent to the second, so that there are only three different choices possible for the quantification domain. The three distinct translations of the distribution function plus the two translations of HEAVY give rise to six possible combinations, two of which do not violate the type restrictions of the translation. These are the combination of (8.105a) with DHEAVY_r and that of (8.105b) with CHEAVY_r. The resulting two EL_r representations of the sentence are, for the distributive reading,

(8.106a) $\cup^*(\text{BOOKS}_{dr}, \{x \in \text{BOOKS}_{dr} | \text{DHEAVY}(x)\}) = \text{BOOKS}_{dr}$

which is readily seen to be equivalent to the more familiar form

(8.106b) $\forall x \in \text{BOOKS}_{dr}: \text{DHEAVY}(x)$

and, for the collective reading,

(8.107a) $\cup^*(\text{BOOKS}_{dr}, \{x \in \{\text{BOOKS}_{dr}\} | \text{CHEAVY}(x)\}) = \text{BOOKS}_{dr}$

which, by the fact that BOOKS_{dr} is the only possible value of x here, is equivalent to

(8.107b) $\text{CHEAVY}(\text{BOOKS}_{dr})$

For constructing representations of sentences with two or more noun phrases we can use the technique, described in the previous section, of combining the representations of the separate NPs into a 'noun phrase sequence' representation, which is subsequently combined with the verb representation (see 8.68). The systematic generation of semantic representations of English sentences with one or more quantifications is described in detail in the formal grammar for a fragment of English presented in section 8.8, and is illustrated below for a variety of sentences with quantified mass nouns and count nouns.

The main points of the approach to quantification outlined so far are summarized below.

1. Three fundamental aspects of every quantification are distinguished:

   a. The *quantification source*. This is usually determined by noun phrase heads and central determiners.
   b. The *quantification domain*. This is sometimes determined by a predeterminer, like 'each', or an adverb, but is often not specified. The relation between the source and domain of a quantification is called its *distribution*.
   c. The absolute or relative quantity of objects involved, the *source involvement*. This is often expressed by a predeterminer, like 'five' or 'all'.

2. These three aspects are accounted for in a uniform way in the EL_f representation of a quantified noun phrase, which has the general form

   (8.108) $(\lambda P: (\lambda z: N(\cup *(S, z)))(\{x \in \delta(K, S) | P(x)\}))$

   In this representation we can identify the following parts:

   a. S represents the quantification source;
   b. $\delta(K, S)$ represents the quantification domain, where the function denoted by δ, the *distribution function*, represents the distribution of the quantification, and K represents a group size (if any);
   c. $(\lambda z: N(\cup *(S, z)))$ represents the source involvement.

3. Those and only those quantificational readings of a sentence that make sense in a given domain of discourse are generated in the translation to the referential level of representation by the constrained translation of the distribution function δ.

This treatment of quantification is clearly limited in various respects. Limitations are, besides the restriction to non-intensional contexts, the neglect of source size presuppositions, of deictic aspects of central determiners, of tense and temporal adverbia (see de Mey, 1981); of negation, and of topic–focus phenomena influencing source involvement (see Szabolcsi, 1983). I wish to emphasize once again that it was not my aim to develop a full-fledged theory of quantification here, but rather to outline a treatment of count noun quantification which is sufficiently rich and interesting to substantiate the claim that ensemble theory can be used to generalize, in principle, any set-based treatment of count noun quantification to an ensemble-based one that includes mass nouns.

8.6 Mass noun quantification

I now turn to the quantification aspects of mass noun phrases. For count noun quantification we have distinguished the following distributions: (a) individual, (b) collective, (c) group, and (d) unspecific. Does this distinction apply to mass nouns as well? Let us consider the following pair of sentences, where a count noun and a mass noun occupy the same position:

(8.109) a. All the concrete blocks were dragged to the backyard
         b. All the concrete was dragged to the backyard

The first of these sentences has a reading in which the concrete blocks were dragged one by one (individual distribution); a reading in which the blocks were dragged all in one go (collective distribution); and a reading in which all the blocks are said to have been dragged to the backyard without specifying how many blocks were dragged at a time (unspecific distribution). Sentence (8.109b), on the other hand, does not have a 'one-by-one' reading for 'all the concrete', for the obvious reason that the mass noun gives no indication as to what 'one concrete' would be. One suspects that it is for the same reason that sentences like

(8.110) c. *Every concrete was dragged to the backyard
         d. *Each (of the) concrete was dragged to the backyard

are deviant. Yet, for mass nouns there is something similar to the individual/non-individual distinction we have seen for count noun quantification. The following sentences illustrate this:

(8.111) This sand is heavy
(8.112) This soup is warm

The first of these sentences, on the reading that comes to mind first, states that a certain quantity of sand, referred to as 'this sand', is heavy as a whole. By contrast, the second sentence in its most plausible reading makes an assertion not about 'this soup' as a whole but about the portions one can take from the soup.

As in the count noun case, I speak of *collective* quantification of a mass noun if something is predicated of the noun extension as a whole. As in the count noun case, the quantification domain is then the set consisting of the source; the difference is that in the mass noun case the source is a general ensemble (continuous, discrete, or mixed) rather than a discrete one.

A reading which is not collective is found in sentence (8.112) and, perhaps even more clearly, in sentences like

(8.113) a. Some of the sand is warm
         b. All the sand is warm

where some or all of the samples of the sand under consideration are said to be warm. In this case the domain of the predicate 'is warm' is the set of samples of the sand. This is the mass noun analogue of individual distribution for count nouns; for reasons which will become clear in a moment I shall call this distribution *homogeneous* rather than individual. A quantification with homogeneous distribution over a source M thus has the quantification domain $\mathscr{P}(M)$.

The reason for speaking of 'homogeneous' rather than 'individual' distribution is that there is a second form of distribution for quantified mass nouns which is *also* analogous in some respects to individual distribution for count nouns. The following sentences illustrate this:

(8.114) a. All this sugar is cubic
         b. All this furniture is heavy

Sentence (8.114a) is, for example, used in the description of a box containing cubic lumps of sugar. Then the domain of the predicate 'is cubic' is clearly not the set of *all* samples of sugar in the box, but a contextually determined subset only: the lumps. Some mass nouns can be combined with a predicate applying to the elements of a subset of the parts of its extension without requiring a particular context to determine the subset. Examples are mass nouns like 'furniture', 'jewellery', and 'poetry', for which the extension usually comes in discrete parts: furniture in articles of furniture, jewellery in jewels, poetry in poems. This phenomenon will be considered in more detail in the next chapter; at this point I merely wish to draw attention to

Quantification and mass nouns 163

the fact that there are cases of mass noun quantification where the domain is a certain subset of the power set of the noun denotation. I call this type of distribution *discrete*.

Group quantification occurs for mass nouns as well as for count nouns, with applied amount terms as indicators of group size. An example is one of the readings of:

(8.115) These machines fill bottles with 5 oz of perfume

In this reading one considers a relation between, say, individual machines, individual bottles, and samples of perfume weighing 5 oz. The quantification domain is thus the set

(8.116) $\{x \in \mathcal{P}(M) | \text{Wght}(x) = 5-\text{oz}\}$

As with a count noun, the group quantification with a mass noun can have local or global source involvement, corresponding to weak and strong group readings. The above example illustrates, in fact, the phenomenon of weak group readings for mass nouns; an example of a strong group reading is found in the sentence

(8.117) 500 tons of steel sank to the bottom

For count nouns we have distinguished two non-collective readings of sentences like:

(8.118) The crane lifted the pipes

On one reading, the crane lifted each of the tubes one-by-one (individual distribution), on the other reading, the crane lifted the pipes in quantities of one, two, or more (unspecific distribution). In both cases all of the source denoted by 'the pipes' is involved. Do we find the same distinctions for mass nouns?

Consider the following example:

(8.119) The crane lifted 500 tons of sand

Since 'sand' does not individuate its reference, this sentence has no 'one-by-one' reading (individual distribution). Besides collective and group readings, the sentence only has a reading that parallels the unspecific reading of (8.118), on which the crane is said to have lifted whatever quantities of sand with a total weight of 500 tons. The quantification domain of the direct object NP is thus $\mathcal{P}(\text{SAND})$, the set of all sand quantities.

Now we have already come across a type of mass noun quantification where the domain is the set of parts of the source: one with homogeneous distribution. Does this mean that individual and unspecific quantification coincide for mass nouns? I think this is indeed the case, but with one exception: there is a difference between quantifications with homogeneous and unspecific distribution if they are combined with complete involvement of the source. This difference is brought out by the following sentences:

(8.120a) All the sand is warm

(8.121a) All the sand was lifted

The first sentence has a reading on which every sample of the sand in question is warm; this is the reading that we called homogeneous. It can be represented by:

(8.120b) $\forall x \in \mathcal{P}(\text{SAND}): \text{WARM}(x)$

or, equivalently, by:

(8.120c) $\forall x \subseteq \text{SAND}: \text{WARM}(x)$

The second sentence, on the other hand, has a preferred reading with unspecific distribution, saying that samples of sand were lifted together making up all of the sand in question. This may be expressed by:

(8.121b) $\cup(\{x \in \mathcal{P}(\text{SAND}) | \text{LIFTED}(x)\}) = \text{SAND}$

According to theorem (5.26) of ensemble theory, the left-hand side of this equation denotes the ensemble formed by those parts of SAND that the predicate LIFTED is true of; thus, (8.121b) is equivalent to:

(8.121c) $[x \subseteq \text{SAND} | \text{LIFTED}(x)] = \text{SAND}$

Two ensembles are equal only if they have the same parts, therefore,

(8.121d) $\forall s: s \subseteq \text{SAND} \leftrightarrow s \subseteq [x \subseteq \text{SAND} | \text{LIFTED}(x)]$

However, as we have seen in chapter 5, this does not necessarily mean that

(8.121e) $*\forall s: s \subseteq \text{SAND} \rightarrow \text{LIFTED}(s)$

(See the discussion of formula (5.12).) Whether (8.121e) follows from (8.121d) depends on the specific properties of the predicate LIFTED. Consequently, (8.121c) does *not* imply that every sample of the sand was lifted, this in contrast with (8.120c).

Another way of bringing out the difference between the preferred readings of the sentences (8.120a) and (8.121a) is to note that (8.120c) and (8.121c) are equivalent to the following formulas (8.120d) and (8.121f), respectively:

(8.120d) $\{x \subseteq \text{SAND}|\text{WARM}(x)\} = \mathscr{P}(\text{SAND})$

(8.121f) $\cup(\{x \subseteq \text{SAND}|\text{LIFTED}(x)\}) = \cup(\mathscr{P}(\text{SAND}))$

Clearly, (8.120d) is a stronger statement than (8.121f), since two sets can have identical unions without being identical themselves.

Note that the predeterminer 'all' in the two sentences under consideration expresses complete involvement of the source in two different ways: in the first sentence it expresses that the entire source ensemble is involved in the sense that the predicate is true of every part of it, whereas in the second it expresses complete involvement in the sense that those parts of which the predicate is true together make up the whole source. This phenomenon is a complication for mass noun quantification that does not arise in connection with count nouns.

In a recent study of mass term quantification, Roeper (1983) has also pointed out the need to distinguish a form of universal quantification where it is not the case that a predicate is true of every part of the quantification source.[12]

Cumulative and subcumulative quantification occur with mass nouns in the same way as with count nouns, except that applied amount terms play the role of numerical quantifiers.

8.7 The representation of mass noun quantification

In this section I consider the semantic representation of sentences with quantified mass nouns, using the ensemble-theoretical constructions of EL_f and EL_r that distinguish Ensemble Languages from traditional set-based representation languages, and I show how these representations can be generated in the two-level model-theoretic framework by means of the grammar described in section 8.8, in combination with the translation method described above.

The grammar is organized according to the general principles of Universal Grammar (Montague, 1970b). It defines a class of ordered trees (syntactic trees), of which the sequences of terminal symbols are expressions of English. For each syntactic tree the grammar defines an EL_f expression, with the formal semantic representation of the English sentence at the leaves. The syntactic trees have unlabelled branches, terminal nodes labelled by English words, and non-terminal nodes labelled by the name of a syntactic category and, optionally, a list of syntactic attributes with their values.

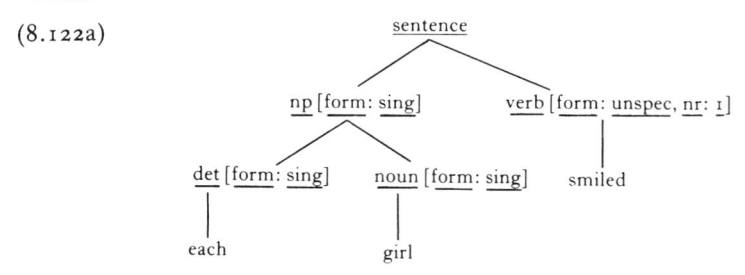

(8.122a)

```
                    sentence
                   /        \
         np [form: sing]    verb [form: unspec, nr: 1]
         /            \              |
  det [form: sing]  noun [form: sing]  smiled
        |              |
      each            girl
```

As an example of a syntactic tree, consider (8.122a). This tree has the sentence 'Each girl smiled' at its leaves. In what follows I shall mostly omit the names of syntactic attributes in the syntactic trees, and indicate only their values. It will be convenient to also have a linear notation for syntactic trees; for this purpose I shall use parentheses instead of branches. For instance, the tree (8.122a) is written in linear form as:

(8.122b) sentence(np(det(each)[sing],
  noun(girl)[sing])[sing],
  verb(smiled)[unspec, 1])

The grammar consists of a lexicon and a set of rules. Lexical entries consist of the syntactic tree of an English word, which is a single branch plus node, and its semantic representation (an EL_f expression). A word which is ambiguous on syntactic or formal semantic grounds has more than one lexical entry.

The grammar rules operate on pairs of syntactic trees and semantic representations. Each rule has a syntactic part and a semantic part. The syntactic part specifies how a syntactic tree is constructed from the syntactic trees of the operands. The semantic part is a compositional rule specifying how a semantic representation is constructed from the semantic representations of the operands. For further details see section 8.8 below.

A point that deserves special consideration is the treatment of central determiners. As central determiners, I consider those determiners that occur in central position in a full-fledged basic noun phrase, and that have the semantic function of determining, together with an NP head, the quantification source of the NP. Examples are definite articles, possessives, and demonstratives. In the fragment of English covered by the grammar of section 8.8 I have included as central determiners the definite article 'the' and the demonstratives 'this' and 'these'. They are treated as indicating that the quantification source of an NP is that part of the head noun extension formed by the items contextually determined as relevant to consider. For example, if the head is the count noun 'books', the effect of 'these' is that the set of the contextually relevant books is chosen as quantification source, rather than the set of all books. Similarly, if the head is the mass noun 'sand', then 'the sand' refers to the quantification source formed by the contextually relevant samples of sand.

It would be outside the scope of the present discussion to deal with the problems of contextual determination of particular members or parts of noun denotations. I have therefore adopted an *ad hoc* method of indicating the function of 'the', 'this', and 'these', when combined with a mass noun or plural count noun. It consists of assuming in EL_f a predicate 'contextually relevant'; given a source set S, the set of those elements of S that this predicate is true of is designated by S_o; similarly, for an ensemble E the subensemble made up by those parts for which the predicate is true is designated by E_o.

The role of referential considerations in the analysis of mass noun quantification can be the same as for count noun quantification, as discussed in section 8.5. Again, we can avoid an explosion of quantificational ambiguities at the formal level of analysis by using a distribution function which is interpreted and disambiguated in the EL_f–EL_r translation. The distribution function for mass nouns is not exactly the same as for count nouns, however, since according to the distinctions made in the previous section the quantification domain D for a mass noun is related to the quantification source S in one of the following ways:

(8.123)   a. homogeneous/unspecific distribution: $D = \mathcal{P}(S)$
           b. collective distribution: $D = \{S\}$
           c. K-group distribution: $D = \{x \in \mathcal{P}(S) | K(x)\}$

(cf. (8.91) for count nouns). I therefore add a separate distribution function for mass nouns in EL_f, designated by the constant δ_m. As in the count noun case, the distribution function operates on pairs consisting of a function representing any group size constraints and the source. The possible EL_r translations of δ_m are thus given by

(8.124) $T_{fr}(\delta_m) = \{(\lambda K, X: \mathcal{P}(X)), (\lambda K, X: \{X\}),$
               $(\lambda K, X: \{z \in \mathcal{P}(X) | K(z)\})\}$

I now turn to the semantic representation of the various types of mass noun quantification using ensemble-theoretical concepts and the derivation of these representations in the two-level model-theoretic framework. The derivation will be described as a two-stage process: the first stage consists of applying the grammar rules of section 8 below, which translate English expressions into EL_f, and the second of translating EL_f expressions into EL_f as described in section 7.5.

A. *Homogeneous quantification*

To illustrate the treatment of homogeneous quantification of a mass NP, we begin by considering the sentence

(8.125)   Five tons of snow melted

This is a mass noun analogue of the sentence 'five boats were lifted', which was analysed in detail in section 8.5. 'Five' and 'tons' have the lexical syntactic/semantic descriptions (8.126) and (8.127), respectively:

(8.126)   a. number(five)[plur]
          b. 5
(8.127)   a. unit(tons)[plur]
          b. (Wght, t.)

Rule B2 of the grammar presented in section 8.8 combines the syntactic parts of these descriptions and includes the particle 'of'. This leads to the syntactic tree

(8.128a) amount(number(five)[plur],
                 unit(tons)[plur], part(of))
          [mass]

The semantic part of the rule constructs the EL_f representation of the applied amount term (in the reading 'exactly five tons of'):

(8.128b) $(\lambda u: Wght(u) = 5\text{-t.})$

Rule D2b of the grammar assigns the status of a determiner to the amount term, constructing the syntactic tree (8.129a) with EL_f representation (8.129b):

(8.129)   a. det(amount(number(five)[plur],
                        unit(tons)[plur], part(of))
                 [mass])
             [mass]

Quantification and mass nouns 169

b. (λX: (λP: (λu: Wght(u) = 5-t.)
 ([x ∈ δ_m((λu: Wght(u) = 5-t.), X)|P(x)])))

Rule F3a combines the determiner and the noun, forming the syntactic tree (8.130a) with EL_f representation (8.130b):

(8.130) a. np(det(amount(number(five)[plur],
                              unit(tons)[plur], part(of))
                    [mass]),
              noun(snow)[mass])
              [mass]
 b. (λP: (λu: Wght(u) = 5-t.)
  ([x ∈ δ_m((λy: Wght(y) = 5-t.), SNOW)|P(x)]))

Rule J1 turns the NP into an NP sequence, which is, of course, a trivial operation for a single noun phrase, that is nonetheless included in the grammar in order to streamline the sentence formation rules. The resulting NP sequence has the syntactic tree

(8.131a) nps(np(det(amount(number(five)[plur],
                                unit(tons)[plur], part(of))
                      [mass]),
                noun(snow)[mass])
                [mass])[mass, 1]

with an EL_f representation of the form:

(8.131b) (λR: np'(λz: R(z)))

where np' stands for the noun phrase representation (8.130b). Finally, rule K1 combines the NP sequence and the verb, thereby deleting the intermediate nps node, leading to the syntactic tree (8.132a) with EL_f representation (8.132b).

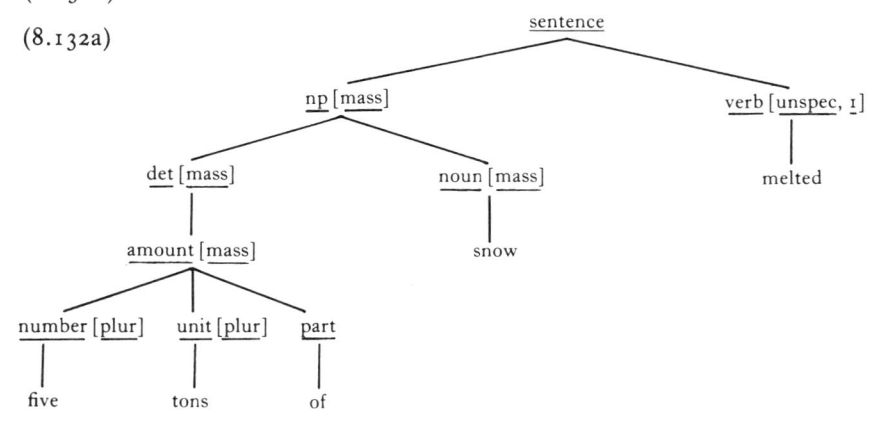

(8.132a)
```
                          sentence
                         /        \
                    np [mass]    verb [unspec, 1]
                   /         \         |
             det [mass]   noun [mass]  melted
                 |             |
           amount [mass]      snow
          /     |      \
   number [plur] unit [plur] part
       |          |         |
      five       tons        of
```

(8.132b)   Wght([x ∈ δ_m((λy: Wght(y) = 5-t.), SNOW)|MELT(x)]) = 5-t.

Assuming that SNOW and MELT have only one interpretation in the domain of discourse, the EL_f–EL_r translation generates the three representations corresponding to the possible instances of the distribution function. The homogeneous interpretation (in this case coinciding with the unspecific one), is the one where the quantification domain is $\mathcal{P}$(SNOW), namely:

(8.133a)   Wght([x ∈ $\mathcal{P}$(SNOW_r)|MELT_r(x)]) = 5-t.

which is, of course, equivalent to

(8.133b)   Wght([x ⊆ SNOW_r|MELT_r(x)]) = 5-t.

As a second example we consider the treatment of the sentence

(8.134a)   All the snow melted

which can be considered as a mass noun analogue of the sentence

(8.135a)   All the snowballs melted

On the distributive reading, the latter sentence has at the referential level the semantic representation

(8.135b)   ∀x ∈ SNOWBALLS_{ro}: MELT(x)

(or rather, a representation equivalent to (8.135b), that can be cast in this form by simplification operations). As mentioned in the previous chapter, the use of ensemble theory is particularly attractive if it is such that, in the semantic analysis of mass noun quantification, ensembles and the part–whole relation play the same role that sets and the member–whole relation play in the analysis of count noun quantification. We thus want the final (EL_r) representation of the homogeneous reading of 'All the snow melted' to be the ensemble analogue of (8.135b), namely

(8.134b)   ∀x ⊆ SNOW_{ro}: MELT(x)

I will now show that this is exactly what the grammar, in combination with the EL_f–EL_r translation, produces.

The noun 'snow' is in the lexicon with the syntactic tree:

(8.136)   noun(snow)[mass]

and with the EL_f ensemble constant SNOW as semantic representation. I

Quantification and mass nouns 171

have already commented on the semantic treatment of 'the' in the grammar. 'The' is in the lexicon with the syntactic tree

(8.137) centraldet(the)[unspec]

and with the EL_f predicate constant CR_o (for 'relevant in context C_o') as semantic representation. The syntactic part of grammar rule E2 combines the syntactic trees (8.136) and (8.137) to form the syntactic tree of a constituent called an 'npcentre', with the result:

(8.138a) npcentre(centraldet(the)[unspec],
                     noun(snow)[mass])[mass]

The semantic part of the rule builds an EL_f expression from the constants SNOW and CR_o, namely:

(8.138b) $[x \subseteq SNOW | CR_o(x)]$

which was announced as being abbreviated as $SNOW_o$. We have seen in the previous section that the predeterminer 'all' in combination with a mass noun can express complete involvement of the source in two ways. It, therefore, has two lexical entries, both with the syntactic tree

(8.139a) predet(all)[mass]

The entries differ in their EL_f representation; for the homogeneous reading of 'all the snow' we need the one with representation

(8.139b) $(\lambda X: (\lambda P: (\lambda z: z = \mathcal{P}(X))(\{x \in \mathcal{P}(X) | P(x)\})))$

Grammar rule F2 combines the syntactic trees (8.138a) and (8.139a) to form:

(8.140a) np(predet(all)[mass],
              npcentre(centraldet(the)[unspec],
                       noun(snow)[mass]))
           [mass]

and combines the corresponding semantic representations to

(8.140b) $(\lambda X: (\lambda P: (\lambda z: z = \mathcal{P}(X))(\{x \in \mathcal{P}(X) | P(x)\})))(SNOW_o)$

or, after simplification by λ-conversion:

(8.140c) $(\lambda P: \{x \in \mathcal{P}(SNOW_o) | P(x)\} = \mathcal{P}(SNOW_o))$

172 Part 1 Model-theoretic semantics of mass terms

This completes the treatment of the NP. The verb form 'melted' is represented in the lexicon by the syntactic tree

(8.141) verb(melted)[unspec, 1]

and the semantic representation MELT. From the intermediate NP sequence, constructed by rule J1 as before (see 8.131), and the representation of the verb, grammar rule K1 forms the syntactic tree (8.142a) for the

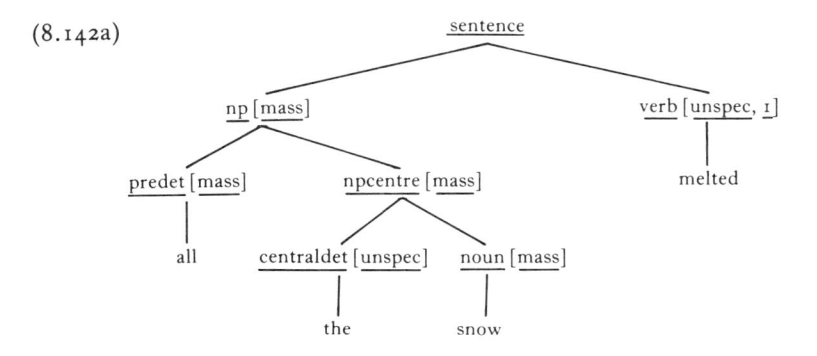

(8.142a)
```
                           sentence
                          /        \
                    np [mass]              verb [unspec, 1]
                   /        \                    |
          predet [mass]   npcentre [mass]      melted
             |            /          \
            all    centraldet [unspec]  noun [mass]
                        |                   |
                       the                 snow
```

sentence. The semantic part of the rule combines the corresponding semantic representations, forming, after λ-conversion, the EL_f expression

(8.142b) $\{x \in \mathcal{P}(SNOW_o) | MELT(x)\} = \mathcal{P}(SNOW_o)$

which is obviously equivalent to

(8.142c) $\forall x \in \mathcal{P}(SNOW_o): MELT(x)$

or also to (8.134b) $\forall x \subseteq SNOW_o: MELT(x)$. This is what we wanted. The EL_f–EL_r translation, which replaces $SNOW_o$ and MELT by $SNOW_{ro}$ and $MELT_r$, is of no particular interest here, as the representation of the quantification aspects is already completely unambiguous at the EL_f level.

B. *Unspecific quantification*

We have seen above that unspecific mass noun quantification differs from homogeneous quantification only in the case of complete source involvement. In the present fragment of English this may occur for the determiner sequences 'the', 'all the', 'all this', and 'all these'. As an example, let us consider the sentence:

(8.143) John carries away the concrete

Quantification and mass nouns 173

Proper names like 'John' have a lexical semantic representation consisting of an EL_f constant, like JOHN. Grammar rule F4 turns the proper name into an NP, generating the syntactic tree

(8.144a) np(propername(John)[sing])[sing]

and the semantic representation

(8.144b) $(\lambda P: P(John))$

The noun phrase 'the concrete' is, as in the above example, construed first as an npcentre with the semantic representation $CONCRETE_o$. Rule F5b subsequently turns this into an NP with complete source involvement and a distribution which is left open, as represented by δ_m. This leads to the syntactic tree

(8.145a) np(npcentre(centraldet(the)[unspec],
      noun(concrete)[mass])[mass])
 [mass]

with EL_f representation

(8.145b) $(\lambda P: [x \in \delta_m((\lambda u: u = CONCRETE_o),$
      $CONCRETE_o)|P(x)] = CONCRETE_o)$

Rule J1 forms an 'NP sequence' from (8.144a) and (8.145a), with the syntactic tree

(8.146a) nps(np(propername(John)[sing])[sing],
    np(npcentre(centraldet(the)[unspec],
      noun(concrete)[mass])[mass])
  [mass]))
 [sing, 2]

and a semantic representation which can be represented schematically as

(8.146b) $(\lambda R: np_1'(\lambda x: np_2'(\lambda y: R(x, y))))$

where np_1' and np_2' stand for the representations of 'John' and 'the concrete', respectively. Substituting (8.144b) for np_1' and (8.145b) for np_2' we obtain, after simplification by λ-conversion:

(8.146c) $(\lambda R: [x \in \delta_m((\lambda u: u = CONCRETE_o),$
      $CONCRETE_o)|R(John, x)] = CONCRETE_o)$

Finally, rule K1 combines the syntactic tree (8.146a) with the one found

174 Part 1 *Model-theoretic semantics of mass terms*

in the lexicon for the two-place verb 'carries away', with the result:

(8.147a) sentence(np(propername(John)[sing])[sing],
        verb(carries away)[sing, 2],
        np(npcentre(centraldet(the)[unspec],
                    noun(concrete)[mass])[mass])
        [mass])

or, in tree form, see (8.147b). The semantic component of the rule applies

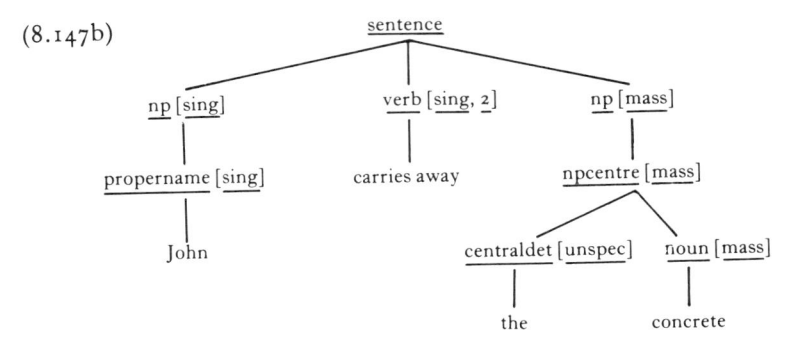

(8.147b)

```
                        sentence
         ┌─────────────────┼─────────────────┐
      np [sing]       verb [sing, 2]      np [mass]
         │                 │                  │
   propername [sing]   carries away      npcentre [mass]
         │                              ┌────┴────┐
       John                    centraldet [unspec]  noun [mass]
                                        │                │
                                       the            concrete
```

the function expression (8.146c) to the lexical EL_f representation of 'carried away', with the result, after λ-conversion:

(8.147c) $[x \in \delta_m((\lambda y: y = CONCRETE_o),$
          $CONCRETE_o)|CARRY(John, x)] = CONCRETE_o$

The unspecific reading is obtained by translating the distribution function δ_m as $(\lambda K, X: \mathcal{P}(X))$, which leads to the EL_r representation:

(8.148a) $[x \in \mathcal{P}(CONCRETE_{ro})|CARRY_r(John, x)] = CONCRETE_{ro}$

or, equivalently,

(8.148b) $[x \subseteq CONCRETE_{ro}|CARRY_r(John, x)] = CONCRETE_{ro}$

This says, concretely, that all the concrete got carried away by John in the 'unspecific' sense that the concrete parts that John carried together make up all the concrete.

C. *Discrete quantification*

We have seen in the previous section that discrete quantification of a mass noun occurs when the quantification domain is a subset of the set of all parts of the source, and when this subset is not explicitly indicated in the NP. (This distinguishes discrete quantification from group quantification.)

Quantification and mass nouns 175

This may happen when a sentence with a quantified mass noun is interpreted with respect to a domain of discourse where the noun refers to a discrete ensemble. For instance, the sentence

(8.149) All the sugar is cubic

has a discrete reading in a domain of discourse in which the word 'sugar' is actually used to refer to sugar lumps. Such considerations, dependent on the choice of discourse domain, are of a referential nature and cannot play a part in formal semantic analysis. From a formal point of view nothing would justify a sentence like (8.149) to be treated differently than, for example, the sentence

(8.150) All the sand is warm

I therefore disregard the phenomenon of discrete quantification at the formal level and consign its handling to the EL_f–EL_r translation. Let us consider, then, how this may be accomplished for the sentence (8.149) interpreted in a domain of discourse where 'sugar' refers to sugar lumps.

We first generate the homogeneous reading of the sentence in the same way as indicated above for the sentence 'All the snow melted', except that here we use for the first time the grammar rule which forms 'verbs' from a copula plus adjective. This rule (rule H) generates the syntactic tree

(8.151) verb(copula(is)[sing, 1], adj(cubic))[nonplur, 1]

and the semantic representation CUBIC. The EL_f representation of the sentence is thus:

(8.152) $\{x \in \mathcal{P}(\text{SUGAR}) | \text{CUBIC}(x)\} = \mathcal{P}(\text{SUGAR})$

(cf. 8.142). The EL_f–EL_r translation replaces SUGAR by an expression that denotes the set of sugar lumps, say SUGAR-LUMPS_r, and translates CUBIC into

(8.153) $(\lambda z: \forall y \in z: \text{CUBIC}_r(y))$

(8.152) is thus translated into the expression (after simplification):

(8.154a) $\{x \in \mathcal{P}(\text{SUGAR-LUMPS}_r) \,|\, \forall y \in x: \text{CUBIC}_r(y)\}$
          $= \mathcal{P}(\text{SUGAR-LUMPS}_r)$

which says that every member of every set of sugar lumps is cubic. This is obviously equivalent to

(8.154b) $\forall x \in \text{SUGAR-LUMPS}_r: \text{CUBIC}_r(x)$

This is clearly a correct representation of the discrete reading of the sentence if 'sugar' is used to refer to sugar lumps.

D. *Collective quantification*

Collective quantification is the case where the quantification domain is the set that has the quantification source as its only element. This characterization applies to collective mass noun quantification as well as to collective count noun quantification. Collectively quantified mass nouns can be treated in the same way as collectively quantified count nouns. For example, the collective reading of 'the sand' in

(8.155)   The sand weighs five tons

is generated by the grammar as follows. 'The sand' is construed first as an npcentre, as before, and subsequently turned into an NP by rule F5b, which constructs the representation

(8.156) $(\lambda P: [x \in \delta_m((\lambda u: u = SAND_o), SAND_o)|P(x)] = SAND_o)$

The isolated amount term 'five tons' is treated by rule A; from the lexical descriptions of 'five' and 'tons' the following syntactic tree is constructed:

(8.157a)   isolamount(number(five)[plur],
                                unit(tons)[plur])

with the semantic representation

(8.157b) $(\lambda Q: Q(5\text{-t.}))$

Rule K2 combines the representations of the NP, the isolated amount term, and the verb, forming the syntactic tree

(8.158a)   sentence(np(npcentre(centraldet(the)[unspec]
                                        noun(sand)[mass])
                            [mass])[mass],
                        measureverb(weighs)[nonplur]
                        isolamount(number(five)[plur],
                                        unit(tons)[plur]))

and an EL_f representation that can be represented schematically as

(8.158b)   np'(λy: isolamount'(λz: measureverb'(y, z)))

Quantification and mass nouns 177

Substituting (8.156), (8.157b) and WEIGH for the primed constituents, we obtain

(8.159) $(\lambda P: [x \in \delta_m((\lambda u: u = SAND_o), SAND_o)|P(x)] = SAND_o)$
$(\lambda y: (\lambda Q: Q(5\text{-t.}))(\lambda z: WEIGH(y, z)))$

Repeated λ-conversion simplifies this expression to

(8.160) $[x \in \delta_m(\lambda u: u = SAND_o, SAND_o)|WEIGH(x, 5\text{-t.})] = SAND_o$

The collective interpretation is obtained by translating the distribution function as $(\lambda K, X: \{X\})$. Translating SAND as $SAND_r$ and WEIGH as $WEIGH_r$, this results, after λ-conversion, in the EL_r representation:

(8.161) $WEIGH_r(SAND_{ro}, 5\text{-t.})$

This example demonstrates in passing the treatment in the grammar of isolated amount terms. Of course, isolated amount terms can also be used in combination with count nouns. Our grammar produces the collective reading of the same sentence with a count noun instead of a mass noun in the same way, constructing for a sentence like:

(8.162) The apples weigh five tons

the semantic representation:

(8.163) $WEIGH_r(APPLES_{ro}, 5\text{-t.})$

E. *Group quantification*

The treatment of group quantification for mass nouns is illustrated with the strong group reading of the sentence

(8.164) Craney lifted five tons of sand

where 'Craney' is supposed to be the proper name of a crane. As a noun phrase, 'Craney' has the representation $(\lambda P: P(Craney))$. 'Five tons of sand' is analysed in the same way as 'Five tons of snow' in sentence (8.125) 'Five tons of snow melted', and thus has the EL_f representation

(8.165) $(\lambda P: (\lambda u: Wght(u) = 5\text{-t.})$
$([x \in \delta_m((\lambda y: Wght(y) = 5\text{-t.}), SAND)|P(x)]))$

As before, the two NPs are combined by grammar rule J1 to form an NP sequence, which is subsequently combined with the lexical description of the verb. The resulting EL_f expression is, after λ-conversion,

(8.166a) $\text{Wght}([x \in \delta_m((\lambda y: \text{Wght}(y) = 5\text{-t.}), \text{SAND})|$
$\text{LIFT}(\text{Craney}, x)]) = 5\text{-t.}$

and the corresponding syntactic tree is as in (8.166b). The strong group

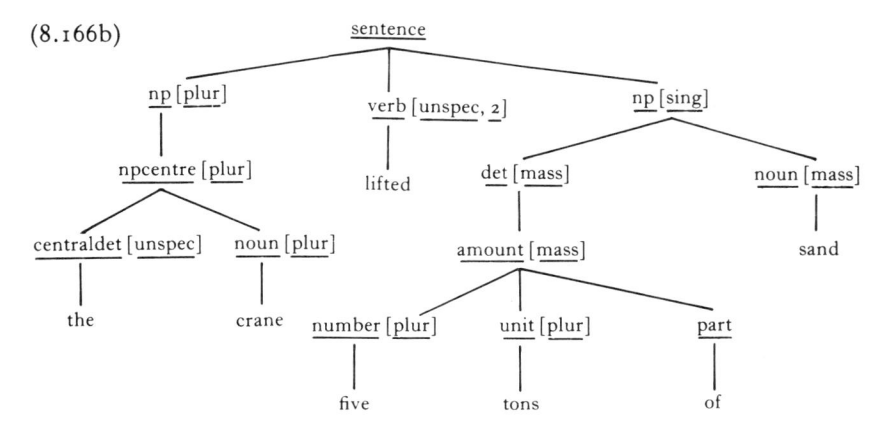

(8.166b)

```
                              sentence
        ┌────────────────────────┼────────────────────┐
     np [plur]            verb [unspec, 2]         np [sing]
        │                        │              ┌──────┴──────┐
   npcentre [plur]             lifted       det [mass]    noun [mass]
    ┌────┴────┐                                 │              │
centraldet   noun [plur]                   amount [mass]      sand
[unspec]                                ┌──────┼──────┐
    │           │                  number    unit     part
   the        crane               [plur]    [plur]
                                    │         │        │
                                   five      tons      of
```

reading is obtained by translating the distribution function into ($\lambda K, X: \{z \in \mathcal{P}(X)|K(z)\}$). Translating SAND into SAND_r, etc., we obtain the EL_r representation:

(8.167) $\text{Wght}_r([x \in \{z \in \mathcal{P}(\text{SAND}_r)|\text{Wght}_r(z) = 5\text{-t.}\}$
$\text{LIFT}_r(\text{Craney}, x)] = 5\text{-t.}$

Note the similarity between this representation and that of strong group quantification for count nouns, illustrated in (8.45).

F. Cumulative and subcumulative quantification
To illustrate the treatment of cumulative and subcumulative quantification for mass nouns we consider the sentence

(8.168)   Three boys drank ten litres of water

in the reading where the boys drank in total ten litres of water and where the water was consumed by these three boys.

The rules G1 and G3 construct for 'three boys' and 'ten litres of water' two so-called 'cumulative NPs' with the syntactic trees (8.169a) and (8.170a), respectively,

Quantification and mass nouns 179

(8.169a)   cumnp(numeral(number(three)[plur])[plur],
                       noun(boys)[plur])[plur]

(8.170a)   cumnp(amount(number(ten)[plur],
                       unit(litres)[plur],
                       part(of))[mass],
                       noun(water)[mass])[mass]

and EL_f representations (8.169b) and (8.170b), respectively:

(8.169b) $((\lambda X: \#(X) = 3), BOYS)$

(8.170b) $((\lambda u: Vol(\cup(u)) = 10\text{-ltrs}), \mathscr{P}(WATER))$

Grammar rule Ia constructs a noun phrase sequence from (8.169) and (8.170) with the syntactic tree

(8.171a)   nps(cumnp(numeral(number(three)[plur])[plur],
                       noun(boys)[plur])[plur],
                       cumnp(amount(number(ten)[plur],
                       unit(litres)[plur],
                       part(of))[mass],
                       noun(water)[mass])[mass])
                       [sing, 2]

and the EL_f representation

(8.171b) $(\lambda R: (\lambda u: \#(proj_1(u)) = 3 \ \& \ Vol(\cup(proj_2(u))) = 10\text{-ltrs})$
           $(\{x \in BOYS \times \mathscr{P}(WATER) | R(x)\}))$

Finally, rule K1 combines the syntactic tree (8.171a) with the lexical

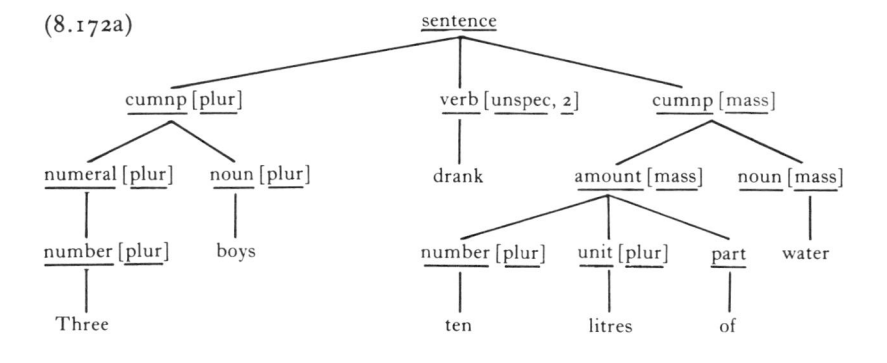

(8.172a)

```
                                    sentence
            ┌──────────────────────────┼──────────────────────────┐
       cumnp [plur]              verb [unspec, 2]            cumnp [mass]
       ┌────┴────┐                     │                    ┌──────┼──────┐
  numeral [plur] noun [plur]         drank            amount [mass]   noun [mass]
       │           │                                  ┌────┼────┐         │
  number [plur]  boys                          number [plur] unit [plur] part   water
       │                                              │           │        │
     Three                                           ten        litres    of
```

syntactic description of 'drank', with the result (8.172a). The semantic part of the rule applies the function expression (8.171b) to the lexical semantic representation of 'drank', resulting in the EL_f expression:

(8.172b) $(\lambda u: \#(proj_1(u)) = 3 \,\&\, Vol(\cup(proj_2(u))) = 10\text{-ltrs})$
$(\{x \in BOYS \times \mathcal{P}(WATER)|DRINK(x)\})$

This representation is transformed by λ-conversion into

(8.172c) $\#(proj_1(\{x \in BOYS \times \mathcal{P}(WATER)|DRINK(x)\})) = 3 \,\&\,$
$Vol(\cup(proj_2(\{x \in BOYS \times \mathcal{P}(WATER)|DRINK(x)\}))) = 10\text{-ltrs}$

which clearly expresses the cumulative reading of the sentence in formal terms. As far as quantification aspects are concerned, the EL_f–EL_r translation is of no interest in this case.

The representation of the subcumulative reading of the sentence is obtained by applying rule Ib instead of Ia, which, instead of (8.171b), creates an NP sequence with EL_f representation

(8.173) $(\lambda R: \exists! z \in \mathcal{P}(\{y \in BOYS \times \mathcal{P}(WATER)|R(y)\}): (\lambda u:$
$\#(proj_1(u)) = 3 \,\&\, Vol(\cup(proj_2(u))) = 10\text{-ltrs})(z))$

Application of rule K1 and λ-conversion lead to the sentence representation

(8.174) $\exists! z \in \mathcal{P}(\{y \in BOYS \times \mathcal{P}(WATER)|DRINK(y)\}):$
$\#(proj_1(z)) = 3 \,\&\, Vol(\cup(proj_2(z))) = 10\text{-ltrs}$

In words, this says that there is precisely one collection of pairs consisting of a boy and a water sample such that the three boys in that collection drank the 10 litres of water in the collection.

8.8 A grammar for a fragment of English

8.8.1 *The fragment*
The fragment of English covered by the grammar described below contains simple sentences, consisting of one or more simple noun phrases and a verb. A verb in this fragment is either a single verb form or a copula plus adjective. By a simple noun phrase is meant: (1) a basic noun phrase (see section 8.1) with count or mass head noun; (2) a proper name; (3) an applied amount term + mass noun or plural count noun; (4) an isolated amount term. The fragment includes a treatment of homogeneous, distribu-

tive, collective, unspecific, cumulative, subcumulative, weak, and strong group quantification.

In view of what was said in section 8.2 about the syntactic and semantic properties of determiners, a distinction is made in the grammar between central determiners and predeterminers. Postdeterminers have not been included, since source size presuppositions have been left out of consideration, but a lexical category of determiners is included that may neither precede a central determiner nor be preceded by a predeterminer. This category is called *determiner*; it includes the cardinals, the indefinite article, and the quantifiers 'each', 'every', 'some', and 'no'. This means that the determiner sequences in the fragment are either single central determiners, predeterminers, or just-so determiners, or predeterminers followed by central determiners.

The predeterminer 'all', and the determiners 'some' and 'no' are treated as imposing no constraints on the possible distributions of quantifications, but as indicating source involvement only. Thus, NPs like 'all sand' and 'all the sand' are treated as differing only in their quantification source. The indefinite article 'a(n)' and the determiners 'each' and 'every' give rise to distributive quantifications only.

The fragment allows the relative scopes of quantifiers in multi-NP sentences to deviate from the left-to-right order of the corresponding noun phrases in a limited way: one quantifier may have wider scope than it would have on the basis of its NP position. For a two-NP sentence this means that both scope orders are allowed; for a three-NP sentence, with quantifiers Q_1, Q_2, Q_3 corresponding to NPs in this left–right order, this means that four of the six logically possible scope orders are allowed: $Q_1-Q_2-Q_3$, $Q_1-Q_3-Q_2$, $Q_2-Q_1-Q_3$, and $Q_3-Q_1-Q_2$. For a four-NP sentence, where I'm afraid our intuitions on the plausibilities of relative scopes already begin to waver, this means that seven of the 24 logically possible scope orders are allowed. This restriction is not based on a serious study of linguistic constraints, but it certainly has the merit of limiting the number of readings of multi-NP sentences while keeping the most plausible interpretations.

It may be noted that in this grammar a lexical distinction is made between mass nouns and count nouns, in spite of the fact that I argued in chapter 2 that the count/mass distinction should not be construed as a distinction among lexical items. This point is discussed in some detail in the next chapter, where a grammar will be presented for an extension of the fragment of English considered here, including grammatical rules for 'deriving' mass nouns from lexical count nouns.

8.8.2 *The grammatical formalism*

The grammar specified below consists of a lexicon and a collection of compositional rules, each consisting of a syntactic part that builds syntactic structures from simpler ones and a semantic rule that builds corresponding semantic structures in parallel. Due to the coupling of syntactic and semantic rules the grammar defines an EL_f expression for each syntactic tree that it generates, the 'formal semantic representation' of the English expression at the leaves of the tree.

The syntactic trees that a rule operates on are indicated by small letters from the beginning of the alphabet: a, b, c, ... Their EL_f representations are indicated by the corresponding primed letters: a', b', c', ... The syntactic category of the top node of a syntactic tree I will call the syntactic category of the tree, and the syntactic attributes of the top node the attributes of the tree.

The syntactic part of a rule consists of three components: (1) a rule that resembles a rewriting rule of a phrase-structure grammar, which I call a *phrase-construction rule* or 'PC rule'; (2) a condition on the values of the syntactic attributes carried by the (top nodes of the) syntactic trees that the rule operates on; (3) a rule specifying how the values of the syntactic attributes of a syntactic tree are determined by the attribute values of the syntactic trees that the rule operates on. Of these components, the PC rules deserve further consideration.

The simplest form of a PC rule, that most of the rules in the grammar described below have, is:

(8.175) a: CATa + b: CATb + ... + j: CATj → CATr

This means that a syntactic tree with the syntactic category CATr may be constructed from a sequence of syntactic trees with the categories CATa, CATb, ..., CATj. In other words, the rule says that the structure (8.176) is a well-formed syntactic tree, for any trees a, b, ..., j. The form (8.175)

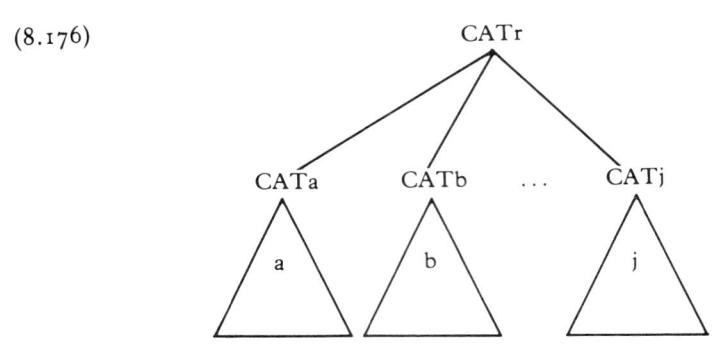

(8.176)

Quantification and mass nouns 183

is of course merely a notational variant of the usual rewrite format. However, there are three respects in which a PC rule may deviate from a rewrite rule.

First, a PC rule may have the effect of 'dissolving' the top node of a syntactic tree that it operates on. Some of the rules below have the more complex form:

(8.177) a: CATa + b: CATb + ... + j: CATj → CATr[z1, ..., zk]

where [z1, ..., zk] is a sequence of syntactic trees which are either elements of the sequence (a, b, ..., j) or 'immediate subtrees' of elements of that sequence. The addition [z1, ..., zk] at the right-hand side of the rule means that the newly formed node of category CATr has the immediate subtrees z1, ..., zk. I call such an addition a *construction clause*. For example, the rule

(8.178) a: CATa + b: CATb → CATc[a_1, a_2, b_1, b_2]

where a_1, a_2, b_1, and b_2 are the immediate subtrees of a and b, has the effect that the categories CATa and CATb are dissolved in the process of constructing the tree at the right-hand side from those at the left-hand side with the effect shown in diagram (8.179). Of course, we do not have to

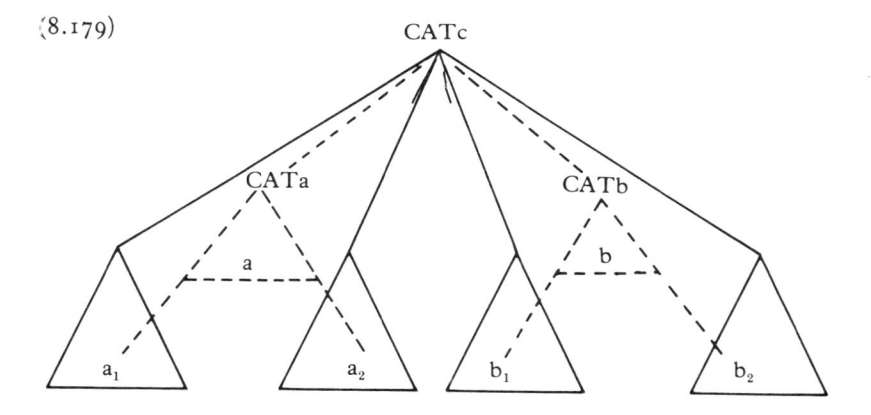

(8.179)

view PC rules as descriptions of construction processes; formally, they are just a way of defining the class of well-formed syntactic trees (further constrained by the attribute conditions considered below).

The second respect in which PC rules may differ from rewriting rules is that they are not necessarily purely concatenating. A rule like (8.178), with the effect shown in (8.179), is in fact not of great interest. The usefulness of constructing and dissolving 'intermediate' syntactic category nodes is in the handling of discontinuous constituents, like in the situation depicted in (8.180). Here, a and b are interlaced discontinuous constituents.

(8.180)

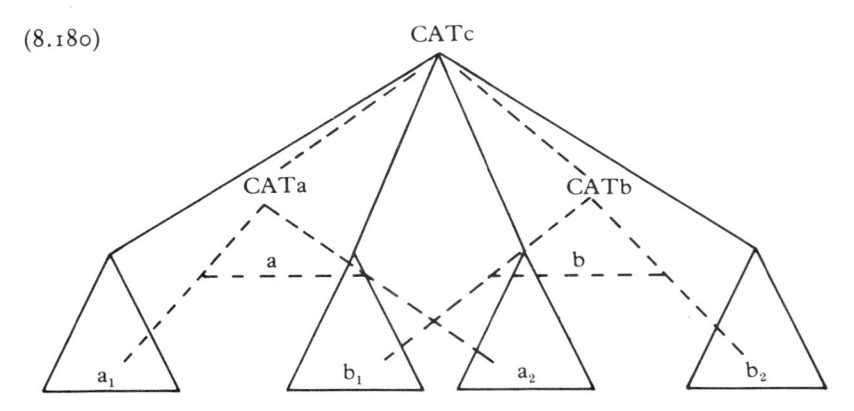

[Diagram: tree with root CATc having four subtrees (triangles with leaves a_1, b_1, a_2, b_2); dashed lines group a_1, a_2 under CATa (with label a) and b_1, b_2 under CATb (with label b).]

The PC rules that combine trees like a and b (and thereby dissolve their top nodes) cannot be concatenating since the trees do not stand in a simple left-to-right order. The placement of tree a to the left of tree b in diagram (8.180) is suggestive, but has no formal significance. We can formulate a rule that would have the effect depicted in (8.180) as (8.181), if we interpret the '+' sign not as mere concatenation, but as saying that the leftmost immediate subtree of b, that is b_1, is immediately to the right of the leftmost immediate subtree of a, that is a_1:

(8.181)   a: CATa + b: CATb → CATc[a_1, b_1, a_2, b_2]

To account for these phenomena, I allow a PC rule to have the form

(8.182)   a: CATa + b: CATb + ... + j: CATj → CATr[z_1, ..., z_k]

where each zi in the construction clause is either an element of the sequence (a, b, ..., j) or an immediate subtree of such an element; where the construction clause is omitted if it is identical to the sequence (a, b, ..., j), and where the '+' sign between two operands a and b has the following significance: going to the right, starting at the top node of a's leftmost immediate subtree, the first node that is encountered which does not belong to a, is the top node of b's leftmost immediate subtree. Note that the simple case of a merely concatenating rule, like (8.175), is a special case of this description.

Both the reinterpretation of the '+' sign and the addition of a clause describing how the syntactic tree of a complex phrase is constructed from the immediate subtrees of dissolved constituents, are deviations from the format of ordinary phrase-structure rules that facilitate the handling of discontinuous constituents. A third respect in which a PC rule may differ from an ordinary rewrite rule is in the description of how a discontinuous constituent-tree is formed. This is as follows. If a phrase of category R may be built up from constituents of categories P and Q, possibly separated by a phrase of category T, this is expressed by a PC rule of the form:

(8.183) p: P+([t: T])+q: Q → R

This rule says that the syntactic tree constructed at the right-hand side consists of the trees p and q, dominated by a new node of category R. The square brackets indicate that t plays the role of 'internal context' of the R phrase, that is a constituent separating the constituents p and q, but not forming part of the R phrase. The round brackets indicate that the presence of t is optional. The relation indicated by the '+' sign is now extended to the effect that an 'internal context' element, like t, also stands in that relation to the newly formed R phrase.

In the rules of a phrase-structure grammar one sometimes finds a notation very much like that in (8.183), used to indicate optional constituency. For instance, the rewrite rule

(8.184) R → P (T) Q

says that a phrase of category R may consist of a sequence of constituents of categories P Q, but may also consist of a sequence of constituents of categories P T Q; in that sense the T-phrase is an optional constituent of an R-phrase. There is an important difference between (8.183) and (8.184), though, in that the constituent in parentheses in the PC rule, even if it is present, is not included in the syntactic structure built up for the R-phrase, while in the rewrite rule the constituent in parentheses will be part of the R-phrase structure. The rule (8.184) is nothing else than an abbreviation of the two rewrite rules

(8.185) a. R → P Q
         b. R → P T Q

and thus generates two syntactic trees (shown in (8.186a) and (8.186b)). The PC rule, by contrast, generates only one syntactic tree, namely (8.186a). The optional character of an operand in the rule only relates to the conditions for application of the rule, not to its effect.

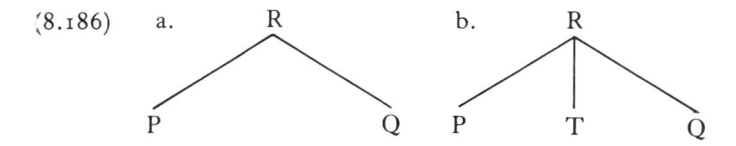

(8.186)   a.   R   b.   R
                   / \   /|\
                  P   Q   P T Q

186   Part 1   Model-theoretic semantics of mass terms

For more details on PC rules as a grammatical formalism, and a more detailed discussion of the left–right neighbourship relation between discontinuous constituents expressed by the '+' sign, see Bunt (1985).

A grammar that consists of phrase-structure rules augmented by procedures that constrain the application of a rule, that add syntactic information to the structure created by the rule, and that assign an interpretation to the resulting structure is called an 'augmented phrase structure grammar' (Robinson, 1982; Paxton, 1978; Heidorn, 1975; see also Bunt, 1985 and Winograd, 1983). By analogy, I call the grammar described here an *augmented phrase-construction grammar*.

Together with the conditions on syntactic attributes and the rules for attribute-value carry-over (in the literature also known as 'feature propagation'), the phrase-construction rules define the class of well-formed syntactic trees. In most cases the conditions on attributes will speak for themselves. It will often be the case that two syntactic trees are required to have identical values for all their attributes; this is indicated by writing the same symbol, β, at the relevant places. For any attribute the value unspec is treated as satisfying any condition.

The values of the syntactic attributes of the syntactic tree at the right-hand side in a PC rule are mostly determined by those of the syntactic trees at the left-hand side. The 'carry-over of attributes' describes this dependence. It will often be the case that the tree at the right-hand side inherits all the attribute values from one of the trees at the left-hand side. This is, again, indicated by writing β at the relevant places. Those values of attributes of the right-hand-side tree which are not explicitly specified by an attribute carry-over rule are unspec. The leftmost immediate subtree of the syntactic tree t will be designated by t_1; the second one from the left by t_2, etc.

8.8.3 *The lexicon*

(A) Verbs

A1 Intransitive verbs

syntactic tree	EL_f translation
verb(fall)[form: plur, nr 1]	FALL
verb(falls)[form: nonplur, nr: 1]	FALL
verb(fell)[form: unspec, nr: 1]	FALL
verb(melted)[form: unspec, nr: 1]	MELT
verb(were lifted)[form: plur, nr: 1]	LIFTED

verb(came down)[form: unspec, nr: 1]   CAMEDOWN
verb(smiled)[form: unspec, nr: 1]   SMILE

A2 Transitive verbs

syntactic tree	EL$_f$ translation
verb(lifts)[form: nonplur, nr: 2]	LIFT
verb(lift)[form: plur, nr: 2]	LIFT
verb(lifted)[form: unspec, nr: 2]	LIFT
verb(carries away)[form: nonplur, nr: 2]	CARRY
verb(drank)[form: unspec, nr: 2]	DRINK
verb(contain)[form: plur, nr: 2]	CONTAIN

A3 Verbs with an indirect object

syntactic tree	EL$_f$ translation
verb(gives)[form: nonplur, nr: 3]	GIVE
verb(give)[form: plur, nr: 3]	GIVE

A4 Two-place verbs with an amount as second argument

syntactic tree	EL$_f$ translation
measureverb(weighs)[form: nonplur]	WEIGH
measureverb(weighs)[form: plur]	WEIGH
measureverb(measures)[form: nonplur]	MEASURE
measureverb(costs)[form: nonplur]	COST

A5 Copulas

syntactic tree	EL$_f$ translation
copula(is)[form: sing, nr: 1]	$(\lambda P: (\lambda x: P(x)))$
copula(are)[form: plur, nr: 1]	$(\lambda P: (\lambda x: P(x)))$

(B) Nouns

B1 Count nouns

syntactic tree	EL$_f$ translation
noun(girl)[form: sing]	GIRLS
noun(girls)[form: plur]	GIRLS
noun(boy)[form: sing]	BOYS
noun(boys)[form: plur]	BOYS
noun(cranes)[form: plur]	CRANES
noun(boxes)[form: plur]	BOXES
noun(jewels)[form: plur]	JEWELS
noun(devices)[form: plur]	DEVICES
noun(puddle)[form: sing]	PUDDLES

188 *Part 1 Model-theoretic semantics of mass terms*

B2 Mass nouns

syntactic tree	EL$_f$ translation
noun(water)[form: mass]	WATER
noun(sand)[form: mass]	SAND
noun(snow)[form: mass]	SNOW
noun(apple)[form: mass]	APPLE
noun(onion)[form: mass]	ONION
noun(concrete)[form: mass]	CONCRETE
noun(glass)[form: mass]	GLASS
noun(furniture)[form: mass]	FURNITURE
noun(sugar)[form: mass]	SUGAR

(C) Proper names

syntactic tree	EL$_f$ translation
propername(John)[form: sing]	John
propername(Mary)[form: sing]	Mary
propername(Craney)[form: sing]	Craney

(D) Adjectives

syntactic tree	EL$_f$ translation
adj(wet)	WET
adj(heavy)	HEAVY
adj(cold)	COLD
adj(sweet)	SWEET
adj(red)	RED
adj(cubic)	CUBIC
adj(round)	ROUND
adj(sharp)	SHARP
adj(hot)	HOT

(E) Numbers

syntactic tree	EL$_f$ translation
number(one)[form: sing]	1
number(two)[form: plur]	2
number(three)[form: plur]	3
number(four)[form: plur]	4
number(five)[form: plur]	5
number(ten)[form: plur]	10

(F) Units

syntactic tree	EL$_f$ translation
<u>unit</u>(litre)[<u>form</u>: <u>sing</u>]	(Vol, litrs)
<u>unit</u>(litres)[<u>form</u>: <u>plur</u>]	(Vol, litrs)
<u>unit</u>(oz)[<u>form</u>: unspec]	(Wght, oz)
<u>unit</u>(kilogramme)[<u>form</u>: <u>sing</u>]	(Wght, kg)
<u>unit</u>(kilogrammes)[<u>form</u>: <u>plur</u>]	(Wght, kg)
<u>unit</u>(ton)[<u>form</u>: <u>sing</u>]	(Wght, t.)
<u>unit</u>(tons)[<u>form</u>: <u>plur</u>]	(Wght, t.)
<u>unit</u>(dollars)[<u>form</u>: <u>plur</u>]	(Val, $)

(G) Partitive particle

syntactic tree	EL$_f$ translation
<u>part</u>(of)	(λ x: x)

(H) Determiners

H1 Predeterminers

syntactic tree	EL$_f$ translation
<u>predet</u>(all)[<u>form</u>: <u>plur</u>]	(λX: (λP: (λu: u = X) (\{x $\in$ δ(λu: u = X, X)|P(x)\})))
<u>predet</u>(all)[<u>form</u>: <u>mass</u>]	(λX: (λP: (λu: u = X) ([x $\in$ δ_m(λu: u = X, X)|P(x)])))
<u>predet</u>(all)[<u>form</u>: <u>mass</u>]	(λX: (λP: (λu: u = $\mathcal{P}$(X)) (\{x $\in$ $\mathcal{P}$(X)|P(x)\})))

H2 Central determiners

syntactic tree	EL$_f$ translation
<u>centraldet</u>(the)[<u>form</u>: unspec]	CR$_\circ$
<u>centraldet</u>(this)[<u>form</u>: nonplur]	CR$_\circ$
<u>centraldet</u>(these)[<u>form</u>: <u>plur</u>]	CR$_\circ$

H3 Just-so determiners

syntactic tree	EL$_f$ translation
<u>det</u>(each)[<u>form</u>: <u>sing</u>] <u>det</u>(every)[<u>form</u>: <u>sing</u>]	(λX: (λP: $\forall$x $\in$ X: P(x)))
<u>det</u>(a)[<u>form</u>: <u>sing</u>] <u>det</u>(some)[<u>form</u>: <u>sing</u>]	(λX: (λP: $\exists$x $\in$ X: P(x)))

190 Part 1 Model-theoretic semantics of mass terms

$$\underline{\text{det}}(\text{some})[\underline{\text{form}}: \underline{\text{plur}}] \qquad (\lambda X: (\lambda P: (\lambda u: \#(u) > 1)$$
$$(\{x \in \delta(\lambda u: \#(u) > 1, X) | P(x)\})))$$

$\underline{\text{det}}(\text{some})[\underline{\text{form}}: \underline{\text{mass}}] \qquad (\lambda X: (\lambda P: \exists x \subseteq^\circ X: P(x)))$

$\left.\begin{array}{l}\underline{\text{det}}(\text{no})[\underline{\text{form}}: \underline{\text{sing}}] \\ \underline{\text{det}}(\text{no})[\underline{\text{form}}: \underline{\text{plur}}]\end{array}\right\} \qquad (\lambda X: (\lambda P: \neg(\exists x \in X: P(x))))$

$\underline{\text{det}}(\text{no})[\underline{\text{form}}: \underline{\text{mass}}] \qquad (\lambda X: (\lambda P: \neg(\exists x \subseteq^\circ X: P(x))))$

8.8.4 The rules of the grammar

Rule A Rule constructing isolated amounts[13]

PC Rule:	a: NUMBER + b: UNIT → ISOLAMOUNT
Conditions on attributes:	β β
Carry-over of attributes:	—
Semantic rule:	a' + b' → $(\lambda P: P(a' - b'_2))$

Rule B Rules constructing applied amounts

All rules (B1–B4) have the same phrase-construction rule and conditions on attributes. The rules are paired differently as far as attribute carry-over and semantic rules are concerned.[14]

PC Rule: a: NUMBER + b: UNIT + c: PART → AMOUNT

Conditions on attributes: β   β

B1
B3 Carry-over of attributes: → <u>form</u>: <u>nonsing</u>

B2
B4 Carry-over of attributes: → <u>form</u>: <u>mass</u>

B1
B2 Semantic rule: a'   + b'   + c' → $(\lambda u: b'_1(u) = a' - b'_2)$

B3
B4 Semantic rule: a'   + b'   + c' → $(\lambda u: b'_1(u) \geq a' - b'_2)$

Rule C Rules constructing numerals
The rules C1 and C2 differ only in their semantic parts.

	PC Rule:	a: NUMBER → NUMERAL
	Conditions on attributes:	—
	Carry-over of attributes:	$\beta \quad \rightarrow \beta$
C1	Semantic rule:	a' $\rightarrow (\lambda X: \#(X) = a')$
C2	Semantic rule:	a' $\rightarrow (\lambda X: \#(X) \geq a')$

Rule D Rules constructing determiners from numerals or applied amounts
Each of the rules is subdivided further into subrules that differ in the conditions on attributes and the semantic parts.

D1	PC Rule:	a: NUMERAL → DET
D2	PC Rule:	a: AMOUNT → DET
	Carry-over of attributes:	$\beta \quad \rightarrow \beta$
D1a D2a	Conditions on attributes:	form: ≠ mass
	Semantic rule:	a' $\rightarrow (\lambda X: (\lambda P: a'(\cup *(X, \{x \in \delta(a', X) | P(x)\}))))$
D1b D2b	Conditions on attributes:	form: mass
	Semantic rule:	a' $\rightarrow (\lambda X: (\lambda P: a' ([x \in \delta_m(a', X) | P(x)])))$

Rule E Rules constructing npcentres

	PC Rule:	a: CENTRALDET + b: NOUN → NPCENTRE
E1	Conditions on attributes:	form: plur ; form: plur
	Carry-over of attributes:	$\beta \quad \rightarrow \beta$
	Semantic rule:	a' + b' $\rightarrow \{x \in b' | a'(x)\}$
E2	Conditions on attributes:	form: mass ; form: mass
	Carry-over of attributes:	$\rightarrow$ form: mass
	Semantic rule:	a' + b' $\rightarrow [x \subseteq b' | a'(x)]$

192 Part 1 *Model-theoretic semantics of mass terms*

Rule F Rules constructing noun phrases
There are six rules, of which F1, F2 and F3a differ only in their phrase-construction parts.

F1	PC Rule:	a: PREDET + b: NOUN	→ NP
F2	PC Rule:	a: PREDET + b: NPCENTRE	→ NP
F3a	PC Rule:	a: DET + b: NOUN	→ NP
	Conditions on attributes:	β β	
	Carry-over of attributes:	β	→ β
	Semantic rule:	a' + b'	→ a'(b')

Rule F3 has two subrules, of which F3a is identical to F1 and F2 except for its phrase-construction rule.

F3b PC Rule: a: DET + b: NOUN → NP
Conditions on attributes: form: nonsing   form: ≠ sing   β
Carry-over of attributes: β   → form: sing
Semantic rule: a'   + b'   → a'(b')

F4 PC Rule: a: PROPERNAME → NP
Conditions on attributes: —
Carry-over of attributes: β   → β
Semantic rule: a'   → (λP: P(a'))

F5 Rule constructing noun phrases from npcentres. The rule has a number of subrules, all sharing the same phrase-construction rule and the same rule for carrying over the values of syntactic attributes:

PC Rule: a: NPCENTRE → NP
Carry-over of attributes: β   → β

F5a Conditions on attributes: form: plur
Semantic rule: a'   → (λP: ∪*(a', {x ∈ δ(λy: y = a', a')|P(x)}) = a')

Quantification and mass nouns 193

F5b Conditions on attributes: form: mass

Semantic rule: a' $\to (\lambda P: [x \in \delta_m(\lambda y: y = a', a)|P(x)] = a')$

F5c Conditions on attributes: form: mass

Semantic rule: a' $\to (\lambda P: \{x \in \mathcal{P}(a')|P(x)\} = \mathcal{P}(a'))$

F6 Rules constructing noun phrases from bare nouns. There are two rules, one for count nouns and one for mass nouns. They have the same phrase-construction rule and attribute carry-over.

PC Rule: a: NOUN $\to$ NP

Carry-over of attributes: β $\to \beta$

F6a Conditions on attributes: form: plur

Semantic rule: a' $\to (\lambda P: (\lambda z: \#(z) > 1)(\{x \in \delta(\lambda u: u = a', a')|P(x)\}))$

F6b Conditions on attributes: form: mass

Semantic rules: a' $\to (\lambda P: (\lambda z: z \neq \emptyset)([x \in \delta_m(u: u = S, S)|P(x)]))$

Rule G Rules constructing 'cumulative noun phrases'

G1 PC Rule: a: NUMERAL + b: NOUN $\to$ CUMNP

Conditions on attributes: form: plur   form: plur

Carry-over of attributes: β $\to \beta$

Semantic rule: a'   + b' $\to (a', b')$

G2 PC Rule: a: AMOUNT + b: NOUN $\to$ CUMNP

Conditions on attributes: form: nonsing   form: plur

Carry-over of attributes: β $\to \beta$

Semantic rule: a'   + b' $\to (a', b')$

194   Part 1 Model-theoretic semantics of mass terms

G3   PC Rule: a: AMOUNT + b: NOUN → CUMNP
        Conditions on
        attributes: form: mass   form: mass
        Carry-over of
        attributes: β   → β
        Semantic rule: a'   + b'   → ((λz: a'(
                                                  ∪(z))), 𝒫(b'))

Rule H Rule constructing 'verbs' from copula + adjective

        PC Rule: a: COPULA + b: ADJ → VERB
        Conditions on
        attributes: —
        Carry-over of
        attributes: β   → β
        Semantic rule: a'   + b'   → a'(b')

Rule I Rules constructing 'noun phrase sequences' with cumulative or subcumulative quantification

   The rules differ only in their semantic parts.[15] For any j > 1 there is a rule as follows:

        PC Rule: a1: CUMNP + ([v: VERB]) + ... + aj: CUMNP → NPS
        Conditions on
        attributes: —
        Carry-over of
        attributes: form: f   → nr: j, form: f
Ia   Semantic rule: a1' + ... + aj' → (λR: (λx: a1'$_1$(proj$_1$(x)) & ...
                                                  & aj'$_1$(proj$_j$(x)))
                                             ({y ∈ a1'$_2$ × ... × aj'$_2$|R(y)}))
Ib   Semantic rule: a1' + ... + aj' → (λR: ∃!x ∈ {y ∈ a1'$_2$ × ... × aj'$_2$|R(y)}:
                                                  a1'$_1$(proj$_1$(x)) & ... & aj'$_1$(proj$_j$(x)))

Rule J Rules constructing 'noun phrase sequences'

   By PERM(x1, ..., xj) is meant any permutation of the sequence (x1, ..., xj).

J1 Rule constructing NP sequences with left-to-right order of relative scopes.
      For any j ≥ 1 there is a rule as follows:

        PC Rule: a1: NP + ([v: VERB]) + ... + aj: NP → NPS
        Conditions on
        attributes: —

Carry-over of attributes: form: f   → form: f, nr: j

Semantic rule: $a_1' + \ldots + a_j' \to (\lambda R: a_1'(\lambda x1: \ldots a_j'(\lambda xj: R(PERM(x1, \ldots, xj))) \ldots)))$

J2 Rule constructing NP sequences where a noun phrase other than the leftmost one has widest scope.[16]

For $m \geq 1, n \geq 0$:

PC Rule: a: NPS + ([v: VERB]) + b: NP + c: NPS →
                  → NPS[$a_1, \ldots, a_m, b, c_1, \ldots, c_n$]

Conditions on attributes: nr: m   nr: n

Carry-over of attributes: form: f   → form: f, nr: m+n+1

Semantic rule: $a' + b' + c' \to$
$(\lambda R: b'(\lambda y: a_1'(\lambda x1: \ldots a_m'(\lambda xm:$
$c_1'(\lambda z1: \ldots c_n'|(\lambda zn:$
$R(PERM(x1, \ldots, xm, y, z1, \ldots, zn)) \ldots))))))$

J3 Rule constructing NP sequences where one of the noun phrases has a wider scope than it would have on the basis of its position in the sequence.

For $k \geq 0, m \geq 1, n \geq 1$:

PC Rule: a: NPS + ([v: VERB]) + b: NPS + c: NPS →
                  → NPS[$a_1, \ldots, a_k, b_1, \ldots, b_m, c_1, \ldots, c_n$]

Conditions on attributes: nr: k   nr: m   nr: n

Carry-over of attributes: form: f   → form: f, nr: k+m+n

Semantic rule: $a' + b' + c' \to$
$(\lambda R: a_1'(\lambda x1: \ldots a_k'(\lambda xk:$
$c_1'(\lambda y1: b_1'(\lambda y2: \ldots (\lambda ym: b_m'(\lambda z1:$
$c_2'(\lambda z2: \ldots c_n'(\lambda zn:$
$R(PERM(x1, \ldots, xk, y1, \ldots, ym, z1, \ldots, zn)) \ldots)$

Rule K   Rules constructing sentences

K1 The rule is split into two subrules that differ only in the conditions on attributes. It is assumed that $n > 0$.

PC Rule: a: NPS + b: VERB → SENTENCE[$a_1, b, a_2, \ldots, a_n$]

Carry-over of attributes: β → β

Semantic rule: a' $+ b'$ → $a'(b')$

K1a Conditions on attributes: β β

K1b Conditions on attributes:
nr: n
form: ≠ plur

nr: n
form: nonplur

K2 PC Rule: a: NP + b: MEASUREVERB + c: ISOLAMOUNT
→ SENTENCE

Conditions on attributes: β β

Carry-over of attributes: —

Semantic rule: a' + b' + c' → a'(λx: c'(λy: b'(x, y)))

9 Modification and mass nouns[1]

9.1 Modification and quantification

Modification is a phenomenon that can be characterized in syntactic terms as the combination of two constituents to form a so-called 'subordinating endocentric construction', that is, a construction that has one constituent which may occupy the same syntactic positions as the construction as a whole. This constituent is called the *head* of the construction, the other the *modifier*.[2] I shall be concerned here with the case where the head is a nominal constituent, in particular, a mass noun.

From a semantic point of view, a modifier typically serves to narrow down the meaning of the head. Thus, in the sentence

(9.1)   The flowers in the desert are beautiful in spring

the modifier 'in the desert' restricts the denotation of 'the flowers' to flowers in the desert. But of course a modifier can function differently, as in the sentence

(9.2)   The Sandinista government in Nicaragua negotiates with the conservative government in El Salvador

Here the modifiers 'Sandinista' and 'conservative' do not narrow down the meanings of the respective noun phrase heads; they are so-called 'non-restrictive modifiers'. Semantically, modification and quantification are closely related, as we can see clearly when we consider the modification of a noun by a relative clause. In the analysis of the modification in a phrase like

(9.3)   The boats lifted by the cranes

we must, just as in the analysis of the quantification in the sentence

(9.4)   The boats were lifted by the cranes

deal with questions such as whether the boats were lifted individually, collectively, or in groups, whether the cranes acted individually or collectively, etc. We can thus speak of the source, distribution, and domain of a modification. The tools, developed in the previous chapter for building semantic representations of quantification while avoiding an explosion of ambiguities, can also be used in the representation of modification. Thus, taking a slightly simpler example than (9.3), the modified phrase

(9.5a)   Boats lifted by Craney

can be represented in EL_f by

(9.6a) $\cup^*(BOATS, \{x \in \delta(\lambda y: y = BOATS, BOATS) | LIFTED(Craney, x)\})$

This may be compared with the EL_f representation of the corresponding quantified sentence:

(9.5b)   Craney lifted the boats

which is

(9.6b) $\cup^*(BOATS, \{x \in \delta(\lambda y: y = BOATS, BOATS) | LIFTED(Craney, x)\})$
         $= BOATS$

We have seen in the previous chapter that a variety of quantificationally different readings is obtained by instantiating the distribution function δ. In the same way we obtain a variety of readings of a modified noun by instantiating the δ function in (9.6b). Rather than going through this process again, I will at once turn to the peculiarities of mass noun modification. Besides considering the representation of adjective–mass noun combinations, I will explore the following questions:

1. Are there co-occurrence restrictions of a formal semantic nature for adjectives and mass nouns, and if so, what are they?
2. Are there reasons to extend the count/mass distinction among nouns to adjectives, and if so, how should 'mass adjectives' and 'count adjectives' be defined?

Concerning the second question, we already noted in chapter 2 that a semantic definition of 'mass terms' based on the criterion of cumulative reference, as suggested among others by Quine and Moravcsik, leads to a distinction between mass adjectives and count adjectives. Adjectives like 'red' and 'ripe' would be mass adjectives, since they satisfy the criterion that 'the sum of parts which are red (ripe) is red (ripe)'; adjectives like 'spherical' or 'light' (= not heavy), on the other hand, would be count adjectives.

It is not immediately clear whether this would be a fruitful distinction. This depends on whether the distinction has grammatical correlates, such as co-occurrence restrictions. There are indications that adjectives which do not refer cumulatively do not combine well with mass nouns. For instance, the combination 'small water' in

(9.7) *There is some small water on the floor

is not acceptable. However, replacing 'small' by 'large', which is cumulative in reference, does not change the situation in this respect. The sentence

(9.8) *There is some large water on the floor

is equally unacceptable. It therefore seems doubtful that cumulativity of reference would make the difference. McCawley (1975) has drawn attention to the fact that the situation is not the same for all mass nouns: whereas 'large water' is unacceptable, 'large furniture' seems reasonable. It therefore seems worth while examining more carefully what co-occurrence restrictions actually obtain.

In order not to rely just on one person's intuitions about the acceptability of certain adjective–mass noun combinations I have carried out an experiment in which a number of informants were asked to judge such combinations in English or in Dutch. The main results of this experiment, reported in Bunt (1980b), will be summarized in section 9.3.

9.2 Theoretical problems with adjective–mass noun combinations

Quine (1960) has proposed to analyse adjective–mass noun combinations such as 'red wine' as denoting the overlap of the mereological wholes denoted by the mass terms 'red' and 'wine'. This raises the question of how to treat an adjective that is not a mass term, such as 'spherical', when applied to a mass noun. Such adjectives would be treated like count nouns, as denoting sets. But since the overlap of a set and a mereological whole is not defined in mereology (nor in set theory), this does not provide a way of interpreting such adjective–noun combinations. Quine's escape is to assume that such combinations do not occur: 'It is reassuring to note that adjectives, not cumulative in reference simply tend not to occur next to mass terms' (1960, p. 104). I shall refer to this conjecture as the *cumulative combination conjecture*. As it stands, the conjecture is surely not correct, as the following counterexample indicates:[3])

(9.9) There is small furniture in the dolls' house

As we have seen in section 3.3, Moravcsik (1973) has suggested two alternative approaches to the semantics of mass terms in which different variants of mereology are used. Both approaches run into the same problem as Quine's, when it comes to mass nouns modified by 'count adjectives'.

We have seen in section 3.4 that Parsons (1970) proposed a semantic theory in which mass nouns are regarded as denoting 'substances'. A 'substance abstraction operator' σ is introduced such that, given a proposition P, the expression $\sigma x[P]$ denotes 'that substance which has as quantities all and only things which the formula inside [the brackets] is true of' (Parsons, 1970, p. 375). For instance, the adjective-noun combination 'soft clay' is analysed as:

(9.10) $\sigma x[\text{SOFT}(x)\ \&\ x\ Q\ \text{CLAY}]$

This analysis is incorrect for adjectives which, unlike 'soft', denote a property which is not cumulative, such as 'spherical'. When we have two bits of matter m_1 and m_2, which are both quantities of a substance M, then the bit of matter m_3 made up by m_1 and m_2 is also a quantity of M. However, if m_1 and m_2 are spherical, m_3 does not need to be spherical. The notion of a substance $\sigma x[\text{SPHERICAL}(x)\ \&\ x\ Q\ M]$, that would have as quantities those and only those objects that are spherical quantities of M, is logically inconsistent. Mass nouns modified by non-cumulative adjectives thus cause equally serious problems for Parsons', Quine's and Moravcsik's proposals.

The theoretical problems in interpreting adjective–mass noun combinations which arise if mereology or substances are used, can be avoided by using ensemble theory. If we analyse a mass adjective–noun combination like 'soft clay' as:

(9.11) $[x \subseteq \text{CLAY} | \text{SOFT}(x)]$

we have a representation which is a well-defined expression in an Ensemble Language, regardless of whether SOFT is cumulative or not. The crucial difference between this representation and Parsons' representation (9.10) is that the ensemble denoted by (9.11) does not have the property of including *only* samples of clay which are soft. It is the 'smallest' ensemble

Modification and mass nouns 201

made up by all clay-samples which are soft, but this does not mean that all its parts are soft (cf. section 6.2). Therefore, the modification of a mass noun with denotation M by an adjective denoting a predicate P, may be represented by

(9.12) $[x \subseteq M | P(x)]$

for any P without a risk of running into theoretical problems concerning the well-formedness of the representation. For any predicate P, formula (9.12) denotes the restriction of the ensemble M to that part which is made up by all M-parts for which P is true. However, P must have certain logical properties if this restriction is to be a non-trivial one.

Consider, for example, the adjective 'heavy' in the sense of exceeding a certain fixed weight. Imagine a situation in which you are carrying a heavy bag of sand. Notice first that the adjective 'heavy', though not cumulative, can be used in predicative position in combination with the mass noun 'sand', as in:

(9.13) The sand in the bag is heavy

Suppose you are now being asked:

(9.14) Put the heavy sand from the bag in this container, please

There is something awkward about this sentence if 'heavy' is interpreted as a restrictive modifier, and this can be explained on semantic grounds. For what would you do to fulfil this request? You might compare the situation with the case where we have a bag of stones, and you are being asked:

(9.15) Put the heavy stones from the bag in this container

A plausible way to proceed in this case might be that you consider each of the stones from the bag, decide whether it is heavy or not, put it in the container if it is and put it back into the bag if it is not. Let us try to apply a similar procedure in the case of (9.14): we take some sand from the bag, decide whether it is heavy or not; if it is we put it in the container, otherwise we put it back into the bag. This procedure runs into problems. For instance, when you have done this I can take a small sample from the container, small enough not to be heavy, and accuse you of having put not only heavy sand but also light sand in the container. This is due to the fact that the predicate 'heavy' has the property that, when x is a part of a mass noun extension that the predicate is true of, x will, in general, have parts that it is not true of. It is therefore impossible to select heavy samples only. If instead of 'heavy', we take a predicate that does not have this property, such as 'dry', this problem does not arise. Accordingly, a sentence like:

(9.16) Put the dry sand from the bag in this container, please

is perfectly all right. The awkwardness of (9.14) is thus indeed caused by the adjective.

Generalizing from this example, we see that a predicate P which is to function as a non-trivial restrictive mass noun modifier should have the property of being *distributive*, that is, if it is true of an ensemble x then it is true of all the parts of x:

(9.17) $(\forall x)(P(x) \rightarrow ((\forall y \subseteq x)P(y)))$

'Heavy' can also have the meaning 'heavy kind of'; this case will be considered below.

It is instructive to state the problem with adjectives like 'heavy' in ensemble-theoretical terms. Treating 'the heavy sand from the bag' as suggested above:

(9.18) $[x \subseteq [y \subseteq \text{SAND} | \text{FROMBAG}(y)] | \text{HEAVY}(x)]$

where FROMBAG represents 'from the bag', etc., we can observe two things. First, the fact that any part x of a mass noun extension M which the predicate 'heavy' is true of has a part y which it is not true of, can be expressed by:

(9.19) $(\forall x \subseteq M)\text{HEAVY}(x) \rightarrow (\exists y \subseteq x)\neg\text{HEAVY}(y)$

Substituting (9.18) for M in this formula, we see that, in the example of putting 'the heavy sand' in the container, the sand we end up with in the container will include parts that are not heavy. Secondly, we see that 'heavy' can only be a restrictive modifier of a trivial kind, since either there was no heavy sand in the bag to begin with, in which case (9.18) is equal to the empty ensemble, or else there was some heavy sand in the bag, in which case (9.18) is equal to the ensemble formed by *all* the sand in the bag. Generally, for any ensemble E we have:

(9.20) $[x \subseteq E | \text{HEAVY}(x)] = \varnothing$ or $= E$

In other words, adjectives like 'heavy', which are not distributive, cannot restrict a mass noun extension in a non-trivial way.

Similar problems arise with 'light sand', as the following example shows:

(9.21) Put the light sand from the bag in this container, please

When trying to imagine how to fulfil this request, we readily see that we get into the same difficulties as in the case of 'heavy sand'. Even if we select only light samples from the bag, we will end up having heavy sand in the container, and in fact having all the sand there. The source of the trouble is here that the property 'light' is not conserved when two or more samples with this property are merged. Conservation of a property P upon merging is expressed in ensemble-theoretical terms by:

(9.22) $(\forall z)((\forall y \subseteq z)P(y)) \rightarrow P(\cup(z))$

that is, the predicate P is true of the merge of any set of objects of which P is true. This is what Quine called 'cumulativity'. Thus, from a semantic point of view, a restrictive mass noun modifier should be required to be *cumulative*.

Again, it is illuminating to consider the ensemble-theoretical analysis. It is easy to see that just as for 'heavy sand' we have for any ensemble 'E':

(9.23) $[x \subseteq E | LIGHT(x)] = \varnothing$ or $= E$

So non-cumulative adjectives like 'light' cannot restrict a mass noun extension in a non-trivial way.

Earlier I introduced the concept of *homogeneous reference* for nouns. I now extend this concept to adjectives, calling an adjective *homogeneously referring* if it denotes a predicate that is both cumulative and distributive (a 'homogeneous predicate'). It follows that homogeneously referring adjectives meet the two requirements we have formulated for restrictive mass noun modification.

It has been argued in chapter 4 that homogeneous reference is characteristic of mass nouns; defining *mass adjectives* as those adjectives that refer homogeneously, we obtain a general notion of 'mass terms', comprising nouns and adjectives, which is characterized uniformly by the semantic property of homogeneous reference. Adjectives that do not refer homogeneously are then 'count adjectives'.

This leads us to the conjecture that only mass adjectives can function as restrictive mass noun modifiers. I call this conjecture the *homogeneous combination principle*:

(9.24) Only homogeneously referring adjectives can function as restrictive mass noun modifiers.

If this principle is valid, it gives us good reasons why it would be of interest to make a count/mass distinction among adjectives.

9.3 Empirical facts about adjective–mass noun combinations

In this section we will examine to what extent the homogeneous combination principle actually holds. Compared to the cumulative combination conjecture, the principle differs in two respects: (1) homogeneous reference (cumulative and distributive reference) is taken as the decisive property, rather than cumulative reference alone; (2) a claim is made only about adjectives functioning as restrictive modifiers, rather than about adjectives that 'occur next to mass terms'. The necessity of this qualification is illustrated by the fact that a sentence such as:

(9.25) I'm tired of carrying all that heavy sand in my bag

that has a reading in which 'heavy' is non-restrictive, is perfectly acceptable.

Sentences with mass nouns modified by count adjectives (in our sense of the term) are usually felt to be more or less tortuous, and often give rise to doubts concerning their syntactic and/or semantic well-formedness. To investigate this point, I performed an experiment in which a number of informants were consulted about a variety of such sentences. Native speakers of English were consulted about English sentences containing adjective–mass noun combinations, and native speakers of Dutch were consulted about similar Dutch sentences. The informants' judgements were assigned numerical values ranging from 0 to 3, the highest number corresponding to the strongest deviance. The average value of the judgements of a sentence will be called its 'degree of deviance'. In addition to being asked to express a judgement on the acceptability of the sentences, the subjects were asked to indicate in a few words what considerations played a role in their judgements for those sentences that were not judged as 'fine' (= degree of deviance 0). Moreover, subjects were asked to answer the question: 'What situation did you try to imagine as being described by the sentence?' The answers to this question provided valuable information, both about the semantic relations between nouns and adjectives that are considered, and about the particular semantic relations relative to which we should take the acceptability judgements. For further details see Bunt (1980b).

It turns out that sentence (9.21) 'Put the light sand from the bag into this container, please' is found unacceptable by most informants (degree of deviance 2.5). Sentence (9.9) 'There is small furniture in the dolls' house' is considerably 'better', having degree of deviance 0.9, but is not quite beyond controversy.

It turns out that there are also quite uncontroversial sentences with a mass noun modified by a count adjective, such as:

(9.26) You have heavy luggage

which has degree of deviance 0.2. Also, sentence (9.9), though criticized by some informants, is found quite normal by a large enough number of informants that we have to take it seriously (degree of deviance 0.9), and the same can be said about the sentence:

(9.27) I have heavy sand in my bag

(degree of deviance 1.4). In order to assess the implications of these observations, which contradict the homogeneous combination principle, we should take a closer look at the semantic relation between the adjective and the noun. We will see that a good understanding of the situation requires the distinction of four different types of (restrictive) modification. Paralleling the quantification types with the same designations, we should distinguish collective, generic, homogeneous, and discrete modification.

A. *Collective modification*

Among the sentences informants were consulted about are the following two:

(9.27) I have heavy sand in my bag

(9.28) Please remove only the heavy sand from my bag

Both sentences contain the count adjective-mass noun combination 'heavy sand', but their average appreciation is quite different: (9.27) has degree of deviance 1.4; (9.28) degree of deviance 2.5. How is this difference explained?

It turns out that the difference comes about because a number of informants found (9.27) just fine, while all informants, without exception, found (9.28) to some extent deviant. Several informants who judged (9.27) 'fine' motivated their judgement by saying that it is fine only if interpreted as

(9.29) I have a heavy bag of sand

In this reading, 'heavy' is considered as applying to the (bag of) sand as a whole, a reading which is not present for (9.28). The difference between (9.27) and (9.28) is paralleled by the difference in quantification type in the sentences:

(9.30)   The sand in my bag is heavy

(9.31)   Most of the sand in my bag is heavy

The first of these sentences has a collective reading, the second one does not. In view of this analogy, I call the type of modification in (9.27) on the reading (9.29) *collective*. Using the terminology suggested in section 9.1, a modification has collective distribution if the modification domain is the set with the modification source as its only element. In the example (9.27), the modification source of the modifier 'heavy' is the ensemble $SAND_b$ denoted by 'sand in my bag', and the modification domain is the set $\{SAND_b\}$.

Mass nouns may clearly be modified collectively by count adjectives. We thus have to qualify the homogeneous combination principle so that it says, more accurately,

(9.32) Only homogeneously referring adjectives can function as non-collective restrictive mass noun modifiers.

B. *Generic modification*

Sentence (9.33)

(9.33)   The ship was loaded with 300 tons of flexible copper and 500 tons of hard copper

presents another case of a mass noun modified by an adjective that may be said to be non-homogeneous, since flexible pieces of copper together may form a piece which is too thick to be flexible. 'Flexible' is clearly restrictive here. This sentence has degree of deviance 0.2, which means that it is generally accepted as correct.

As in the case of collective modification, it is instructive to consider a parallel case of quantification. Take the sentences

(9.34)   a. Copper is more flexible than steel
         b. Bolivian copper is more flexible than Antarctic copper

(9.35)   This bracelet is made of flexible copper

The quantification in the sentences (9.34) is usually called 'generic', since something is said about kinds (genera) of copper and steel. Interpreting (9.35) as

(9.36)   This bracelet is made of a flexible kind of copper

we can say the same about (9.35). It therefore seems appropriate to call this type of modification *generic*. It is in this way that sentence (9.35) is accepted by our informants, that is, on the reading

(9.37) The ship was loaded with 300 tons of a flexible kind of copper and 500 tons of a hard kind of copper

This type of modification is also present in such expressions as 'heavy syrup' and 'light oil', where 'heavy' and 'light' refer to the *specific weights* of these liquids.

Since adjectives which are not homogeneous can be applied to mass nouns as generic modifiers, we add a further qualification to the homogeneous combination principle:

(9.38) Only homogeneously referring adjectives can function as non-collective, non-generic restrictive mass noun modifiers.

C. *Homogeneous and discrete modification*

There are still other cases of acceptable count adjective–mass noun combinations, which cannot be explained in terms of collective or generic modification. We already came across the examples (9.9) 'There is small furniture in the dolls' house', and (9.26) 'You have heavy luggage'. One might think that 'small furniture' and 'heavy luggage' are acceptable due to the fact that furniture and luggage usually come in certain discrete parts: chairs, tables, etc. and suitcases, bags, etc. However, the following sentences show that this explanation does not work:

(9.39) *There is small apple in the salad

(9.40) *You have heavy sausage on your plate

Though apple and sausage usually come in the form of discrete apples and sausages, the combinations 'small apple' and 'heavy sausage' in these sentences are deviant (degrees of deviance 2.2 and 2.4, respectively). Apparently, the existence of a strong association between a mass noun and a discrete class of objects is not sufficient to allow a count adjective to modify the noun restrictively in a non-collective, non-generic way.

Let us consider a mass noun of which the extension does not naturally come in discrete parts, such as 'sugar'. Imagine the following situation. We are in a sugar refinery and are being given an explanation of the process. We are being told that

(9.41) The wet sugar, resulting from the second stage of the process, is dried here

(9.42)   This container contains only wet sugar

The sugar leaves the refinery in various forms, among which are lumps of two different sizes: small cubic lumps and larger rectangular lumps. At the packing department, we are being told that

(9.43)   The blue boxes are filled with cubic sugar, the red boxes with rectangular sugar, and the white boxes with a mixture of cubic and rectangular sugar

(9.44)   The blue box contains only cubic sugar

Let us consider the sentences (9.42) and (9.44) more closely. Cases of quantification paralleling the cases of modification are:

(9.45)   All the sugar in this container is wet

(9.46)   All the sugar in the blue box is cubical

There is a difference between these sentences in that (9.45) can very well be understood as asserting that all sugar samples in the container are wet, while (9.46) cannot sensibly be understood as asserting that all sugar samples in the box are cubic – only the lumps of sugar are meant to be cubic. Whereas the quantification in (9.45) ranges over all the sugar samples in the container, in (9.46) it ranges only over the set of sugar *lumps* in the box.

Similarly, the domain of application of the modifier 'wet' in (9.42) consists of all sugar samples, while in (9.44) the domain of application of 'cubic' is restricted to a particular subset of sugar samples (the lumps). In view of the obvious parallels with mass noun quantification, I call the former type of modification *homogeneous*, the latter type *discrete*. Homogeneous modification occurs when a mass noun modifier has the power set of the modification source (the extension of the noun) as its domain of application; discrete modification occurs when the modification domain is a contextually determined subset of the power set of the modification source.

Since count adjectives are typically adjectives of size, shape, or other aspects of outward appearance, which can be applied sensibly only to well-delineated objects, the use of a mass noun homogeneously modified by a count adjective mostly leads to nonsensical situations, as we have seen in section 9.2. It is therefore not surprising that sentences like (9.14) and (9.21) are judged as highly deviant. However, a count adjective can apply to a mass noun as a discrete modifier if the intended individuation of the referent is contextually clear. For some mass nouns there are fairly standard ways of individuating the referent (as for 'furniture', 'luggage', 'footwear', 'fruit'). For other mass nouns certain individuations are common in special contexts; for instance, restaurants and bars provide a context in which mass nouns referring to food or drinks individuate. It seems possible for almost any mass noun to construct a context where the noun can be used with a particular individuation in mind – which means that it can be used semantically as a count noun. (In such cases, these mass nouns also tend to be used syntactically as count nouns; think of 'one coffee', 'two beers', etc.) Does this undermine the homogeneous combination principle? I think not.

First of all, the possibility of non-generic, non-collective modification of a mass noun by a count adjective is restricted to discrete modification, which is only possible if the use of the mass noun is understood as elliptic for a non-mass expression: 'sugar' for 'lumps of sugar', 'beer' for 'glasses of beer', etc.

Secondly, there is a class of mass nouns for which discrete modification does not seem possible at all. This is the class of mass nouns that are also commonly used as count nouns, and where the count noun denotes a certain set of parts of the mass use denotation. Another way of characterizing this class is in terms of the Universal Grinder (Pelletier, 1975; see also chapter 2): the count use refers to the discrete objects considered as inputs to the grinder, the mass use to the homogeneous mass produced by the grinder. We might therefore call the latter *ground nouns*. Examples of ground nouns are: 'apple', 'cake', 'stone', 'onion', 'hair', 'rope', 'diamond', 'rock', 'ice cream', etc.

Sentences like:

(9.47)   *This box is filled with heavy stone

(9.48)   *There is round pancake on the plate

(9.49)   *Don't put such big onion in the salad

are considered highly deviant by our informants, with the explanation that one ought to say, instead:

(9.50)   This box is filled with heavy stones

(9.51)   There is a round pancake on the plate

(9.52)   Don't put such big onions in the salad

The acceptability judgements of count adjective–mass noun combinations on the collective, homogeneous, and discrete interpretations are summarized in table (9.53).[4]

(9.53)	Collective modification	Homogeneous modification	Discrete modification
Ground nouns	1.2	2.3	2.3
Other mass nouns	0.8	2.4	1.4

Generally, we can say that discrete modification of a ground noun is deviant because there are two possibilities for the individuation that the modifier presupposes: either it is the standard individuation of the count use of the noun, in which case one is supposed to use the noun as a count noun instead of a mass noun, or it is a non-standard individuation, in which case one is expected to indicate explicitly which individuation is intended (which will mostly give rise to a count noun phrase with embedded mass noun).

In summary, what is left of the homogeneous combination principle are the following constraints on restrictive mass noun modification:

(9.54) a. Restrictive, non-generic modification of a mass noun by a count adjective is only possible in the form of collective or discrete modification. Homogeneous modification of a mass noun can only be achieved by a mass adjective (homogeneously referring adjective).

b. 'Ground nouns', mass uses of nouns also commonly used as count nouns and where the two uses are semantically related by the Universal Grinder, cannot be modified discretely. Non-generic, non-collective modification of such nouns can only be achieved by mass adjectives.

The importance of this principle is not so much that it tells us that certain adjective–mass noun combinations are ill-formed, but that it enables us to filter out unintended readings of sentences involving count adjective–mass noun combinations. In particular, if we meet a count adjective–ground noun combination, only a collective or a generic interpretation is possible; the homogeneous interpretation, which would be semantically deviant (examples (9.15), (9.21)), and the discrete reading, which would be syntactically deviant (examples (9.47)–(9.49)), are ruled out by clause (b) of the principle. It thus seems useful to make a count/mass distinction among adjectives.

In order to make use of the principle, one should not only distinguish between count adjectives and mass adjectives but also between ground nouns and other mass nouns. Would it be feasible to make this distinction in a grammar? I think it would be very sensible to make this distinction anyway: as the idea of the Universal Grinder makes clear, virtually every concrete count noun has a potential mass noun use of which the meaning can be derived from the count noun meaning; it would be uneconomical to include both the mass use and the count use in the lexicon. It would surely be preferable to include as lexical mass nouns only those which are not ground nouns, such as 'water', 'furniture', 'sand', etc., and to derive the ground nouns from lexical count nouns by means of a rule corresponding to the Universal Grinder. This rule could mark the mass nouns in question as ground nouns, thus giving us the desired grammatical distinction.

The question as to how a count/mass distinction among adjectives could be made, has been answered here by taking homogeneity of reference as the defining characteristic of mass adjectives. Is it really feasible to identify mass adjectives on this basis? It seems that there are very few adjectives in the language of which we can say with certainty that they denote a homogeneous property (examples are 'ripe' and 'well done'). For many adjectives this is either unclear or would require the distinction of various senses, some of which refer homogeneously and some of which do not. This does not seem very attractive. Fortunately, in order to make use of the homogeneous combination principle it is required in the first place that we identify *count* adjectives, adjectives that do *not* refer homogeneously. There is a number of adjectives of which we can safely say that they do not refer homogeneously, such as adjectives of size or amount ('large', 'small', 'great', 'tiny', 'huge', 'heavy', 'light', etc.), or of shape or other aspects of outward appearance ('spherical', 'oval', 'round', 'cubic', 'dusty', 'shiny', 'scratched', 'sharp', 'dull', etc.) The extent to which it is worth while making a count/mass distinction among adjectives depends on the comprehensiveness of the class of adjectives for which we can decide that they do not refer homogeneously.

In section 9.6 I shall present a formal grammar, including a lexicon, for a fragment of English which makes clear how the distinctions between count adjectives and mass adjectives, and between ground nouns and other mass nouns, can effectively be made in a grammar.

9.4 The representation of mass noun modification

In this section I turn to the representation in Ensemble Languages of adjective–mass noun combinations and the generation of these representations by the grammar described in section 9.5. I shall restrict myself to adjectives that are *intersective*, that is, have the property that the extension of an adjective–noun combination depends only on the extensions of the noun and the adjective. The modification by adjectives that are not intersective cannot be treated in an extensional framework (see Bennett, 1974; Kamp, 1975; Montague, 1970a). The grammar in section 9.5, which is used here to obtain ensemble-theoretical representations of expressions with modified mass nouns, is an extension of the grammar in section 8.8. Again, the lexicon and the rules of the grammar accomplish a translation from English to EL_f, and purely lexical translation rules may be used to translate from EL_f to EL_r, as described in section 7.5.

A. *Homogeneous modification*

Homogeneous modification is the most typical form of mass noun modification. I shall analyse the homogeneous modification of a mass noun *m* denoting the ensemble M, by an adjective *a* denoting the predicate A, as denoting the restriction of M to the part formed by all M-parts having the property A, that is, as:

(9.55) $[x \subseteq M \,|\, A(x)]$

Grammar rule M1 combines adjectives and mass nouns to this effect. Via the process described in the previous chapter, a sentence like

(9.56)   John drank some cold water

is thus assigned the syntactic tree

(9.57a)   sentence(np(propername(John)[sing])[sing],
             verb(drank)[unspec, 2],
             np(det(some)[mass],
                nom(adj(cold)[unspec],
                   nom(noun(water)[mass])[mass])
                [mass])[mass])

and the EL_f representation, after λ-conversion:[5]

(9.57b) $\exists y \subseteq^\circ [x \subseteq \text{WATER} \,|\, \text{COLD}(x)]: \text{DRINK}(\text{John}, y)$

According to the homogeneous combination principle (9.54), homogeneous modification cannot be achieved by count adjectives; grammar rule M1 thus requires that the *form* attribute of the adjective does not have the value *count*.

B. *Discrete modification*

Discrete modification of a mass noun occurs when a modifier has a certain subset of the power set of the modification source as its domain. It parallels discrete quantification, as the following sentence pair illustrates:

(9.58) a. These boxes contain cubic sugar
 b. The sugar in these boxes is cubic

Discrete modification presupposes a certain individuation of the source; as in the case of discrete quantification, the determination of this individuation is usually a referential matter, belonging to the EL_r level of analysis. Representations of discrete modification are thus generated in the EL_f–EL_r translation, rather than in the English–EL_f translation. We have seen in section 8.7 that this may be accomplished in the case of discrete quantification by combining the EL_f–EL_r translation with the generation of the homogeneous reading. This works for discrete modification as well. To illustrate this we shall consider the interpretation of sentence (9.58a) in a domain of discourse in which sugar takes the form of sugar lumps.

First we generate the EL_f representation of the sentence reading with homogeneous modification. For 'cubic sugar' we construct a syntactic structure of category <u>nom</u> with an EL_f representation that I abbreviate as CS:

(9.59a) $CS =_D [s \subseteq SUGAR | CUBIC(s)]$

Rule F6b turns the nominal into a noun phrase, with representation

(9.60) $(\lambda P: (\lambda z: z \neq \varnothing)([y \in \delta_m(\lambda u: u = CS, CS) | P(y)]))$

Rule J1 combines this representation with that of 'These boxes' (see example (8.101) in the previous chapter) into a noun phrase sequence representation which is subsequently applied to the verb representation by rule K1. This gives the following EL_f representation:

(9.61a) $(\lambda R:$
 $(\lambda Q: \cup *(BOXES_o, \{x \in \delta(\lambda y: y = BOXES_o, BOXES_o) | Q(x)\}) = BOXES_o)$
 $(\lambda x_1: (\lambda P: (\lambda z: z \neq \varnothing)([y \in \delta_m(\lambda u: u = CS, CS) | P(y)]))$
 $(\lambda x_2: R(x_1, x_2))))(CONTAIN)$

which is simplified by repeated λ-conversion to:

(9.61b) $\cup*(BOXES_o, \{x \in \delta(\lambda y: y = BOXES_o, BOXES_o) | [y \in \delta_m(\lambda u: u = CS, CS) | CONTAIN(x, y)] \neq \varnothing\}) = BOXES_o$

Let the EL_f–EL_r translation replace SUGAR by SUGAR-LUMPS$_r$, BOXES$_o$ by BOXES$_{ro}$, CONTAIN by (λu: CONTAIN$_r$(u)), and CUBIC by (λz: $\forall y \in z$: CUBIC$_r$(y)). The EL_f representation of 'cubic sugar' (9.59a) is thus translated into an expression that I abbreviate as CSLUMPS$_r$:

(9.59b) $CSLUMPS_r =_D [s \subseteq SUGAR\text{-}LUMPS_r | (\lambda z: \forall y \in z: CUBIC_r(y))]$

Moreover, I take the quantifications in the noun phrases 'These boxes' and 'cubic sugar' to be distributive and homogeneous, respectively. This gives, altogether, the following EL_r representation:

(9.62a) $\cup*(BOXES_{ro}, \{x \in BOXES_{ro} | [y \in \mathcal{P}(CSLUMPS_r) |$
$(\lambda u: CONTAIN_r(u)(x, y)] \neq \varnothing)\}) = BOXES_{ro}$

which can be simplified to

(9.62b) $\{x \in BOXES_{ro} | [y \in \mathcal{P}(CSLUMPS_r) | CONTAIN_r(x, y)] \neq \varnothing\}$
$= BOXES_{ro}$

This says that the set of those boxes that contain a non-empty set of cubic sugar lumps is the same as the set of boxes. This is obviously equivalent to saying that each of these boxes contains at least one cubic sugar lump, that is, (9.62b) is equivalent to the more familiar form

(9.62c) $\forall x \in BOXES_{ro}: \exists y \subseteq^\circ CSLUMPS_r: CONTAIN(x, y)$

This demonstrates the possibility of handling discrete modification at the EL_r level.

I think the phenomenon of discrete modification is indeed preferably accounted for at the EL_r level, like the phenomenon of discrete quantification, since the presupposed individuation of the source is, in general, not determined on formal grounds but depends on referential considerations. Yet it may be argued that for certain mass nouns a context-independent individuating reading exists. This view is most reasonable for ground nouns and for other mass nouns having morphologically related count noun counterparts in the language, such as 'jewellery' ('jewels'), 'poetry' ('poems'), etc. Mass nouns of the latter kind, which are not ground nouns and which have a context-independent individuating reading, can be viewed syntactically as mass nouns and semantically as plural count nouns. For such mass nouns it might be considered appropriate to deal with discrete modification at the formal level of analysis. It is technically of some interest to see how we might accommodate this view. To illustrate this, I have included 'collective mass nouns' in the grammar of section 9.6 as nouns with the form feature coll. Examples are 'jewellery' and 'poetry', considered as semantically synonymous to the count nouns 'jewels' and 'poems', respectively. Grammar rule M2, which handles in the first place ordinary count noun modification, constructs for the combination of an adjective and a collective mass noun like

(9.63a) expensive jewellery

the syntactic tree

(9.63b) nom(adj(expensive)[count],
            nom(noun(jewellery)[coll])[coll])
         [coll]

with the semantic representation:

(9.63c) $\{x \in \text{JEWELS} \mid \text{EXPENSIVE}(x)\}$

Clearly, 'expensive jewellery' upon this analysis is semantically indistinguishable from 'expensive jewels'. There is a syntactic distinction, however, which is expressed by the value of the form attribute.

C. *Collective modification*

Collective modification by an adjective occurs, for instance, in the sentence

(9.64) John has heavy sand in his bag

if we take it in the reading

(9.65) The sand in John's bag is heavy

(The majority of subjects in the above mentioned experiment considered this to be the interpretation of the sentence.) It is easy enough to write down an EL_f expression representing this reading, for instance:

(9.66) $\text{HEAVY}([x \subseteq \text{SAND} \mid \text{IN}(x, \text{bag}_j)])$

where bag_j abbreviates an EL_f representation of 'John's bag'. In the previous chapter I showed how such a representation can, in principle, be generated for sentences of the form of (9.65), but the derivation of the representation from the original sentence (9.64) presents a problem since the surface structure differs greatly from the structure of the representation. This is not a problem specific to mass nouns, but a problem of collective modification in general. A sentence like

(9.67) John has heavy books in his bag

involving only count nouns, poses exactly the same problems for the representation of the collective reading 'The books in John's bag are heavy'.

The root of the problem is that, while 'heavy' is, syntactically speaking, a modifier of the noun 'sand', semantically it applies to the sand John has in his bag, but there is no phrase in the sentence with this denotation. So we have to resolve a conflict between syntactic and semantic structure and design compositional grammar rules that construe 'heavy' as a constituent of the noun phrase 'heavy sand' while constructing a semantic representation in which HEAVY is applied to $[x \subseteq SAND | IN(x, bag_j)]$. Rule F7 has been included in the grammar to accomplish this. For instance, in the analysis of the sentence

(9.68) John carries heavy sand

rule F7 constructs the syntactic tree

(9.69a) np(adj(heavy)[count],
　　　　　nom(noun(sand)[mass])[mass])[mass]

with EL_f representation

(9.69b) $(\lambda P: HEAVY([x \subseteq SAND | P(x)]))$

For the rest, the same construction process is carried out as described in the previous chapter. In particular, (9.69b) and the representation of 'John' are combined into that of an NP sequence which looks, in this case, after λ-conversion, as follows:

(9.70) $(\lambda R: HEAVY([x \subseteq SAND | R(JOHN, x)]))$

This representation is applied to the verb representation by the semantic part of rule K1a with the result:

(9.71) $HEAVY([x \subseteq SAND | CARRY(John, x)])$

This is precisely what we wanted.

D. *Generic modification*
Generic modification parallels the phenomenon of generic quantification, as the following pair of sentences illustrates:

(9.72)   This bracelet is made of flexible copper

(9.73)   The copper of which this bracelet is made is flexible

In the generic reading of these sentences, 'flexible' is used to indicate a 'specific' property, on a par with such properties as specific weight, specific heat, and specific conductibility.

As in the case of generic quantification, it is questionable whether generic modification can be treated adequately in an extensional framework. Like generic quantification, it is therefore left out of further consideration here (see also section 8.2).

9.5 Augmented phrase-construction grammar for an extended fragment of English

In this section I present an augmented phrase-construction grammar for an extension of the fragment of English, covered by the grammar in section 8.8. The extensions consist of the treatment of the following phenomena:

1. The homogeneous modification of a mass noun by a sequence of adjectives (and thereby, indirectly, of discrete modification as well).
2. The discrete modification, by a sequence of adjectives, of mass nouns having an (alleged) context-independent individuating reading ('collective mass nouns').
3. The 'ordinary' non-collective, non-generic modification of a count noun by a sequence of adjectives.
4. The collective modification of a count noun or mass noun by an adjective.
5. The phenomenon that, in principle, every singular count noun can be used as a mass noun, a so-called 'ground noun'.
6. The distinction between 'count adjectives' and 'mass adjectives', as well as adjectives which are not clearly 'count' or 'mass'.
7. The occurrence of a mass noun in predicative position after a copula.

Most of these extensions have been considered above. Extension 3 is simply that expressions like

(9.74)   cubic red boxes

are translated, by grammar rule M2, into:

(9.75a) $\{x \in \{y \in \text{BOXES} \mid \text{RED}(y)\} \mid \text{CUBIC}(x)\}$

which is equivalent to

(9.75b) $\{x \in \text{BOXES} | \text{RED}(x) \,\&\, \text{CUBIC}(x)\}$

Extension 7 is that an expression of the form

(9.76) x is water

is translated by rule N into an EL_f expression of the form (after λ-conversion):

(9.77) $x \subseteq \text{WATER}$

This has, for instance, the result that the grammar (plus the logic of ensembles) resolves Quine's well-known 'puddle puzzle' (see section 3.2). The puzzle is that from the premises:

(9.78) All the puddles are water

(9.79) All water is wet

it should follow that

(9.80) All the puddles are wet

For the first premise the grammar generates the EL_f representation:

(9.81) $\cup^*(\{x \in \delta(\lambda y: y = \text{PUDDLES}_o, \text{PUDDLES}_o) | x \subseteq \text{WATER}\})$
        $= \text{PUDDLES}_o$

As before, the possible interpretations of the sentence are generated at the EL_r level by translating the distribution function while observing the type restrictions imposed by the translation of the other EL_f constants. Suppose that WATER is translated as the EL_r constant WATER_r of type E(water), where water is a referential atomic type and E(water) an ensemble type (see chapter 6), then by the type conditions on the partselection construction $x \subseteq \text{WATER}_r$, the variable x must either have the type E(water) or the type S(water) or the union of the two. Assuming further that PUDDLES_o is translated into PUDDLES_{ro} of type S(E(water)), which means that an individual puddle is viewed at the referential level as a water sample, then a little calculation shows that the subexpression $\delta(\lambda y: y = \text{PUDDLES}_o, \text{PUDDLES}_o)$ in (9.81), denoting the quantification domain, has only one translation in EL_r, namely PUDDLES_{ro} (only the distributive reading of the quantification survives). The translation of (9.81) is thus:

(9.82a) $\cup^*(\{x \in \text{PUDDLES}_{ro} | x \subseteq \text{WATER}_r\}) = \text{PUDDLES}_{ro}$

Modification and mass nouns 219

which is obviously equivalent to

(9.82b) $\forall x \in PUDDLES_{ro}: x \subseteq WATER_r$

The second premise, on the intended reading with homogeneous quantification, has the EL_r representation

(9.83) $\forall x \subseteq WATER: WET(x)$

(cf. the treatment of (8.134) 'All the snow melted', and the use of grammar rule H for 'is wet'). For the hoped-for consequence (9.80) the grammar generates the EL_f representation

(9.84) $\cup^*(\{x \in \delta(\lambda y: y = PUDDLES_o, PUDDLES_o) | WET(x)\})$
        $= PUDDLES_o$

Assuming that WET is translated into $(\lambda z: WET_r(z))$, where WET_r is an EL_r predicate applicable to individual puddles but not to sets of puddles, there is one translation of the distribution function δ that survives the EL_f–EL_r translation, namely the translation $(\lambda X: X)$. We thus obtain the following EL_r translation of (9.84):

(9.85a) $\cup^*(\{x \in PUDDLES_{ro} | WET_r(x)\}) = PUDDLES_{ro}$

which is obviously equivalent to

(9.85b) $\forall x \in PUDDLES_{ro}: WET_r(x)$

This is indeed a logical consequence of (9.82) and (9.83).

Compared to the grammar described in section 8.8, the grammar described below is extended with a number of rules and lexical items implementing the extensions 1–7 of the fragment of English mentioned above. Rule group F has been extended with rule F7 to deal with collective modification. The new rules M produce modifications with homogeneous or discrete distribution. Rule L has been added in order to do justice to the observation that many nouns, like 'apple', 'onion', 'cake', and 'rope' occur both as singular count nouns and as mass nouns (ground nouns). These words are included in the lexicon as singular count nouns and transformed by rule L into ground nouns. For instance, application of this rule to the lexical entry for 'onion' leads to the syntactic tree

(9.86) noun(noun(onion)[sing])[ground]

We have seen in chapter 2 that most nouns which are ordinarily used as mass nouns, such as 'wine', can be used as count nouns with the readings 'kind of ...' and 'conventional serving of ...'. This suggests that we should also have rules in the grammar that go in the opposite direction, from mass to count. I have not included any rules to this effect, however, since it is not clear to me what their semantic parts should be. One might be tempted to introduce special functions that assign to each mass noun the classes of its (conventionally recognized) kinds and its conventional servings or portions. This would be helpful for analysing sentences such as:

(9.87) Hungary produces excellent wines

(9.88) I want to have a large ice cream

But it would be insufficient for sentences like:

(9.89) Seagram now produces wines without alcohol

(9.90) I was dreaming of an ice cream as big as the Eiffel Tower.

Clearly, wines without alcohol do not belong to the conventionally recognized kinds of wine, and an ice cream of the size of the Eiffel Tower falls outside the class of conventional servings.

In chapter 2 I have argued that the count/mass distinction should not be drawn between words, but between occurrences of words. This would suggest that nouns should not be labelled as mass etc. in the lexicon, but that such a labelling should only take place as a noun occurs in a syntactic configuration where it can be classified as such. There are two reasons why I have nonetheless assigned the features 'mass', 'collective mass', 'singular' and 'plural' to nouns in the lexicon. First, we have seen earlier in this chapter that there is empirical evidence that we should distinguish ordinary mass nouns, ground nouns, and collective mass nouns. This calls for lexical distinctions. Secondly, the count and mass uses of a noun are semantically different, and although it would of course be possible to represent nouns as syntactically 'neutral' in the lexicon, I don't think it is possible to give them satisfactory 'neutral' semantic representations.[6]

Rule N has been added to deal with copula + mass noun constructions, as illustrated by (9.76)–(9.77). For the rest the grammar is essentially the same as that of section 8.8, with minor modifications due to the fact that, where formerly a rule would have a constituent of syntactic category noun, now a constituent of category nom (noun preceded by adjectives) is allowed; moreover, the new values ground and coll of the form attribute turn up in some of the rules.

The lexicon of this grammar is the same as the one in section 8.8 except for the entries of adjectives and the addition of 'collective mass nouns'. Adjectives now carry a <u>form</u> attribute in order to distinguish count adjectives and mass adjectives. Adjectives which are neither clearly 'count' nor 'mass' have the value <u>unspec</u> for this attribute. As before, an attribute with the value <u>unspec</u> satisfies any attribute condition.

Only the new parts of the lexicon are given here; for convenience, the grammar is specified completely, though some of the rules are identical to those in section 8.8. The rules A–K of the present grammar are adapted versions of the corresponding rules in section 8.8. Rules F7, L, M, and N are new.

In those parts of the rules that stipulate conditions on syntactic attributes, the notation <u>v</u>|<u>w</u> is used to indicate that the value of an attribute be either <u>v</u> or <u>w</u>.

An algorithm for parsing the sentences of the fragment and translating them into EL_f (and subsequently into EL_r) according to the rules of this grammar has been implemented in the TENDUM system (Bunt and thoe Schwartzenberg, 1982).[7]

9.5.1 Additions and changes in the lexicon

(B) *Nouns*

'Collective mass nouns'. Nouns with form feature <u>coll</u>.

syntactic tree	EL_f translation
<u>noun</u>(jewellery)[<u>form</u>: <u>coll</u>]	JEWELS
<u>noun</u>(poetry)[<u>form</u>: <u>coll</u>]	POEMS

(D) *Adjectives*

syntactic tree	EL_f translation
<u>adj</u>(wet)[<u>form</u>: unspec]	WET
<u>adj</u>(heavy)[<u>form</u>: count]	HEAVY
<u>adj</u>(cold)[<u>form</u>: unspec]	COLD
<u>adj</u>(sweet)[<u>form</u>: mass]	SWEET
<u>adj</u>(ripe)[<u>form</u>: mass]	RIPE
<u>adj</u>(red)[<u>form</u>: unspec]	RED
<u>adj</u>(cubic)[<u>form</u>: count]	CUBIC
<u>adj</u>(round)[<u>form</u>: count]	ROUND
<u>adj</u>(expensive)[<u>form</u>: count]	EXPENSIVE

9.5.2 *The rules of the grammar*[8]

Rule A Rule constructing isolated amounts

PC Rule:	a: NUMBER + b: UNIT → ISOLAMOUNT
Conditions on attributes:	β β
Carry-over of attributes:	–
Semantic rule:	a' + b' → $(\lambda P: P(a' - b'_2))$

Rule B Rules constructing applied amounts

All rules (B1–B4) have the same phrase-construction rule and conditions on attributes. The rules are paired differently as far as attribute carry-over and semantic rules are concerned.

PC Rule: a: NUMBER + b: UNIT + c: PART → AMOUNT

Conditions on attributes: β β

B1, B3 Carry-over of attributes: → form: nonsing

B2, B4 Carry-over of attributes: → form: mass

B1, B2 Semantic rule: a'   + b'   + c' → $(\lambda u: b'_1(u) = a' - b'_2)$

B3, B4 Semantic rule: a'   + b'   + c' → $(\lambda u: b'_1(u) \geq a' - b'_2)$

Rule C Rules constructing numerals

The rules C1 and C2 differ only in their semantic parts.

PC Rule:	a: NUMBER → NUMERAL
Conditions on attributes:	–
Carry-over of attributes:	β → β
C1 Semantic rule:	a' → $(\lambda X: \#(X) = a')$
C2 Semantic rule:	a' → $(\lambda X: \#(X) \geq a')$

Rule D Rules constructing determiners from numerals or applied amounts

Each of the rules is subdivided further into subrules that differ in the conditions on attributes and the semantic parts.

Modification and mass nouns 223

D1	PC Rule:	a: NUMERAL → DET		
D2	PC Rule:	a: AMOUNT → DET		
	Carry-over of attributes:	β	·	$\to \beta$
D1a *D2a*	Conditions on attributes:	form: $\neq$ mass		
	Semantic rule:	a'		$\to (\lambda X: (\lambda P: a'(\cup^*(X, \{x \in \delta(a', X) \mid P(x)\}))))$
D1b *D2b*	Conditions on attributes:	form: mass		
	Semantic rule:	a'		$\to (\lambda X: (\lambda P: a' ([x \in \delta_m(a', X) \mid P(x)])))$

Rule E Rules constructing 'npcentres'

	PC Rule:	a: CENTRALDET + b: NOM → NPCENTRE		
E1	Conditions on attributes:	form: plur	form: plur	
	Carry-over of attributes:		β	$\to \beta$
	Semantic rule:	a'	+ b'	$\to \{x \in b' \mid a'(x)\}$
E2	Conditions on attributes:	form: mass	form: mass| ground|coll	
	Carry-over of attributes:			form: mass
	Semantic rule:	a'	+ b'	$\to [x \subseteq b' \mid a'(x)]$

Rule F Rules constructing noun phrases

There are seven rules, of which F1 and F2 differ only in their phrase construction parts.

F1	PC Rule:	a: PREDET + b: NOM		→ NP
F2	PC Rule:	a: PREDET + b: NPCENTRE → NP		
	Conditions on attributes:	β	β	
	Carry-over of attributes:		β	$\to \beta$
	Semantic rule:	a'	+ b'	$\to a'(b')$

Rule F3 has two subrules, of which F3a is identical to F1 and F2 except for its phrase-construction rule.

224   *Part 1 Model-theoretic semantics of mass terms*

F3   PC Rule: a: DET + b: NOM → NP

F3b Conditions on   <u>form</u>:   <u>form</u>:
       attributes: nonsing   ≠ sing

       Carry-over of   → <u>form: sing</u>
       attributes:

       Semantic rule: a'   + b'   → a'(b')

F4   PC Rule: a: PROPERNAME → NP
       Conditions on   —
       attributes:

       Carry-over of   β   → β
       attributes:

       Semantic rule: a'   → (λP: P(a'))

F5   Rule constructing noun phrases from npcentres. The rule has a number of subrules, all sharing the same phrase-construction rule and the same rule for carrying over the values of syntactic attributes:

       PC Rule: a: NPCENTRE → NP
       Carry-over of   β   → β
       attributes:

F5a Conditions on   <u>form</u>:
       attributes: plur | coll
       Semantic rule: a'   → (λP: ∪*(a', {x ∈ δ(λy:
                                              y = a', a') | P(x)}) = a')

F5b Conditions on   <u>form</u>:
       attributes: mass | ground
       Semantic rule: a'   → (λP: [x ∈ δ_m(λy:
                                              y = a', a') | P(x)] = a')

F5c Conditions on   <u>form</u>:
       attributes: mass | ground
       Semantic rule: a'   → (λP: {x ∈ 𝒫(a') | P(x)} = 𝒫(a'))

F6   Rules constructing noun phrases from bare noms. There are two rules, one for count noms and one for mass noms. They have the same phrase-construction rule and attribute carry-over.

       PC Rule: a: NOM   → NP
       Carry-over of   β   → β
       attributes:

Modification and mass nouns 225

F6a Conditions on   form:
      attributes: plur|coll
      Semantic rule: a' $\rightarrow (\lambda P: (\lambda z: \#(z) > 1)(\{x \in \delta(\lambda u: u = a', a') | P(x)\}))$

F6b Conditions on   form:
      attributes: mass|ground
      Semantic rules: a' $\rightarrow (\lambda P: (\lambda z: z \neq \emptyset)([x \in \delta_m(\lambda u: u = S, S) | P(x)]))$

F7   Rules forming adjective–nominal combinations for collectively modifying adjectives. The two subrules have the same phrase-construction rule and carry-over of attribute values.

      PC Rule: a: ADJ   +b: NOM $\rightarrow$ NP
      Carry-over of
      attributes: β $\rightarrow \beta$

F7a Conditions on   form: form: mass|
      attributes: $\neq$ mass   ground
      Semantic rule: a'   +b' $\rightarrow (\lambda P: a'([x \subseteq b' | P(x)]))$

F7b Conditions on   form:
      attributes: plur|coll
      Semantic rule: a'   +b' $\rightarrow (\lambda P: a'(\{x \in b' | P(x)\}))$

Rule G   *Rules constructing 'cumulative noun phrases'*

G1   PC Rule: a: NUMERAL +b: NOM $\rightarrow$ CUMNP
       Conditions on
       attributes: form: plur   form: plur
       Carry-over of
       attributes: β $\rightarrow \beta$
       Semantic rule: a'   +b' $\rightarrow (a', b')$

G2   PC Rule: a: AMOUNT   +b: NOM $\rightarrow$ CUMNP
       Conditions on
       attributes: form: nonsing   form: plur
       Carry-over of
       attributes: β $\rightarrow \beta$
       Semantic rule: a'   +b' $\rightarrow (a', b')$

226   *Part 1 Model-theoretic semantics of mass terms*

G3   PC Rule: a: AMOUNT + b: NOM   → CUMNP
     Conditions on   form: mass   form: mass |
     attributes: ground | coll
     Carry-over of
     attributes: → form: mass
     Semantic rule: a'   + b'   → (λ z: a'($\cup$ (z),
                                                $\mathcal{P}$(b')))

Rule H Rule constructing 'verbs' from copula + adjective

     PC Rule: a: COPULA + b: ADJ → VERB
     Conditions on
     attributes: —
     Carry-over of
     attributes: β → β
     Semantic rule: a'   + b'   → a'(b')

Rule I Rules constructing 'noun phrase sequences' with cumulative or subcumulative quantification

The rules differ only in their semantic parts.[9] For any j > 1 there is a rule as follows:

     PC Rule: a1: CUMNP + ([v: VERB]) + ... + aj: CUMNP
                                            → NPS
     Conditions on
     attributes: —
     Carry-over of   form: f   → nr: j, form: f
     attributes:
Ia   Semantic rule: a1' + ... + aj'   → (λ R: (λ x: a1'$_1$(proj$_1$(x)) & ...
                                                ... & aj'$_1$(proj$_j$(x)))
                                                (\{y \in a1'_2 \times ... \times aj'_2 | R(y)\}))
Ib   Semantic rule: a1' + ... + aj'   → (λ R: $\exists$!x $\in$ \{y $\in$ a1'_2 $\times$ ... $\times$ aj'_2 | R(y)\}:
                                                a1'$_1$(proj$_1$(x)) & ... & aj'$_1$(proj$_j$(x)))

Rule J Rules constructing 'noun phrase sequences'

By PERM(x1, ... xj) is meant any permutation of the sequence (x1, ... , xj).

J1   Rule constructing NP sequences with left-to-right order of relative scopes.

     For any j ≥ 1 there is a rule as follows:

Modification and mass nouns 227

PC Rule:	a1: NP+([v: VERB])+...+aj: NP →	
		→ NPS
Conditions on attributes:	–	
Carry-over of attributes:	form: f	→ form: f, nr: j
Semantic rule:	a1'+...+aj'	→ (λR: a1'(λx1: ... aj'(λxj: R(PERM(x1, ..., xj))...)))

J2 Rule constructing NP sequences where a noun phrase other than the leftmost one has widest scope.[10]

For m ≥ 1, n ≥ 0:

PC Rule:	a: NPS+([v: VERB])+b: NP+c: NPS →		
		→ NPS[a₁, ..., aₘ, b, c₁, ..., cₙ]	
Conditions on attributes:	nr: m	nr: n	
Carry-over of attributes:	form: f	→ form: f, nr: m+n+1	
Semantic rule:	a'+b'+c' →		
	(λR: (λy: a₁'(λx1: ... aₘ'(λxm: c₁'(λz1: ... cₙ'(λzn: R(PERM(x1, ..., xm, y, z1, ..., zn)) ...))))))		

J3 Rule constructing NP sequences where one of the noun phrases has a wider scope than it would have on the basis of its position in the sequence.

For k ≥ 0, m ≥ 1, n ≥ 1:

PC Rule:	a: NPS+([v: VERB])+b: NPS+c: NPS →		
		→ NPS[a₁, ..., aₖ, b₁, ..., bₘ, c₁, ..., cₙ]	
Conditions on attributes:	nr: k	nr: m	nr: n
Carry-over of attributes:	form: f	→ form: f, nr: k+m+n	
Semantic rule:	a'+b'+c' →		
	(λR: a₁'(λxi: ... aₖ'(λxk: c₁'(λy1: b₁'(λy2: ... (λym: bₘ'(λz1: (c₂'(λz2: ... cₙ'(λzn: R(PERM(x1, ..., xk, y1, ..., ym, z1, ..., zn))...)		

Rule K Rules constructing sentences

K1 The rule is split into two subrules that differ only in the conditions on attributes. It is assumed that n > 0.

228   Part I Model-theoretic semantics of mass terms

	PC Rule:	a: NPS + b: VERB → SENTENCE[a_1, b, a_2, ..., a_n]
	Carry-over of attributes:	β → β
	Semantic rule:	a' + b' → a'(b')
K1a	Conditions on attributes:	β β
K1b	Conditions on attributes:	nr: n nr: n form: form: ≠plur nonplur
K2	PC Rule:	a: NP + b: MEASUREVERB + c: ISOLAMOUNT → SENTENCE
	Conditions on attributes:	β β
	Carry-over of attributes:	—
	Semantic rule:	a' + b' + c' → a'(λx: c'(λy: b'(x, y)))

Rule L Rule forming 'ground nouns' from singular count nouns

	PC Rule:	a: NOUN → NOUN
	Conditions on attributes:	form: sing
	Carry-over of attributes:	→ form: ground
	Semantic rule:	a' → $\cup$(a')

Rule M Rules forming adjective (-sequence)–noun combinations

The rules M1 and M2 have the same phrase-construction rule and carry-over of attribute values.

	PC Rule:	a: ADJ + b: NOM → NOM
	Carry-over of attributes:	β → β
M1	Conditions on attributes:	form: form: ≠count mass|ground
	Semantic rule:	a' + b' → [x ⊆ a' | b'(x)]
M2	Conditions on attributes:	form: plur|coll
	Semantic rule:	a' + b' → {x ∈ a' | b'(x)}

M3 PC Rule: a: NOUN   → NOM

    Conditions on attributes: —

    Carry-over of attributes: β   → β

    Semantic rule: a'   → a'

Rule N Rule constructing 'verbs' from copula + mass nouns

    PC Rule: a: COPULA + b: NOUN   → VERB

    Carry-over of attributes: β   → β

    Conditions on attributes: form: mass
                                            ground|coll

    Semantic rule: a'   + b'   → (λx: x ⊆ b')

PART 2
ENSEMBLE THEORY

10 Axiomatic ensemble theory

10.1 The logical system

In this chapter I offer a formal axiomatic account of ensemble theory. In this section I describe the logical framework in which ensemble theory is formulated. In section 10.2 the theory is derived step by step from an axiomatic base, the proofs of a number of theorems of fundamental importance are presented, and some derived concepts are defined which are useful for the formulation or application of the theory. Section 10.3 is devoted to a discussion of the notions of 'merge', 'overlap', and 'completion', the ensemble analogues of the union, intersection, and complement in set theory. In section 10.4 I shall discuss two particularly interesting kinds of ensemble, called 'continuous' and 'discrete'.

For the formulation of the axioms and the proofs of the theorems, I shall use a variant of a well-known logical system, often used in the formulation of set theory (see Fraenkel *et al.*, 1973, pp. 283-4).

A. The *logical language* in which axioms, theorems, etc. are stated is a first-order predicate language, defined as follows:

1. *s* is a *primitive symbol* if and only if it is one of the following symbols:
    a. *Individual variables*: x, x_1, x_2, ... (*ad infinitum*). Occasionally, other names of variables will be used as well, such as y, z, u, v, etc.
    b. *Primitive predicates*: the binary predicates $\subseteq$, $\in$.
    c. *Logical constants*:
        (i) Connectives: ¬, &, v, →, ↔.
        (ii) Quantifiers: the universal quantifier ∀.
                        the existential quantifier ∃.

233

d. *Auxiliary symbols*:), (. Occasionally, square brackets], [will be used instead of ordinary parentheses in order to increase the readability of formulas.

2. S is a *formula* if and only if it has one of the following forms:
   a. $\alpha \subseteq \beta$ or $\alpha \in \beta$, where α and β are variables; a formula of one of these forms is called *atomic*.
   b. $\neg(S_1)$, $(S_1) \lor (S_2)$, $(S_1) \& (S_2)$, $(S_1) \rightarrow (S_2)$, $(S_1) \leftrightarrow (S_2)$, where S_1 and S_2 are formulas. Parentheses will often be omitted if no confusion is likely to arise.
   c. $(\forall \alpha)(S_1)$, $(\exists \alpha)(S_1)$, where α is a variable and S_1 is a formula. Quantifier sequences like $(\forall x)(\forall y)(\forall z)$ will often be abbreviated as $(\forall x, y, z)$. I shall occasionally abbreviate expressions of the form $(\forall x)((x \subseteq y) \rightarrow S)$ or $(\exists x)((x \subseteq y) \& S)$, where S is a formula, as $(\forall x \subseteq y)$ S and $(\exists x \subseteq y)$ S, respectively. Likewise for the $\in$-relation and for the derived relations defined in section 10.2.

B. The *axioms and rules of inference* are the following:

3. X is an axiom if and only if it has one of the following forms:
   a. Axiom schemata of the propositional calculus:
   $(S_1) \rightarrow ((S_2) \rightarrow (S_1))$,
   $(S_1 \rightarrow S_2) \rightarrow ((S_1 \rightarrow (S_2 \rightarrow S_3)) \rightarrow (S_1 \rightarrow S_3))$,
   $(S_1 \rightarrow S_2) \rightarrow ((S_1 \rightarrow \neg S_2) \rightarrow \neg S_1)$,
   $\neg \neg S_2 \rightarrow S_2$,
   $S_1 \rightarrow (S_2 \rightarrow S_1 \& S_2)$,
   $(S_1 \& S_2) \rightarrow S_1$, $(S_1 \& S_2) \rightarrow S_2$,
   $S_1 \rightarrow (S_1 \lor S_2)$, $S_2 \rightarrow (S_1 \lor S_2)$,
   $(S_1 \rightarrow S_3) \rightarrow ((S_2 \rightarrow S_3) \rightarrow ((S_1 \lor S_2) \rightarrow S_3))$,
   $(S_1 \leftrightarrow S_2) \rightarrow (S_1 \rightarrow S_2)$, $(S_1 \leftrightarrow S_2) \rightarrow (S_2 \rightarrow S_1)$,
   $(S_1 \rightarrow S_2) \rightarrow ((S_2 \rightarrow S_1) \rightarrow (S_1 \leftrightarrow S_2))$,
   where S_1, S_2, and S_3 range over formulas.
   b. Axiom schemata of the predicate calculus: $(\forall \alpha)(S) \rightarrow S'$, $S' \rightarrow (\exists \alpha)(S)$, where S ranges over all formulas, α ranges over all variables, and S' is a formula obtained from S by replacing one or more of the free occurrences of α in S by some variable α', provided that those occurrences are not within the scope of a quantifier $(\forall \alpha')$.

4. S₁ is *immediately derivable* from the formulas S₂ and S₃ if:
   a. (Rule of Modus Ponens): S₃ is S₂→S₁ or else if S₂ has the form S₄→S₅ and S₁ has the form
   b. (Rule of consequent universalization): S₄→($\forall \alpha$)S₅, where α is not free in S₄, or
   c. (Rule of antecedent existentialization): ($\exists \alpha$)(S₄)→S₅, where α is not free in S₅.

10.2 Ensemble theory built up from a system of axioms

10.2.1 *Axiom of transitivity*
This axiom postulates the transitivity of the part–whole relation:

AXIOM 1. $(\forall x, y, z)((x \subseteq y \,\&\, y \subseteq z) \rightarrow x \subseteq z)$

The following derived concepts are defined in terms of the primitive $\subseteq$. (All definitions of derived concepts in this chapter can be regarded as *abbreviations*: the expression at the left-hand side of a definition is regarded as a short notation for the expression at the right-hand side.)

Definition 2.1.1 (*Equality*).[1] Two ensembles are equal iff they include each other.
   In formula: $x = y =_D x \subseteq y \,\&\, y \subseteq x$

Definition 2.1.2 (*Emptiness*). An ensemble is empty iff it is equal to all its parts.
   In formula: $\text{EMPTY}(x) =_D (\forall y \subseteq x)(y = x)$

Definition 2.1.3 (*Non-empty part*). An ensemble x is a non-empty part of an ensemble y iff x is a part of y and x is not empty.
   In formula: $x \subseteq^\circ y =_D x \subseteq y \,\&\, \neg\text{EMPTY}(x)$

Definition 2.1.4 (*Proper part*). An ensemble x is a proper part of an ensemble y iff x is a part of y and x is not equal to y.
   In formula: $x \subset y =_D x \subseteq y \,\&\, \neg(x = y)$

Definition 2.1.5 (*Genuine part*). An ensemble x is a genuine part of an ensemble y iff x is a non-empty part of y and x is not equal to y.
   In formula: $x \subset^\circ y =_D x \subseteq^\circ y \,\&\, \neg(x = y)$

Definition 2.1.6 (*Overlap*). Two ensembles overlap iff they have a common non-empty part.
   In formula: $x \,\hat{o}\, y =_D (\exists u)(u \subseteq^\circ x \,\&\, u \subseteq^\circ y)$

Definition 2.1.7 (*Atomicity*). An ensemble is atomic iff it is not empty and it is equal to each of its non-empty parts.
In formula: $AT(x) =_D \neg EMPTY(x) \& (\forall y \subseteq^\circ x)(x = y)$

A few elementary properties of these notions are established by the following corollaries and theorems.

Corollary 2.1.1. An atomic ensemble has no genuine parts.

Since every ensemble is either empty or not, and every non-empty ensemble either has a genuine part or not, we have:

Corollary 2.1.2. Every ensemble is either atomic or empty or possesses a genuine part.

Theorem 2.1.1. All parts of an empty ensemble are empty.
In formula: $(\forall x)(EMPTY(x) \rightarrow (\forall y \subseteq x)EMPTY(y))$

Proof: Let y be an arbitrary part of an empty ensemble x. By definition 2.1.2, this means $y = x$. Let z be an arbitrary part of y; according to axiom I, $z \subseteq x$. Therefore, again, $z = x$. The latter implies (definition 2.1.1) $x \subseteq z$. We already had $y = x$; combining this with $x \subseteq z$, by axiom I: $y \subseteq z$. By assumption, $z \subseteq y$; therefore (definition 2.1.1) $y = z$. We thus see that an arbitrary part of y is equal to y, which means (definition 2.1.2) $EMPTY(y)$. Therefore, an arbitrary part y of x is EMPTY.

Theorem 2.1.2. An atomic ensemble has no genuine parts.
In formula: $(\forall x)(AT(x) \rightarrow \neg(\exists y)(y \subset^\circ x))$

Proof: Let x be an atomic ensemble, and y a non-empty part of x. This means that y is not a proper part of x, for if it were, then by definition 2.1.7 it would be empty. So we have $\neg(y \subset x)$. Substituting definition 2.1.4 in this formula, we have $\neg(y \subseteq x \& \neg(y = x))$, or: $\neg(y \subseteq x) \vee \neg(\neg(y = x))$. Since y is a part of x, the first element in this disjunction is false, hence the second is true: $\neg(\neg(y = x))$, or $y = x$. So every non-empty part of x is equal to x, which means that x has no genuine parts.

10.2.2 Axiom of equality

This axiom ensures that the relation $=$, defined by definition 2.1.1, has the substitution properties that are desired for the equality relation.

AXIOM II. $(\forall x, y, z)(((x = y \,\&\, z \subseteq x) \to z \subseteq y) \,\&\, ((x = y \,\&\, x \in z) \to y \in z))$

The axiom says that equal ensembles may be substituted to the left and to the right of the relation sign $\in$. The following theorem establishes that $=$ therefore has the desired substitution properties.

Theorem 2.2.1. If S is a formula of the logical language, and x and y are two variables such that $x = y$, then the replacement of any free occurrence of x in S, which is not in the scope of a quantifier binding y, by an occurrence of y does not affect the truth value of S.

Proof: Follows immediately from axioms I and II plus the fact that, according to rule 2a of the syntax definition of the logical language, free occurrences of a variable are always immediately preceding or following the $\subseteq$ relation or the $\in$ relation.

An alternative approach to equality is to incorporate this notion in the underlying logical system; in that case we have an axiom corresponding to axiom II among the collection of logical axioms. See Fraenkel *et al.* (1973, pp. 25–30), for a discussion of alternative approaches to the equality relation.

10.2.3 *Axiom of unicles*

AXIOM III. $(\forall x)([AT(x) \to (\exists! y)(y \in x)] \,\&\, [\neg AT(x) \to \neg(\exists y)(y \in x)])$

The notation $\exists! y$ is an abbreviation of: 'there is one and only one y', that is, formally:

Definition 2.3.1 (*Unique existence*). $(\exists! y)S =_D (\exists y)S \,\&\, (\forall z)(S \to z = y)$

where 'S' stands for any formula of the logical language.

The axiom of unicles in fact says two things: (1) For an atomic ensemble x there is always exactly one ensemble y such that $y \in x$; I shall call this the *unicle* of x; (2) A non-atomic ensemble does not have a unicle. Later, in chapter 13, I will consider the possibility of allowing atomic ensembles that do not have a unicle.

238   Part 2 Ensemble theory

The unicle-relation can be used as the basis for defining a new, derived relation that I call *membership* and symbolize as ∈; its relation to the notion of membership in set theory will be established in section 13.1. The definition of membership in ensemble theory is:

Definition 2.3.2 (*Membership*). $x \in y =_D (\exists z \subseteq y)(x \underline{\in} z)$

The following theorems and colloraries capture a few elementary properties of this notion of membership.

Theorem 2.3.1. All members of a part of an ensemble are members of that ensemble.
In formula: $(\forall x, y)(x \subseteq y \rightarrow (\forall z \in x)(z \in y))$

Proof: Let x and y be two ensembles such that $x \subseteq y$. Let z be a member of x. By definition 2.3.2, $z \in x$ implies $(\exists u \subseteq x)(z \underline{\in} u)$. According to the axiom of transitivity, $u \subseteq x$ and $x \subseteq y$ imply $u \subseteq y$. Therefore, $(\exists u \subseteq y)(z \underline{\in} u)$. This means, according to definition 2.3.2, that $z \in y$.

Corollary 2.3.1. Equal ensembles have the same members.
$(\forall x, y)(x = y \rightarrow (\forall z)(z \in x \leftrightarrow z \in y))$

Corollary 2.3.2. Equal ensembles are members of the same ensembles.
$(\forall x, y)(x = y \rightarrow (\forall z)(x \in z \leftrightarrow y \in z))$

Theorem 2.3.2. An empty ensemble has no members.
In formula: $(\forall x)(EMPTY(x) \rightarrow \neg(\exists y)(y \in x))$

Proof: Let x be an empty ensemble. If x had a member y, then by definition 2.3.2 y would be the unicle of some part of x. According to the axiom of unicles, this part of x would be atomic. But according to theorem 2.1.1 all parts of an empty ensemble are empty. In view of the definition of atomicity, this is a contradiction. Therefore, x does not have a member.

10.2.4 *Axiom of extensionality*
This axiom establishes under what conditions one ensemble is part of another.

AXIOM IV. $(\forall x, y)([(\forall z \subseteq° x)(z \hat{o} y) \vee (\exists u)(u \underline{\in} x \,\&\, u \underline{\in} y)] \rightarrow x \subseteq y)$

The two clauses of the disjunction in this axiom correspond to two cases in which an ensemble x is part of an ensemble y. The first case is that every non-empty part of x overlaps with y; the second is that x and y have a common unicle. These cases are distinguished because, if x is an ensemble which is not empty or atomic, then it is part of an ensemble y if every non-empty part of x overlaps with y (first clause). Now an atomic ensemble has no other non-empty parts than itself (theorem 2.2.1); therefore, if this criterion is to be used to prove that an atomic ensemble x is part of an ensemble y, it has to be proved that x overlaps with y. In order to prove that, it must be proved that x and y have a common non-empty part. But since x has no non-empty part besides itself, this means that it has to be proved that x itself is part of y. Which is what we wanted to prove in the first place. We thus see that the first clause of the axiom leads to a circular procedure if we try to use it for atomic ensembles. This is why the second clause is needed; it says that an ensemble x is included in an ensemble y if x's unicle is the unicle of y. According to the axiom of unicles, something can be the unicle of y only if y is atomic. The axiom of extensionality thus only specifies under what conditions an atomic ensemble is included in another *atomic* ensemble. From this it can easily be deduced under what conditions an atomic ensemble is included in an arbitrary other ensemble (see below, theorem 2.4.3).

Theorem 2.4.1. Every ensemble is part of itself.
In formula: $(\forall x)(x \subseteq x)$

Proof: According to corollary 2.1.2, every ensemble is either atomic, or empty, or possesses a genuine part. We consider the three cases one by one.

1. If x is atomic, then by the axiom of unicles, $(\exists u)(u \underline{\in} x)$, therefore $(\exists u)(u \underline{\in} x \& u \underline{\in} x)$, from which follows, by the second clause of the axiom of extensionality, that $x \subseteq x$.
2. If x is empty, by theorem 2.1.1 x has no non-empty parts. Therefore, any implication of the form $(\forall y)(y \subseteq^\circ x \to S)$, where S is an arbitrary formula of the logical language, is trivially true. In particular it is true for the formula y ô x. Therefore, we have $(\forall y)(y \subseteq^\circ x \to y \hat{o} x)$, which is just the first clause of the axiom of extensionality. Therefore $x \subseteq x$.

3. Let z be an arbitrary genuine part of x. So $z \subset^\circ x$ and $\neg\text{EMPTY}(z)$. This z is either atomic or not. If $AT(z)$, we just proved that $z \subseteq z$; therefore, z is a non-empty common part of z and x, so $z \, \hat{o} \, x$. We thus see that any atomic part of x overlaps with x. If z is a non-atomic genuine part of x, then by corollary 2.1.1 z has a genuine part y. It follows from the transitivity of the $\subseteq$-relation that $y \subseteq^\circ x$. Thus, y is a non-empty common part of z and x, so $z \, \hat{o} \, x$. We thus see that any non-empty non-atomic part of x overlaps with x. Combined with the case of atomic parts, this means that we have proved that any non-empty part of x overlaps with x. According to the first clause in the axiom of extensionality, this means that $x \subseteq x$.

Corollary 2.4.1. Every ensemble is equal to itself.
$(\forall x)(x = x)$

Corollary 2.4.2. The unicle of an ensemble is a member of that ensemble.
$(\forall x)(\forall y)(y \subseteq x \to y \in x)$

Corollary 2.4.3. Two atomic ensembles are equal if they have the same unicle.
$(\forall x, y)((AT(x) \, \& \, AT(y)) \to [(\forall z)(z \subseteq x \to z \subseteq y) \to x = y])$

A slightly different way of saying essentially the same thing is: if y is an ensemble containing the unicle of an ensemble x, then y is equal to x. This is expressed by the following corollary.

Corollary 2.4.4. If x is an ensemble having the unicle z, then all ensembles having that same unicle are equal to x.
$(\forall x, z)(z \subseteq x \to (\forall y)(z \subseteq y \to y = x))$

In view of this corollary, an atomic ensemble is uniquely determined by its unicle.

Definition 2.4.1. The *singleton of z* is the atomic ensemble with unicle z.

Notation 2.4.1. I will use the notation $\{z\}$ to designate the singleton of z.

Using this notation, we can formulate corollary 2.4.4 as:

Corollary 2.4.4a. $(\forall x, z)(z \subseteq x \to x = \{z\})$

Corollary 2.4.5. Two atomic ensembles overlap iff they are equal.

Corollary 2.4.6. An atomic ensemble x overlaps with an ensemble y iff x is a part of y.

Theorem 2.4.2. Empty ensembles are part of every ensemble.
In formula: $(\forall x)(\text{EMPTY}(x) \to (\forall y)(x \subseteq y))$

Proof: Let x be an empty ensemble, and y an arbitrary ensemble. According to the axiom of extensionality, x is a part of y if every non-empty part of x overlaps with y. Theorem 2.1.1 established that an empty ensemble has no non-empty parts. Thus, if z is a part of x, all formulas of the form $z \subseteq^\circ x \to S$, where S is an arbitrary formula, are true. In particular, the formula $z \subseteq^\circ x \to z \,\hat{o}\, y$ is true. This holds for any z, so we have proved $(\forall z)(z \subseteq^\circ x \to z \,\hat{o}\, y)$.

Corollary 2.4.7. There is only one empty ensemble.
$(\forall x, y)((\text{EMPTY}(x) \,\&\, \text{EMPTY}(y)) \to x = y)$

This means that the definition of emptiness defines a unique empty ensemble.

Notation 2.4.2. The empty ensemble will be designated by $\varnothing$.

We shall see later that there exists at least one empty ensemble.

Theorem 2.4.3. An atomic ensemble x is part of an ensemble y iff x's unicle is a member of y.
In formula:
$(\forall x, y)(\text{AT}(x) \to ((\forall z)(z \underline{\in} x \to z \in y) \leftrightarrow x \subseteq y))$

Proof: The 'only if' part of the theorem is obvious. To prove the 'if' part, consider an atomic ensemble x with the unicle z. We prove that $z \in y$ implies $x \subseteq y$.
By definition, $z \in y$ means $z \underline{\in} u$ for some $u \subseteq y$. According to corollary 2.4.4, $z \underline{\in} u$ implies $u = \{z\}$. Also, by the same token, $x = \{z\}$. From the definition of $=$ and the transitivity of $\subseteq$ it follows that $u = x$ and that therefore $x \subseteq y$.

Corollary 2.4.8. An ensemble x is a member of an ensemble y iff the singleton of x is a part of y.
$(\forall x, y)(x \in y \leftrightarrow \{x\} \subseteq y)$

Theorem 2.4.4. The singleton of an ensemble x has x as its one and only member.
In formula: $(\forall x)(\forall y)(y \in \{x\} \leftrightarrow y = x)$

242 Part 2 Ensemble theory

Proof: Let x and y be two equal ensembles. By the definition of singleton (definition 2.4.1), x ∈ {x}. By the axiom of equality, it follows that y ∈ x. By corollary 2.4.2, y ∈ x.
Suppose y ∈ {x}. By corollary 2.4.8, {y} ⊆ {x}. Since {y} is not empty, it follows from the atomicity of {x} that {y} = {x}. According to corollary 2.3.1, this implies y = x.

Corollary 2.4.9. An ensemble x is atomic iff it is the singleton of its unicle.

Theorem 2.4.5. A non-atomic ensemble x is part of an ensemble y if all x's proper parts are parts of y.
In formula: $(\forall x, y)(\neg AT(x) \to [(\forall z \subset x)(z \subseteq y) \to x \subseteq y])$

Proof: The case that x is empty is trivial, in view of theorem 2.4.2. Let x be non-empty; by corollary 2.1.1, it has a genuine part z. By definition, z is also a *proper* part of x. The supposition is that all proper parts of x are parts of y, so z ⊆ y; we have to prove that x ⊆ y.
Being a genuine part, z is not empty. Since z ⊆ z and z ⊆ y, z has a non-empty part (*viz.* itself) in common with y. So z ô y. Thus, every non-empty proper part of x overlaps with y; applying the axiom of extensionality, we have x ⊆ y.

Combining corollary 2.4.6 with the axiom of extensionality, we obtain the following result:

Corollary 2.4.10. An ensemble x is part of an ensemble y if every non-empty part of x overlaps with y.
$(\forall x, y)(\forall z \subseteq° x)(z \,ô\, y \to x \subseteq y)$

Corollary 2.4.11. A non-empty ensemble x is part of an ensemble y iff every non-empty part of x overlaps with y.
$(\forall x, y)(x \neq \emptyset \to (x \subseteq y \leftrightarrow (\forall z \subseteq° x) z \,ô\, y))$

These corollaries will prove to be very useful for showing that one ensemble is part of another.

10.2.5 *Axiom of pairing*
The axiom of pairing establishes that it is possible to form pairs of ensembles, and that pairs of ensembles are themselves ensembles. The notion of pairing that is defined here is exactly the same as the one in

set theory. The reason for introducing it here is that it allows us to define ensemble theory in such a way that set theory is integrated in it, in the sense that sets are particular kinds of ensembles. Ensemble theory is thus formulated in a way that does not presuppose set-theoretical concepts; therefore, notions like 'pair' are defined within the theory.[2] The axioms VI (powers), IX (infinity), and X (regularity) are included for similar reasons.

In order to formulate the axiom of pairing in a concise and accurate way, the following notation is introduced.

Notation 2.5.1. If S is a formula of the logical language, then by S[x/y] is meant the formula, obtained by replacing all free occurrences of x in S by y. (If y already occurred in S, then we first replace all occurrences of y by some variable y', not already occurring in S.)

Notation 2.5.2. By $(\underline{\exists}x)S$ is meant: there is an x such that S and such that $x \subseteq y$ for any y such that S. In other words, if $(\underline{\exists}x)S$ is true, then S is true for x, and x is included in every y for which S is true; I will then say that x is the 'smallest' or 'minimal' ensemble such that S. The formal definition of this notation is:

Definition 2.5.1. $(\underline{\exists}x)S =_D (\exists x)(S \;\&\; (\forall y)(S[x/y] \rightarrow x \subseteq y))$

Using this notation, the axiom of pairing can be formulated as follows:

AXIOM V. $(\forall x, y)(\underline{\exists}p)(x \in p \;\&\; y \in p)$

The axiom says that for any two ensembles x and y there is a minimal ensemble p, having x and y as members. The following theorem establishes that there is only one such minimal ensemble.

Theorem 2.5.1. For any two ensembles x and y there is only ensemble p which is the minimal ensemble having both x and y as members.

Proof: If p_1 and p_2 were both minimal ensembles, having x and y as members, it would follow from p_1 being minimal that $p_1 \subseteq p_2$, and from p_2 being minimal that $p_2 \subseteq p_1$. Therefore $p_1 = p_2$.

Definition 2.5.2. The uniquely determined minimal ensemble, having x and y as members, is called the *pair* of x and y, and designated by {x, y}.

An elementary property of this notion of pairing is:

Theorem 2.5.2. For any ensemble x, the pair of x and x is the same as the atomic ensemble with x as unicle.
In formula: $(\forall x)(\{x, x\} = \{x\})$

Proof: By definition of $\{x\}$, $x \in \{x\}$. Also by definition, $\{x, x\}$ is the minimal ensemble having x as member, therefore $\{x, x\} \subseteq \{x\}$. On the other hand, corollary 2.4.8 establishes that $x \in \{x, x\}$ implies $\{x\} \subseteq \{x, x\}$. Therefore, $\{x, x\} = \{x\}$.

10.2.6 *Axiom of powers*

The axiom of powers postulates for any ensemble x the existence of a minimal ensemble that has the parts of x as its members.

AXIOM VI. $(\forall x)(\exists p)(\forall z)(z \subseteq x \rightarrow z \in p)$

The following theorem tells us that for a given ensemble x there is at most one minimal ensemble having the parts of x as members:

Theorem 2.6.1. For every ensemble x there is only one ensemble p, which is the minimal ensemble having all parts of x as members.

Proof: If p and q are both minimal ensembles, having all parts of x as members, their minimality implies mutual inclusion.

Definition 2.6.1. The uniquely determined minimal ensemble having the parts of x as members is called the *power* (ensemble) of x, and designated by $\mathscr{P}(x)$.

10.2.7 *Axiom of merging (or sums)*

The axiom of merging will be the basis for defining an ensemble analogue of the union in set theory.

AXIOM VII. $(\forall x)(\exists u)[(\forall z \in x)(z \subseteq u) \& (\forall y \subseteq^\circ u)(\exists w \in x)(w \, ô \, y)]$

In words, the axiom says: for every ensemble x there exists an ensemble u having all the members of x as parts, and only having non-empty parts that overlap with a member of x.

Definition 2.7.1. A *merge* of an ensemble x is an ensemble including all members of x and only having non-empty parts that overlap with a member of x.

Corollary 2.7.1. For any ensemble x, if u is a merge of x then every non-empty part of u overlaps with at least one member of x.

The following theorem establishes that every ensemble has, at most, one merge.

Theorem 2.7.1. For every ensemble x there is only one ensemble that is a merge of x.

Proof: Suppose u and v are both merges of x. I shall prove that $u = v$. Three cases must be distinguished: (1) the case that x has no members, (2) the case that x has exactly one member, and (3) the case that x has at least two members.

1. Suppose x has no members. All non-empty parts of u overlap with a member of x, so for any y: $y \subseteq^\circ u \to (\exists w \in x)(y \hat{o} w)$. The consequent of this implication is false, since u has no members, therefore the antecedent must be false too. So u has no non-empty parts. Since $u \subseteq u$, this means that u is empty. By corollary 2.4.7, this implies that u is uniquely determined.

2. Suppose x has exactly one member. Let w be this member. Then, by the definition of merge, u has the property $w \subseteq u$ & $(\exists y \subseteq^\circ u)(y \hat{o} w)$. The second clause of this conjunction implies, by corollary 2.4.10, $u \subseteq w$. Combined with the first clause, we have $u = w$. By the same token, $v = w$. Therefore $u = v$.

3. Suppose x has at least two different members. In that case u and v both have at least two different parts, hence at least one non-empty part (Corollary 2.4.7: all empty ensembles are equal). Let y be a non-empty part of u. According to corollary 2.7.1, y overlaps with at least one member of x. Let w be such a member; w and y thus have a common non-empty part w'. Since $w \in x$, by the definition of merge, $w \subseteq v$. By the transitivity of the $\subseteq$ relation, $w' \subseteq^\circ v$. On the other hand, we already had $w' \subseteq^\circ y$. So w' is a non-empty common part of v and y. So $y \hat{o} v$. We have now proved that an arbitrary non-empty part y of u overlaps with v. According to the axiom of extensionality, this means $u \subseteq v$. In the same way we can prove $v \subseteq u$, therefore $u = v$.

Notation 2.7.1. The uniquely determined merge of an ensemble x will be denoted by $\cup(x)$. I shall frequently consider the merge of a pair {x, y}; in that case I shall also write '$x \cup y$' instead of '$\cup(\{x, y\})$'.

The proof of the last theorem contains two results, established in passing, that are worth stating separately:

Corollary 2.7.2. The merge of an ensemble that has no members is $\varnothing$.

$$(\forall x)(\neg(\exists y)(y \in x) \rightarrow \cup(x) = \varnothing)$$

Corollary 2.7.3. The merge of an atomic ensemble is its unicle.

$$(\forall x)[AT(x) \rightarrow (\forall y)(y = \cup(x) \leftrightarrow y \subseteq x)]$$

Another way of saying essentially the same as the latter corollary is:

Corollary 2.7.3a. The merge of the singleton of an ensemble is that ensemble.

$$(\forall x)(\cup(\{x\}) = x).$$

The axiom of merging is rather cumbersome due to the stipulation that all non-empty parts of the merge of an ensemble x overlap with at least one of the members of x. This is a way of stipulating that the merge should not include 'superfluous' parts; it should only include those parts which are members of x or which are 'made up from' members of x. To see this clearly, let us try to define the notion of union in set theory in terms of the subset-relation only.

If X is the set consisting of the sets A and B, that is, X = {A, B}, the union of X (what we usually call the union of A and B), should have A and B as subsets, but also those sets which can be 'made up from' A and B. The phrase 'made up from' is easily formalized in terms of the membership-relation: a set S is made up from A and B if it contains only members from A or B. However, if we want to use the subset-relation only, this is difficult to express: we would like to say that S is made up from A and B if it is the union of a subset of A and a subset of B. The problem with this formulation is that we use the term 'union' here, and that is just what we are trying to define.

In 10.2.5, I introduced the concept of a 'minimal' ensemble satisfying a certain predicate. It would be attractive to use that notion in the axiom of merging, defining the merge of an ensemble x simply as the minimal ensemble having all the members of x as parts. Unfortunately, that definition seems not to be restrictive enough if we want to construct a formalism with close analogues of the set-theoretical notions of union, intersection, and complement, forming a Boolean algebra in the same way as in set theory (see below, section 10.3). Definition 2.7.1 is more restrictive than a definition stipulating that the merge should be '⊆ minimal' (see definition 2.5.1). The following theorem establishes this.

Theorem 2.7.2. For every ensemble x, the merge $\cup(x)$ is the minimal ensemble having all members of x as parts.
In formula: $(\forall x)(\exists u)(\forall z \in x)(z \subseteq u \;\&\; u = \cup(x))$

Proof: Consider an ensemble x having at least two members; the case that x has less than two members is trivial, in view of corollaries 2.7.2 and 2.7.3. From the axiom of merging it follows that there exist ensembles including all members of x. Let u be an arbitrary such ensemble. We prove that $\cup(x) \subseteq u$.
Since x has at least two members, $\cup(x)$ has at least one non-empty part e. According to the definition of $\cup(x)$, $e \subseteq \cup(x)$ implies that there is a $w \in x$ such that $e \:\hat{o}\: w$. Let w' be a non-empty common part of e and w. Since $w \in x$, $w \subseteq^\circ u$; therefore $w' \subseteq^\circ u$. Also, $w \subseteq^\circ e$. Therefore $e \:\hat{o}\: u$. We have now proved that any non-empty part e of $\cup(x)$ overlaps with u. Therefore $\cup(x) \subseteq u$. Therefore $u = \cup(x)$.

Theorem 2.7.3 (Theorem of submerging). The merge of certain parts of an ensemble is again a part of that ensemble.
In formula: $(\forall x)(\forall y)((\forall z \in y)(z \subseteq x) \rightarrow \cup(y) \subseteq x)$

Proof: Let y be a non-empty ensemble, having only parts of x as members. (Such a y exists, according to the axiom of powers.) By definition of $\cup(y)$, all members of y are parts of $\cup(y)$. On the other hand, all members of y were parts of x. According to theorem 2.7.2, $\cup(y)$ is the minimal ensemble including all members of y, therefore $\cup(y) \subseteq x$.

Theorem 2.7.4. The pair of two ensembles is the merge of their singletons.
In formula: $(\forall x, y)(\{x, y\} = \{x\} \cup \{y\})$

Proof: By the definition of pair, $\{x\} \in \{\{x\}, \{y\}\}$, so $x \subseteq \{x\} \cup \{y\}$. By corollary 2.4.8, $x \in \{x\} \cup \{y\}$. Similarly $y \in \{x\} \cup \{y\}$. Since the pair $\{x, y\}$ is by definition the minimal ensemble containing x and y as members, $\{x, y\} \subseteq \{x\} \cup \{y\}$. On the other hand, $x \in \{x, y\}$, therefore $\{x\} \subseteq \{x, y\}$. Similarly, $\{y\} \subseteq \{x, y\}$. Therefore, according to theorem 2.7.3, $\{x\} \cup \{y\} \subseteq \{x, y\}$. Therefore $\{x, y\} = \{x\} \cup \{y\}$.

10.2.8 Axiom (schema) of replacement

The axiom of replacement, which is really an axiom schema (a schematic description of an infinite collection of axioms), has the primary purpose of establishing that, if we select from a given ensemble those members that have a certain property, these members form an ensemble. To formulate this accurately, we must first formalize what is meant by saying that an ensemble has a certain property.

I define a *condition on x* as any formula of the logical language in which x occurs freely.

Notation 2.8.1. The notation C(z) will be used to represent a condition on z, and I will say that 'z has the property C' instead of: the formula C[x/z] is true.

I define a *functional condition on x* as a condition on two variables x and y such that for every x there exists at most one y for which the condition is true.

Notation 2.8.2. The notation $C(z_1, z_2)$ will be used as short for $C[x/z_1, y/z_2]$.

I shall use the expression: 'C is a functional condition on the ensemble z' as short for: 'for every x ∈ z there is at most one y such that C(x, y)'. Notice that a functional condition C on the ensemble x defines a function F_C, having as its domain the set of those members x of z for which there is a y such that C(x, y), and assigning to an argument x_i in its domain the value $F_C(x_i) = y_i$, where y_i is the unique object such that $C(x_i, y_i)$.

Using this terminology and notation, the axiom (schema) of replacement can be formulated as follows:

AXIOM VIII. For any functional condition C on the ensemble x,
$$(\forall x)(\exists y)(\forall z)(z \in y \leftrightarrow (\exists u \in x) C(u, z))$$

This axiom says that, given an ensemble x and a functional condition C on the ensemble x, there exists a minimal ensemble y having as members exactly those objects that constitute the value-range of the function F_C.

The following important theorem can be derived from this axiom:

Theorem 2.8.1 (*Theorem of subensembles*). For every ensemble x and condition C there exists a minimal ensemble y having as members those and only those members z of x having the property C.
In formula: $(\forall x)(\exists y)(\forall z)[z \in y \leftrightarrow (z \in x \ \& \ C(z))]$

Proof: If C is a condition on z, then the formula C', defined as
C' =_D C & u = z, is a functional condition on u, since it is obviously a condition on u, and C'(u, z₁) as well as C'(u, z₂) would imply z₁ = z₂. Thus, for any ensemble x, C' is a functional condition on the ensemble x. According to axiom VIII we thus have:
($\exists$y)($\forall$z)[z $\in$ y $\leftrightarrow$ ($\exists$u)(u $\in$ x & u = z & C(z))].
According to corollary 2.3.2, this is equivalent to:
($\exists$y)($\forall$z)[z $\in$ y $\leftrightarrow$ ($\exists$u)(z $\in$ x & C(z))], or to:
($\exists$y)($\forall$z)[z $\in$ y $\leftrightarrow$ (z $\in$ x & C(z))].

Theorem 2.8.2. The minimal ensemble y having as members those and only those members of a given ensemble x having a certain property C, is uniquely determined.

Proof: Suppose y₁ and y₂ are two such ensembles. From their being minimal it follows that y₁ $\subseteq$ y₂ and that y₂ $\subseteq$ y₁. Therefore y₁ = y₂.

Notation 2.8.3. For the unique minimal ensemble having as members those and only those members of x having the property C, I shall use the notation:
{z $\in$ x | C(z)}

Theorem 2.8.3. The power ensemble of an ensemble x only has parts of x as members.
In formula: ($\forall$x)($\forall$y)(y $\in$ $\mathcal{P}$(x) $\rightarrow$ y $\subseteq$ x)

Proof: Suppose $\mathcal{P}$(x) contains a member u which is not a part of x. Let P' be the ensemble defined by: P' = {y $\in$ $\mathcal{P}$(x) | $\neg$(y = u)}. The existence of P' is guaranteed by the theorem of subensembles. I prove that P' contains all parts of x, but that not $\mathcal{P}$(x) $\subseteq$ P', which contradicts the minimality assumption in the definition of $\mathcal{P}$(x). Since u $\notin$ x, and P' contains all members of $\mathcal{P}$(x) not equal to u, it follows that all parts of x are members of P' (see corollary 2.3.2). We assumed that u $\in$ $\mathcal{P}$(x), therefore {u} $\subseteq$ $\mathcal{P}$(x) (corollary 2.4.8). On the other hand, u $\notin$ P' implies {u} $\not\subseteq$ P'. So $\mathcal{P}$(x) has a non-empty part which is not a part of P'. This contradicts the minimality assumption $\mathcal{P}$(x) $\subseteq$ P'.

By definition of the power ensemble of x, all parts of x are members of $\mathcal{P}$(x). Theorem 2.8.3 thus establishes that the propositions z $\subseteq$ x and

$z \in \mathcal{P}(x)$ are equivalent. Therefore:

Notation 2.8.4. As well as writing $\{z \in \mathcal{P}(x) | C(z)\}$, I shall also write: $\{z \subseteq x | C(z)\}$.

Theorem 2.8.4. For every ensemble x and condition C, the ensemble $\{z \in x | C(z)\}$ is a part of x.

Proof: Given an ensemble x, let x' be the ensemble, defined by:
$x' =_D \{y \in \mathcal{P}(x) | (\exists z)(z \subseteq y \ \& \ C(z))\}$. The existence of x' follows from the theorem of subensembles. The proof goes in two steps. First we prove that $\cup(x') \subseteq x$ and subsequently that $\{z \in x | C(z)\} \subseteq \cup(x')$. By the transitivity of $\subseteq$, the theorem follows.

According to theorem 2.8.3, all members of x' are parts of x. Therefore, $\cup(x') \subseteq x$ (theorem of submerging).

Let y be an arbitrary member of x such that C(y). Then $\{y\} \in \mathcal{P}(x)$ and $(\exists z)(z \subseteq y \ \& \ C(z))$, so $\{y\} \in x'$. Therefore $\{y\} \subseteq \cup(x')$. Therefore $y \in \cup(x')$. Since $\{z \in x | C(z)\}$ is by definition the *minimal* ensemble containing all members of x such that C, it follows that $\{z \in x | C(z)\} \subseteq \cup(x')$. This completes the proof.

Corollary 2.8.1. Every ensemble is equal to the merge of its parts.
$(\forall x) x = \cup(\{z \subseteq x | z = z\})$

Notation 2.8.5. In what follows, I shall use the notation x_* to designate the minimal ensemble having the atomic parts of x as members. Formally:

Definition 2.8.1. $x_* =_D \{z \subseteq x | AT(z)\}$.

Theorem 2.8.5. For every ensemble x and condition C there exists one and only one minimal ensemble having as parts all x-parts z such that C(z).
In formula: $(\forall x)(\exists u)(\forall z)([z \subseteq x \ \& \ C(z)] \rightarrow z \subseteq u)$

Proof: Given x and C, let u be the merge of the ensemble $\{z \subseteq x | C(z)\}$. From theorem 2.8.3 it follows that all x-parts having the property C are parts of u. According to corollary 2.7.3, u is the minimal ensemble having all these parts; the uniqueness of such an ensemble follows, as before, from the minimality condition. So u satisfies the requirements mentioned in the theorem, and its existence is guaranteed by the theorems 2.8.2 and 2.8.3 and the axiom of merging.

Notation 2.8.6. The unique minimal ensemble including all parts of an ensemble x having the property C will be designated by:
$[z \subseteq x | C(z)]$.

Theorem 2.8.6. For every ensemble x and condition C, the ensemble $[z \subseteq x | C(z)]$ is equal to the merge of those parts of x having the property C.
In formula: $(\forall x)([z \subseteq x | C(z)] = \cup(\{z \subseteq x | C(z)\}))$

Proof: See the proof of the previous theorem.

Corollary 2.8.2. For every ensemble x and condition C, the ensemble $[z \subseteq x | C(z)]$ is included in x.

Corollary 2.8.3. For every ensemble x and condition C, the ensemble $[z \subseteq x | C(z)]$ includes all parts of x having the property C.
$(\forall x)(\forall y \subseteq x)(C(y) \to y \subseteq [z \subseteq x | C(z)])$

It is worth noting that the reverse of this corollary is not true, as theorem 2.8.7 establishes.

Theorem 2.8.7. Given an ensemble x, it is *not* the case that, for any condition C:
$(\forall y \subseteq x)(y \subseteq [z \subseteq x | C(z)] \to C(y))$

Proof: Take for C the condition: $y \in \{y_1, y_2\}$, where y_1 and y_2 are two parts of x. This is a condition on y. Since $C(y_1)$ and $C(y_2)$, $y_1 \subseteq [z \subseteq x | C(z)]$ and $y_2 \subseteq [z \subseteq x | C(z)]$; therefore, $y_1 \cup y_2 \subseteq [z \subseteq x | C(z)]$. However, $\neg C(y_1 \cup y_2)$.

Theorem 2.8.8. There exists an empty ensemble.

Proof: Take any ensemble x, and a condition C which is always false, such as the condition $z \neq z$. The ensemble $[z \subseteq x | z \neq z]$ has no members. According to corollary 2.7.2, the merge of this ensemble, whose existence is ascertained by the axiom of merging, is empty.

10.2.9 *Axiom of infinity*
This axiom postulates the existence of ensembles with infinitely many members. In passing, it postulates the very existence of ensembles at all.

AXIOM IX. $(\exists x)[(\exists y)(y \in x) \ \& \ (\forall z)(z \in x \to \{z\} \in x)]$

10.2.10 *Axiom of regularity*
This axiom has the purpose of excluding ensembles with an undesirable membership structure. It excludes, for instance, the possibility that an ensemble is a member of itself.

AXIOM X. $(\forall x)[(\exists y)(y \in x) \to (\exists z \in x)\neg(\exists w \in z)(w \in x)]$

10.3 Operations on ensembles

10.3.1 *Merge*
In section 10.2.7 the notion 'merge of x', written as $\cup(x)$ was introduced, which is the ensemble analogue of the union in set theory. Following the usual practice with unions, I shall use the notation '$y_1 \cup y_2 \cup \ldots \cup y_n$' if x has the members $y_1, y_2, \ldots, y_n$, besides the notation $\cup(x)$, and refer to 'the merge of $y_1, y_2, \ldots,$ and y_n'.

Some fundamental properties of the merge have been established in 10.2.7 and 10.2.8; further properties will be derived below (10.3.4 and 10.3.5).

10.3.2 *Overlap*
An ensemble analogue of the set-theoretical concept of intersection is also defined, and called *overlap*. I first prove the following theorem about the existence of those ensembles that will be defined as overlaps.

Theorem 3.2.1 For every ensemble x there exists a uniquely determined ensemble w which includes as parts all the common parts of the members of x, and which is the minimal ensemble for which this is true.
In formula: $(\forall x)(\exists w)(\forall z)[(\forall y \in x)(z \subseteq y) \to z \subseteq w]$

Proof: Take, for a given ensemble x, for w the ensemble:
$w = \cup(\{u \in \mathcal{P}(\cup(x)) \mid (\forall y \in x)(u \subseteq y)\})$.
If x has no members then $\cup(x)$ is empty, so $w = \varnothing$.
Suppose that x has members. Let z be an arbitrary part of some of the members of x. Since all members of x are parts of $\cup(x)$, the transitivity of $\subseteq$ implies that $z \subseteq \cup(x)$. By definition of the power ensemble, $z \in \mathcal{P}(\cup(x))$. So $\mathcal{P}(\cup(x))$ is an ensemble containing as members all parts of at least one of the members of x; *a fortiori*, $\mathcal{P}(\cup(x))$ contains all parts of each member of x.
To the ensemble $\mathcal{P}(\cup(x))$ we now apply the theorem of

subensembles (2.8.1) with $C = (\forall y \in x)(u \subseteq y)$, obtaining the ensemble $v = \{u \in \mathscr{P}(\cup(x)) | (\forall y \in x)(u \subseteq y)\}$.
This ensemble contains all and only those ensembles which are part of each member of x. The ensemble w, being the merge of v, has all these ensembles as parts.
Theorems 2.8.2 and 2.7.2 in combination with corollary 2.7.3 ensure that w is the minimal ensemble having this property, and is therefore uniquely determined.

Definition 3.2.1. The *overlap* of an ensemble x is the minimal ensemble that includes the common parts of all members of x.

Notation 3.2.1. The overlap of x is denoted by $\cap(x)$. If x contains the members $y_1, y_2, \ldots, y_n$ I shall also write $y_1 \cap y_2 \cap \ldots \cap y_n$ instead of $\cap(x)$, and refer to 'the overlap of $y_1, y_2, \ldots, y_n$'.

In section 2.4 I introduced the overlap relation ô; this relation is related to the overlap operator $\cap$ by:

Corollary 3.2.1. The overlap relation holds between two ensembles x and y iff the overlap of x and y is not empty.
$(\forall x, y)(x \, ô \, y \leftrightarrow x \cap y \neq \emptyset)$

In the course of proving theorem 3.2.1 we noted in passing the following result:

Corollary 3.2.2. The overlap of an ensemble that has no members is empty.
$(\forall x)((\neg(\exists y)(y \in x)) \to \cap(x) = \emptyset)$

In section 10.2.7 we have seen that the merge of parts of an ensemble is again a part of that ensemble (theorem 2.7.3). We can prove something similar about overlaps.

Theorem 3.2.2. The overlap of a number of parts of some given ensembles is part of each of these ensembles.
In formula: $(\forall x, y)(y \in x \to \cap(x) \subseteq y)$.

Proof: If x is an ensemble having no members, which means that we are considering the overlap of zero ensembles, the proof is trivial in view of corollary 3.2.2. Similarly if x contains only empty members. Suppose x has a non-empty member, so $\cap(x)$ is not empty. Let z be an arbitrary non-empty part of $\cap(x)$. By the definition of $\cap(x)$, $z \subseteq$

$\cap(x)$ implies $z \,\hat{o}\, u_1$, for a certain member u_1 of the ensemble $\{u \in (\cup(x)) | (\forall y)(y \in x \to u \subseteq y)\}$, that is, $u_1 \subseteq \cup(x)$ and $u_1 \subseteq y$ for all $y \in x$. Now $z \,\hat{o}\, u_1$ and $z \neq \emptyset$ implies $z \,\hat{o}\, y$, for all $y \in x$. So an arbitrary non-empty $z \subseteq \cap(x)$ overlaps with all $y \in x$; therefore $\cap(x) \subseteq y$ for all $y \in x$.

Further properties of the $\cap$-operation will be discussed in 10.3.5.

Corollary 3.2.3. The overlap of an ensemble x is the maximal common part of the members of x.
$(\forall x, y)[(\forall z \in x) y \subseteq z \to y \subseteq \cap(x)]$

10.3.3 *Completion*

Next I shall define an ensemble analogue of the set-theoretical concept of complement. I call it *completion*. To do this, I first prove the following theorem concerning the existence and uniqueness of the ensembles to be defined as completions.

Theorem 3.3.1. For every two ensembles x and E such that $x \subseteq E$ there exists a unique ensemble w which is the smallest ensemble such that $x \cup w = E$.
In formula: $(\forall x)(\forall E)(x \subseteq E \to (\exists w)(x \cup w = E))$

Proof: The cases that $x = \emptyset$ and that $x = E$ are trivial, so suppose x is a genuine part of E: $x \subset^\circ E$.
Consider the ensemble $w = [z \subseteq E | z \cap x = \emptyset]$. Since w is the merge of parts of E, by the theorem of submerging, $w \subseteq E$. We also had $x \subseteq E$, so by the same token $x \cup w \subseteq E$. We next prove that $E \subseteq x \cup w$, from which it follows that $x \cup w = E$. This goes by reduction *ad absurdum*.

Suppose that it was not the case that $E \subseteq x \cup w$. Then by corollary 2.4.11 E would have a non-empty part y such that $y \cap (x \cup w) = \emptyset$, which would imply that $y \cap x = \emptyset$ and $y \cap w = \emptyset$. (Since if, e.g., $y \cap x \neq \emptyset$, then $x \subseteq (x \cup w)$ would imply $y \cap (x \cup w) \neq \emptyset$.)
But this can't be, since $y \cap x = \emptyset$ implies $y \subseteq w$, which contradicts $y \neq \emptyset$ & $y \cap w = \emptyset$.
Therefore $x \cup w = E$.

It remains to be proved that w is the minimal ensemble which, upon merging with x, gives E. The most convenient way to prove this is with the help of a powerful theorem, the 'partition theorem', that has not yet

Axiomatic ensemble theory 255

been established. I therefore present that theorem first and subsequently complete the present proof.

Note that, by theorem 2.8.5, the ensemble $[z \subseteq E | z \cap x = \varnothing]$ is uniquely determined.

Definition 3.3.1. The *completion* of an ensemble x relative to an ensemble E in which x is included, is the merge of those parts of E that do not overlap with x.

Notation 3.3.1. The notation $\bar{x}^E$ is used to designate the completion of x relative to E.

10.3.4 The partition theorem

I now establish a result which turns out to be very useful in proving certain properties of the merge, overlap, and completion of ensembles.

Theorem 3.4.1. If an ensemble x is equal to the merge of an ensemble y, then every part of x is equal to the merge of certain parts of members of y.
In formula:
$(\forall x, y)[x = \cup(y) \to (\forall z \subseteq x)[(\exists w)(z = \cup(w) \, \& \, (\forall t \in w)(\exists s \in y)(t \subseteq s))]]$

Proof: Given two ensembles x and y such that $x = \cup(y)$, we consider an arbitrary part z of x. The case $x = \varnothing$ is trivial, so let us consider a non-empty ensemble x. Consider a non-empty part z of x (again, the case $z = \varnothing$ is trivial). We define the ensemble w, as occurring in the theorem in formula form, as $w = \{m \subseteq x | (\exists a)(a \in y \, \& \, m = z \cap a)\}$. That is, w is the minimal ensemble containing the overlaps of z with the members of x. We prove that this ensemble w has the desired properties: its merge is z, and all its members are parts of x-members. According to theorem 3.2.2, all members of w are parts of z, therefore their merge is part of z: $\cup(w) \subseteq z$.

Next we prove that $z \subseteq \cup(w)$. Let $p \subseteq^\circ z$. Since $z \subseteq x$ and $x = \cup(y)$, $z \subseteq \cup(y)$. So $p \subseteq^\circ \cup(y)$. By corollary 2.7.1, every non-empty part of $\cup(y)$ overlaps with at least one member of y. Hence there is a member s of y such that p ô s. So we have $p \cap s \subseteq^\circ s$, as well as $p \cap s \subseteq^\circ p$ and thus, since $p \subseteq^\circ z \subseteq x$, $p \cap s \subseteq^\circ x$. Hence $p \cap s$ is a member of w, so $p \cap s \subseteq^\circ \cup(w)$. Thus, p has a non-empty part in common with $\cup(w)$: w ô $\cup(w)$. We have now proved that an arbitrary non-empty part of z overlaps with $\cup(w)$, therefore, by corollary 2.4.10, $z \subseteq \cup(w)$.

256 *Part 2 Ensemble theory*

This means that we have now established that $z = \cup(w)$.
It remains to be proved that for every member t of w there is a member s of y such that $t \subseteq s$.
By the definition of w, $t \in w$ implies $t = z \cap s$ for some $s \in y$.
According to theorem 3.2.2, $t = z \cap s$ implies $t \subseteq s$.

In order to facilitate the remaining part of the proof of theorem 3.3.1, I first prove the following result with the help of the partition theorem.

Theorem 3.4.2. For any two ensembles x and E, such that $x \subseteq E$, the completion of x with respect to E does not overlap with x.
In formula: $(\forall x, E)(x \subseteq E \rightarrow \neg(\bar{x}^E \hat{o} x))$

Proof: Suppose $\bar{x}^E$ and x have a common non-empty part y. It then follows from theorem 2.8.6 and corollary 2.7.1 that y has a non-empty part w in common with a certain member z of the ensemble $[z \subseteq E \mid \neg(z \hat{o} x)]$. Therefore $w \subseteq° z$, as well as $w \subseteq° y$. Since y is a part of x, it follows that w is a non-empty common part of z and x. This contradicts that z is a member of $[z \subseteq E \mid \neg(z \hat{o} x)]$. So the assumption that $\bar{x}^E$ and x have a common non-empty part must be wrong.

I now prove the remaining part of theorem 3.3.1, which is:

Theorem 3.4.3. For any two ensembles x and E such that $x \subseteq E$, the completion of x with respect to E is the minimal ensemble y such that $x \cup y = E$.
In formula: $(\forall x, E)(x \subseteq E \rightarrow (\forall y)(x \cup y = E \rightarrow \bar{x}^E \subseteq y))$

Proof: Let x and E be two ensembles such that $x \subseteq E$. The cases that x is empty or equal to E are trivial, so let us consider the case that x is a genuine part of E. Let y be an arbitrary ensemble such that $x \cup y = E$.
Consider an arbitrary non-empty part z of $\bar{x}^E$. Since $\bar{x}^E$ is a part of E, $z \subseteq E$, and since $E = x \cup y$, also $z \subseteq x \cup y$. This implies, by the definition of merging, that z overlaps with x or with y or both. By theorem 3.4.2, z does not overlap with x. So $z \hat{o} y$. We have now proved that an arbitrary non-empty part of $\bar{x}^E$ overlaps with y; therefore, by corollary 2.4.9, $\bar{x}^E \subseteq y$.

10.3.5 *The Boolean algebra of ensemble operations*

In this subsection I show that the operations of merging, overlapping, and completion with respect to a given ensemble, form a Boolean algebra

Axiomatic ensemble theory 257

in the same way as the operations of union, intersection, and taking the complement with respect to a given set.

Definition 3.5.1. A Boolean algebra is a 6-tuple (E, +, *, ′, o, 1) such that:
1. + and * are commutative.
2. + and * are associative.
3. + and * are distributive, that is, for any a, b, and c ∈ E:
    (i) a+(b*c) = (a+b)*(a+c)
    (ii) a*(b+c) = (a*b)+(a*c)
4. + and * are reciprocal, that is, for any a and b ∈ E:
    (i) (a*b)′ = a′+b′
    (ii) (a+b)′ = a′*b′
5. (i) a+a = a
   (ii) a*a = a
6. a″ = a.
7. (i) a+a′ = 1
   (ii) a*a′ = o
8. (i) a+o = a
   (ii) a*1 = a
9. (i) a+1 = 1
   (ii) a*o = o

Theorem 3.5.1. For every ensemble x, the members of which are all parts of an ensemble E, the 6-tuple (x*, ∪, ∩, $^{-E}$, ∅, E), where x* is the ensemble {z ∈ x | z = z}, is a Boolean algebra.

Proof: We check the points 1–9 from definition 3.5.1 one by one for a given ensemble x and a fixed ensemble E including x. Let a, b, and c be arbitrary members of x. Instead of $\bar{a}^E$ we will write a′.

1. Commutativity of ∪ and ∩: From the axiom of pairing it follows immediately that {a, b} = {b, a}; therefore a ∪ b =$_D$ ∪({a, b}) = ∪({b, a}) =$_D$ b ∪ a.
   Likewise for a ∩ b.
2. Associativity of ∪ and ∩: According to theorem 2.7.2, a ∪ (b ∪ c) =$_D$ ∪({a, ∪({b, c})}) is the minimal ensemble including a and b ∪ c as parts. It is easily proved that it is also the minimal ensemble including a, b, and c, and also the minimal ensemble including a ∪ b and c. Therefore, a ∪ (b ∪ c) = (a ∪ b) ∪ c.
   Likewise for ∩.

258 *Part 2 Ensemble theory*

3. Of the two distributive laws, we prove the second one:
   $a \cap (b \cup c) = (a \cap b) \cup (a \cap c)$.
   We prove the equality by proving mutual inclusion of the ensembles denoted by the expressions at the left- and right-hand sides. Consider an arbitrary non-empty part e of $a \cap (b \cup c)$. By definition of overlap, $e \subseteq^\circ a$ and $e \subseteq^\circ (b \cup c)$. By corollary 2.7.1, $e \, ô \, b$ or $e \, ô \, c$. Suppose $e \, ô \, b$. Then $e \cap b$ is a non-empty part of b and also of e and thus of a. So $e \cap b \subseteq^\circ a \cap b$. By the definition of merge, this implies that $e \cap b$ is also part of any ensemble merged with $a \cap b$. So $e \cap b \subseteq^\circ (a \cap b) \cup (a \cap c)$. By theorem 3.2.2, it follows that the left-hand ensemble is part of the right-hand ensemble.
   Now from right to left. Let e be an arbitrary non-empty part of $(a \cap b) \cup (a \cap c)$. By corollary 2.7.1, $e \, ô \, (a \cap b)$ or $e \, ô \, (a \cap c)$ or both. Suppose $e \, ô \, a \cap b$. Let e_{ab} be their overlap: $e_{ab} = e \cap (a \cap b)$. Then $e_{ab} \subseteq a$ and $e_{ab} \subseteq b$ and therefore, trivially, $e_{ab} \subseteq b \cup c$. So $e_{ab} \subseteq a \cap (b \cup c)$. So e_{ab} overlaps with $a \cap (b \cup c)$; therefore the right-hand ensemble is part of the left-hand ensemble. Therefore the two are equal.

4. Of the two laws of reciprocity, we prove $(a \cup b)' = a' \cap b'$. Let e be a non-empty part of $(a \cup b)'$. According to theorem 3.4.2, $(a \cup b)'$ does not overlap with $(a \cup b)$, therefore e does not overlap with $(a \cup b)$. It is easily seen that $\neg(e \, ô \, (a \cup b))$ implies $\neg(e \, ô \, a)$ and $\neg(e \, ô \, b)$. Consequently, $e \subseteq a'$ and $e \subseteq b'$. So $e \subseteq (a' \cap b')$. Therefore $(a \cup b)' \subseteq a' \cap b'$. So the left-hand side ensemble is included in the right-hand side ensemble.
   Next, let e be a non-empty part of the ensemble to the right. This means that $e \subseteq a'$ and $e \subseteq b'$, hence (theorem 3.4.2) e overlaps neither with a nor with b. This implies that e does not overlap with $a \cup b$. Since $(a \cup b) \cup (a \cup b)' = E$, it follows from corollary 2.7.1 that $e \, ô \, a \cup b$. So the right-hand ensemble is part of the left-hand ensemble. Therefore the two are equal.

5. To prove that $a \cup a = a$, we first note that the pair $\{a, a\}$ is equal to the singleton $\{a\}$ (theorem 2.5.2). Using corollary 2.7.3, we see that $a \cup a = \cup(\{a, a\}) = \cup(\{a\}) = a$.
   To prove that $a \cap a = a$, we note first that $a \cap a = \cap(\{a, a\}) = \cap(\{a\}) = a$; the latter equality follows from the fact that, by the definition of overlap, $\cap(\{a\})$ is the merge of the common parts of all members of $\{a\}$ – which is the merge of all the parts of a – which is a itself (corollary 2.8.1).

Axiomatic ensemble theory 259

6. To prove a″ = a, we prove mutual inclusion of the two ensembles. Note that a″ = [z ⊆ E | ¬(z ô a′)]. Consider an arbitrary non-empty part e of a. According to theorem 3.4.2, e does not overlap with a′. Therefore e ⊆ a″, hence e ô a″. So a ⊆ a″.

   Next, consider an arbitrary non-empty part e of a″. Applying theorem 3.4.2 again (and making use of the obvious commutativity of ô), we see that e ⊆ a″ implies ¬(e ô a′). Since a ∪ a′ = E, ¬(e ô a′) implies e ô a (corollary 2.7.1). Therefore a″ ⊆ a. Therefore a″ = a.

7. a ∪ a′ = E by definition.
   a ∩ a′ = ∅ according to theorem 3.4.2.

8. a ∪ ∅ = a since a ⊆ a and ∅ ⊆ a, therefore a ∪ ∅ ⊆ a, etc.
   a ∩ E = a, as follows from corollary 3.2.3.

9. a ∪ E = E and a ∩ ∅ = ∅ follow immediately from theorem 2.7.2 and corollary 3.2.3.

   This completes the proof.

This theorem makes clear that the operations of merging, taking overlaps, and taking completions, have all the properties we would intuitively like them to have. The following immediate consequences of the theorem are worth noting.

Corollary 3.5.1. For every ensemble x, the 6-tuple (x, ∪, ∩, $^{-x}$, ∅, ∪(x)). is a Boolean algebra.

Corollary 3.5.2. For every ensemble x, the 6-tuple ($\mathscr{P}$(x), ∪, ∩, $^{-x}$, ∅, x) is a Boolean algebra.

11 *Continuous, discrete, and mixed ensembles*

11.1 Continuous ensembles

Two particularly interesting kinds of ensembles are those called 'continuous' and those called 'discrete'. This chapter is devoted to a discussion of these ensembles and to the 'mixing' of continuous and discrete ensembles. In this section I consider continuous ensembles.

Definition 1.1. An ensemble is *continuous* iff it is non-empty, and each of its non-empty parts has a genuine part.

I will use the notation CONT(x) to indicate that the ensemble x is continuous. In formal notation, we thus have the definition:

Definition 1.1a. $\text{CONT}(x) =_D \neg(x = \varnothing) \,\&\, (\forall z \subseteq^\circ x)(\exists y)(y \subset^\circ z)$

An immediate consequence of the definition is:

Corollary 1.1. A continuous ensemble has no minimal parts.
$(\forall x)(\text{CONT}(x) \to \neg(\exists z)[\neg(\exists y)(y \subset^\circ z)])$

This corollary stresses what is characteristic of continuous ensembles: in a continuous ensemble one can continue indefinitely to take ever smaller, 'genuine' parts. A continuous ensemble differs in this respect from a set: in a set one can consider 'smaller parts' in the sense of non-empty proper subsets until one hits the singleton sets, and no further. See also corollary 1.3.

Another immediate consequence of the definition is:

Corollary 1.2. The empty ensemble is not continuous.

I shall now establish some fundamental properties of this notion of continuity.

Continuous, discrete, and mixed ensembles 261

Theorem 1.1. Every non-empty part of a continuous ensemble is continuous.
In formula: $(\forall x)(CONT(x) \rightarrow (\forall z \subseteq^\circ x)CONT(z))$

Proof: Let x be a continuous ensemble and z a non-empty part of x. We have to prove that every non-empty part of z has a genuine part. Let $y \subseteq^\circ z$. By $z \subseteq x$, $y \subseteq^\circ x$. By CONT(x), y has a genuine part.

Theorem 1.2. The merge of one or more continuous ensembles is a continuous ensemble.
In formula: $(\forall x)([(\exists y)(y \in x) \& (\forall y \in x)CONT(y)] \rightarrow CONT(\cup(x)))$

Proof: Let x be an ensemble of which all members are continuous, and which contains at least one member. The latter implies that $\cup(x)$ is not empty. We have to prove that every non-empty part of $\cup(x)$ has a genuine part.
Let z be some non-empty part of $\cup(x)$. According to corollary 10.2.7.1, z overlaps with at least one member y_i of x. So $z \cap y_i$ is not empty. Since $z \cap y_i \subseteq y_i$ (theorem 10.3.2.2), and CONT(y_i) due to $y_i \in x$, by theorem 1.1, CONT($z \cap y_i$). Therefore $z \cap y_i$ has a genuine part w. Since $z \cap y_i \subseteq z$, w is also a genuine part of z. This completes the proof.

Theorem 1.3. The overlap of one or more continuous ensembles, if not empty, is continuous.
In formula:
$(\forall x)([(\exists y)(y \in x) \& (\forall y \in x)CONT(y)] \rightarrow [\cap(x) = \varnothing \vee CONT(\cap(x))])$

Proof: Let x be an ensemble of which all members are continuous, which contains at least one member y, and of which the overlap $\cap(x)$ is not empty. By the definition of overlap, $\cap(x) \subseteq y$. Being a member of x, y is continuous. By theorem 1.1, it follows that $\cap(x)$ is continuous.

Theorem 1.4. The completion of a continuous ensemble x with respect to a continuous ensemble U is continuous.
In formula: $(\forall x, U)[x \subseteq U \& CONT(x) \& CONT(U)] \rightarrow CONT(\bar{x}^U)$

Proof: Let x and U be two continuous ensembles such that x is included in U. By definition, $\bar{x}^U$ is the merge of certain parts of U. By theorem 1.2, all parts of U are continuous so that, according to theorem 1.2, their merge is continuous too.

Roughly speaking, the theorems 1.2, 1.3, and 1.4 establish that the operations of merging, taking overlaps, and completing conserve the property of continuity.

I shall now turn to the question of membership for continuous ensembles.

Theorem 1.5. Atomic ensembles are not continuous.

Proof: By definition, an atomic ensemble x is not empty. By theorem 10.2.4.1, $x \subseteq x$, so $x \subseteq^\circ x$. If x were continuous, then by the definition of continuity x should have a genuine part. But, by theorem 10.2.1.2, this is not the case. Therefore x is not continuous.

Combined with theorem 1.1, this leads to the following corollary:

Corollary 1.2. A continuous ensemble has no atomic parts.
 $(\forall x)(CONT(x) \to \neg(\exists y \subseteq x)AT(y))$

From the definition of the membership relation it follows immediately that:

Corollary 1.3. A continuous ensemble has no members.
 $(\forall x)(CONT(x) \to \neg(\exists z)(z \in x))$

This last result emphasizes once again that continuous ensembles are fundamentally different from sets.

We also establish the reverse of the last corollary: if an ensemble has no members, then it is continuous (provided that the ensemble is not empty, of course).

Theorem 1.6. A non-empty ensemble that has no members is continuous.
 In formula: $(\forall x)([x \neq \emptyset\ \&\ \neg(\exists z)(z \in x)] \to CONT(x))$

Proof: Let x be a non-empty ensemble having no members. We prove that an arbitrary non-empty part of x has a genuine part.
 Having no members, x is not atomic (axiom of unicles and corollary 10.2.4.2). According to corollary 10.2.1.1, this implies that x has a genuine part y. As a good genuine part, y is not empty. Moreover, y has no members, for any of its members would be members of x (theorem 10.2.3.1), contradicting the assumption. Therefore, y is not atomic. Applying corollary 10.2.1.2 again, we see that y thus has a genuine part.

11.2 Discrete ensembles

In this section I introduce the notion of a 'discrete ensemble'. Discrete ensembles will be seen to be the antipodes of continuous ensembles, and to be in every respect like ordinary sets.

Definition 2.1. An ensemble is *discrete* iff it is equal to the merge of its atomic parts.

I will use the notation DISCR(x) to indicate that the ensemble x is discrete. In formal notation, we thus have the definition:

Definition 2.1a. $\text{DISCR}(x) =_D x = \cup(x_*)$

(x_* designates the minimal ensemble having the atomic parts of x as members; see definition 10.2.8.1).

Since the empty ensemble has no atomic parts, it follows trivially that $\varnothing_* = \varnothing$. Therefore:

Corollary 2.1. The empty ensemble is discrete.
    DISCR($\varnothing$)

I now establish a few fundamental properties of the notion of discreteness.

Theorem 2.1. Every non-empty discrete ensemble has a member.
    In formula: $(\forall x)([\text{DISCR}(x) \& x \neq \varnothing] \rightarrow (\exists z)(z \in x))$

Proof: Consider a non-empty discrete ensemble x. Thus, $x = \cup(x_*)$. Since x is not empty, neither is $\cup(x_*)$. By corollary 10.2.7.2, this implies that x_* has a member y. From $y \in x_*$ it follows that $y \subseteq \cup(x_*)$, therefore $y \subseteq x$ and AT(y). By theorem 10.2.4.3, it follows that y's unicle is a member of x.

Theorem 2.2. Every part of a discrete ensemble is discrete.
    In formula: $(\forall x)(\text{DISCR}(x) \rightarrow (\forall y \subseteq x)\text{DISCR}(y))$

Proof: Let x be a non-empty discrete ensemble. In view of corollary 2.1, we only need to consider non-empty parts of x. Let y be such a part. We prove that $y = \cup(y_*)$.
Since $x = \cup(x_*)$, $y \subseteq \cup(x_*)$. According to the partition theorem (10.3.4), this implies that $y = \cup(w)$ for a certain w having only members that are parts of members of x_*. Since the members of x_* are atomic, all members of w are either empty or members of x_*.

Let w' be the minimal ensemble containing all and only those members of w that are not empty: $w' = \{z \in w \mid z \neq \emptyset\}$, so all members of w' are atomic. From theorem 10.2.7.2 it follows that $\cup(w') = \cup(w) = y$. By the definition of merge, all members of w' are parts of y, so $w' \subseteq y_*$. We have now proved that y is equal to the merge of certain of its atomic parts. To prove that y is equal to the merge of *all* its atomic parts, that is, $y = \cup(y_*)$, we show that every atomic part of y is a member of w'.

Let z be an atomic part of y. Since $y = \cup(w')$, $z \subseteq \cup(w')$. Therefore, $z \hat{o} w_i$ for some $w_i \in w'$, and since z as well as w_i is atomic, it follows (by corollary 10.2.4.6) that $z = w_i$. Therefore $z \in w'$. It follows that $y_* \subseteq w'$. We already had $w' \subseteq y_*$, so $w' = y_*$. We already proved $y = \cup(w')$, therefore $y = \cup(y_*)$. This completes the proof.

Corollary 2.2. Every non-empty part of a discrete ensemble has a member.
$(\forall x)(\mathrm{DISCR}(x) \to (\forall y \subseteq^\circ x)(\exists z)(z \in y))$

The reverse of this corollary is also true, but is less easily proved.

Theorem 2.3. An ensemble is discrete if each of its non-empty parts has at least one member.
In formula: $(\forall x)(\forall y \subseteq^\circ x)(\exists z)(z \in y) \to \mathrm{DISCR}(x)$

Proof: Consider an ensemble x of which every non-empty part has a member. Let y be such a part, and z a member of y. We first prove that $x \subseteq \cup(x_*)$.
$z \in y$ implies $\{z\} \subseteq y$, therefore $\{z\} \subseteq x$, therefore $\{z\} \in x_*$, therefore $\{z\} \subseteq \cup(x_*)$. On the other hand we had $\{z\} \subseteq y$, so $\{z\}$ is a non-empty common part of y and $\cup(x_*)$, hence $y \hat{o} \cup(x_*)$. We thus see that an arbitrary non-empty part of x overlaps with $\cup(x_*)$, therefore $x \subseteq \cup(x_*)$.
On the other hand, all members of $\cup(x_*)$ are parts of x, therefore their merge is part of x: $\cup(x_*) \subseteq x$.
Therefore $x = \cup(x_*)$.

Corollary 2.3. An ensemble is discrete iff each of its non-empty parts has a member.

This is a possible alternative definition of discreteness.

Corollary 2.4. A non-empty memberless ensemble is continuous.
$(\forall x)([x \neq \emptyset \ \& \ \neg(\exists y)(y \in x)] \to \text{CONT}(x))$

Corollary 2.5. Atomic ensembles are discrete.

Theorem 2.4. For every ensemble x and condition C, the ensemble $\{z \in x | C(z)\}$ is discrete.
In formula: $(\forall x)\text{DISCR}(\{z \in x | C(z)\})$

Proof: Given an ensemble x and a condition C, let y be the ensemble defined as $y =_D \{z \in x | C(z)\}$. We prove that $y = \cup(y_*)$. All members of y_* are parts of y, therefore their merge is too: $\cup(y_*) \subseteq y$. On the other hand, we prove $y \subseteq \cup(y_*)$ as follows. Let w be a member of x having the property C. Being a member of x such that C(z), $w \in y$. Therefore $\{w\} \subseteq y$. Since $\{w\}$ is an atomic part of y, $\{w\} \in y_*$. Therefore $\{w\} \subseteq \cup(y_*)$, so $w \in \cup(y_*)$. We thus see that $\cup(y_*)$ contains all members of x having the property C, and since y is by definition the minimal ensemble for which this is the case, we have $y \subseteq \cup(y^*)$. Therefore $y = \cup(y^*)$. This completes the proof.

Theorem 2.5. The pair of two ensembles is discrete.
In formula: $(\forall x, y)\text{DISCR}(\{x, y\})$

Proof: Let p designate the pair of two ensembles x and y. We prove that $p = \cup(p_*)$.
Let z be an atomic part of p, that is, $z \subseteq p$ and $z \in p_*$. According to theorem 10.2.7.4, $p = \{x\} \cup \{y\}$, therefore, by corollary 10.2.7.1 z overlaps with $\{x\}$ or with $\{y\}$. Therefore, by corollary 10.2.4.5, either $z = \{x\}$ or $z = \{y\}$. By the definition of p_* and the definition of pair, it follows that $p_* = \{\{x\}, \{y\}\}$. Therefore $p = \cup(p_*)$.

Corollary 2.6. Singletons are discrete.
$(\forall x)\text{DISCR}(\{x\})$

Theorem 2.6. The power of an ensemble is discrete.
In formula: $(\forall x)\text{DISCR}(\mathcal{P}(x))$

Proof: Consider an ensemble x and its power ensemble p. Let z be an arbitrary part of x, then $z \in p$. Therefore, $\{z\} \subseteq p$. Moreover, $\{z\}$ is atomic, so $\{z\} \in p_*$. Therefore $\{z\} \subseteq \cup(p_*)$. Therefore z is a member of $\cup(p_*)$. In other words, any part of x is a member of $\cup(p_*)$. Since p is by definition the minimal ensemble having all parts of x as members, it follows that $p \subseteq \cup(p_*)$.
On the other hand, since by definition of p_* all members of p_* are

parts of x, by the theorem of submerging $\cup(p_*) \subseteq p$. Therefore $p = \cup(p_*)$, i.e. p is discrete.

Theorem 2.7. A discrete ensemble x is part of a discrete ensemble y iff all members of x are members of y.

In formula:

$(\forall x, y)([DISCR(x) \& DISCR(y)] \rightarrow [x \subseteq y \leftrightarrow (\forall z)(z \in x \leftrightarrow z \in y)])$

Proof: Consider two discrete ensembles x and y, with $x \neq \emptyset$ (otherwise the theorem is trivial).

(a) Suppose $x \subseteq y$. If z is a member of x, then $\{z\} \subseteq x$, therefore, by the transitivity of $\subseteq$, $\{z\} \subseteq y$, therefore $z \in y$.

(b) Suppose all members of x are members of y. Let w be an atomic part of x, with unicle z (so $w = \{z\}$). Then $z \in x$, therefore by assumption $z \in y$. Therefore $\{z\} \subseteq y$, or $w \subseteq y$. So any atomic x is a part of y, or, in other words, any member of x_* is a part of y. By the theorem of submerging, it follows that $\cup(x_*) \subseteq y$. Since x is discrete, $x = \cup(x_*)$. Therefore $x \subseteq y$.

Theorem 2.8. The merge of any number of discrete ensembles is discrete.

Proof: Let x be a non-empty ensemble having only discrete members (for x having zero members the theorem is trivial). Let z be a non-empty part of $\cup(x)$. By corollary 10.2.7.1, z overlaps with a member y of x. Since y is discrete, and $z \cap y \subseteq y$, by corollary 2.2 $z \cap y$ has a member. This is also a member of y; therefore we see that every non-empty part of $\cup(x)$ has a member. By corollary 2.3, it follows that $\cup(x)$ is discrete.

Corollary 2.7. The overlap of any number of discrete ensembles is discrete.

Corollary 2.8. The completion of a discrete ensemble relative to a discrete ensemble is discrete.

The operations of merging, completing, and taking overlaps thus conserve the property of discreteness.

11.3 Continuity versus discreteness

In this section I consider the relations between continuous and discrete ensembles. First, it is proved that an ensemble cannot be both continuous and discrete.

Theorem 3.1. The properties of continuity and discreteness are mutually exclusive.
In formula:
$(\forall x)([CONT(x) \to \neg DISCR(x)] \ \& \ [DISCR(x) \to \neg CONT(x)])$

Proof: According to corollary 1.3, a continuous ensemble has no members. According to theorem 2.1, a non-empty discrete ensemble does have a member. Therefore, a non-empty ensemble cannot be both continuous and discrete. Moreover, by corollary 1.2 and corollary 2.1, the empty ensemble is discrete and not continuous.

Theorem 3.2. The overlap of a continuous ensemble and a discrete ensemble is empty.
In formula: $(\forall x, y)([CONT(x) \ \& \ DISCR(y)] \to x \cap y = \varnothing)$

Proof: Let x be a continuous ensemble and y a discrete ensemble. Suppose $x \cap y$ is not empty. Let z be a non-empty common part of x and y. Being a non-empty part of a continuous ensemble, z is continuous (theorem 1.1). Being a part of a discrete ensemble, z is discrete (theorem 2.2). According to the previous theorem, this is a contradiction. Therefore the supposition that $x \cap y$ is non-empty is false.

It is not the case that every ensemble is either continuous or discrete. This is obvious when we consider what happens upon merging a continuous ensemble x and a discrete ensemble y. The result is an ensemble which has a continuous part (x), and is therefore not discrete, and which also has a discrete part (y), and is therefore not continuous. I call such an ensemble 'mixed'.

Definition 3.1. An ensemble is *mixed* iff it has a continuous part and a non-empty discrete part.

Notation 3.1. The notation MIX(x) is used to indicate that x is a mixed ensemble. Formally:

Definition 3.2. $MIX(x) =_D (\exists y \subseteq x) CONT(y) \ \& \ (\exists z \subseteq^\circ x) DISCR(z)$

In view of the theorems 1.1 and 2.2, two direct consequences of the definition are:

Corollary 3.1. The merge of a continuous ensemble and a discrete ensemble is a mixed ensemble.
$(\forall x, y)([CONT(x) \ \& \ DISCR(y)] \to MIX(x \cup y))$

Corollary 3.2. An ensemble is mixed iff it is neither continuous nor discrete.
$$(\forall x)(MIX(x) \leftrightarrow [\neg CONT(x) \,\&\, \neg DISCR(x)])$$

Alternatively, we could have defined an ensemble to be mixed if it is neither continuous nor discrete, and proved that a mixed ensemble has both a continuous part and non-empty discrete part. In any case, it is obvious that continuous, discrete, and mixed ensembles exhaust all possible types of ensembles. When considering ensembles of arbitrary type, I shall sometimes use the term *general ensemble* in order to emphasize that we are not considering a particular kind of ensemble. Correspondingly, I shall occasionally refer to *general ensemble theory* when referring to the theory of general ensembles, as defined by the axioms I–X in section 10.2.

12 A model for ensemble theory[1]

In this chapter I shall describe a model for ensemble theory in a more detailed and formal way than in chapter 5. Section 12.1 discusses the structure of the model, section 12.2 contains the proofs that the axioms of ensemble theory are satisfied in the model.

I shall refer to the axiom system, described in chapter 10, as ETX. For convenience of reference, I list the axioms here.

ETX1. $(\forall x, y, z)((x \subseteq y\ \&\ y \subseteq z) \to x \subseteq z)$
(Transitivity)

ETX2. $(\forall x, y, z)(((x = y\ \&\ z \underline{\in} x) \to z \underline{\in} y)\ \&\ ((x = y\ \&\ x \underline{\in} z) \to y \underline{\in} z))$
(Equality)

ETX3. $(\forall x)([AT(x) \to (\exists! y)(y \underline{\in} x)]\ \&\ [\neg AT(x) \to \neg(\exists y)(y \underline{\in} x)])$
(Unicles)

ETX4. $(\forall x, y)([(\forall z \subseteq^\circ x)(z\ \hat{o}\ y) \vee (\exists u)(u \underline{\in} x\ \&\ u \underline{\in} y)] \to x \subseteq y)$
(Extensionality)

ETX5. $(\forall x, y)(\exists p)(x \in p\ \&\ y \in p)$
(Pairing)

ETX6. $(\forall x)(\exists p)(\forall z)(z \subseteq x \to z \in p)$
(Powers)

ETX7. $(\forall x)(\exists u)[(\forall z \in x)(z \subseteq u)\ \&\ (\forall y \subseteq^\circ u)(\exists w \in x)(w\ \hat{o}\ y)]$
(Merging)

ETX8. For any functional condition C on the ensemble x,
$(\forall x)(\exists y)(\forall z)(z \in y \leftrightarrow (\exists u \in x)C(u, z))$
(Replacement)

ETX9. $(\exists x)[(\exists y)(y \in x)\ \&\ (\forall z)(z \in x \to \{z\} \in x)]$
(Infinity)

ETX10. $(\forall x)[(\exists y)(y \in x) \to (\exists z \in x)\neg(\exists w \in z)(w \in x)]$
(Regularity)

269

12.1 The model structure

The axioms of ensemble theory contain an individual constant (∅) and variables which are all of the same type, and two primitive two-place predicates, ⊆ and ∈, both applicable to pairs of objects of that type. A model of the axiom system ETX is therefore a triple

(12.1) $M = (U, \subseteq_U, \in_U)$

where U is the domain of values that the variables may take, and from which the interpretation of the constant '∅' is to be picked, and $\subseteq_U$ and $\in_U$ are both relations in $U \times U$. The model described in section 5.5 is an example of such a triple (see (5.42)).

Every variable and individual constant in the language of the ETX axioms stands for an ensemble; as we have seen in the previous chapter, an ensemble, in general, has both a discrete part and a continuous part. What was called a 'discrete ensemble' may be viewed as an ensemble with an empty continuous part, and what was called a 'continuous ensemble' as having an empty discrete part. Therefore, I construct the interpretation domain U as consisting of pairs (d, c), where d is the interpretation of the discrete part of an ensemble and c that of the continuous part. For the 'discrete' components (d) of these pairs I will use subsets of U, with the empty subset as a special case (see the recursive definition given below). For the 'continuous' components (c) I will take the elements of a non-atomic, complete Boolean algebra, that is, a structure

(12.2) $B = (A, +, *, ', 0, 1)$

where:

1. B is a Boolean algebra (see definition 10.3.5.1)
2. For all $a \in A$ and $b \in A$, $a+b \in A$, $a*b \in A$, and $a' \in A$ (Completeness).
3. If ≤ is the ordering relation on A defined by $b \leq a =_D a+b = a$, then for every $a \in A$, $a \neq 0$, there is an element $b \in A$, $b \neq a$ and $b \neq 0$, such that $b \leq a$.

The components of B designated by +, *, and ' will serve as the interpretations of the merge, overlap, and completion of ensembles; the Boolean algebra we see playing a role in the construction of a model reflects the Boolean properties of the ensemble operations, established in section 10.3.5. The ordering relation ≤ will serve as the interpretation of

A model for ensemble theory 271

the part–whole relation among ensembles; the fact that continuous ensembles have no minimal parts is reflected in that the algebra B is non-atomic.

Given such an algebra B, the interpretation domain U is defined formally as follows:

Definition 1.1. Given a complete, non-atomic Boolean algebra B = (A, +, *, ', o, 1) the set U is defined by:

1. $(\emptyset, c) \in U$ if $c \in A$ and $\emptyset$ is the empty set.
2. $(d, c) \in U$ if d is a subset of U and $c \in A$.
3. U has no other elements than those described by 1 and 2.

The relations $\subseteq_U$ and $\in_U$, which together with U make up the model M (12.1), are defined as follows:

Definition 1.2. Let $a = (d_a, c_a)$ and $b = (d_b, c_b)$ be elements of the domain U defined by definition 1.1. Then: $a \subseteq_U b =_D d_a \subseteq d_b$ and $c_a \leq c_b$ where $\subseteq$ designates the ordinary subset relation and $\leq$ the Boolean ordering relation on A.

Definition 1.3. Let $a = (d_a, c_a)$ and $b = (d_b, c_b)$ be elements of the domain U defined by definition 1.1. Then: $a \in_U b =_D d_b = \{(d_a, c_a)\}$ and $c_b = o$, where o designates the null element of the Boolean algebra.

With U, $\subseteq_U$, and $\in_U$ thus defined, the triple M (12.1) will be a model for ensemble theory.

12.2 Satisfaction of the ETX axioms

From the definitions of $\subseteq_U$ and $\in_U$ it follows immediately that the axioms of transitivity (ETX1), equality (ETX2), and unicles (ETX3) are satisfied. (See also section 5.5.) The satisfaction of the axioms of replacement (ETX8), infinity (ETX9), and regularity (ETX10) follows immediately from their purely set-theoretic character and the fact that the universe U encloses a subuniverse V, of purely set-theoretical constructs, of a model for set theory.[2]

It remains to be proved that the axioms of extensionality (ETX4), pairing (ETX5), powers (ETX6), and merging (ETX7) are satisfied. In providing these proofs I shall use the following notation:

– the object in the domain U that is used as the interpretation

(value) of a variable x will be indicated by the same variable but with an accent: x';
- the discrete and continuous components of an object x' in U will be indicated by d_x and c_x, respectively. Thus, the interpretation of a variable x is represented as x' or as (d_x, c_x);
- the symbol $\emptyset$ will be used only as a constant of the ETX language, designating the empty ensemble;
- the empty set will be designated by $\emptyset_s$;
- the symbol $\subseteq$ will be used only as a constant of the ETX language, designating the part–whole relation;
- the subset-relation, element-relation, and union-operation of set theory will be represented by $\subseteq_s$, $\in_s$, and $\cup_s$, respectively.

Theorem 2.1. The axiom of extensionality (ETX4) is satisfied in the model $M = (U, \subseteq_U, \in_U)$.

Proof: We consider the two cases, distinguished in the axiom, separately; first the case of two ensembles having a common unicle, and subsequently the case of two ensembles where all non-empty parts of the one overlap with the other.

1. Suppose $(\exists u)(u \in x \,\&\, u \in y)$.
   The assumption $u \in x$ means that in the interpretation domain we have $u' \in_U (d_x, c_x)$ which, by the definition of $\in_U$, means $d_x = \{u'\}$ and $c_x = 0$. By the same token, $u \in y$ means that in the interpretation domain $u' \in_U (d_y, c_y)$ which, by the definition of $\in_U$, means $d_y = \{u'\}$ and $c_y = 0$. Therefore, $(d_x, c_x) = (d_y, c_y)$, and hence, trivially, $(d_x, c_x) \subseteq_U (d_y, c_y)$, which is the interpretation of $x \subseteq y$.

2. Suppose $(\forall z)(z \subseteq^\circ x \to z \,\hat{o}\, y)$.
   Suppose that not $x \subseteq y$. Then in the interpretation domain it is not the case that $(d_x, c_x) \subseteq_U (d_y, c_y)$. Then either (a) it is not the case that $c_x \leq c_y$, or (b) d_x is not a subset of d_y.
   (a) If it is not the case that $c_x \leq c_y$ then the complement c'_y of c_y (complement in the sense of the Boolean algebra) has a non-empty overlap with c_x: $c'_y * c_x \neq 0$. By the completeness of the algebra, $c'_y * c_x$ belongs to A, therefore the pair $(d_x, c'_y * c_x)$ is a non-empty part of (d_x, c_x) which does not 'overlap' with (d_y, c_y) in the sense of having no other common $\subseteq_U$-part than the 'empty' object $(\emptyset, 0)$.

This means that x has a non-empty part that does not overlap with y, which violates the assumption.

(b) If it is not the case that d_x is a subset of d_y then d_x has an element z' which is not an element of d_y, and since d_x and d_y are both subsets of U, this must be an element of U. It follows that ($\{z'\}$, o) is a non-empty part (in the sense of $\subseteq_U$) of (d_x, c_x) which does not 'overlap' with (d_y, c_y) in the sense of having no other common $\subseteq_U$-part than the 'empty' object ($\emptyset$, o). This means that x has a non-empty part that does not overlap with y, which violates the assumption.

Therefore $x \subseteq y$.

Therefore the axiom of extensionality is satisfied.

Theorem 2.2. The axiom of pairing (ETX5) is satisfied in the model $M = (U, \subseteq_U, \in_U)$.

Proof: With x' and y' elements in U, the set $\{x', y'\}$ is a subset of U, hence the pair ($\{x', y'\}$, o) is in U. This is the 'smallest' (in the sense of the $\subseteq_U$-relation) object in U containing both x' and y'. Its existence in the interpretation domain means that the axiom of pairing is satisfied.

Theorem 2.3. The axiom of powers (ETX6) is satisfied in the model $M = (U, \subseteq_U, \in_U)$.

Proof: With $x' = (d_x, c_x)$ in U, what we are looking for in the interpretation domain is the pair ($\{y' | y' \subseteq_U x'\}$, o), which would be the interpretation of the smallest ensemble having all parts of x as its members.

Suppose $y \subseteq x$. Then $y' \subseteq_U x'$, so $d_y \subseteq_s d_x$ and $c_y \leqslant c_x$.

From $d_y \subseteq_s d_x$ and $d_x \subseteq_s U$ it follows that $d_y \subseteq_s U$.

From $c_y \leqslant c_x$ and $c_x \in_s A$ it follows that $c_y \in_s A$.

Combining the two, it follows that the pair (d_y, c_y) is a member of U. Since this is true for any $y \subseteq x$, it follows that the collection of all pairs (d_y, c_y) such that $(d_y, c_y) \subseteq_U (d_x, c_x)$ is a subset of U. Hence the pair ($\{y' | y' \subseteq_U x'\}$, o) is an element in U. This means that the axiom of powers is satisfied.

Theorem 2.4. The axiom of merging (ETX7) is satisfied in the model $M = (U, \subseteq_U, \in_U)$.

Proof: I consider the merge of two ensembles; the proof is easily generalized for the merge of any set of ensembles.

With $x' = (d_x, c_x)$ and $y' = (d_y, c_y)$ in U we have:
(1) $d_x \subseteq_s U$ and $d_y \subseteq_s U$, therefore their union $d_x \cup_s d_y \subseteq_s U$;
(2) $c_x \in_s A$ and $c_y \in_s A$ therefore $c_x + c_y \in_s A$, by the completeness of the Boolean algebra;
Combining (1) and (2) we have $(d_x \cup_s d_y, c_x + c_y) \in_s U$.

This pair is the smallest (in the sense of the $\subseteq_U$ relation) element in the interpretation domain that has both x' and y' as $\subseteq_U$-parts. Its existence in U means that the axiom of merging is satisfied.

This completes the proof that $M = (U, \subseteq_U, \in_U)$ is a model for the axiom system ETX, and thereby of the consistency of ensemble theory. The triple $(V, \subseteq_U, \in_U)$, with $V = \{(d, c) \in_s U \mid c = 0\}$ constitutes an embedded model for set theory. Moreover, the universe A of the Boolean algebra used in the definition of U has 'non-zero' elements, namely the element 1, and therefore, by clause 3 of 12.2, others as well. The model therefore includes objects of the form $(\emptyset, a)$, that have the part–whole structure of a continuous ensemble. The model thus shows that ensemble theory offers us something beyond classical set theory.

13 *Ensemble theory, set theory, and mereology*

In this chapter I shall discuss the formal relations between ensemble theory, set theory, and mereology (or the 'calculus of individuals'). Section 13.1 contains the proof that ensemble theory incorporates set theory in the sense that sets are formally indistinguishable from discrete ensembles. In section 13.2 it is shown that, by weakening one of the axioms of ensemble theory (the axiom of unicles), a variant of the theory is obtained that incorporates mereology as well.

13.1 Ensemble theory and set theory

In this section discrete ensembles are proved to be formally indistinguishable from sets. By 'sets' are meant objects that satisfy the axioms of the Zermelo–Fraenkel system, to which I shall refer as ZFX. By 'discrete ensembles' I mean objects that satisfy the axioms I–X of chapter 10 and, in addition, have the property of discreteness (definition 11.2.1). The system formed by the axioms I–X is referred to as ETX.

The proof consists of showing that, when ETX is extended with an axiom saying that all ensembles have the property of discreteness, the resulting system is equivalent to the Zermelo–Fraenkel system: all axioms of ZFX can be derived from the axioms of the extended system and vice versa. I shall refer to the extended system as ETX*; thus, ETX* consists of the axioms I–X plus the additional axiom:

AXIOM XI (Axiom of discreteness). $(\forall x)x = \cup(x_*)$

I shall prove the equivalence of ETX* and ZFX using the following formulation of the ZFX axioms:

ZFX1. $(\forall x, y, z)((x = y \,\&\, x \in z) \to y \in z)$
(Extensionality/Equality)

ZFX2. $(\forall x, y)(\exists p)(\forall z)(z \in p \leftrightarrow (z = x \vee z = y))$
(Pairs)
ZFX3. $(\forall x)(\exists P)(\forall z)(z \in P \leftrightarrow z \subseteq x)$
(Powers)
ZFX4. $(\forall x)(\exists u)(\forall z)(z \in u \leftrightarrow (\exists y \in x)(z \in y))$
(Unions)
ZFX5. For any functional condition C on the set x:[1]
$(\forall x)(\exists y)(\forall z)(z \in y \leftrightarrow (\exists w \in x)C(w, z))$
(Replacement)
ZFX6. $(\exists x)[(\exists y)(y \in x \ \& \ (\forall z \in x)(\{z\} \in x))]$
(Infinity)
ZFX7. $(\forall x)[(\exists y)(y \in x) \rightarrow (\exists z \in x)\neg(\exists w \in z)(w \in x)]$
(Regularity)

It is worth noting that this formulation of the axioms of Zermelo–Fraenkel set theory assumes an underlying logical framework which does not contain the notion of equality; the equality relation occurring in axiom ZFX1 is a defined notion, as in the axiomatic formulation of ensemble theory given in chapter 10.[2]

To compare the axiom systems of ensemble theory and set theory, we must first consider the logical languages in which the axioms are formulated. These are the same except for their predicate symbols. The language of the ensemble axioms has two primitive two-place predicates, designated by the symbols $\subseteq$ and $\in$, and six defined predicates, designated by AT, =, $\subseteq°$, ô, $\in$, and $\{\ldots\}$. The language in which the ZFX axioms are formulated, on the other hand, has one primitive predicate, designated by $\in$, and three defined predicates: =, $\subseteq$, and $\{\ldots\}$. The meanings of the primitive predicate symbols are determined by the axiom systems in which they occur, those of the defined predicates by their definitions in terms of the primitive predicates. Therefore, although the languages of the ETX and ZFX systems have several symbols in common, these do not necessarily have the same meaning in the two formalisms. For instance, the = predicate as defined in set theory does not have the same meaning as the one defined in ensemble theory. The former, which I will designate temporarily by $=_s$ to avoid confusion, is defined by: $x =_s y =_D (\forall z)(z \in x \leftrightarrow z \in y)$. If we introduce this equality notion in ensemble theory, that is, we regard the symbol $\in$ as designating the membership relation in ensemble theory, then by the fact that a continuous ensemble has no members we would have that any two continuous ensembles are equal. Consequently, when we see the same formulas in both axiom systems, such as ETX9 and ZFX6, we may not yet conclude that the axioms have the same meaning. We must first establish the precise relations between the primitive and defined predicates of the languages in which the axioms are formulated. In fact, the enterprise of comparing the formalisms of set theory and ensemble theory *is* that of comparing their predicates.

The rest of this section is devoted to proving the claim that the concept of a discrete ensemble is the same as that of a set. This means that we have the task of showing that:

(13.1) 1. Discrete ensembles satisfy the axioms of ZFX. That is, for any objects satisfying the axioms of ETX* we can indicate a relation $\in$ such that the axioms of ZFX are satisfied.
2. Sets satisfy the axioms of ETX*. That is, for any objects satisfying the axioms of ZFX we can indicate relations $\subseteq$ and $\underline{\in}$ such that the axioms of ETX* are satisfied.

When we want to prove (1), we have to keep in mind that the predicate symbols in the ZFX axioms have different definitions than the same symbols in the language of ensemble theory. To avoid any confusions, I shall label the predicate symbols of set theory with the subscript 's' and those of ensemble theory with the subscript 'e'. The procedure for proving the equivalence of the axiom systems for set theory and discrete ensemble theory is as follows:

(13.2) 1. (i) Consider objects that satisfy the axioms of ETX*, where all predicate symbols are subscripted with 'e'.
   (ii) Identify a two-place predicate that plays the role of element relation, and use the symbol $\in_s$ to designate it.
   (iii) Define predicates $=_s$, $\subseteq_s$, and $\{\ldots\}_s$ in terms of the predicate $\in_s$ in the way that is usual in set theory.
   (iv) Show that the objects chosen in 1(i) satisfy the ZFX axioms with all predicate symbols subscripted with 's'.
2. (i) Consider objects that satisfy the axioms of ZFX, where all predicate symbols are subscripted with 's'.
   (ii) Identify two two-place predicates that play the role of part–whole relation and member–whole relation, and designate these by $\subseteq_e$ and $\underline{\in}_e$, respectively.

278 Part 2 Ensemble theory

(iii) Define predicates $=_e$, $\subseteq_e^\circ$, $\hat{o}_e$, AT_e, $\in_e$, and $\{\ldots\}_e$ in terms of the $\subseteq_e$ and $\underline{\in}_e$ predicates in the way that is usual in ensemble theory.

(iv) Show that the objects chosen in 2(i) satisfy the ETX* axioms with all predicate symbols subscripted with 'e'.

13.1.1 Sets in ensemble theory

I will now show that discrete ensembles satisfy the Zermelo–Fraenkel axioms, going through the procedure 1(i–iv) just outlined. So we consider objects that satisfy the ETX* axioms, and our first task is to identify a predicate $\in_s$ that can play the role of the element relation. For this purpose we take of course the membership relation defined in ensemble theory:

Definition 1.1.1. $x \in_s y =_D (\exists z)(z \subseteq_e y \ \& \ x \underline{\in}_e z)$

We define the predicates $=_s$, $\subseteq_s$ and $\{\ldots\}_s$ in terms of the $\in_s$ relation in the same way as in set theory:

Definition 1.1.2. $x \subseteq_s y =_D (\forall z)(z \in_s x \to z \in_s y)$

Definition 1.1.3. $x =_s y =_D (\forall z)(z \in_s x \leftrightarrow z \in_s y)$

Definition 1.1.4. $\{\ldots\}_s$ is the atomic ensemble such that $x \in_s \{x\}_s$.

The last definition presupposes that there is only one atomic ensemble z such that $x \in_s z$. But this follows immediately from definition 1.1.1 plus the fact that an atomic ensemble has by definition one unicle.

The next task is to show that discrete ensembles satisfy the ZFX axioms in which the predicate symbols are replaced by the corresponding subscripted ones introduced by the above definitions. The easiest way to do this is by showing first that the predicates $=_s$, $\subseteq_s$, $\in_s$, and $\{\ldots\}_s$ as defined above, are equivalent to the predicates $=_e$, $\in_e$, $\subseteq_e$, and $\{\ldots\}_e$, as long as we restrict their application to discrete ensembles.

For convenience I rephrase the definitions of $=_e$, $\in_e$, $\{\ldots\}_e$ from chapter 10 using the notation with subscripts.

Definition 1.1.5. $x \in_e y =_D (\exists z)(z \subseteq_e y \ \& \ x \underline{\in}_e z)$

Definition 1.1.6. $x =_e y =_D x \subseteq_e y \ \& \ y \subseteq_e x$

Definition 1.1.7. $\{x\}_e$ is the atomic ensemble with unicle x.

Ensemble theory, set theory, and mereology   279

Note that the definitions 1.1.1 and 1.1.5 have the same right-hand side, therefore:

Corollary 1.1.1. $(\forall x, y)(x \in_s y \leftrightarrow x \in_e y)$

In view of this, I shall drop the subscripts of the $\in$ symbol.

Theorem 11.2.7 tells us that a discrete ensemble x is part of a discrete ensemble y iff all members of x are members of y—which is precisely the definition of $\subseteq_s$. Consequently:

Corollary 1.1.2. $(\forall x, y)(\text{DISCR}(x) \& \text{DISCR}(y) \to (x \subseteq_s y \leftrightarrow x \subseteq_e y))$

In view of this, I shall drop the subscripts of the $\subseteq$ symbol.

Combining the last corollary with the definitions of $=_s$ and $=_e$, the equivalence of the two notions of equality for discrete ensembles follows immediately:

Corollary 1.1.3. $(\forall x, y)(\text{DISCR}(x) \& \text{DISCR}(y) \to (x =_s y \leftrightarrow x =_e y))$

In view of this, I shall also drop the subscripts of the $=$ symbol.

The equivalence of the concepts expressed by $\{\ldots\}_s$ and $\{\ldots\}_e$ follows immediately from their definitions combined with corollary 1.1.1:

Corollary 1.1.4. $(\forall x)(\{x\}_s = \{x\}_e)$

Hence we may also drop the subscripts in the representation of singletons.

Establishing the equivalence of the predicates in the ZFX axioms and those in the ETX* axioms has simplified our task to showing that the formulas of the ZFX axioms can be derived in ensemble theory from the ETX* axioms, where the symbols in the ZFX axioms may be treated as those of the ETX system.

I now turn to these derivations.

Theorem 1.1.1. ZFX1: $(\forall x, y, z)((x = y \& x \in z) \to y \in z)$
            (Extensionality/Equality)

Proof: ZFX1 follows immediately from the second clause of ETX2.

Theorem 1.1.2. ZFX2: $(\forall x, y)(\exists p)(\forall z)(z \in p \leftrightarrow (z = x \vee z = y))$
            (Pairing)

Proof: Let p be the pair of x and y, as defined by definition 10.2.5.2. It follows from the definition that $x \in p$ and $y \in p$. Next I prove that p has no other members than x and y. Let z be an atomic part of p, so $z \in p_*$.[3] By theorem 10.2.7.4, $p = \{x\} \cup \{y\}$, therefore (corollary 10.2.7.1), z overlaps with $\{x\}$ or with $\{y\}$. Therefore, by corollary 10.2.4.5, either $z = \{x\}$ or $z = \{y\}$. So p has $\{x\}$ and $\{y\}$ as only atomic parts. Therefore p has x and y as its only members. Therefore, $(\forall z)(z \in p \leftrightarrow (z = x \vee z = y))$. The existence of p is postulated by ETX5.

Theorem 1.1.3. ZFX3: $(\forall x)(\exists P)(\forall z)(z \in P \leftrightarrow z \subseteq x)$
(Powers)

Proof: The power $\mathcal{P}(x)$ of a given ensemble x, as defined by definition 10.2.6.1, is shown to have the desired properties of containing all parts of x and having no other members.
By definition 10.2.6.1, $(\forall z)(z \subseteq x \rightarrow z \in \mathcal{P}(x))$.
By theorem 10.2.8.3, $\mathcal{P}(x)$ only has parts of x as members.
The existence of $\mathcal{P}(x)$ is postulated by ETX6.

Theorem 1.1.4. ZFX4: $(\forall x)(\exists u)(\forall z)(z \in u \leftrightarrow (\exists y \in x)(z \in y))$
(Unions)

Proof: We show that for u, occurring in ZFX4, we can take the merge $\cup(x)$ of x. For $x = \emptyset$ the case is trivial, so suppose x is not empty.

1. We first prove the implication from right to left.
   By theorem 11.2.1, x has a member y. If $y \in x$, then $y \subseteq \cup(x)$, so all members of y are members of $\cup(x)$ (theorem 10.2.3.1). In other words, all members of members of x are members of $\cup(x)$.

2. We now prove the implication from left to right.
   Consider a member z of $\cup(x)$. (There is such a member, since we assumed x to be non-empty.) We prove that z is a member of y for some $y \in x$. Since $z \in \cup(x)$, $\{z\} \subseteq \cup(x)$. By corollary 10.2.7.1, $\{z\}$ overlaps with some member y of x. Since $\{z\}$ is atomic, by corollary 10.2.4.6 $\{z\}$ ô y implies $\{z\} \subseteq y$. Therefore $z \in y$.
   This completes the proof.

Theorem 1.1.5. ZFX5: $(\forall x)(\exists u)(\forall z)(z \in u \leftrightarrow (\exists w \in x)C(w, z))$
(Replacement)

Proof: ZFX5 is identical to ETX8, except that ETX8 stipulates that u is 'minimal' in the sense of definition 10.2.5.1. ETX8 thus implies ZFX5: if there is a 'minimal' u having as members those and only those z such that $C(w, z)$ for some $w \in s$, then *a fortiori* there is some such u.

Theorem 1.1.6. ZFX6: $(\exists x)[(\exists y)(y \in x) \& (\forall z \in x)(\{z\} \in x)]$
(Infinity)

Proof: ZFX6 is identical to ETX9.

Theorem 1.1.7. ZFX7: $(\forall x)[(\exists y)(y \in x) \to (\exists w \in x)\neg(\exists w \in z)(w \in x)]$
(Regularity)

Proof: ZFX7 is identical to ETX10.

Theorems 1.1.1 through 1.1.7 establish that discrete ensembles have all the properties that sets have. Now it might be the case that the axioms of set theory can be derived from those of ETX* because the addition of the axiom of discreteness to the system ETX of general ensemble theory leads to an inconsistent axiom system, from which we could derive just anything. In section 13.1.2 I shall show that the axioms of ETX* can be derived from those of ZFX, which implies that ETX* is not inconsistent. That the addition of the axiom of discreteness does not cause inconsistencies in ensemble theory can also be verified directly, by carefully examining the effect of the addition on those axioms that ascertain the existence of certain axioms; this has been done in Bunt (1981a), chapter 12, section 1.1.

13.1.2 *Ensembles in set theory*

To prove that sets satisfy the axioms of ETX*, I follow the procedure 2(ii)–(iv) described in (13.3). We are now working in the language of the Zermelo–Fraenkel axioms, which has a single primitive predicate, symbolized as $\in_s$, and the non-primitive predicates $\subseteq_s$, $=_s$, and $\{\ldots\}_s$ with their usual definitions. Our first task is to identify two predicates that can take the roles of the part–whole and unicle–whole relations in discrete ensemble theory. The following definitions serve this purpose.

Definition 1.2.1. $x \subseteq_e y =_D (\forall z)(z \in_s x \to z \in_s y)$

Definition 1.2.2. $x \underline{\in}_e y =_D x \in_s y \& (\forall z)(z \in_s y \to z =_s x)$

The non-primitive predicates in the ETX* axioms are defined in terms of the $\subseteq_e$ and $\underline{\in}_e$ predicates in the same way as usual in ensemble theory:

Definition 1.2.3. $x \in_e y =_D (\exists z)(z \subseteq_e y \& x \underline{\in}_e z)$

Definition 1.2.4. $x =_e y =_D x \subseteq_e y \& y \subseteq_e x$

Definition 1.2.5. $\text{EMPTY}(x) =_D (\forall z)(z \subseteq_e x \rightarrow z =_e x)$

Definition 1.2.6. $\text{AT}(x) =_D (\forall y)(y \subseteq^\circ x \rightarrow y =_e x) \,\&\, \neg\text{EMPTY}(x)$

Definition 1.2.7. $x \subseteq^\circ y =_D x \subseteq_e y \,\&\, \neg\text{EMPTY}(x)$

Definition 1.2.8. $x \,\hat{o}\, y =_D (\exists z)(z \subseteq^\circ x \,\&\, z \subseteq^\circ y)$

Definition 1.2.9. $\{x\}_e$ is the set s such that $x \in_e s$ and $\text{AT}(s)$

Since the symbols EMPTY, AT, $\subseteq^\circ$, and ô are not used in set theory, no subscripts are used in connection with them. The predicate EMPTY has been introduced only to facilitate the other definitions. Note that definition 1.2.9 presupposes that there is precisely one atomic set containing a given element x (containing in the sense of the $\in_e$-relation). I shall return to this point below. First, it is again convenient to establish the equivalence of the symbols with different subscripts, as well as the equivalence of the concept of an empty set as defined in definition 1.2.5 and that of the usual concept of an empty set. For convenience I list the definitions of the predicate symbols with subscript 's' here:

Definition 1.2.10. $x \subseteq_s y =_D (\forall z)(z \in_s x \rightarrow z \in_s y)$

Definition 1.2.11. $x =_s y =_D (\forall z)(z \in_s x \leftrightarrow z \in_s y)$

Definition 1.2.12. $\{x\}_s$ is the singleton set with element x.

Comparing the definitions 1.2.1 and 1.2.10, we see that the predicates $\subseteq_e$ and $\subseteq_s$ have the same definition. Thus:

Corollary 1.2.1. $(\forall x, y)(x \subseteq_e y \leftrightarrow x \subseteq_s y)$

In view of this I shall drop the subscripts of the $\subseteq$ symbol.

From this corollary and the respective definitions it follows immediately that the equality concepts represented by $=_e$ and $=_s$ are equivalent:

Corollary 1.2.2. $(\forall x, y)(x =_e y \leftrightarrow x =_s y)$

I will therefore drop the subscripts of the $=$ symbol.

The equivalence of the $\in_e$ and $\in_s$ relations is somewhat less obvious.

Lemma 1.2.1. $(\forall x, y)(x \in_e y \leftrightarrow x \in_s y)$

Proof:

(a) Let x and y be two sets such that $x \in_e y$. By definition, this means that $(\exists z)(z \subseteq y \,\&\, x \in_e z)$. By the definition of $\in_e$, this implies that $(\exists z)(z \subseteq y \,\&\, x \in_s z)$, and hence $x \in_s y$.

(b) To prove the implication in the other direction, let x and y be two sets such that x is a member of y, that is, $x \in_s y$. This is equivalent to the singleton $\{x\}_s$ being a subset of y. By the definition of singleton sets, this means that y has a subset z containing x as its one and only element: $(\exists z)(z \subseteq y \,\&\, x \in_s z \,\&\, (\forall w)(w \in_s z \to w = x))$. The second and third conjuncts in this formula form the definition of $x \in_e z$, hence we have $(\exists z)(z \subseteq y \,\&\, x \in_e z)$. But this is precisely the definition of $x \in_e y$.

In view of this result I drop the subscript of the $\in$ symbol.

The last equivalence of subscripted predicates to be proved concerns the two notions of singleton. The ensemble notion of a singleton is closely related to that of atomic ensembles, which in turn depends on the concept of emptiness as expressed in definition 1.2.5. The following lemma establishes that this is the same concept as that of being the empty set (that is, as with all the equivalences considered here, as long as we restricted the ensemble concept to discrete ensembles).

Lemma 1.2.2. $(\forall x)(\text{EMPTY}(x) \leftrightarrow x = \varnothing)$, where $\varnothing$ represents the empty set.

Proof:

(a) Let x be a set such that EMPTY(x). The empty set $\varnothing$ is a subset of every set, hence, by the definition of EMPTY, $\varnothing = x$.

(b) The empty set $\varnothing$ by definition has no elements, hence by the definition of the subset relation, for any set x we have: $x \subseteq \varnothing \to x = \varnothing$. Therefore EMPTY($\varnothing$).

In view of this result we may replace the expression EMPTY(x) in the definitions 1.2.6 and 1.2.7 (and anywhere else) by: $x = \varnothing$. Thus, the predicate $\subseteq^\circ$ means non-empty subset of, and the predicate AT means not empty, and equal to any of its non-empty subsets. It is now readily seen that the presupposition that there is precisely one atomic set containing a given element, underlying definition 1.2.9, is correct.

Lemma 1.2.3. $(\forall x)(\exists! y)(\text{AT}(y) \,\&\, x \in y)$

Proof: By definition 1.2.9, $x \in \{x\}_e$ and $\text{AT}(\{x\}_e)$ for any set x. Hence there exists a set y such that $(\text{AT}(y) \,\&\, x \in y)$.

Moreover, there is only one such set. For suppose y_1 and y_2 are both atomic sets containing the element x. Then $x \in y_1$ implies $\{x\}_s \subseteq y_1$; from $AT(y_1)$ it follows that $y_1 = \{x\}_s$.
By the same token, $y_2 = \{x\}_s$.
Hence $y_1 = y_2$.

In the proof of this corollary we have seen, in passing, that the atomic set with element x is in fact the good old singleton $\{x\}_s$. On the other hand, applying lemma 1.2.1 to definition 1.2.9, we see that the atomic set with element x is also $\{x\}_e$. Hence the two notions of singleton are equivalent:

Corollary 1.2.3. $(\forall x)(\{x\}_e = \{x\}_s)$

Hence we may also drop the subscripts in the notation $\{\ldots\}$.

This means that we have now eliminated all the subscripts of predicate symbols.

We have now reduced the task to showing that the formulas of the ETX* axioms can be derived from those of the ZFX axioms, where the predicate symbols in the ETX* formulas may be read as the corresponding symbols in set theory.

I now turn to these derivations.

Theorem 1.2.1. ETX1: $(\forall x, y, z)((x \subseteq y \text{ \& } y \subseteq z) \to x \subseteq z)$
(Transitivity)

Proof: Follows immediately from definition 1.2.1.

Theorem 1.2.2. ETX2: $(\forall x, y, z)(((x = y \text{ \& } z \in x) \to z \in y) \text{ \&}$
$((x = y \text{ \& } x \in z) \to y \in z))$
(Equality)

Proof: The two main clauses of the axiom are proved separately.
Consider two equal sets x and y.
1. We prove that $(\forall x, y, z)((x = y \text{ \& } z \in x) \to z \in y)$
Suppose z is a unique element of x. By definition 1.2.2, $z \in x$. By definition 1.2.1, $z \in y$.
Suppose $w \in y$. By definition 1.2.2, $w \in x$. We already assumed that $z \in x$; by definition 1.2.2, this implies that any member of x is equal to z. Thus $w = z$. By definition 1.2.2, this means that $z \in y$.

2. We prove that $(\forall x, y, z)((x = y \;\&\; x \subseteq z) \rightarrow y \subseteq z)$.
   Suppose $x \subseteq z$. By corollary 1.2.1, $x \in z$. By ZFX1, $y \in z$.
   Suppose $w \in z$. It follows, from $x \subseteq z$ and definition 1.2.2, that $w = x$. Since $x = y$, by the transitivity of equality $w = y$. In other words, $y \in z$ and any member of z is equal to y, that is, $y \subseteq z$.

Theorem 1.2.3. ETX3: $(\forall x)([AT(x) \rightarrow (\exists! y)(y \in x)] \;\&\;$
$\qquad\qquad\qquad [\neg AT(x) \rightarrow \neg(\exists y)(y \subseteq x)])$
(Unicles)

Proof: The two clauses of the axiom are proved separately.

1. Let x be atomic; we already established that this means the same as that x is the singleton of a certain y (cf. corollary 10.2.4.9). Suppose $x = \{y\}$. By theorem 10.2.4.4, this implies that $(\forall z)(z \in x \rightarrow z = y)$. This means $y \subseteq x$. Thus: $(\exists y)(y \subseteq x)$. Suppose $z \subseteq x$. By definition 1.2.2, $z \in x$. From $y \subseteq x$ it follows that $z = y$; therefore $(\exists! y)(y \subseteq x)$.
2. Suppose x is not atomic. This means that there is no y which is the one and only member of x. Now there are two possibilities: either x has no members at all, or x has several members.
   If x has no members at all, then from definition 1.2.2 it follows that there is no y such that $y \subseteq x$. If x has several members, then by definition 1.2.2 there is no y such that $y \subseteq x$ either.

Theorem 1.2.4. ETX4: $(\forall x, y)([(\forall z \subseteq^\circ x)(z \;\hat{o}\; y) \;\vee\;$
$\qquad\qquad\qquad (\exists u)(u \subseteq x \;\&\; u \subseteq y)] \rightarrow x \subseteq y)$
(Extensionality)

Proof: The case $x = \emptyset$ is trivial. We prove the two clauses of the disjunction separately for a set x having at least one member.

1. We prove $(\forall x, y)((\forall z \subseteq^\circ x)(z \;\hat{o}\; y) \rightarrow x \subseteq y)$.
   Consider a set x of which every non-empty subset overlaps with y, that is, has a member in common with y. We must prove that $x \subseteq y$. Let w be a member of x. Then $\{w\} \subseteq x$. Since $\{w\}$ is not empty, it has a member in common with y. This must be w, so $w \in y$. Thus, every member of x is a member of y. By definition 1.2.1, $x \subseteq y$.

286 *Part 2 Ensemble theory*

2. We prove $(\forall x, y)((\exists u)(u \in x \& u \in y) \to x \subseteq y)$.
Suppose x and y have a unique element u in common. Then x = {u} as well as y = {u}; hence x = y. So trivially x ⊆ y.

Theorem 1.2.5. ETX5: $(\forall x, y)(\exists p)(x \in p \& y \in p)$
(Pairing)

Proof: According to the Zermelo–Fraenkel axiom of pairs (ZFX2) there exists, given any two sets x and y, a set p having only x and y as members. We show that such a set p satisfies ETX5, by proving that p is a subset of any set of which x and y are members.
Let p' be a set of which x and y are members. Let z be a member of p. By the definition of p, either z = x or z = y. Therefore, by ZFX1, z ∈ p'. Thus, all members of p are members of p', therefore p ⊆ p'. This completes the proof.

Theorem 1.2.6. ETX6: $(\forall x)(\exists p)(\forall z)(z \subseteq x \to z \in p)$
(Powers)

Proof: According to the Zermelo–Fraenkel axiom of powers (ZFX3) there exists, for any x, a set P having as members the subsets of x. Such a set P satisfies ETX6 since it is a subset of any set of which the subsets of x are members. Thus, P is '⊆-minimal'.

Theorem 1.2.7. ETX7: $(\forall x)(\exists u)[(\forall z \in x)(z \subseteq u) \&$
$(\forall y \subseteq° u)(\exists w \in x)(w \hat{o} y)]$
(Merging)

Proof: According to the Zermelo–Fraenkel axiom of unions (ZFX4) there exists, for any set x, a set u having as members those and only those sets that are members of a member of x. We show that u satisfies ETX7, by proving that: (i) all members of x are subsets of u; (ii) every non-empty subset of u overlaps with a member of x. For x = ∅ the theorem is trivial, so consider a non-empty set x.

1. Let z be a member of x. By definition of u, all members of z are members of u. Therefore z ⊆ u.
2. Let y be a non-empty subset of u. Let w be a member of y; since y ⊆ u, w ∈ u. Therefore, by definition of u, w is a member of some member of x. In other words, y has a member in part with a member of x: y overlaps with a member of x.

Theorem 1.2.8. ETX8.
   For any functional condition C on the ensemble x:
   $(\forall x)(\exists y)(\forall z)(z \in y \leftrightarrow (\exists u \in x)C(u, z))$
   (Replacement)

Proof: ETX8 is identical to the Zermelo–Fraenkel axiom of replacement ZFX5, except that ETX8 stipulates that the y, whose existence is postulated by ZFX5, is '$\subseteq$-minimal'; however, this minimality is obvious from its very definition plus the Zermelo–Fraenkel definition of $\subseteq$.

Theorem 1.2.9. ETX9: $(\exists x)[(\exists y)(y \in x) \, \& \, (\forall z)(z \in x \to \{z\} \in x)]$
   (Infinity)

Proof: ETX9 is identical to ZFX6.

Theorem 1.2.10. ETX10: $(\forall x)[(\exists y)(y \in x) \to (\exists z \in x)\neg(\exists w \in z)(w \in z)]$
   (Regularity)

Proof: ETX10 is identical to ZFX7.

Theorem 1.2.11. ETX*11: $(\forall x)x = \cup(x_*)$
   (Discreteness)

Proof: Notice that x_* is the '$\subseteq$-minimal' set containing the atomic subsets of x; it is readily established that in Zermelo–Fraenkel terms this is the set having as members those and only those sets that are atomic subsets of x.
 Since all members of x_* are subsets of x, $\cup(x_*) \subseteq x$. On the other hand, if $y \in x$ then $\{y\} \in x_*$, so $\{y\} \subseteq \cup(x_*)$, and hence $y \in \cup(x_*)$. Therefore $x \subseteq \cup(x_*)$. Therefore $x = \cup(x_*)$.

 In deriving the axioms of ETX*, we have, in passing, derived the axioms of ETX from those of ZFX. This implies the relative consistency of the axiom system ETX: *assuming Zermelo–Fraenkel set theory to be consistent, general ensemble theory is consistent*. For suppose ETX were inconsistent. This would mean that there is a formula S of the logical language, defined in section 10.1, such that both S and its negation ¬S can be derived from the ETX axioms. But in that case the proofs of S and ¬S, starting at the ETX axioms, can be turned into proofs starting at the ZFX axioms, having the ETX axioms as intermediate stages. Therefore, if ensemble theory were inconsistent, so would be Zermelo–Fraenkel set theory.

13.2 Ensemble theory and mereology

13.2.1 *Mereology, or the theory LLG*
In this section we consider the formal relation between ensemble theory and mereology. Mereology was developed by Lesniewski between 1911 and 1922 as part of a comprehensive logical framework for the foundations of mathematics. This framework consisted of a hierarchy of three axiomatic systems, called 'Protothetics', Ontology' and 'Mereology'. Protothetics and Ontology together formed a system of logic, comparable in scope and power to the system of *Principia Mathematica* (Whitehead and Russell, 1910–13). Mereology was devised as an alternative to set theory, which at the time was struggling with antinomies like the Russell paradox. Unfortunately, Lesniewski's writings were extremely inaccessible; several of the most important papers appeared only in Polish, and, as Fraenkel *et al.* (1973) complain, 'Lesniewski wrote his German papers in a style that made no concessions to the reader – some of them are printed in an esoteric symbolism with hardly a word of explanation in ordinary language'.[4] Therefore, Leonard and Goodman did a useful thing by reformulating mereology, as they say: 'in a more usable form, with additional definitions, a practical notation, and a transparent English terminology' (1940, p. 46). This reformulation is in terms of the framework and the notation of *Principia Mathematica*; the authors call their reformulation of mereology 'the calculus of individuals'. I shall refer to mereology, formulated in this way, as 'the theory LLG' (Lesniewski–Leonard–Goodman).

Leonard and Goodman introduce the notion of an *individual* by contrasting individuals with sets (classes) in the following way:

(13.3) An individual ... we understand to be whatever is represented in any given discourse by signs belonging to the lowest logical type of which that discourse makes use. ... The concept of an individual and that of a class may be regarded as different devices for distinguishing one segment of the total universe. ... In both cases, the differentiated segment is potentially divisible, and may even be physically discontinuous. The difference in the concepts lies in this:

that to conceive a segment as ... an individual offers no suggestion as to what these subdivisions, if any, must be, whereas to conceive a segment as a class imposes a definite schema of subdivision into subclasses and members (Leonard and Goodman, 1940, p. 45).[5]

The authors argue that domains of discourse often cannot be modelled adequately in set-theoretical terms, because set theory has no means to describe the internal structure of individuals: 'The ordinary logistic defines no relations between individuals except identity and diversity. A calculus of individuals that introduces other relations, such as the part–whole relation, would obviously be very convenient' (1940, p. 46).

The theory LLG rests on three axioms and three definitions. There is one primitive notion, the dyadic relation 'is disjoint with'.[6] I represent this relation by the symbol $/\!/$. In terms of this primitive, the notions of 'part–whole', 'overlap', and 'fusion' are defined as follows.[7]

Definition 2.1.1. An individual x *is part of* an individual y iff any individual disjoint with y is disjoint with x.

To avoid confusion with the part–whole relation of ensemble theory, I shall call the part–whole relation of LLG '*L-part of*'. I designate this relation by $\leq$. So, formally, we have:

Definition 2.1.1a. $x \leq y =_D (\forall z)(z /\!/ y \rightarrow z /\!/ x)$

Definition 2.1.2. An individual x overlaps with an individual y iff there is an individual x which is a common L-part of x and y.

(Since there are no 'empty individuals' in LLG, it need not be stipulated in this definition that the common L-part should be non-empty.)

To avoid confusion with the overlap relation of ensemble theory, I shall call the overlap relation of LLG 'L-overlap'. I designate this relation by $\underline{o}$. So, formally, we have:

Definition 2.1.2a. $x \underline{o} y =_D (\exists z)(z \leq x \,\&\, z \leq y)$

Definition 2.1.3. An individual u is a fusion of a set s of individuals iff every individual is disjoint with u iff it is disjoint with all members of s.[8]

I use the notation $u\, F^u\, s$ for indicating that u is a fusion of s. It is provable in LLG that for every non-empty set of individuals there is exactly one individual that is a fusion of it; it is thus permitted to refer to 'the fusion of a set of individuals'. The formal definition of fusion is:

Definition 2.1.3a. $u \, F^u \, s =_D (\forall z)(z /\!/ u \leftrightarrow (\forall y \in s)(z /\!/ y))$

The axioms of LLG are the following.

Axiom LLG 1. $(\forall x, y)(x \mathrel{\underset{\sim}{o}} y \leftrightarrow \neg(x /\!/ y))$
  In words: Two individuals overlap iff they are not disjoint.

Axiom LLG 2. $(\forall x, y)((x \leq y \,\&\, y \leq x) \rightarrow x = y)$
  In words: Two individuals that are L-parts of each other are equal.

Axiom LLG 3. $(\forall \alpha)((\exists z)(z \in \alpha) \rightarrow (\exists u)(u \, F^u \, \alpha))$
  In words: A non-empty set of individuals has a fusion.

13.2.2 Ensembles and individuals

The individuals of LLG are entities that have no members, only parts. In ensemble theory we also have such entities: continuous ensembles. There is, however, a difference between these two conceptions of a memberless, part–whole structured entity: in a continuous ensemble one can continue always to take ever smaller parts; for an LLG-individual this need not be the case. There is nothing in the axioms of LLG that prevents an individual from having minimal parts, nor is there anything that forces an individual to have minimal parts. A continuous ensemble therefore seems to be a special kind of individual.

The various kinds of ensemble that the axioms of general ensemble theory allow are represented in diagram (13.4).

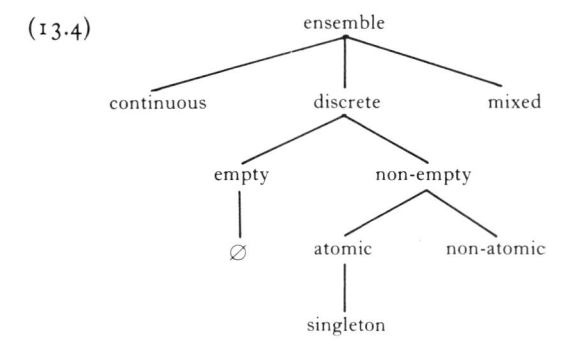

(13.4)
```
                    ensemble
         ┌─────────────┼─────────────┐
   continuous       discrete        mixed
                  ┌─────┴─────┐
                empty      non-empty
                  │         ┌────┴────┐
                  ∅       atomic   non-atomic
                            │
                        singleton
```

For the comparison of ensemble theory and the theory LLG it is more instructive to represent these distinctions in a slightly different way, as in diagram (13.5), with the understanding that singletons and the empty ensemble are special cases of discrete ensembles.

(13.5)

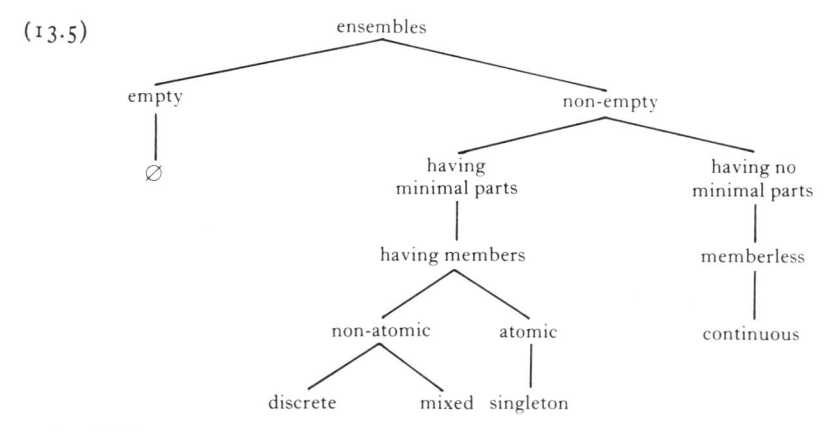

```
                        ensembles
                   /              \
               empty              non-empty
                 |              /          \
                 ∅         having        having no
                        minimal parts   minimal parts
                            |                |
                        having members   memberless
                         /      \            |
                    non-atomic  atomic    continuous
                    /     \       |
                discrete mixed  singleton
```

An LLG individual is non-empty, has no members (the concept of membership is alien to LLG), and may have minimal parts. For the latter reason, if LLG individuals were ensembles we should find them in two parts of the family tree in diagram (13.5): in the part headed by 'having minimal parts' and in that headed by 'having no minimal parts'. But since an LLG individual has no members, the former part of the tree is excluded. Therefore, according to this diagram, an LLG individual would necessarily have the infinite part–whole structure of a continuous ensemble. This is not the case.

Ensemble theory and LLG would be more similar if we had ensembles that have minimal parts without having members. The reason why such ensembles do not exist in ensemble theory as defined in chapter 10 is that the axiom of unicles stipulates that every atomic ensemble has a member: its unicle. As it stands, the axiom in fact says two things: every atomic ensemble has exactly one unicle, and every non-atomic ensemble has no unicles. Let us consider the effect of weakening the first clause to: every atomic ensemble has *at most one* unicle. A more compact formulation of the axiom in this weaker form is: if an ensemble has a unicle, then it is atomic and has only one unicle. In formula:

AXIOM III'. $(\forall x)((\exists y)(y \subseteq x) \rightarrow [AT(x) \& (\forall z \subseteq x)(z = y)])$
 (*Weak axiom of unicles*)

Choosing axiom III' instead of ETX III has the effect that we now have two kinds of atomic ensemble, with and without a unicle. I define:

Definition 2.2.1. An *atomic individual ensemble* is an atomic ensemble that has no unicle.

Notation 2.2.1. The notation ATIND(x) will be used to indicate that x is an atomic individual ensemble.

Those atomic ensembles that do have a unicle are just like the atomic ensembles in general ensemble theory; we have seen that these are singletons (corollary 10.2.4.9).

The introduction of atomic individuals necessitates a modification of the axiom of extensionality, which in its present form would not allow us to prove that an individual atomic ensemble is a part of itself. The simplest modification consists of adding to the axiom the clause saying that an atomic individual includes itself. We then obtain:

AXIOM IV'. $(\forall x, y)([[(\forall z \subseteq^\circ x)(z \hat{o} y) \vee (\exists u)(u \underset{=}{\in} x \& u \underset{=}{\in} y)] \rightarrow (x \subseteq y)]$
$\& [\text{ATIND}(x) \rightarrow x \subseteq x])$
(*Modified axiom of extensionality*)

Replacing the ensemble axioms III and IV by III' and IV', respectively, we obtain a modified version of ensemble theory to which I shall refer as ET'; to the modified axiom system I shall refer as ETX'. In ET' we can define the new concept of an 'individual ensemble' as follows:

Definition 2.2.2. An *individual ensemble* is a non-empty ensemble that has no members.

Obviously, an atomic individual ensemble is an individual ensemble.

Notation 2.2.2. I will use the notation IND(x) to indicate that x is an individual ensemble.

Formally, we thus have:

Definition 2.2.2a. $\text{IND}(x) =_D x \neq \emptyset \& \neg(\exists z)(z \in x)$

According to this definition, a continuous ensemble is clearly an individual ensemble, but, due to the weaker axiom of unicles, in ET' it is not the case that an individual ensemble necessarily has an infinite part–whole structure.

The various types of ensemble in the modified theory ET' are represented in diagram (13.6).

(13.6)

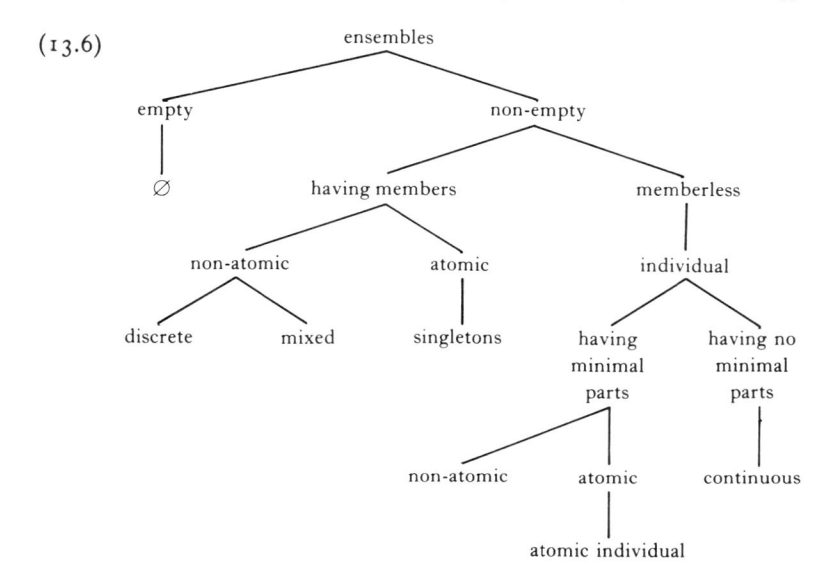

```
                                    ensembles
                        ┌───────────────┴──────────────┐
                     empty                          non-empty
                       │                    ┌───────────┴──────────┐
                       ∅              having members           memberless
                              ┌───────────┴─────────┐              │
                         non-atomic              atomic         individual
                         ┌────┴────┐                │         ┌──────┴──────┐
                     discrete    mixed          singletons  having      having no
                                                            minimal      minimal
                                                             parts        parts
                                                      ┌────────┴──────┐     │
                                                 non-atomic       atomic  continuous
                                                                     │
                                                              atomic individual
```

The definition of an individual ensemble, definition 2.2.2, has the following immediate consequences:

Corollary 2.2.1. There is no empty individual ensemble.

Corollary 2.2.2. Every non-empty part of an individual ensemble is an individual ensemble.

The following theorem concerning individual ensembles will be useful:

Theorem 2.2.1. The merge of one or more individual ensembles is an individual ensemble.
In formula:
$(\forall x)[[(\exists z)(z \in x) \& (\forall y \in x)\text{IND}(y)] \to \text{IND}(\cup(x))]$

Proof: Let x be an ensemble having at least one member, and of which all members are individual ensembles. Suppose $\cup(x)$ is not an individual ensemble. Then $\cup(x)$ contains a member z. Thus, $\{z\} \subseteq \cup(x)$. According to corollary 10.2.7.1, $\{z\}$ overlaps with a member y of x. Since $\{z\}$ is atomic, by corollary 10.2.4.6 $\{z\} \subseteq y$. Therefore $z \in y$. This contradicts the assumption that every member of x is an individual ensemble.

I shall now show that individual ensembles and LLG individuals represent the same concept, in that they have the same part–whole structure, they do not have an additional member–whole structure, and they are not empty. Individual ensembles by their very definition are not empty and have no member–whole structure. LLG individuals have no member–whole structure because there is no concept of membership in LLG, and there is no such thing as an empty individual in LLG. To show that individual ensembles and LLG individuals have the same part–whole structure, I shall prove the equivalence of the LLG axioms and the ETX' axioms insofar as they relate to the part–whole relation in ensemble theory. I shall follow a similar procedure as in section 13.1 when ensemble theory and set theory were compared.

Again, the comparison of the axiom systems must begin with a comparison of the formal languages in which the axioms are expressed and of the further logical frameworks that are used. For the ensemble axioms the logical framework and formal language have been described earlier in this chapter. The LLG axioms are formulated within a logical framework that includes classical set theory. We have seen in chapter 10 that the formulation of ensemble theory, by contrast, does not presuppose set theory (see section 5.2). The logical framework of the LLG system is thus more elaborate than that described in section 10.1. In addition to the axiom schemata of the propositional calculus and the predicate calculus it also includes an axiomatization of set theory. The language of the framework contains, for this reason, the symbol $\in$ denoting the element relation in set theory, and symbols for the defined predicates of set theory which are used in the set axioms. These are not the ZFX axioms, since in Zermelo–Fraenkel set theory all objects are considered to be sets; that is, the elements of a set are supposed also to be sets. Formally, this means that the variables in the ZFX axioms always stand for sets. This is brought out by the fact that from the ZFX axioms it can be deduced that two objects are equal if and only if they have the same elements: $(\forall x, y)(x = y \leftrightarrow (\forall z)(z \in x \leftrightarrow z \in y))$. Clearly, this notion of equality would be unacceptable if variables such as x and y could denote other entities than sets. Underlying LLG is a version of set theory where a set may consist of elements which themselves are not sets; see, for example, Suppes (1960) for an axiomatization of such a set theory. In particular, in the present version a set may consist of LLG individuals. To distinguish between sets and individuals, the language of LLG has two types of variables, for which I will use Greek and Roman letters. Greek letters will denote sets, Roman letters individuals. This convention was already used above in the formulation of axiom LLG3. The use of the ∈ symbol is only permitted if the expression to its right denotes a set, so the string x ∈ y is not well-formed, but x ∈ α is.

The LLG language has one symbol that designates a primitive predicate not belonging to the underlying framework, namely the symbol ∥ designating the relation 'disjoint with' among individuals. The predicate symbols ≤, o̬, and F^u are added, for convenience, by the definitions 2.1.1, 2.1.2, and 2.1.3, respectively. Note that the symbols ∥, ≤, and o̬ may only be flanked by individual variables, and that the F^u symbol must have an individual variable to its left and a set expression to its right. The equality concept in LLG belongs to the underlying logic and may relate to sets as well as to individuals.

After these preliminaries I shall now turn to the proof that individual ensembles and LLG individuals have the same part–whole structure. First I show that individual ensembles satisfy the LLG axioms; and subsequently, that LLG individuals satisfy the ETX' axioms.

13.2.3 *LLG individuals in ensemble theory*
In order to derive the LLG axioms from the ETX' axioms, we must first extend the language of ensemble theory with the necessary concepts for expressing the LLG axioms. The LLG primitive ∥ is defined as follows:

Definition 2.3.1. $x \parallel y =_D \neg(x \hat{o} y)$

The other predicates of LLG are defined in terms of the ∥-relation by the definitions 2.1.1, 2.1.2, and 2.1.3. The following lemmas establish that the notions of L-part and L-overlap, defined by definitions 2.1.1 and 2.1.2, are equivalent to the corresponding notions of ensemble theory, restricted to individual ensembles.

Lemma 2.3.1. Between any two individual ensembles the relation of L-part holds if and only if the one is part of the other.
In formula: $(\forall x, y)((IND(x) \& IND(y)) \rightarrow (x \leq y \leftrightarrow x \subseteq y))$

Proof: Let x and y be two individual ensembles.

1. Suppose $x \leq y$. By definition 2.1.1, $(\forall z)(z \parallel y \rightarrow z \parallel x)$. By definition 2.3.1, $(\forall z)(\neg(z \hat{o} y) \rightarrow \neg(z \hat{o} x))$ or, equivalently, $(\forall z)(z \hat{o} x \rightarrow z \hat{o} y)$. Since x is not empty, x has a non-empty part w. Thus, there is a

w such that w ô x. By the supposition, w ô y. We have now proved that any non-empty part of x overlaps with y, therefore $x \subseteq y$ (corollary 10.2.4.10).

2. Suppose $x \subseteq y$. Since x and y are not empty, this implies that any non-empty part of x overlaps with y (corollary 10.2.4.11). Let z be an ensemble not overlapping with y: $\neg(z \hat{o} y)$. Then $z /\!/ x$, for if z ô x then there would be a w such that $w \subseteq^\circ z$ and $w \subseteq^\circ x$ which, by the supposition, would imply $w \subseteq^\circ y$; w would thus be a non-empty common part of z and y. So $z /\!/ x$. We have now proved that any z disjoint with y is disjoint with x, that is, $x \leq y$.

Corollary 2.3.1. An ensemble x is L-part of an ensemble y iff x is not empty and x is a part of y.

Lemma 2.3.2. Two ensembles L-overlap if and only if they overlap. In formula: $(\forall x, y)(x \underline{o} y \leftrightarrow x \hat{o} y)$

Proof:

1. From left to right.
 By definition 2.1.2, $x \underline{o} y$ implies $(\exists z)(z \leq x \,\&\, z \leq y)$. According to corollary 2.3.1, this is equivalent to $(\exists z)(z \neq \varnothing \,\&\, z \subseteq x \,\&\, z \subseteq y)$. The last expression is the definition of ô. Therefore x ô y.
2. From right to left.
 By definition x ô y means $(\exists z)(z \neq \varnothing \,\&\, z \subseteq x \,\&\, z \subseteq y)$, which by corollary 2.3.1 is equivalent to $(\exists z)(z \leq x \,\&\, z \leq y)$. The last expression is the definition of o. Therefore $x \underline{o} y$.

I now turn to the proofs of the LLG axioms for individual ensembles, given the ET' axioms.

Theorem 2.3.1. LLG1: $(\forall x, y)(x \underline{o} y \leftrightarrow \neg(x /\!/ y))$
 In words: Two (individual) ensembles L-overlap if and only if they are not disjoint.

Proof:

1. Suppose $x \underline{o} y$. By lemma 2.3.1, x ô y. By definition 2.3.1, $\neg(x /\!/ y)$.
2. Suppose $\neg(x /\!/ y)$. By definition 2.3.1, $\neg\neg(x \hat{o} y)$, or x ô y. By lemma 2.3.2, $x \underline{o} y$.

Theorem 2.3.2. LLG2: $(\forall x, y)((x \leq y \,\&\, y \leq x) \rightarrow x = y)$
 In words: Two (individual) ensembles that are L-parts of each other are equal.

Proof: Consider two ensembles x and y such that x≤y and y≤x. By lemma 2.3.1, x⊆y and y⊆x. By definition 10.2.1.1, this means x=y.

Theorem 2.3.3. LLG3: $(\forall s)[(\exists z)(z \in s) \to (\exists u)(u \ F^u \ s)]$

In words: For every non-empty collection s of individual ensembles there is an individual ensemble which is a fusion of s.

Proof: Consider a non-empty ensemble s, having individual ensembles as members. By theorem 2.2.1, the merge of s is an individual ensemble. We show that ∪(s) is a fusion of s, that is $(\forall z)(z \| \cup(s) \leftrightarrow (\forall x \in s) z \| x)$.

1. Let z be an individual ensemble disjoint with ∪(x). Suppose z is not disjoint with every member of s. Let x be a member of s such that z ô x. Since x⊆∪(x), this would imply that z∩x is a non-empty common part of z and ∪(x), which contradicts the assumption z∥∪(x). So any individual z disjoint with ∪(x) is disjoint with all members of x.
2. Consider an individual ensemble z disjoint with all members of s. Suppose z is not disjoint with ∪(s). Then z∩(∪(x)) would be a non-empty part of ∪(x); according to corollary 10.2.7.1, this means that z∩(∪(x)) overlaps with a member of s, which contradicts the assumption. Therefore, any individual z disjoint with all members of s is disjoint with ∪(x).

We thus see that individual ensembles satisfy the LLG axioms; therefore, whatever can be proved in LLG about individuals can be proved about individual ensembles in this variant of ensemble theory. In other words, individual ensembles are LLG individuals. In this sense we may say that ensemble theory incorporates mereology.

13.2.4 *Ensembles in the theory LLG*

Finally, I shall show that LLG individuals may be regarded as individual ensembles, by proving that LLG individuals satisfy those axioms of ETX′ that describe the part–whole structure of these ensembles. These axioms are: the axiom of transitivity (ETX1), the modified axiom of extensionality (ETX4′), and the axiom of merging (ETX7). The other ensemble axioms either formulate properties of the unicle–whole relation or they describe ways in which ensembles may be built up in terms of their members.

In order to prove ensemble-theoretical statements about LLG individuals we must first enrich the language of LLG with the necessary predicates. The part–whole relation of ensemble theory is defined by:

Definition 2.4.1. $x \subseteq y =_D x \leq y$

where the $\leq$ relation is defined in LLG by definition 2.1.1.

In view of the absence of an 'empty individual' in LLG, there is no such difference as in ensemble theory between the predicates 'part of' and 'non-empty part of'. Hence I define the ensemble predicate $\subseteq^\circ$ as identical to the general $\subseteq$ relation:

Definition 2.4.2. $x \subseteq^\circ y =_D x \leq y$

We also need the ensemble notion of overlap, which is defined in the usual way:

Definition 2.4.3. $x \, \hat{o} \, y =_D (\exists z)(z \subseteq^\circ x \,\&\, z \subseteq^\circ y)$

From these definitions and that of L-overlap (definition 2.1.2) we obtain:

Corollary 2.4.1 $(\forall x, y)(x \, \hat{o} \, y \to x \, \underline{o} \, y)$

We also need the predicate 'atomic individual', which means being atomic in the ensemble-theoretical sense but having no members. Since LLG individuals by their very nature do not have members, the property of being an atomic individual coincides with that of just being atomic. Hence the definition:

Definition 2.4.4. $\text{ATIND}(x) =_D (\forall y)(y \subseteq x \to y = x)$

Armed with these definitions, we now turn to the derivation of the relevant parts of the ensemble axioms from the LLG axioms.

Theorem 2.4.1. ETX1: $(\forall x, y, z)(x \subseteq y \,\&\, y \subseteq z \to x \subseteq z)$

Proof: Let x, y, and z be individuals such that $x \subseteq y$ and $y \subseteq z$. By definition 2.4.1, $x \leq y$ and $y \leq z$. By the definition of L-part, this means that $(\forall w)(w \| y \to w \| x)$ and $(\forall w)(w \| z \to w \| y)$. By combining these two we obtain: $(\forall w)(w \| z \to w \| x)$. That is, $x \leq z$. Therefore $x \subseteq z$.

As for an LLG equivalent of the (modified) axiom of extensionality ETX4', note that this has the form:

(13.7) $(\forall x, y)((A \vee B) \to x \subseteq y) \,\&\, C$

where A is the condition that all non-empty parts of x overlap with y, B

Ensemble theory, set theory, and mereology 299

is the condition that x and y have a common unicle, and C is the clause that an atomic individual is part of itself. This form is logically equivalent to the following three-part conjunction:

(13.8) $(\forall x, y)(A \rightarrow x \subseteq y)$ & $(\forall x, y)(B \rightarrow x \subseteq y)$ & C

The axiom ETX4′ is thus really a conjunction of three subaxioms, which I shall refer to as ETX4′a, ETX4′b, and ETX4′c:

ETX4′a: $(\forall x, y)[(\forall z)(z \subseteq^\circ x \rightarrow z \,\hat{o}\, y) \rightarrow x \subseteq y]$
ETX4′b: $(\forall x, y)[(\exists u)(u \in x \,\&\, u \in y) \rightarrow x \subseteq y]$
ETX4′c: $(\forall x)(ATIND(x) \rightarrow x \subseteq x)$

The formula ETX4′b contains the symbol $\in$, which has not been defined in the language of LLG. Moreover, this predicate *cannot* be defined in LLG – not as a relation among individuals, that is. We have already seen in section 13.2.1 that the LLG system has only one primitive relation among individuals, that of 'being disjoint with', in terms of which all other predicates have to be defined. The notion of being a unicle of something cannot be defined in terms of this primitive, just as the element relation in set theory cannot be defined in terms of the subset relation. Therefore, ETX4′b cannot be a statement in LLG and hence this subaxiom cannot be derived from the LLG axioms. Note that this is precisely as it should be, since ETX4′b is that part of the axiom of extensionality that specifies under what conditions one singleton ensemble is part of another. Since there are no LLG individuals corresponding to singleton ensembles, there should be no corresponding axiom in the LLG system.[9]

The formulas ETX4′a and ETX4′c, with the predicate symbols as defined by definitions 2.4.1–2.4.4, are statements in the LLG language, and they constitute those parts of the extensionality axiom which are relevant here. They are derived from the LLG axioms in the following theorems.

Theorem 2.4.2. ETX4′a: $(\forall x, y)((\forall z)(z \subseteq^\circ x \rightarrow z \,\hat{o}\, y) \rightarrow x \subseteq y)$

Proof: Let x and y be two individuals such that $(\forall z)(z \subseteq^\circ x \rightarrow z \,\hat{o}\, y)$. I prove that this implies $x \subseteq y$ by deriving a contradiction from the assumption that not $x \subseteq y$.

In view of definition 2.4.2 and corollary 2.4.1, our assumptions are equivalent to:

1. $(\forall z)(z \leq x \rightarrow z \, \underline{o} \, y)$
2. $\neg(x \leq y)$

Assumption (2) means, by the definition of L-part, that there is an individual w such that

3. $w \mathbin{/\mkern-6mu/} y$ & $\neg(w \mathbin{/\mkern-6mu/} x)$.

For such an individual w, by axiom LLG1, $w \mathrel{\underline{o}} x$; hence w has an L-part v such that $v \leq w$ & $v \leq x$. By assumption (1), this v overlaps with y. But this implies that w also overlaps with y, which contradicts assumption (3). Hence assumption (3) is incompatible with the assumptions (1) and (2), and hence $x \leq y$. Therefore, by definition 2.4.2, $x \subseteq y$.

Theorem 2.4.3. ETX4'c: $(\forall x)(\text{ATIND}(x) \rightarrow x \subseteq x)$

Proof: The statement $z \mathbin{/\mkern-6mu/} x \rightarrow z \mathbin{/\mkern-6mu/} x$ is trivially true for any z and x. Therefore $(\forall x)((\forall z)(z \mathbin{/\mkern-6mu/} x \rightarrow z \mathbin{/\mkern-6mu/} x))$. By definition 2.1.1, this means $(\forall x)(x \subseteq x)$, that is, every individual is part of itself. Hence *a fortiori* every atomic individual is part of itself.

The third ensemble axiom to be proved in LLG is that of merging, which says that any collection of ensembles has a merge. Since the notion of a collection is formalized in ensemble theory as that of a discrete ensemble, the formula expressing the axiom in ensemble theory has a universally quantified variable ranging over ensembles – as all variables in the language of ensemble theory do. In the LLG formalism, however, the notion of a collection is formalized in the underlying logical framework in set-theoretical terms. Therefore, in the language of LLG the axiom should contain a quantified variable ranging over sets, a variable represented by a Greek letter. Moreover, the ensemble axiom says that *any* collection of ensembles has a merge; in the case of an empty collection (an ensemble without any members) this is the empty ensemble. But since there is no empty individual in LLG, which could serve as the merge of an empty set of individuals, the quantified variable should be restricted to range over non-empty sets. Hence the axiom of merging takes the following form in LLG:

ETX7': $(\forall \alpha)((\exists x)(x \in \alpha) \rightarrow (\exists u)[(\forall y \in \alpha)(y \subseteq u)$ &
$(\forall z \subseteq^\circ u)(\exists w \in \alpha)(w \hat{o} z)])$

Theorem 2.4.4. ETX7'.

Proof: Let α be a non-empty set. By axiom LLG3 there exists an individual u such that:

(1) $(\forall z)(z \| u \leftrightarrow (\forall y \in \alpha)(z \| y))$

Suppose ETX7′ were not true, that is, there exists an individual x such that $\neg((\forall y \in \alpha)(y \subseteq x) \& (\forall z \subseteq^\circ x)(\exists w \in \alpha)(w \hat{o} z))$. This means that either $(\exists y \in \alpha)(\neg(y \subseteq x))$ or $(\exists z \subseteq^\circ x)(\neg(\exists w \in \alpha)(w \hat{o} z))$. We consider the two cases separately.

1. Suppose α has a member y such that $\neg(y \subseteq x)$. By definition 2.4.1 and definition 2.1.1, this is equivalent to: $\neg(\forall z)(z \| x \to z \| y)$, and thus to: $(\exists z)(z \| x \& \neg(z \| y))$. This contradicts (1).
2. Suppose x has a non-empty part z such that $\neg(\exists w \in \alpha)(w \hat{o} z)$. By the definitions 2.4.2 and 2.4.3 this means that $(\exists z)(z \leq x \& \neg(\exists w \in \alpha)(w \underset{\sim}{o} z))$ or, equivalently, that $(\exists z)(z \leq x \& (\forall w \in \alpha)(w \| z))$. Since $z \leq x$ implies $\neg(z \| x)$, it follows that $(\exists z)(\neg(z \| x) \& (\forall w \in \alpha)(w \| z))$. This contradicts (1).

This completes the proof.

The theorems 2.4.1 through 2.4.4 show that LLG individuals satisfy those parts of the axiom system of ensemble theory that relate to their part–whole structure. In section 13.2.3 we established that, conversely, individual ensembles satisfy the axioms of LLG. Individual ensembles therefore have the same part–whole structure as LLG individuals. Altogether, this shows that individual ensembles and LLG individuals represent the same concept.

Notes

2 Mass terms

1 Allan has collected a great deal of interesting material relating to the count/mass distinction. I have reservations about his analysis, however. Allan's countability scores are based only on his personal judgements of the 'grammaticality' of certain phrases, and are influenced by how common certain expressions are. The count noun 'lamb', of which the Universal Grinder mass noun equivalent is very common in Australia, is therefore classified differently from the noun 'cat'. For example, Allan judges the NP 'all lamb' grammatical, the NP 'all cat' ungrammatical. I suspect, however, that this reflects culinary habits rather than a linguistic distinction.
2 By an 'amount phrase' I mean an expression consisting of a numeral, followed by a noun designating a unit of measurement, followed by the particle 'of'. For more details see section 6.2.
3 Unless there are grammatical differences between concrete and abstract mass nouns, this distinction is irrelevant to formal semantics.
4 This may be taken as a more general objection to the cumulative reference condition. When we have a red book and a bouquet of red roses, would it make sense to say that 'the sum' of the book and the roses is red?

3 Approaches to mass term semantics

1 A brief description of mereology is presented in section 13.2. See also Tarski (1936).
2 I think the analysis (3.19) is highly questionable, but it is the consequence of analysing 'water' before the copula as referring to the totality of all water. Besides, independent of how we analyse the sentence 'All water is water', it may be argued that the totality of all water is itself water; see Cocchiarella (1976, p. 212).
3 I have said that mereology and the calculus of individuals are theories of a part–whole relation. This is indeed what they are, but it so happens that, for the sake of obtaining a concise axiom system, Lesniewski (and following him Leonard and Goodman) have chosen as primitive the relation of being 'discrete' (=disjoint) with. Formally we thus have: x overlaps y $=_D$ not (x discrete with y).
4 Ter Meulen has recognized the need of a part–whole relation in the description of mass noun denotation, and has introduced a non-logical predicate 'part of' for this purpose. This has the disadvantage that the logical properties of the predicate,

such as its cumulativity and distributivity, have to be stipulated separately by means of meaning postulates like (3.70). From a methodological point of view this is undesirable: meaning postulates are meant to capture meaning aspects of natural language terms via their translations into the logical representation language, but 'part of' is, in ter Meulen's approach, not the translation of a natural language term. Instead, it functions as a logical concept, on a par with the element-relation of set theory. It should therefore have the status of a *logical* concept, of which the properties are captured in the underlying logic, rather than by means of meaning postulates.

4 Towards a semantic theory of mass nouns

1 Intuitively speaking, 'furniture' and 'wood' belong to two different classes of mass nouns: 'wood' belongs to the 'material names', together with 'gold', 'dust', 'water', 'air', 'meat', 'butter', etc., while 'furniture' belongs to a class that we might call 'collective mass nouns', together with such nouns as 'footwear', 'clothing', 'jewellery', 'pottery', and 'luggage'. This distinction may be relevant to formal semantics if it can be given a syntactic basis. I have found two phenomena that point in this direction. One is that 'collective mass nouns' display a type of modification that is not found with other mass nouns: so-called 'discrete modification' (see section 9.3, and Bunt (1980b)). The other is the phenomenon that 'collective mass nouns' seem to form an exception to the rule in the Dutch language that mass nouns have a diminutive form that can be used to designate (small) samples of the mass noun extension. For instance, 'hout-je' (small) piece of wood, 'ijs-je' an ice cream, 'muziek-je' a piece of music, 'water-tje' a creek or small canal, etc. 'Collective mass nouns', such as 'meubilair' (furniture), 'vee' (cattle), 'gereedschap' (tools), 'aardewerk' (pottery), or 'bagage' (luggage), typically have no diminutive forms.
2 Empirical data concerning the possibility of combining adjectives, not cumulative in reference, with mass nouns are discussed in section 9.3, and in Bunt (1980b).

5 Ensemble theory

1 The symbol '$\exists!$' stands for: 'There is exactly one'. Formally, the notation $(\exists!x)P(x)$ is an abbreviation of: $(\exists x)[P(x) \& (\forall y)(P(y) \rightarrow y = x)]$.

6 Semantic representations based on ensemble theory

1 Instead of $\cup(t_1, \ldots, t_n)$, I also write $t_1 \cup \ldots \cup t_n$.
2 The type inclusion relation $<_t$ holds between a type $\underline{t}$ and a type $\underline{t}'$ if and only if one of the following conditions is satisfied.

   1. $\underline{t}$ is atomic, and $\underline{t}'$ is identical to $\underline{t}$.
   2. $\underline{t} = S(t_1)$ and $\underline{t}' = S(t_2)$ or $\underline{t}' = E(t_2)$ for some types $\underline{t_1}$ and $\underline{t_2}$, such that $\underline{t_1} <_t \underline{t_2}$.
   3. $\underline{t} = E(t_1)$ and $\underline{t}' = E(t_2)$ for some types $\underline{t_1}$ and $\underline{t_2}$ such that $\underline{t_1} <_t \underline{t_2}$.
   4. $\underline{t} = (t_1 \rightarrow t_2)$ and $\underline{t}' = (t_3 \rightarrow t_4)$ for some types $\underline{t_1}$, $\underline{t_2}$, $\underline{t_3}$, and $\underline{t_4}$ such that $\underline{t_1} <_t \underline{t_3}$, $\underline{t_3} <_t \underline{t_1}$, and $\underline{t_2} <_t \underline{t_4}$.

5. $\underline{t} = \text{Tr}(\underline{t}_1)$ and either $\underline{t}' = \text{Tr}(\underline{t}_2)$ or $\underline{t}' = (\langle \underline{t}_2, \underline{t}_2 \rangle \to \text{real})$, with $\underline{t}_1 <_t \underline{t}_2$.
6. $\underline{t} = \text{amt}(\underline{t}_1)$ and either $\underline{t}' = \text{amt}(\underline{t}_2)$ or $\underline{t}' = S(\langle \text{real}, \underline{t}_2 \rangle)$ for some types $\underline{t}_1$ and $\underline{t}_2$ such that $\underline{t}_1 <_t \underline{t}_2$.
7. $\underline{t} = \langle \underline{t}_1, \ldots, \underline{t}_n \rangle$ and either for each type component $\underline{t}_c$ of $\underline{t}$ there is a type component $\underline{t}_c'$ of $\underline{t}'$ such that $\underline{t}_c <_t \underline{t}_c'$ (for the notion of type component see below), or else $\underline{t}' = \langle \underline{t}_1', \ldots, \underline{t}_n' \rangle$ for some types $\underline{t}_1, \ldots, \underline{t}_n, \underline{t}_1', \ldots, \underline{t}_n'$ such that $\underline{t}_i <_t \underline{t}_i'$ for every i with $1 \le i \le n$.
8. $\underline{t} = (\underline{t}_1 \cup \ldots \cup \underline{t}_n)$ and for each type component $\underline{t}_c$ of $\underline{t}$ there is a type component $\underline{t}_c'$ of $\underline{t}'$ such that $\underline{t}_c <_t \underline{t}_c'$ (for the notion of type component see below), or else $\underline{t}' = (\underline{t}_1' \cup \ldots \cup \underline{t}_n')$ for some types $\underline{t}_1, \ldots, \underline{t}_n, \underline{t}_1', \ldots, \underline{t}_n'$ such that $\underline{t}_i <_t \underline{t}_i'$ for every i with $1 \le i \le n$.
9. $\underline{t} <_t \underline{t}_c'$ for some type component $\underline{t}_c'$ of $\underline{t}'$. (For the notion of type component see below.)

The notion of a 'type component' is defined by the following recursive rules:

1. If $\underline{t}$ is a type of the form $\underline{t}_1 \cup \ldots \cup \underline{t}_n$ then a type component of $\underline{t}_1$, of $\underline{t}_2$, or ... or of $\underline{t}_n$ is a type component of $\underline{t}$.
2. If $\underline{t}$ is a type of the form $\langle \underline{t}_1, \ldots, \underline{t}_n \rangle$ then a type of the form $\langle \underline{t}_1', \ldots, \underline{t}_n' \rangle$ is a type component of $\underline{t}$ if $\underline{t}_i'$ is a type component of $\underline{t}_i$ for every i such that $1 \le i \le n$.
3. In all other cases a type $\underline{t}$ has itself as its one and only type component.

3 The complete specification of the type restrictions on the various EL constructions, expressed by the predicate TR, is given by the following rules.

1a. TR(abstraction, $\underline{t}_1, \underline{t}_2$) = TRUE.
That is, there are no type restrictions on the variable or the description part of an abstraction.
1b. TR(application, $\underline{t}_1, \underline{t}_2$) = TRUE iff $\underline{t}_1 = (\underline{t} \to \underline{t}')$ for some types $\underline{t}$ and $\underline{t}'$ such that $\underline{t}_2 <_t \underline{t}$.
2a. TR(non, $\underline{t}$) = TRUE iff $\underline{t}$ = truthvalue.
2b. TR(conj, $\underline{t}_1, \underline{t}_2$) = TRUE iff $\underline{t}_1 = \underline{t}_2$ = truthvalue.
2c. TR(disj, $\underline{t}_1, \underline{t}_2$) = TRUE iff $\underline{t}_1 = \underline{t}_2$ = truthvalue.
3a. TR(universal-quantification, $\underline{t}_1, \underline{t}_2$) = TRUE iff $\underline{t}_1$ is a set type and $\underline{t}_2 = (\underline{t}_2' \to \text{truthvalue})$ for some type $\underline{t}_2'$ such that $\underline{t}_{1c} <_t S(\underline{t}_2')$ for every type component $\underline{t}_{1c}$ of $\underline{t}_1$. The most important cases are: (1) $\underline{t}_1 = S(\underline{t}_2)$; (2) $\underline{t}_1 = S(\underline{t}_3)$ for some type $\underline{t}_3$ such that $\underline{t}_2' = (\underline{t}_3 \cup \underline{t}_4)$ for some type $\underline{t}_4$, and (3) $\underline{t}_1 = (S(\underline{t}_3) \cup S(\underline{t}_4))$ for some types $\underline{t}_3$ and $\underline{t}_4$ such that $\underline{t}_2 = (\underline{t}_3 \cup \underline{t}_4)$. (For the notion of a set type see below; for the notion of a type component see note 2.)
3b. TR(existential-quantification, $\underline{t}_1, \underline{t}_2$) = TR(universal-quantification, $\underline{t}_1, \underline{t}_2$)).
4a. TR(power, $\underline{t}$) = TRUE iff $\underline{t}$ is an ensemble type (see below).
4b. TR(cartesian-product, $\underline{t}_1, \ldots, \underline{t}_n$) = TRUE iff $\underline{t}_1, \ldots, \underline{t}_n$ are ensemble types (see below).
4c. TR(union, $\underline{t}_1, \ldots, \underline{t}_n$) = TRUE iff $\underline{t}_1, \ldots, \underline{t}_n$ are ensemble types (see below).
4d. TR(unionstar, $\underline{t}_0, \underline{t}_1, \ldots, \underline{t}_n$) = TRUE iff $\underline{t}_0$ is a set type, and for every i with $1 \le i \le n$ there is a type component $\underline{t}_{oc}$ of $\underline{t}_o$ such that either $\underline{t}_i <_t \underline{t}_{oc}$ or $S(\underline{t}_i) <_t \underline{t}_{oc}$. (For the notion of a set type see below; for the notion of a type component see note 2.)

306 *Notes*

4e. TR(selection, t_1, t_2) = TRUE iff t_1 is a set type, $t_2 = t_{2d} \rightarrow$ truthvalue) for some type t_{2d}, and for every type of component t_c of t_1, with $t_c = S(t_c')$, $t_c' <_t t_{2d}$. (This ensures that the modifier expression in a selection construction denotes a predicate with a domain that contains all the elements of the denotation of the head expression. For the notion of a set type see below; for the notion of a type component see note 2.)

4f. TR(partselection, t_1, t_2) = TRUE iff t_1 is an ensemble type and $t_2 = (t_{2d} \rightarrow$ truthvalue) for some type t_{2d}, such that $t_{1c} <_t t_{2d}$ for every type component of t_1. (For the notion of an ensemble type see below; for the notion of a type component see note 2.)

4g. TR(membership, t_1, t_2) = TRUE iff t_2 is an ensemble type (see below).

4h. TR(inclusion, t_1, t_2) = TRUE iff t_1 is an ensemble type (see below).

5a. TR(set, $t_1, \ldots, t_n$) = TRUE. (No type restrictions.)

5b. TR(card, t) = TRUE iff t is a set type (see below).

5c. TR(iteration, t_1, t_2) = TRUE iff t_1 is a set type, $t_2 = (t_{2d} \rightarrow t_{2r})$ for some types t_{2d} and t_{2r}, and for every type component t_c of t_1, with $t_c = S(t_c')$, $t_c' <_t t_{2d}$.

6a. TR(equality, t_1, t_2) = TRUE. (No type restrictions.)

6b. TR(conditional, t_1, t_2, t_3) = TRUE iff t_1 = truthvalue.

6c. TR(function-union, $t_1, \ldots, t_n$) = TRUE iff, for every i with $1 \le i \le n$, $t_i = (t_{id} \rightarrow t_{ir})$ for some types t_{id}, t_{ir}, such that t_{id} and t_{jd} have no type components in common if $i \ne j$. (For the notion of a type component see note 2.)

6d. TR(n-tuple, $t_1, \ldots, t_n$) = TRUE. (No type restrictions.)

6e. TR(element$_i$, t) = TRUE iff $t = \langle t_1, \ldots, t_n \rangle$ for some types $t_1, \ldots, t_n$, with $n \ge 1$.

6f. TR(amount, t_1, t_2) = TRUE iff t_1 = integer or real, and $t_2 = \langle t_2', Tr(t_2') \rangle$ for some type t_2'.

The notion of a set type is defined recursively by the following rules:

1. A type t is a set type if $t = S(t')$ for some type t'.
2. A type t is a set type if $t = (t_1 \cup \ldots \cup t_n)$ for some types $t_1, \ldots, t_n$ which are all set types.
3. No other type is a set type.

This means that, if t is a set type, then every type component (see note 2) of t is of the form $S(t')$. An EL expression having a set type always denotes a set.

Similarly, the notion of an ensemble type is defined as follows:

1. A type t is an ensemble type if $t = E(t')$ or $t = S(t')$ for some type t'.
2. A type t is an ensemble type if $t = (t_1 \cup \ldots \cup t_n)$ for some types $t_1, \ldots, t_n$ which are all ensemble types.
3. No other type is an ensemble type.

4 The function TYPE, that computes the type of any EL expression, is defined by the following rules.

1a. TYPE(abstraction(var: x, descr: E)) = (TYPE(x) $\rightarrow$ TYPE(E))
1b. TYPE(application(fun: F, arg: a)) = t_2, if TYPE(F) = $(t_1 \rightarrow t_2)$

Notes 307

2a. TYPE(non(arg: p)) = truthvalue
2b. TYPE(conj(1: p, 2: q)) = truthvalue
2c. TYPE(disj(1: p, 2: q)) = truthvalue
3a. TYPE(universal-quantification(forall: A, holds: P)) = truthvalue
3b. TYPE(existential-quantification(forsome: A, holds: P)) = truthvalue
4a. TYPE(power(arg: E)) = S(TYPE(E))
4b. TYPE(cartesian-product(1: E_1, ..., n: E_n))
     = S($\langle$TYPE(E_1), ..., TYPE(E_n)$\rangle$)
4c. TYPE(union(1: E_1, ..., n: E_n)) = (TYPE(E_1) $\cup$ ... $\cup$ TYPE(E_n))
4d. TYPE(unionstar(reference: S_o, el_1: S_1, ..., el_n: S_n)) = TYPE(S_o)
4e. TYPE(selection(head: S, mod: P)) = TYPE(S)
4f. TYPE(partselection(head: E, partmod: P)) = TYPE(E)
4g. TYPE(membership(member: a, ensemble: E)) = truthvalue
4h. TYPE(inclusion(part: a, whole: E)) = truthvalue
5a. TYPE(set(1: a_1, ..., a_n)) = S(TYPE(a_1) $\cup$ ... $\cup$ TYPE(a_n))
5b. TYPE(card(arg: A)) = integer
5c. TYPE(iteration(for: A, apply: F)) = S(t_2), if TYPE(F) = ($t_1 \to t_2$)
6a. TYPE (equality(arg_1: A, arg_2: B)) = truthvalue
6b. TYPE(conditional(if: C, then: A, else: B)) = (TYPE(A) $\cup$ TYPE(B))
6c. TYPE(function-union(1: F_1, ..., n: F_n))
     = (($t_{1d} \cup ... \cup t_{nd}$) $\to$ ($t_{1r} \cup ... \cup t_{nr}$)) if TYPE($F_i$) = ($t_{id} \to t_{ir}$)
6d. TYPE(n-tuple(1: e_1, ..., n: e_n)) = $\langle$TYPE(e_1), ..., TYPE(e_n)$\rangle$
6e. TYPE($element_i$(arg: T)) = t_i, if TYPE(T) = $\langle t_1, ..., t_i, ..., t_n \rangle$
6f. TYPE(amount(num: n, unit: u)) = amt(TYPE(u))

7 Two-level model-theoretic semantics

1 In a purely extensional framework of analysis the denotation of a declarative sentence is a truth value, in an intensional framework it is a function from possible worlds to truth values.
2 For a discussion of the Principle of Compositionality and its significance in the development of semantic theories see Janssen (1983) and Bach (1983).
3 The translations of the EL_f constants become more complex, however. For example, suppose we want to translate the EL_f expression AGE(Mary). Translation rule (7.38b) involves translating AGE by AGE_a, which is an EL_r constant of type (person $\to$ integer). The EL_f constant, on the other hand, has type (entity $\to$ integer). Since entity covers any type of object in the discourse domain, it is translated into a giant union of $ELTL_r$ types: TT(entity) = (person $\cup$ article of furniture $\cup$ city ...). This means that the translation of AGE by AGE_a does not satisfy the condition (7.41). To meet this condition, we must translate AGE into a union of EL_r functions, applicable to arguments of types person, article of furniture, city, etc. Using the 'function union' construction defined by (6.35) rule 6c and (6.36) rule 6c, we obtain: T_{fr}(AGE) = AGE_a f $\cup$ AGE_i f $\cup$ AGE_c f $\cup$ ...
4 The proof goes as follows.
   Consider a complex EL_f expression e, built up from EL_f constants with three

constructions. Let us designate the branching categories of these constructions by $\underline{brc_a}$, $\underline{brc_b}$ and $\underline{brc_c}$, and their selectors by sel_{a1}, sel_{a2}, etc. To simplify matters, suppose the $\underline{brc_a}$-construction has only two selectors. Thus, the expression has the following structure:

1. $e = \underline{brc_a}(sel_{a1}: \underline{brc_b}(sel_{b1}: C_1, \ldots, sel_{bm}: C_m),$
   $sel_{a2}: \overline{brc_c}(sel_{c1}: C_{m+1}, \ldots, sel_{cn}: C_{m+n}))$

Assuming e to be a well-formed El_f expression, the following type restriction is satisfied:

2. $TR(\underline{brc_a}, TYPE_f(\underline{brc_b}(sel_{b1}: C_1, \ldots, sel_{bm}: C_m)),$
   $TYPE_f(\overline{brc_c}(sel_{c1}: C_{m+1}, \ldots, sel_{cn}: C_{m+n})))$
   $= TRUE$

All translations of e are of the form

3. $z = \underline{brc_a}(sel_{a1}: \underline{brc_b}(sel_{b1}: Z_1, \ldots, sel_{bm}: Z_m),$
   $sel_{a2}: \overline{brc_c}(sel_{c1}: Z_{m+1}, \ldots, sel_{cn}: Z_{m+n}))$

with $Z_i \in T_r(C_i)$. We have to prove that

4. $TYPE_r(z) <_t TT(TYPE_f(e))$

From (7.41) we know that $TYPE_r(Z_i) <_t TT(TYPE_f(C_i))$. Therefore, by (7.42), both $\underline{brc_b}(sel_{b1}: Z_1, \ldots, sel_{bm}: Z_m)$ and $\underline{brc_c}(sel_{c1}: Z_{m+1}, \ldots, sel_{cn}: Z_{m+n})$ satisfy the type restrictions for their respective branching categories, and hence are well-formed EL_r expressions. By (7.43), the following relation holds between the types of these expressions:

5. $TYPE_r(\underline{brc_b}(sel_{b1}: Z_1, \ldots, sel_{bn}: Z_m)) <_t$
   $\overline{TYPE_r(\underline{brc_b}, sel_{b1}: TT(TYPE_r(Z_1)), \ldots,}$
   $sel_{bm}: TT(TYPE_r(Z_m)))$

6. $TYPE_r(\underline{brc_c}(sel_{c1}: Z_{m+1}, \ldots, sel_{cn}: Z_{m+n})) <_t$
   $\overline{TYPE_r(\underline{brc_c}, sel_{c1}: TT(TYPE_r(Z_{m+1})), \ldots,}$
   $sel_{cn}: TT(TYPE_r(Z_{m+n})))$

Therefore, by (7.42) these expressions satisfy the type restrictions for the branching category $\underline{brc_a}$. Applying (7.43) now at the level of the $\underline{brc_a}$ construction in (3), the desired result follows.

5 See Montague's treatment of the transitive and intransitive uses of 'walk' in 'Universal Grammar' (Montague 1974, pp. 190–1).
6 This is a slightly modified version of an example due to Landsbergen (1976).

8 Quantification and mass nouns

1 In view of the restriction throughout this study to non-intensional aspects of mass terms, the three classes of occurrences distinguished below are illustrated with examples that allow a purely extensional treatment. (See also note 2, however.) For the notion of the head of a grammatical construction see Lyons (1968) or section 9.1.

2 I am not sure that (8.13) is the most desirable analysis of (8.12); it does find support, though, in the following quotation from Cocchiarella: 'The individual which is correlated with the concept of a natural kind of stuff ... is the spatio-temporally scattered individual which is the mereological sum of all the individuals of that kind' (Cocchiarella, 1976, p. 212).
3 See section 1.2 for a discussion of the deviance.
4 Examples taken from Quirk et al. (1972). See also Leech and Svartvik (1975) section 550, and the study of English noun phrase structure by Pack and Henrichsen (1979).
5 De Mey (forthcoming) uses the term 'predicate set' for this purpose.
6 There is no unanimity in the usage of the term 'quantifiers' in the literature. Cushing (1977) writes:

> a quantifier is a semantic operator that answers one of the questions 'How many?' or 'How much?'. The sentence 'Some things are worth while' for example, answers the question 'How many things are worthwhile?'. Another way of formulating this intuitive characterisation of quantifiers is to say that quantifiers give some indication of the sizes of sets. (Cushing 1977, p. 101).

Leech and Svartvik (1975) define quantifiers as 'determiners or pronouns indicating quantity or amount'. Pronoun-quantifiers are words like 'everybody', 'someone', 'anything', etc., and pronouns followed by an of-construction, as in 'some of the men'. A rather different usage of the term 'quantifiers' is suggested by Barwise and Cooper (1981), who use the term for complete noun phrases. They argue that noun phrases are the natural language counterpart of (generalized) quantifiers in logic.

7 It may be argued that the question which quantitative indication a quantifier gives is at least partly a question for referential semantics, rather than for formal semantics. For certain quantifiers, such as 'many' and 'much', it is impossible to specify in a universe of discourse independent way what quantitative indication they give; therefore, for these quantifiers this question cannot be handled at the formal level of analysis.
8 Sets containing no elements would be pathological cases, the inclusion of which can only cause trouble. There would be no point in including singleton sets, unless there were reasons to distinguish between such things as lifting an individual tube and lifting the set consisting of that tube.
9 For a recent study of quantifier scope phenomena see Cooper (1983).
10 A λ-expression of the form $(\lambda x: E(x))$, where $E(x)$ designates any well-formed expression containing a free occurrence of the variable x, denotes a function of x which is defined as follows: for any argument a, the value of the function is the value of the expression $E(x)$ when a is substituted for x. The application of this function to the argument a is written as $(\lambda x: E(x))(a)$. The operation of λ-conversion draws the obvious consequence from the above definition that the latter expression has the same value as the simpler expression $E(a)$. For the formal definition of λ-conversion see Church (1941).
11 See note 10. In what follows I shall occasionally apply λ-conversion to simplify semantic representations, without explicit mention.

12 Roeper's example is: 'All phosphorus is red or black', which may be true without each quantity of phosphorus being either red or black, if the totality of all phosphorus can be "decomposed" into red and black parts, or, to put it differently, if the red and the black quantities together make up all phosphorus. In the language of ensemble theory this is expressed by: $[x \subseteq \text{PHOSPHORUS}|\text{RED}(x) \vee \text{BLACK}(x)] = \text{PHOSPHORUS}$. This is the EL representation of the reading that I call 'unspecific' (cf. 8.121c). Incidentally, in a footnote to his paper Roeper says that 'ensemble theory' is another name for mereology. This is not correct; the precise relation between the formalisms of mereology and ensemble theory is the subject matter of section 13.2.

13 The EL_f representation b' of the operand b, of syntactic category <u>unit</u>, is a 2-tuple (see part F of the lexicon). In accordance with the notation introduced in chapter 6, (6.35), rule 6e, b'_2 is the second element of b'.

14 See note 13; b'_1 and b'_2 are the first and second elements of b', respectively.

15 The indices $1, \ldots, j$, standing on the line, serve to distinguish the operands of the rule. The EL_f representation of each operand ai is a 2-tuple ai' (see rule G); ai'_1 thus denotes the first element of ai', ai'_2 the second.

16 Earlier in this section the following notation was used for the immediate subtrees of a syntactic tree. The leftmost immediate subtree of the tree designated by a is designated by a_1, the second one from the left by a_2, etc. This notation is also used here. Thus, $a_1{'}$ designates the EL_f representation of the leftmost immediate subtree of a, etc.

9 Modification and mass nouns

1 Most of the material presented in sections 9.2 and 9.3 has been published separately in Bunt (1980a).
2 See Lyons (1968), section 6.4.
3 See Allan (1980) for other counterexamples.
4 See Bunt (1980b) for a more detailed presentation and discussion of the data.
5 In what follows I shall freely apply λ-conversions to simplify expressions.
6 Whether it is possible to represent nouns as semantically neutral depends, of course, on whether the semantic differences between count and mass nouns are reflected in their representations. It may be technically possible to make the semantic distinctions by means of meaning postulates rather than directly in the representations; we have seen the drawback of such an approach, however, when discussing ter Meulen's work in section 3.5. Note that, technically speaking, it is irrelevant whether a count/mass distinction is made in the lexicon or by grammar rules that convert neutral nouns to count nouns and mass nouns. Pelletier and Schubert (forthcoming) argue that, if the count/mass distinction is viewed as a semantic distinction between noun occurrences, this distinction should not be expressed in terms of syntactic features or categories, but in terms of semantic representation, since the syntactic properties would not rule out any natural language expression as being ungrammatical. It should be noted, however, that in a grammar with paired syntactic/semantic rules as I propose here (and as they propose), syntactic features and categories do not so much serve to distinguish

between grammatical and ungrammatical expressions, but are used to characterize the class of expressions on which a semantic rule operates (and, together, the syntactic rules define the fragment of the language that can be interpreted by the semantic rules).
7 Most of the implementation work was done by Gemme thoe Schwartzenberg and Jurgen van der Linden at the Institute for Perception Research in Eindhoven.
8 See chapter 8, notes 13 and 14.
9 See chapter 8, note 15.
10 See chapter 8, note 16.

10 Axiomatic ensemble theory

1 Some remarks on terminology and notation: the term 'inclusion' will be used as synonymous with 'part-whole'; thus, saying that x is included in y means the same as that x is a part of y. Occasionally, I shall also say that y 'contains' x; this is meant as synonymous with 'x is a member of y'.
2 Depending on how a theory is grafted upon an underlying logic, there may be another reason to have axioms like the axiom of pairs. In the usual setup of set theory there is an axiom of pairs postulating the existence (as sets, that is) of pairs *of sets*. However, we want to establish that pairs *of ensembles* are sets. We do this by postulating that pairs of ensembles are ensembles, proving later that pair ensembles have the property of 'discreteness' (see definition 11.2.1 and theorem 11.2.5), and finally showing that discrete ensembles are formally indistinguishable from sets (section 13.1).

12 A model for ensemble theory

1 In constructing a model for ensemble theory I have benefited from suggestions by several people, in particular by Peter van Emde Boas, Freek Wiedijk, and an anonymous referee for Reidel Publishing Company.
2 See the closing paragraph of this chapter.

13 Ensemble theory, set theory, and mereology

1 A functional condition C on the set x is a condition on two variables y and z, such that for every member y of x there is at most one z such that C(y, z). (Cf. section 10.2.8.)
2 See also section 10.2.2.
3 See definition 10.2.8.1.
4 Fraenkel *et al.* (1973), p. 200. See also Luschei (1962, pp. 44ff), and Leonard and Goodman (1940, p. 46).
5 Note the similarity between this characterization of the distinction between sets and individuals and the characterization of the distinction between count term reference and mass term reference, given in section 4.2.
6 In LLG this relation is called 'is discrete with'. I prefer the term 'disjoint', in order to avoid confusion with the notion of discreteness in ensemble theory.

7 Cf. note 3 to chapter 3.
8 The theory LLG presupposes a logical framework that includes the theory of sets. Set-theoretical concepts are therefore allowed in the definitions and axioms of LLG (cf. definition 2.1.3a and axiom LLG3).
9 Singleton ensembles correspond, of course, to singleton sets rather than to individuals. Therefore, a statement corresponding to ETX4'b should be derivable from the set axioms that form part of the logical basis of LLG. This is indeed the case.

Bibliography

Allan, K. (1980) Nouns and countability. *Language* 56, 451–567.
Bach, E. (1983) Semi-compositionaliteit. *GLOT* 6, 113–30.
Bartsch, R. (1973) The semantics and syntax of number and numbers. In J. P. Kimball (ed.), *Syntax and semantics* vol. 2. Seminar Press, London & New York.
Barwise, J. and Cooper, R. (1981) Generalized quantifiers in natural language. *Linguistics and Philosophy* 4, 159–218.
Bealer, G. (1975) Predication and matter. In F. J. Pelletier (ed.), *Mass terms*. Reidel, Dordrecht.
Bennett, M. R. (1974) Some extensions of a Montague fragment of English. Unpublished Ph.D. Dissertation, University of California, Los Angeles.
Bennett, M. R. (1975) Some extensions of a Montague fragment of English. Corrected version of Bennett (1974). Indiana University Linguistics Club, Bloomington.
Bennett, M. R. (1978) Demonstratives and indexicals in Montague grammar. *Synthese* 39, 1–80.
Bernays, P. and Fraenkel, A. A. (1958) *Axiomatic set theory*. North-Holland, Amsterdam.
Birkhoff, G. and Bartee, T. C. (1967) *Modern applied algebra*. McGraw-Hill, New York.
Bronnenberg, W. J., Bunt, H. C., Landsbergen, S. P. J., Scha, R. J. H., Schoenmakers, W. J., and van Utteren, E. P. C. (1980) The question answering system PHLIQA 1. In L. Bolc (ed.), *Natural communication with computers*, MacMillan, London; Hanser Verlag, München.
Bunt, H. C. (1976) The formal semantics of mass terms. In F. Karlsson (ed.) *Papers from the Third Scandinavian Conference of Linguistics*. Academy of Finland, Turku.
Bunt, H. C. (1978) A formal semantic analysis of mass terms and amount terms. In J. A. G. Groenendijk and M. B. J. Stokhof (eds.), *Amsterdam papers in formal grammar* vol. 2. University of Amsterdam, Amsterdam.
Bunt, H. C. (1979) Ensembles and the formal semantic properties of mass terms. In F. J. Pelletier (ed.), *Mass terms*. Reidel, Dordrecht.
Bunt, H. C. (1980a) On the why, the how, and the whether of a count-mass distinction among adjectives. In J. A. G. Groenendijk, T. M. V. Janssen, and M. B. J. Stokhof (eds.), *Formal methods in the study of language*. Mathematical Centre, Amsterdam.

Bibliography

Bunt, H. C. (1980b) An experimental study of semantic relations and syntactic restrictions for mass nouns and adjectives. *IPO annual progress report* 15, 100–4.
Bunt, H. C. (1981a) The formal semantics of mass terms. Unpublished Ph.D. Dissertation, University of Amsterdam.
Bunt, H. C. (1981b) Rules for the interpretation, evaluation and generation of dialogue acts. *IPO annual progress report* 16, 99–113.
Bunt, H. C. (1982) IPO Dialogue Project. *SIGART newsletter* 80, 60–1.
Bunt, H. C. (1983) A grammar formalism with augmented phrase-construction rules. *IPO annual progress report* 18, 92–8.
Bunt, H. C. (1984a) The resolution of quantificational ambiguity in the TENDUM system. *COLING84 Preprints*, Palo Alto.
Bunt, H. C. (1985) The formal representation of (quasi-) continuous concepts. In J. R. Hobbs and R. C Moore (eds.), *Formal theories of the common sense world*, Contributions to Artificial Intelligence vol. 1. Ablex, Norwood, NJ.
Bunt, H. C. and thoe Schwartzenberg, G. O. (1982) Syntactic, semantic and pragmatic parsing for a natural language dialogue system. *IPO annual progress report* 17, 123–9.
Bunt, H. C., Beun, R. J., Dols, F. J. H., van der Linden, J. A., and thoe Schwartzenberg, G. O. (1984) The TENDUM dialogue system and its theoretical basis. In *IPO annual progress report* 19.
Burge, T. (1972) Truth and mass terms. *Journal of philosophy* 69 (10), 263–82.
Burge, T. (1975) Mass terms, count nouns, and change. *Synthese* 31, 459–78.
Burge, T. (1977) A theory of aggregates. *Noûs* 11, 97–117.
Cartwright, H. M. (1965) Heraclitus and the bath water. *Philosophical review* 74, 466–85.
Cartwright, H. M. (1970) Quantities. *Philosophical review* 79, 466–85.
Cartwright, H. M. (1975) Some remarks on mass nouns and plurality. *Synthese* 31, 395–410.
Cocchiarella, N. (1976) On the logic of natural kinds. *Philosophy of science* 43, 202–22.
Cooper, R. (1983) *Quantification and syntactic theory*. Reidel, Dordrecht.
Cheng, C. Y. (1973) Response to Moravcsik. In Hintikka *et al.* (1973).
Church, A. (1941) *The calculi of lambda-conversion*. Princeton University Press, Princeton, NJ.
Clarke, D. S. (1970) Mass terms as subjects. *Philosophical studies* 21, 25–9.
Cushing, S. (1977) The formal semantics of quantification. Indiana Linguistics Club, Bloomington.
Dahl, Ö. (1978) On generics. *Formal semantics of natural language*, ed. Edward L. Keenan. Cambridge University Press, Cambridge.
Dik, S. C. (1973) Sets in semantic structures. *Publikaties van het Instituut voor Algemene Taalwetenschap* 4, University of Amsterdam.
Dik, S. C. (1975) Universal quantification in Dutch. *Publikaties van het Instituut voor Algemene Taalwetenschap* 6, University of Amsterdam.
Fraenkel, A. A., Bar-Hillel, Y., Levy, A., and van Dalen, D. (1973) *Foundations of set theory*. North-Holland, Amsterdam.
Gazdar, G. (1982) Phrase Structure Grammar. In P. Jacobson and G. K. Pullum (eds.), *The nature of syntactic representation*. Reidel, Dordrecht.

Gazdar, G. and Pullum, G. K. (1982) Generalized Phrase Structure Grammar: A Theoretical Synopsis. Indiana University Linguistics Club, Bloomington.
Gil, D. (1982) Quantifier scope, linguistic variation, and natural language semantics. *Linguistics and philosophy* 4, 421–72.
Gleason, H. A. (1965) *Linguistics and English grammar*. Holt, Rinehart & Winston, New York.
Goodman, N. (1951) *The structure of appearance*. Harvard University Press, New Haven & Cambridge, Mass.
Grandy, R. (1973) Response to Moravcsik. In Hintikka *et al.* (1973).
Grandy, R. (1975) Stuff and things. *Synthese* 31, 479–85.
Guenthner, F. and Rohrer, Chr. (1978) (eds.) *Studies in formal semantics*. North-Holland, Amsterdam.
Halmos, P. R. (1950) *Measure theory*. Van Nostrand, Princeton, NJ.
Hausser, R. R. (1974) Quantification in an extended Montague grammar. Unpublished Ph.D. Dissertation, University of Texas at Austin.
Hausser, R. R. (1980) Surface compositionality and the semantics of mood. In J. R. Searle, F. Kiefer, and M. Bierwisch (eds.), *Speech act theory and Pragmatics*. Reidel. Dordrecht.
Heidorn, G. (1975) Augmented phrase-structure grammar. In R. Schank and B. Nash-Webber (eds.), *Theoretical issues in natural language processing*. MIT, Cambridge, Mass.
Higginbotham, J. and May, R. (1981) Questions, quantifiers and crossing. *The linguistic review* 1, 41–80.
Hintikka, K. J. J., Moravcsik, J. M. E., and Suppes, P. (1973) *Approaches to natural language*. Reidel, Dordrecht.
Hoepelman, J. (1976) Mass nouns and aspect, or: Why we can't eat gingercake in an hour. In J. A. G. Groenendijk and M. B. J. Stokhof (eds.) *Amsterdam papers in formal grammar* vol. 1, University of Amsterdam, Amsterdam.
Janssen, T. M. V. (1983) Foundations and applications of Montague grammar. Unpublished Ph.D. Dissertation, University of Amsterdam.
Jespersen, O. (1924) *The philosophy of grammar*. Allen & Unwin, London.
Kamp, H. (1975) Two theories about adjectives. In E. Keenan (ed.) *Formal semantics of natural language*. Cambridge University Press, London & New York.
Klooster, W. G. (1972) The structure underlying measure phrase sentences. Unpublished Ph.D. Dissertation, University of Utrecht.
Landsbergen, S. P. J. (1976) Syntax and formal semantics of English in PHLIQA1. *COLING76 preprints*, Ottawa.
Landsbergen, S. P. J. and Scha, R. J. H. (1979) Formal languages for semantic representation. In S. Allén & J. S. Petöfi (eds.), *Aspects of automatized text processing*. Buske, Hamburg.
Laycock, H. (1975) Theories of matter. *Synthese* 31, 411–442.
Leech, G. and Svartvik, J. (1975) *A communicative grammar of English*. Longman, London.
Leonard, H. S. and Goodman, N. (1940) The calculus of individuals and its uses. *Journal of symbolic logic* 5, 45–55.

Lesniewski, S. (1927–31) O podstawach matematyki. *Przeglad Filozoficzny* 30, 164–206; 31, 261–91; 32, 60–101, 33, 75–105, 34, 142–70.

Lesniewski, S. (1929) Grundzüge eines neuen Systems der Grundlagen der Mathematik. *Fundamenta mathematicae* 14, 1–81.

Luschei, E. C. (1962) *The logical systems of Lesniewski*. North-Holland, Amsterdam.

Lyons, J. (1968) *Introduction to theoretical linguistics*. Cambridge University Press, London & New York.

Lyons, J. (1977) *Semantics*. Cambridge University Press, Cambridge.

McCawley, J. D. (1975) Lexicography and the count-mass distinction. *Proceedings of the 1st Annual Meeting of the Berkeley Linguistics Society*, 314–21.

McCawley, J. D. (1981) *Everything that linguists have always wanted to know about logic*. Basil Blackwell, Oxford, & University of Chicago Press, Chicago.

Medema, P., Bronnenberg, W. J., Bunt, H. C., Landsbergen, S. P. J., Schoenmakers, W. J., and Utteren, E. P. C. van (1975) PHLIQA1: Multilevel semantics in question-answering. *American journal of computational linguistics* microfiche 32.

Meulen, A. G. B. ter (1980) Substances, quantities, and individuals. Unpublished Ph.D. Dissertation, Stanford University.

Meulen, A. G. B. ter (1981) An intensional logic for mass terms. In J. A. G. Groenendijk, T. M. V. Janssen, and M. B. J. Stokhof (eds.), *Formal methods in the study of language*. Mathematical Centre, Amsterdam.

Mey, S. de (1980) Stages and extensionality: the Carlson problem. In S. Daalder and M. Gerritsen (eds.), *Linguistics in the Netherlands 1980*, 191–202, North-Holland, Amsterdam.

Mey, S. de (1981) Intensional and extensional interpretation in Montague grammar. In S. Daalder and M. Gerritsen (eds.), *Linguistics in the Netherlands 1981*, 181–92. North-Holland, Amsterdam.

Mey, S. de (1982) Aspects of the interpretation of bare plurals. Paper presented at the Annual Meeting of Linguists in the Netherlands, Amsterdam, January 1982.

Montague, R. (1970a) English as a formal language. In B. Visentini (ed.), *Linguaggi nella società e nella technica*. Edizionedi communità, Milano, 189–224. Reprinted in Montague (1974).

Montague, R. (1970b) Universal grammar. *Theoria* 36, 373–98. Reprinted in Montague (1974).

Montague, R. (1973) The proper treatment of quantification in ordinary English. In Hintikka *et al.* (eds.), *Approaches to natural language*, Reidel, Dordrecht.

Montague, R. (1974) *Formal philosophy, selected papers*. Yale University Press, New Haven & London.

Moravcsik, J. M. E. (1973) Mass terms in English. In Hintikka *et al.* (1973).

Pack, A. and Henrichsen, L. E. (1979) Order of modifiers in the English noun phrase. *TESL reporter*, Fall 1979, p. 12.

Parsons, T. (1970) Mass terms and amount terms. *Foundations of language* 6, 353–88.

Parsons, T. (1975) Afterthoughts on mass terms. *Synthese* 31, 517–21.

Partee, B. (1975) Comments on C. J. Fillmore's and N. Chomsky's papers. In D. Austerlitz (ed.), *The scope of American linguistics*. De Ridder Press, Lisse, the Netherlands.

Partee, B. (1976) (ed.) *Montague grammar*. Academic Press, New York.
Paxton, W. H. (1978) Part E, the language definition system. In Walker (1978).
Pelletier, F. J. (1974) On some proposals for the semantics of mass terms. *Journal of philosophical logic* 3, 87–108.
Pelletier, F. J. (1975) Non-singular reference: some preliminaries. *Philosophia* 5.
Pelletier, F. J. (1979) (ed.) *Mass terms*. Reidel, Dordrecht.
Pelletier, F. J. and Schubert, L. K. forthc. Mass expressions. In D. Gabbay and F. Guenthner (eds.), *Handbook of philosophical logic*.
Putnam, H. (1975) The meaning of 'meaning'. In *Mind, language, and reality*. Cambridge University Press, Cambridge.
Quine, W. V. O. (1960) *Word and object*. MIT Press, Cambridge, Mass.
Quirk, R., Greenbaum, S., Leech, G., and Svartvik, J. (1972) *A grammar of contemporary English*. Longman, London.
Robinson, J. (1982) DIAGRAM: a grammar for dialogues. *Communications of the ACM* 25, 27–47.
Roeper, P. (1983) Semantics for mass terms with quantifiers. *Noûs* 17, 251–65.
Scha, R. J. H. (1976) Semantic types in PHLIQA1. *COLING76 preprints*, Ottawa.
Scha, R. J. H. (1978) A formal treatment of some aspects of quantification in English (Abstract). *Preprints of Seventh International Conference on Computational Linguistics*, Bergen, Norway.
Scha, R. J. H. (1981) Distributive, collective, and cumulative quantification. In J. A. G. Groenendijk, T. M. V. Janssen, and M. B. J. Stokhof (eds.), *Formal methods in the study of language*. Mathematical Centre, Amsterdam.
Schoenflies, A. (1921) Zur Axiomatik der Mengenlehre. *Mathematische Annalen* 131, 173–200.
Strawson, P. F. (1959) *Individuals*. Methuen, London.
Suppes, P. (1960) *Axiomatic set theory*. Princeton University Press, Princeton, NJ.
Szabolcsi, A. (1983) Focussing properties, or the trap of first order. *Theoretical linguistics* 10 (2/3), 125–45.
Tarski, A. (1936) Der Wahrheitsbegriff in den formalisierten Sprachen. *Studia Philosophica* 1, 261–405.
Thomason, R. H. (1972) Some extensions of a Montague fragment of English. In Partee (1976).
Thomason, R. H. (1974) Introduction to Montague (1974).
Thomason, R. H. (1979) On the semantic interpretation of the Thomason 1972 fragment. Indiana University Linguistics Club, Bloomington.
Walker, D. E. (1978) *Understanding spoken language*. North-Holland, Amsterdam.
Ware, R. X. (1975) Some Bits and Pieces. *Synthese* 31, 379–93.
Wegel, H. (1956) Axiomatische Mengenlehre ohne Elemente von Mengen. *Mathematische Annalen* 131, 757–58.
Whitehead, A. N. and Russell, B. (1910–13) *Principia mathematica*. Cambridge University Press, Cambridge.
Winograd, T. (1983) *Language as a cognitive process*, vol. 1, *Syntax*. Addison-Wesley, Reading, Massachusetts.
Zemach, E (1975) On the adequacy of a type ontology. *Synthese* 31, 509–15.

Index

abstract mass nouns, 10-1, 15, 129-30, 303
activity verbs, 17-18
adjectives
  count 16-17, 198-200, 203-11, 217
  intersective, 212
  mass, 16-17, 19, 27, 51, 135, 198-9, 203, 210-11, 217
Allan, K., 7, 12, 14, 303, 310
Allén, S., 315
ambiguity
  in formal languages, 115-24
  quantificational, 141, 143, 152-9
  referential, 111-12, 114-18, 123-4
  structural semantic, 111, 113
  syntactic, 111-12, 113
amount, 76-81, 87, 88, 100
amount construction in EL, 92, 94, 98-9, 306, 307
amount expression in EL, 90, 92, 94, 168-70, 176-80
amount phrases, 7, 39, 41, 75, 303
amount terms
  applied, 76, 163, 168, 180, 190, 191, 222, 223
  attributive, 75, 81
  isolated, 76, 176, 177, 180, 190, 222
  predicative, 75, 76, 81
amount type, 86, 87-8, 82, 90, 94
applied amount term, 76, 180, 163, 168, 190, 191, 222, 223
artificial intelligence, 4
atomic
  ensemble, 55, 59-60, 236, 290-5
  individual ensemble, 291-2, 298-300
  type, 84-5, 99
attributive amount term, 75, 81
augmented phrase-construction
  grammar, xi, 186, 217
  rule, 186, 217
Austerlitz, D., 317
axiom of
  discreteness, 275, 281, 287
  equality, 56, 60, 235, 237

equality in set theory, 237, 276
extensionality, 60, 238-9, 269, 285-6
extensionality in set theory, 53-4, 275
extensionality, modified, 292, 297, 298
infinity, 243, 251, 269
merging, 244-5, 269, 287-8
pairing, 62, 69, 70, 242-3, 269, 287
pairing in set theory, 276, 286
powers, 62, 243, 244, 269
powers in set theory, 276, 286
regularity, 243, 252, 269
regularity in set theory, 276, 286
replacement, 247-8, 269, 287
replacement in set theory, 276
transitivity, 56, 69, 235, 269, 284
unicles, 60, 69-72, 237, 269, 285
unicles, weak, 291-2
unions, 276, 286

Bach, E., 307, 313
Bar-Hillel, Y., 314
Bartee, T. C., 78, 313
Bartsch, R. 315
Barwise, J., 146, 309, 313
basic noun phrase, 133, 138, 166, 180
Bealer, G., 5, 313
Bennett, M., 111, 115, 139, 212
Benthem, J. F. van, xiii, 311
Bernays, P., 237, 313
Bierwisch, M., 315
Birkhoff, G. 78, 313
Bolc, L., 313
Boolean algebra
  definition, 257
  non-atomic, 270, 271
  of ensembles, 246, 256-9
branching category, 88-9, 95, 99, 119-22, 308
Bronnenberg, W. J., 82, 118, 119, 313
Bunt, H. C., xii, 10, 11, 15, 46, 79, 82, 83, 89, 96, 118, 119, 186, 199, 204, 221
Burge, T., 5, 9, 13, 14, 15, 19, 22, 24, 25, 29, 31, 33, 36, 43, 134

319

calculus of individuals, see mereology
cardinality construction, in EL, 91, 94, 100, 306, 307
Cartwright, H. M., 14, 22, 33, 36, 37, 314
central determiner, 136, 138–9, 160, 181, 189, 191, 223
Cheng, C. Y., 20, 45, 314
Cheng's condition, 20, 45
Chomsky, N., 317
Church, A., 309, 314
Clarke, C. S., 33, 37, 314
Cocchiarella, N., 303, 309, 314
collective distribution
 of count nouns, 141, 161
 of mass nouns, 167, 206
collective mass nouns, 214–15, 217, 219, 220, 221, 304
collective modification, xi, 205–6, 209, 210, 215–6, 217, 219
collective quantification
 of count nouns, 216
 of mass nouns, 155–6, 158–9, 160, 162–3
completion, 58, 64, 254–5
compositionality, principle of, 106, 307
condition
 Cheng's, 20, 45
 formal, 248
 functional, 248, 249
conditional construction, 92, 94, 158, 306, 307
constitution relation, 30–1, 41
construction, in EL, see branching category
construction clause, 183–5
continuity, in ensemble theory, 63–5, 260–3, 290–5
continuous ensemble, 63–5, 260–3, 290–5
conversion
 factor, 76–9
 function, 76–9, 94, 99
Cooper, R., 309, 314
count adjectives, 16–17, 198–200, 203–11, 217
count nouns, 3–6, 9–20
count verbs, 17–18
count/mass distinction, 3–5, 9–20, 43–7, 198–211, 220–1
 of adjectives, 16–17, 198–211
countability, 12, 303
culinary habits, 303
cumulative combination principle, 200, 204
cumulative predicate, 96, 203
cumulative reference, 18, 35, 43, 51, 135, 199, 200–1, 304
 condition of, 16–20, 22, 45, 98, 198, 303
cumulative quantification,
 for count nouns, 144–5, 150, 152, 153
 for mass nouns, 165, 178–80

Cushing, S., 309, 314

Daalder, S., 316
Dahl, Ö., 142, 314
Dalen, D. van, 314
D-amount, 78, 79, 80
data base, 119
definite descriptions with mass nouns, 40, 95–6
determiner,
 central, 136, 138–9, 160, 181, 189, 191, 223
 post-, 136, 138–9, 181
 pre-, 136, 138–9, 181, 189
Dik, S. xiii, 5, 140, 314
dimension, 76–81
discontinuous constituents, 183–5
discrete
 ensembles, 64, 71, 263–8, 275–81
 distribution, 163, 219
 modification, 205, 207–10, 213–5, 217
 quantification, 174–7, 213
discreteness,
 axiom of, 275, 281, 287
 definition, 64, 263
 in ensemble theory, 71, 263–8, 275–81
distribution
 collective, for count nouns, 141, 161
 collective, for mass nouns, 167, 206
 discrete, 163, 219
 function, 156, 160, 167, 173, 174, 177, 218, 219
 group, 141, 143–4, 152–3, 161, 167, 177–8
 group, for mass nouns, 167, 177–8
 homogeneous, 162, 164, 167, 219
 individual, 141, 152, 153, 161
 of modification, 198
 of quantification, 140–1, 154, 156–7, 160
 unspecific, 141, 144, 149, 161, 164, 167
distributive
 predicates, 202–3
 quantification, 140, 142, 147, 149, 181
 reference, 43, 202, 204
 reference, condition of, 20, 98
division of reference, 4, 15–6, 22, 46
domain
 assignment to type, 85–8
 categorization of, 84, 85, 109–10
 of a modification, 198, 206, 208, 213
 of a quantification, 140–1, 149, 155–6, 158–9, 160–3, 218
 of a type, 85, 86–8, 94
D-unit, 77, 79

Emde Boas, P. van, 311
emptiness, in emsemble theory, 56, 235

Index

empty ensemble, 54–5, 56, 235, 341
endocentric construction, 197
  subordinating, 197
ensemble
  atomic, 55, 59–60, 236, 290–5
  atomic individual, 291–2, 298–300
  continuous, 63–5, 260–3, 290–5
  discrete, 64, 71, 263–8, 275–81
  empty, 54–5, 56, 235, 341
  general, 130, 268
  individual, 292–7
  maximal, 58
  minimal, 57–8, 62, 64, 65, 243
  mixed, 65, 68, 85, 267–8
  pair, 62, 243
  power, 62, 244, 287
  singleton, 61, 64, 240, 290–5
equality
  axiom of, 236, 269, 284–5
  in ensemble theory, 56, 60, 235, 237
  in set theory, 237, 275–6
extensionality
  axiom of, 60, 238–9, 269, 285–6
  in ensemble theory, 53–4, 60–1, 238–9
  in set theory, 53–4, 275
  modified axiom of, 292, 297, 298

formal atomic type, 85
Fraenkel, A. A., 7, 53, 233, 237, 275, 276, 278, 281, 282, 287, 288, 294, 311, 314
function union, in EL, 92, 94, 158, 306, 307
functional condition, 248
fusion, 22, 289–90, 297

Gazdar, G., xi
general ensembles 130, 268
generalized quantifiers, 309
generic
  modification, 205, 206–7, 210, 216–17
  modifier, 207
  quantification, 142
genuine part, 63, 235–6
Gerritsen, M. 316
Gil, D., 147, 315
Gleason, H. A., 315
global source involvement, 143, 163
Goodman, N., 22, 27, 51, 288, 303, 311
GPSG, xi
Grandy, R., 22, 33, 37, 315
Greenbaum, S., 317
Groenendijk, J. 313, 315, 316, 317
ground nouns, 209–11, 214, 217, 219, 220
group distribution,
  for count nouns, 141, 143–4, 152–3, 161
  for mass nouns, 167, 177–8

group quantification,
  for count nouns, 144, 145
  for count nouns, strong, 144, 148, 153–5, 178
  for count nouns, weak, 144, 148, 153–5
  for mass nouns, 144, 145
  for mass nouns, strong, 163, 177
  for mass nouns, weak, 163
group size, 141, 156, 160, 167
  indicator of, 144, 148, 163
Guenthner, F., 102, 103, 315

Halmos, P., 80, 315
Hausser, R., 103, 315
head, 197
Heidorn, G., 175, 315
Higginbotham, J., 315
Hintikka, J., 314, 315, 316
Hobbs, J. R., 314
Hoepelman, J., 18, 315
homogeneous
  combination principle, 203–7, 209, 210, 213
  distribution, 162, 164, 167, 219
  modification, 205, 207–9, 210, 212–13, 217
  quantification, 168–72, 214, 219
  reference, 39, 46, 203, 211
  reference hypothesis, 46–7, 97, 129

individual, 39, 49, 51–2, 71–2, 84, 137, 146, 288–301, 309
  atomic ensemble, 291–2, 298–300
  distribution, 141, 152, 153, 161
  ensemble, 292–7
  quantification, 141, 143, 144
individuation, 4, 20, 36, 43, 47, 52, 97, 136, 208–10, 214
infinity, axiom of, in ensemble theory, 243, 251, 269
  in set theory, 276
intensional contexts with mass nouns, 6, 22, 37–8, 48, 49, 50, 161, 307
interface problems between formalisms, 50–2, 54–5
internal context, 185–6
interpretation, see model
interpretation domain, 66–70, 270–4
intersective adjectives, 212
involvement, source-, 139–41, 143–4, 155, 160, 165
  global, 143, 163
  local, 143, 163
  total, 143, 144, 148, 152
isolated amount terms, 76, 176, 177, 180, 190, 222

iteration construction in EL, 91, 94, 306, 307

Jacobson, P., 314
Janssen, T. M. V., 307, 313, 316, 317, 315
Jespersen, O. 7, 9, 315

Kamp, H., 212, 315
Karlsson, F., 313
Keenan, E., 314, 315
Kiefer, F., 315
Kimball, J. P., 313
Klooster, W. G., 76, 315

lambda
  abstraction, 90, 309
  conversion, 147, 309
Landsbergen, J. 89, 116, 308, 315
Laycock, H., 5, 315
Leech, G., 139, 309, 316, 317
Leonard, H., 22, 27, 51, 288, 303, 311, 316
Lesniewski, S., 5, 22, 50, 288, 303, 316
Levy, A., 314
Linden, J. van der, xii, 311
LLG, theory of, 288-91, 294-301
local source involvement, 143, 163
L-overlap, 295-300
L-part, 295-98
Luschei, E. C., 311, 316
Lyons, J., 73, 105, 308, 310, 316

mass adjectives, 16-17, 19, 27, 51, 135, 198-9, 203, 210-11, 217
mass nouns, 3-6, 9-20
  abstract, 10-11, 15, 129-30, 303
  collective, 214-15, 217, 219, 220, 221, 304
mass terms, 3-6, 9-20, 204-211
mass verbs, 17
material names, 304
maximal
  ensemble, 58
  portion, 41, 96
McCawley, J. D., 199, 316
measure
  function, 80-1
  phrase, *see* amount phrase
Medema, P., 118, 316
member-whole relation in ensemble theory, 61, 238, 294
merge, 57, 244, 252
merging, axiom of, 244-5, 269, 287-8
mereological sum, 22, 28, 33, 35, 52; *see also* fusion
  overlap 51, 199, 203
  wholes, restricted, 26-8, 32, 44-7, 97

mereology, 5, 22-4, 26-8, 31-3, 35, 43-4, 47-52, 288-301
  subsumption in ensemble theory, 295-7, 301
Meulen, A. ter, 5, 10, 14, 17, 22, 23, 33, 37-42, 46, 48-50, 111, 137, 303, 304, 310, 316
Mey, S. de, xiii, 161, 309, 316
minimal ensembles, 57-8, 62, 64, 65, 243
minimal parts, 24, 26, 28, 36-7, 45-6, 49, 50, 63, 97, 290-1
  hypothesis, 24, 26, 30, 35-6, 44-8, 130, 134
mixed ensemble, 65, 68, 85, 267-8
model
  assignment, 107, 108-10, 114, 270
  in formal semantics, 118-24
  of ensemble theory, ix, 56, 66-71, 269-74
  structure, 107, 108-10, 114, 270
model-theoretic semantics, 105-18
  two-level, x, 5, 118-24, 129-32, 146, 152-60, 165, 167-80, 212-16
modification
  collective, xi, 205-6, 209, 210, 212-13, 217
  discrete, 205, 207-10, 213-5, 217
  distribution of, 198
  domain of a, 198, 206, 208, 213
  generic, 205, 206-7, 210, 216-17
  homogeneous, 205, 207-9, 210, 212-13, 217
  nonrestrictive, 197, 204
  source, 198, 206, 208, 213
modifier, 197
  generic, 207
Montague, R., 6, 37, 42, 50, 74, 96, 111, 113, 115, 128, 146, 165, 212, 308
Moore, R., 314
Moravcsik. J. M. E., xiii, 16, 17, 18, 22, 24, 25, 26-9, 32, 43, 44, 47, 50, 55, 97, 135, 198, 200, 316
multilevel semantics, 118-19

nominal mass terms, 37-8
non-empty part, 63, 235
nonrestrictive modification, 197, 204
noun phrase sequence, 148-9, 151, 160, 213
npcentre, 171, 172-3, 176, 191, 223
null amount, 79-80

overlap relation
  in ensemble theory, 57-8, 64, 235, 252-4
  in mereology, 34, 35, 51, 199, 289, 290, 295-6, 298-300, 303

Pack, A., 309
pair ensemble, 62, 243
pairing, axiom of,
 in ensemble theory, 62, 69, 70, 242–3, 269, 287
 in set theory, 276, 286
Parsons, T., 5, 9, 10, 12, 15, 22, 25, 29–33, 43, 44, 47, 48, 55, 59, 76, 97, 200, 317
Partee, B., 144, 152–3, 317
partselection construction, in EL, 91, 93, 95–7, 100, 130–2, 218, 306, 307
partition theorem, 255–6
Paxton, W. H., 186, 317
PC rule, see phrase-construction rule
Pelletier, F. J., 9, 11, 12, 14, 15, 22, 24, 25, 29, 32, 33, 36, 37, 47, 48, 209, 313
performance verbs, 17–8
Petöfi, J., 315
PHILIQA1, xii, 82, 115, 118
phrase-construction rule, 182–6, 217
 augmented, 186, 217
possible denotation, 86–8, 90, 107–10, 128
postdeterminer, 136, 138–9, 181
power ensemble, 62, 244, 287
powers, axiom of,
 in ensemble theory, 62, 69, 70, 242–3, 269, 287
 in set theory, 276, 286
predeterminer, 136, 138–9, 160, 171, 181, 189
predicate,
 cumulative, 96, 203
 distributive, 202–3
 homogeneous, 203, 211
 set, 309
predicative amount term, 75, 76, 81
predicative mass term, 23, 26, 37–9, 49
projection, in EL, 101, 145, 150–1
proper part, in ensemble theory, 56, 235
PTQ, 146
puddle puzzle, 25, 27, 28–9, 218–19
Pullum, G. K., xi, 314
Putnam, H., 103, 317

quantification,
 collective, of count nouns, 140–1, 143, 147, 149
 collective, of mass nouns, 162, 176–7
 cumulative, of count nouns, 144–5, 150, 152, 153
 cumulative, of mass nouns, 165, 178–80
 discrete, 174–7, 213
 distribution, 140–1, 154, 156–7, 160
 distributive, 140, 142, 147, 149, 181, 214
 domain, 140–1, 149, 155–6, 158–9, 160, 162–3, 218

quantification (*cont.*)
 group, of count nouns, 144, 145
 group, of mass nouns, 163
 homogeneous, 168–72, 214, 219
 individual, 141, 143, 144
 source, 138–41, 143, 150, 156, 160, 162–3, 218
 strong group, of count nouns, 144, 148, 153–5, 178
 strong group, of mass nouns, 163, 177
 subcumulative, of count nouns, 145, 150, 153
 subcumulative, of mass nouns, 165, 178–80
 weak group, of count nouns, 144, 148, 153–5 178
 weak group, of mass nouns, 163
quantificational ambiguity, 141, 143, 152–9
quantifier, 139, 309
 generalized, 309
 scope, 142, 309
 subscripted, 147
quantities, 22, 29–33, 37–42, 46–7, 49, 200
quantity-of relation, 30–1, 43
Quine, W.V. O., 4, 5, 7, 13, 14, 15, 16, 17, 18, 19, 21–6, 27, 36, 43, 44, 45, 47, 51, 95, 96, 130, 134, 135, 198, 199, 200, 203, 218, 317
Quirk, R., 10, 11, 309, 317

reference,
 cumulative, 18, 35, 43, 51, 135, 199, 200–1, 304
 distributive, 43, 202, 204
 division of, 4, 15–6, 22, 46
 homogeneous, 39, 46, 203, 211
 recursive, 323
referential
 ambiguity, 111–12, 114–18, 123–4
 atomic type, 85–6, 109, 126
regularity, axiom of
 in ensemble theory, 243, 252, 269
 in set theory, 276
replacement, axiom (schema) of
 in ensemble theory, 247–8, 269, 287
 in set theory, 276
restricted
 mereological wholes, 26–8, 32, 44–7, 97
 part–whole relation, 18–19, 44
Robinson, J., xi, xiii, 133, 186, 317
Roeper, P., ix, 165 310, 317
Russell, B., 288, 318

Scha, R., xi, xiii, 118, 119, 144, 148, 150–1, 317
Schank, R., 315

Schoenflies, A., 53, 317
Schoenmakers, W. J., 118, 313
Schwartzenberg, G. O. thoe, 83, 221, 311, 314
scope, 142, 309
Searle, J. R., 315
selector, 88–9, 95, 99, 119, 308
semantic ambiguity
 quantificational, 141, 143, 152–9
 referential, 111–12, 114–18, 123–4
 structural, 111, 113
semantic type, see type
singleton ensemble, 61, 64, 240, 290–5
Socrates, 33, 34
source,
 global involvement, 143, 163
 involvement, 139–41, 143–4, 155, 160, 165
 local involvement, 143, 163
 modification-, 198, 206, 208, 213
 quantification-, 138-41, 143, 150, 153, 160, 162, 166–7
 of denotations, 108, 110
 total involvement, 143–4, 148, 152
Stokhof, M., 313, 315, 316, 317
Strawson, P. F., 37, 317
strong group quantification
 of count nouns, 144, 148, 153–5, 178
 of mass nouns, 163, 177
structural semantic ambiguity, 111, 113
subensembles, theorem of, 248–9, 252–3
subcumulative quantification
 of count nouns, 145, 150, 153
 of mass nouns, 165, 178–80
submerging, theorem of, 247
subscripted
 power symbol, 144
 quantifier, 147
substance abstraction operator, 32, 200
substances, 18, 22, 29–33, 37–9, 43–4, 46–7, 49, 55
 Parsons, 29–33 43–4, 59, 97, 200
sum, mereological; see fusion; mereological sum
Suppes, P., 294, 314, 317
Svartvik, J., 139, 309, 316, 317
syntactic ambiguity, 111-12, 113
Szabolcsi, A., 161, 317

Tarski, A., 105, 303, 317
TENDUM, 83, 124, 221, 314
term valuation, 92, 109, 110, 124
terms, in EL, 88, 90, 92, 109
theorem
 of partitions, 255–6
 of subensembles, 248–9, 252, 3
 of submerging, 247

Thomason, R. H., 104, 111, 317
total source involvement, 143, 144, 148, 152
transitive function, 77, 86–7, 99
transitivity, axiom of, 56, 69, 235, 269, 284
translation
 as interpretation, 114, 117–18, 120
 formal, 113–14, 119–24
 type-, 121-2, 308
two-level model-theoretic semantics, x, 5, 118–24, 129–32, 146, 152–60, 165, 167–80, 212–16
type (semantic), 83–8, 89–90, 92, 94, 95, 99, 109–10, 117, 120–3, 124–8, 157–9, 218, 304–8
 assignment, 92, 94, 306–7
 atomic, 84–5, 99
 complex, 84–6
 component, 304–5
 domain of, 85, 86–8, 94
 ensemble-, 305, 306
 formal atomic, 85
 inclusion, 87, 120–2, 304–5, 309
 referential atomic, 85–6, 109, 126
 restrictions, 89–90, 120, 158–9, 305–6, 308
 set-, 305, 306
 translation, 121–2, 308
 union, 84, 86, 305, 306, 307, 218

unicle, 60–1, 71–2, 80, 237
unicles, axiom of, 60, 69–72, 237, 269, 285
 weak, 291–2
unicle–whole relation, 60, 237
union
 function-, 92, 94, 158, 306, 307
 of types, 84, 86, 88, 218, 305, 306, 307
unions, axiom of, 276, 287
unionstar, 91, 93, 99, 149–50, 154–60, 213–14, 218–19, 305, 307
units, 75–8, 94, 136–7
Universal Grammar, 165
Universal Grinder, 11, 209–11
Universal Sorter, 11
unspecific distribution
 for count nouns, 141, 144, 149, 161
 for mass nouns, 164, 167
Utteren, E. van, 118, 313

valuation function, 92
 for EL, 92–4
 term-, 92, 109, 110, 124
verbs,
 activity-, 17–18
 count-, 17
 mass-, 19
 performance-, 17–18

Visentini, B., 316

Walker, D. E., 317
Webber, B., 315
weak group quantification
　of count nouns, 144, 148, 153–5
　of mass nouns, 163
Wegel, H., 53, 317

Whitehead, A. N., 288, 318
Wiedijk, F., 311
Winograd., T., xi, 186, 318

Zemach, E., 5, 318
Zermelo, E., 7, 53, 233, 237, 275, 276, 278, 281, 282, 287, 294, 311, 311, 314